CONFERENC
IN CHINA

MW01519785

In this landmark project, Professor Riccardo Moratto and Professor Irene A. Zhang evaluate how conference interpreting developed as a profession in China, and the directions in which it is heading.

Bringing together perspectives from leading researchers in the field, Moratto and Zhang present a thematically organized analysis of the trajectory of professional conference interpreting in China. This includes discussion of the pedagogies used both currently and historically, the professionalization of interpreter education, and future prospects for virtual reality, multimodal conferences, and artificial intelligence. Taken as a whole, the contributors present a rich and detailed picture of the development of conference interpreting in China since 1979, its status today, and how it is likely to develop in the coming decades.

This is an essential resource for scholars and students of conference interpreting in China.

Riccardo Moratto is Professor of Translation and Interpreting Studies at the Graduate Institute of Interpretation and Translation, Shanghai International Studies University.

Irene A. Zhang is Professor and Dean of the Graduate Institute of Interpretation and Translation, Shanghai International Studies University.

Routledge Studies in East Asian Interpreting

Routledge Studies in East Asian Interpreting aims to discuss practical and theoretical issues in East Asian interpreting. This series encompasses scholarly works on every possible interpreting activity and theory involving the use of Chinese (Mandarin, Cantonese, and other topolects), Japanese, Korean and other East Asian languages/dialects. At a time when Western interpreting studies has reached its maturity and scholars are looking for inspiration from elsewhere in the world, the field of East Asian interpreting offers the greatest potential for discovery of new frontiers and formulation of new theories. The topics included in this series set out to include all the subfields of interpreting in the broader East Asian region, with Chinese, Japanese, and Korean being the main research languages. Topics can range from interpreter education, conference interpreting, medical or healthcare interpreting, educational interpreting, public service interpreting (also known as community interpreting), sign language interpreting, police interpreting, legal interpreting, interpreting for children, diplomatic interpreting, interpreting in war zones, social services interpreting, liaison or dialogue interpreting, business interpreting, remote interpreting, new models in consecutive and simultaneous interpreting, chuchotage or whispered interpreting, simconsec interpreting, telephone interpreting, shadowing, and respeaking. The series primarily consists of focus/shortform books, monographs, edited volumes, handbooks, and companions dedicated to discussing the above issues in East Asia.

Conference Interpreting in China
Practice, Training and Research
Edited by Riccardo Moratto and Irene A. Zhang

Professional Interpreting Programmes in China
Constructing a Curriculum Improvement Model
Yinying Wang

Conference Interpreting in China

Practice, Training and Research

Edited by Riccardo Moratto and Irene A. Zhang

Routledge
Taylor & Francis Group

LONDON AND NEW YORK

First published 2023
by Routledge
4 Park Square, Milton Park, Abingdon, Oxon OX14 4RN

and by Routledge
605 Third Avenue, New York, NY 10158

Routledge is an imprint of the Taylor & Francis Group, an informa business

© 2023 selection and editorial matter, Riccardo Moratto and Irene A. Zhang; individual chapters, the contributors

British Library Cataloguing-in-Publication Data
A catalogue record for this book is available from the British Library

ISBN: 978-1-032-41341-9 (hbk)
ISBN: 978-1-032-41342-6 (pbk)
ISBN: 978-1-003-35762-9 (ebk)

DOI: 10.4324/9781003357629

Typeset in Galliard
by Apex CoVantage, LLC

Contents

Foreword: Western impressions about Chinese conference interpreting research

Introduction

When the editors asked me to write about conference interpreter training in China, I had to excuse myself: I may have participated modestly in one capacity or another in the setting up and activities of some Chinese training programs over the years, but I cannot claim to have a solid, accurate knowledge of the present scene. Chinese authors are in an infinitely better position to report and reflect on it, as indeed is done in the literature and in this collective volume. On the other hand, while monitoring international developments in conference interpreting research (CIR) as reflected in the *CIRIN Bulletin* since 1991 (https://cirin-gile.fr), I have had the opportunity to observe the spectacular development of Chinese research over the past two decades and am only too glad to write a few comments about some of its noteworthy features as a foreword to this volume.

"Interpreting" vs. conference interpreting

The existence of conference interpreting (CI) as a distinct profession was formalized in the early 1950s (Baigorri-Jalón 2000, 2015); the International Association of Conference Interpreters (AIIC) was created in Geneva in 1953. Academic and semi-academic publications on CI started in the 1960s in Europe and North America – and in Japan (Gile 1988). In the 1970s, interest in CI gave rise to a trickle of research publications, which turned into a regular, albeit small, flow in the 1980s (see the bibliographies on the CIRIN site). By the end of the decade, the flow had strengthened to a sufficient extent to justify the creation of a specialized journal, *The Interpreters' Newsletter*, which was set up in 1988 by the University of Trieste, in Italy. It was followed in 1991 by *Interpreting Research* 通訳理論研究, which was set up in Tokyo by the Interpreting Research Association of Japan 通訳理論研究会, and in 1996 by *Interpreting*, an international journal published by John Benjamins. All three included papers on various types of interpreting beyond CI but were grounded in primary interest in research into conference interpreting.

In China, as pointed out in Dawrant et al. (2022), the distinction between conference interpreting and other types of interpreting, in particular business interpreting, is not as clear as in the West, but many authors, including several who contribute in this volume, report that conference interpreting as a formally distinct category of interpreting started developing in the late 1970s, with the establishment of a training program in Beijing by the UN in cooperation with the Chinese government. Chinese publications on conference interpreting and on topics directly related to conference interpreting in English and other European languages were few until the end of the 1990s. Publications on interpreting started booming at the beginning of the 21st century, rising to 839 by 2007 (Wang and Mu 2009, 278). According to Dawrant et al. (2022), the foundation of three Chinese PhD programs in 2004 did a lot to boost research into interpreting in China. But the Chinese government's decision to set up MTI degrees in 2007 (their number reached 316 in 2021 according to Dong and Chen, this volume) was arguably an even stronger driver of research production, because of the theses and publications requirements that came with them.

As is the case in the global literature on interpreting, the largest number of publications on interpreting in China addresses interpreter training. This goes from textbooks (58 Chinese interpreting textbooks were reviewed in Yang and Li 2022) to articles published in conference proceedings, in collective volumes, in journals. When reading texts written in English and abstracts of texts written in Chinese, the impression is that the overwhelming majority of them addresses interpreter training in general as opposed to conference interpreting as it is defined in Europe and the Americas, even if they address techniques in the consecutive and simultaneous modes which, in the Western model, are generally discussed in relation to conference interpreting. This may be due to the fact that in China, save for a few exceptions, interpreter training is part of language teaching and enhancement, and only a small fraction of the students will eventually become conference interpreters.

According to the AIIC paradigm (Mackintosh 1995), which set the standards for conference interpreting in the 1950s and has been dominant ever since, only students with excellent mastery of their future working languages should be trained in interpreting. Those who do not meet this requirement run the risk of doing word-for-word "transcoding" instead of analyzing the input and formulating the output on the basis of the meaning they extracted from the speech. Field experience and research by some authors, including myself (Gile 1982) and Ersöz Demırdağ (2013), tell a slightly different story. If input speeches are adapted appropriately and the principles of "interpretive" interpreting are explained properly, language students can be expected to acquire the basics of meaning-based, communication-oriented interpreting in line with what is taught in conference interpreter training programs. Many of the Chinese interpreting textbooks published so far explain the effort models and interpretive theory (Yang and Li 2022) and provide appropriate guidance, and genuine interpreting competence acquisition may well be found in many

Chinese interpreter training classes, even at the undergraduate level. To what extent this is the case is worth investigating.

A related question linked to the fact that training in consecutive and simultaneous interpreting in China often starts when students are still weak in their foreign language is the presence of lexical and phrasal suggestions and drills in Chinese interpreting textbooks. As suggested earlier, this runs counter to the AIIC paradigm. On the other hand, even in AIIC-approved training programs, many students fail to graduate because of language weaknesses. Could language drills help? Gérard Ilg, a highly respected interpreter and interpreter training pioneer from Switzerland who taught in Geneva and Paris over several decades starting in the 1950s, thought so – this was a major bone of contention between him and Seleskovitch. According to Ilg, by creating automatic or semi-automatic connections between frequently used phrases in one's working languages, interpreters obtain cognitive relief, which frees resources for better analysis and reformulation of less-formulaic language solutions to translation. Assuming this is true, the next step would be to conduct lexicometric and phraseometric analyses of relevant corpora and establish frequency rankings so as to select the best candidates for drills depending on the type of market.

The AIIC paradigm remains valid for highly selective conference interpreter training programs which prepare students for immediate employment at high-level conferences within a short time. But the Chinese example offers an opportunity to investigate the possibility of a gradual development of interpreting skills starting while still in advanced language training.

High research productivity

Chinese texts on interpreting (beyond CIR) have become far more numerous than publications on interpreting in any other country. In his analysis five years ago, Xu (2017) processed data from 1,289 MA theses and 2,900 research papers. When considering the potential Chinese contribution to the IS (interpreting studies) community, the most relevant texts are those that are published in English in widely distributed journals and in collective volumes. As regards CIR, the latter may be even more relevant than journal articles, as they represent a large part of the total research text production (probably varying between 20 and 50% according to CIRIN data), and collective volumes often focus on a particular theme or topic (quality expectations and perception, training, cognitive issues, etc.), which makes it possible for interested researchers to find relevant Chinese contributions without having to go through a keyword search, as is the case of journal articles. Also, both Gile (2005) and Zhu and Aryadoust (2022) observe that in the IS literature, books tend to be quoted more often than papers published in journals.

At the time this text is being written, for the 1990s, the 52 entries for China in the CIRIN bibliography (which is updated periodically) represent less than 4% of the total number of 1,402 entries. For the years 2000 to 2009, out of a total of 1,741 entries, there are 561 papers in English (32% of the total number of entries for all languages). The largest contribution comes from Italy (64 texts), followed by France (61 texts, but 25 of them were written by the same author), by Korea (46 papers), Austria (41 papers), Switzerland (31 papers), and China (28 papers). For the years 2010 to 2019, China accounts for 19.6% of the 1,261 entries. The total number of papers is 866, 525 of which are in English. Chinese contributions (from China's mainland and other Chinese-speaking territories, as well as contributions by Chinese authors affiliated with overseas institutions) are by far the most numerous, with 80 entries. They are followed by Spain (48 entries) and Italy (45 entries).

These numbers should be taken as rough indications since CIRIN, an independent, self-funded initiative, relies on manual data collection by its editor and on contributions by colleagues as opposed to comprehensive databases. However, these statistics highlight how salient Chinese CIR presence has become in the global CIR landscape.

They also highlight the small size of the corpus of published CIR entries worldwide. In a recent analysis, Baxter (2022), who mined 50 translation journals for papers on spoken language interpreting (of all categories) published in the past 20 years, found about 1,300 texts, that is, an average of slightly more than 60 per year, CIR representing only a fraction of that number. Interestingly, he found that by far the most productive author was a Chinese, Andrew Cheung, with a total of 17 entries. Carmen Valero Garcés from Spain follows with 15 entries, and Bart Defrancq from Belgium is third with 13 entries. With 11 papers, Han Chao is another Chinese author in the top group. The numbers and rankings for individual research production are very different in the CIRIN bibliographies, which only include conference interpreting but cover articles in collective volumes besides MA theses and doctoral dissertations. Be that as it may, the list remains small, which means that it is enough for a small group of authors to adopt a new approach, new research methods or produce new findings to potentially have significant influence on the CIR community at large. The implications as regards Chinese CIR are clear.

Institutional resources

With hundreds of BTI and MTI programs, China is arguably by far the country in the world with the largest population of translation and interpreting students and teachers. The total institutional investment in this population is necessarily large and has made it possible to organize academic and research-related operations at a scale not found elsewhere. One striking example is that of a four-year nationwide research project funded by the government to develop interpreting competence scales in China, which involved surveying about 30,000 students (Wang et al. 2020).

Such institutional resources have made it possible to organize many national Chinese IS conferences, held initially every two years, general translation and interpreting conferences, conferences on specialized interpreting and translation-related themes, training workshops, and so on – with frequent participation of scholars from overseas. Such meetings and other functions are likely to foster national and international contacts and interaction between researchers at an activity level far above that found in Europe or the Americas. The present COVID pandemic and its aftermath may have inflicted a severe blow to these dynamic exchanges, and economic conditions can vary as well. But basically, the demographics of the T&I academic population should remain very large when compared to the demographics of any other country, and institutional resources in China should remain at a far higher level than anywhere else in the world. The resulting potential for research and research-related initiatives is obvious.

Innovative input from linguistics

Among conference interpreter trainers, a widely accepted ideal is that of the interpreters' output sounding like a well-formulated, convincing native speaker's speech. A similar ideal for written translation is prevalent among translators of non-literary texts. In both cases, reality is different, even when the translators or interpreters work into their native language. The phenomenon has been under investigation in written translation, with intensive use of electronic corpora, but lags behind as regards conference interpreting, where reasons for distinctive features of the interpreters' output are partly different. In particular, there is substantial evidence to suggest that in conference interpreting, the way the output is verbalized in the target language is largely shaped by cognitive pressure which results from time constraints during the interpreting process.

A stimulating aspect of Chinese CIR has been the innovative input of linguists interested in the links between such cognitive factors and linguistic aspects of the output. They have been investigating linguistic features of interpretations using constructs and tools such as dependency distance, lexical simplification, formulaic language, lexical category bias, the ratio between sentence length and number of clauses, all of which help shed light on cognitive economics in different interpreting modes. A number of Chinese researchers are quite active in this promising direction (see reviews in recent issues of the *CIRIN Bulletin*).

Interesting angles in the literature on interpreter training

Overall, as is the case in other parts of the world, interpreter training seems to remain the most popular topic of Chinese research on interpreting, as it has been since the start (see Wang and Mu 2009 for data up to 2007). Many studies are similar to Western studies in that they look at curricula, interpreting tactics, training methods, note-taking in consecutive with similar approaches. But many innovate, for instance by experimenting with different assessment methods, including student peer assessments, comparative judgment, semi-automatic assessment, by exploring the relative severity/leniency of assessors, by looking at teaching material selection and ways of evaluating their relative difficulty for students, by investigating the motivations of students and teachers, by conducting a longitudinal study of students' evolution over five years, from undergraduate to graduate status, by looking at the effect of anxiety in the classroom. These studies provide much food for thought.

Sometimes, Chinese research initiatives offer methodological tools as well. Such is the case of the very innovative consecutive note-taking fluency scales (Han et al. 2022), which could be put to good use in the classroom.

Conclusion

CIR is a small branch in a small discipline in the academic world. In most countries, there are no research centers dedicated to CIR or even to IS in general, and the number of active CIR researchers, those who publish more than an occasional text every few years, is often no more than a handful. If only for that reason, a country that puts a few hundred, or even a few dozen, active CI researchers on the map can have a major influence on the CIR landscape, as has been the case of Spain, which had a very low profile until the 1990s, and then became a major actor with the academization of interpreting schools (MEC 1991). Besides noteworthy individual studies by Chinese researchers (highlighted in the *CIRIN Bulletin*), at the level of a national research community, the potential of Chinese production is considerable and deserves much attention from scholars overseas. This collective volume published in English by a prestigious publisher is a welcome contribution that should help in this respect.

Daniel Gile
Professor Emeritus
Université Sorbonne Nouvelle, Paris

References

Baigorri-Jalón, Jesús. 2000. *La interpretación de conferencias: El nacimiento de una profesión. De París a Nuremberg.* Granada: Editorial Comares.

Baigorri-Jalón, Jesús. 2015. "The History of the Interpreting Profession." In *The Routledge Handbook of Interpreting*, edited by Holly Mikkelson and Renée Jourdenais, 11–28. London and New York: Routledge.

Baxter, Robert Neal. 2022. "Trending Topics in Current Interpreting Research: An Overview of Twenty Years of Interpreting Studies Seen Through the Lens of T&I Journals." *Transletters* 6. 1–30.

CIRIN Bulletin. https://cirin-gile.fr.

Dawrant, Andrew C., Binhua Wang, and Hong Jiang. 2022. "Conference Interpreting in China." In *The Routledge Handbook of Conference Interpreting*, edited by Michaela Albl-Mikasa and Elisabet Tiseliust, 182–96. London and New York: Routledge.

Ersöz Demirdağ, Hande. 2013. "L'enseignement de l'interprétation consécutive: une étude de cas turc-français." Unpublished doctoral dissertation, Université Paris III Sorbonne-Nouvelle.

Gile, Daniel. 1982. "Initiation à l'interprétation consécutive à l'INALCO." *Meta* 27(3): 347–51.

Gile, Daniel. 1988. "Les publications japonaises sur la traduction: un aperçu." *Meta* 33(1): 115–26.

Gile, Daniel. 2005. "Citation Patterns in the T&I Didactics Literature." *Forum* 3(2): 85–103.

Han, Lili, Jing Lu, and Jisheng Wen. 2022. "Note-Taking Proficiency in Interpreting Teaching: Putting the Note-Taking Fluency Scale to the Test." *Theory and Practice in Language Studies* 12(10): 2024–35.

Mackintosh, Jennifer. 1995. "A Review of Conference Interpretation: Practice and Training." *Target* 7(1): 119–33.

MEC (Ministerio de Educación y Ciencia). 1991. Real Decreto 1385/1881. BOE 234, 31773–75.

Wang, Binhua, and Lei Mu. 2009. "Interpreter Training and Research in Mainland China." *Interpreting* 11(2): 267–83.

Wang, Weiwei, Yi Xu, Binhua Wang, and Lei Mu. 2020. "Developing Interpreting Competence Scales in China." *Front. Psychol.* 11(481). doi: 10.3389/fpsyg.2020.00481.

Xu, Ziyun. 2017. "The Ever-changing Face of Chinese Interpreting Studies: A Social Network Analysis." *Target* 29(1): 7–38.

Yang, Yuan, and Xiandong Li. 2022. "Which Theories Are Taught to Students and How They Are Taught: A Content Analysis of Interpreting Textbooks." *Círculo de Lingüística Aplicada a la Comunicación* 92: 167–85. https://dx.doi.org/10.5209/clac.78327.

Zhu, Xuelian, and Vahid Aryadoust. 2022. "A Scientometric Review of Research in Translation Studies in the Twenty-First Century." *Interpreting* https://doi.org/10.1075/target.20154.zhu.

Acknowledgments

We are truly indebted to all the contributors of this volume, who provided the erudition and wisdom of each chapter. Thank you for answering with patience our editorial queries and responding to our suggestions. Working with you has been a pleasure, and notwithstanding the names on the spine of the book, this volume is really yours.

We would also like to extend our most heartfelt gratitude to the editorial team at Routledge, in particular Katie Peace, Simon Bates, and Khin Thazin, for your unwavering support, and all the copyeditors at Routledge, for your patience and professionality.

Our immense gratitude also goes to all past and future interpreters for your enormous yet oftentimes underappreciated efforts. This volume is dedicated to all of you.

Notes on editors

Riccardo Moratto is Professor of Translation and Interpreting Studies at the Graduate Institute of Interpretation and Translation (GIIT), Shanghai International Studies University (SISU), Chartered Linguist and Fellow Member of the Chartered Institute of Linguists (CIoL), Editor in Chief of Interpreting Studies for Shanghai Foreign Language Education Press (外教社), General Editor of *Routledge Studies in East Asian Interpreting*, and General Editor of *Routledge Interdisciplinary and Transcultural Approaches to Chinese Literature*. Professor Moratto is a conference interpreter and renowned literary translator. He has published extensively in the field of translation and interpreting studies and Chinese literature in translation.

Irene A. Zhang is Professor of Translation and Interpreting Studies and Dean of the Graduate Institute of Interpretation and Translation (GIIT), Shanghai International Studies University (SISU). A conference interpreter by training, Prof. Zhang has published extensively in the field of translation and interpreting studies. She is also General Editor of *Routledge Studies in East Asian Interpreting* and General Editor of the *Journal of Translation Studies* published by Peter Lang.

Notes on contributors

BAI Xuejie has been teaching in Lanzhou University and working as a part-time interpreter after graduating with a master's degree in applied linguistics with a focus on translation and interpretation from Lanzhou University. She has published three papers on translation and interpretation, has been teaching such courses as entry-level interpreting and high-level public speaking for undergraduates and simultaneous interpreting, sight translation, as well as interpreting theories and skills. She has interpreted for over a hundred conferences, symposiums, lectures, business negotiations and has tutored students to participate in and win prizes in national and provincial public speaking and interpreting contests.

CHEN Yihui was formerly a full-time university lecturer of English–Chinese interpreting. He is now a PhD student in the School of English Studies at Shanghai International Studies University. His research interests include interpreter education and interpreter identity.

CHEN Yiqiang is a PhD student at the Centre for Translation, Interpreting, and Cognition (CSTIC), University of Macao, and his research interest lies in interpreting process research and conference interpreting.

DONG Jiqing is a lecturer in translation and interpreting at Shanghai International Studies University. Sponsored by China Scholarship Council, she undertook her doctoral project (2012–2016) on public service interpreting at Heriot-Watt University, UK. From 2017 to 2019, she worked as a lecturer at the University of Leicester, UK, convening MA modules in translation studies and supervising postgraduate students in various fields of interpreting.

GAO Bin is Professor of Translation Studies at the School of English and International Studies, Beijing Foreign Studies University, China. She accomplished the training in conference interpreting in SCIC EU (Brussels). Her research interests include interpreter education and conference interpreting.

GAO Yu is currently a lecturer at the School of Interpreting and Translation, Beijing International Studies University (BISU), China. She is also a PhD

xviii   *Notes on contributors*

candidate at the School of English and International Studies, Beijing Foreign Studies University (BFSU), China. Her research interests include cognitive processing in interpreting and corpus-based interpreting.

HE Yinghua holds a master's degree in translation studies from the School of Interpreting and Translation Studies, Guangdong University of Foreign Studies. Her main research interests include translation policy and translation pedagogy.

JIA Hui received her MA degree in foreign linguistics and applied linguistics from Beijing Foreign Studies University in 2013. She is currently working as a lecturer at the School of Interpreting and Translation, Beijing International Studies University, and pursuing a doctoral degree at the Faculty of Humanities, the Hong Kong Polytechnic University. Her current research interests include corpus-based interpreting, interpreting pedagogy, and multilingual interpreting studies.

JIANG Yu received his master's degree of translation and interpreting from the University of Bath in 2013 and from Shandong University in 2014. He is now pursing his doctoral degree at China University of Foreign Affairs. He is now working as the vice dean of the School of Interpreting and Translation, Beijing International Studies University. His research interests include interpreting and translation studies and international political linguistics.

LEI Victoria is Associate Professor at the University of Macao. She has a PhD in English literature from the University of Glasgow, UK, and is a life member of Clare Hall, University of Cambridge. She provides conference interpreting service at local, national, and international levels. From 2003 to 2009, she was an invited translator/presenter at Teledifusão de Macao. She studies comparative studies, translation/interpreting studies, and 19th-century studies. Her interpreting practice and teaching have led her to focus her research on cognition and interpreting in recent years. She joined UM's Centre for Cognitive and Brain Sciences in 2019.

LI Dechao is Associate Professor at the Department of Chinese and Bilingual Studies, the Hong Kong Polytechnic University. His main research areas include corpus-based translation studies, empirical approaches to translation process research, history of translation in the late Qing and early Republican periods, and problem-based learning and translator/interpreter training.

LI Defeng is Distinguished Professor of Translation Studies and Director of Centre for Studies of Translation, Interpreting, and Cognition (CSTIC) at the University of Macao. Previously, he taught at the School of Oriental and African Studies of the University of London, where he served as Chair of the Centre for Translation Studies. He also taught at the Department of Translation, the Chinese University of Hong Kong, for a decade. He publishes in cognitive translation studies, corpus-assisted translation studies, translation education, and second language education.

LI Xiaoyan is currently a PhD candidate at Shanghai International Studies University with a specialization in interpreting studies. She is also a lecturer at the College of Foreign Languages, Xinjiang Normal University. Her research interests include interpretation theory and teaching.

LI Zhi is Associate Professor in the School of Western Languages at Harbin Normal University. She is working to promote translation technology education and is in charge of MTI translation technology courses in her department. Her research interests include interpreting and translation theories and practice, as well as interpreting and translation technologies. She has published more than ten articles in translation journals, and seven of them are in core journals. She is the coauthor of two books on interpreting and technologies, one of the authors of two translation textbooks, and the leader of four research programs relating to interpreting and technology.

LIU Xinyuan is a PhD student of translation and interpreting studies at the School of English Studies in Shanghai International Studies University. Her research interests include empirical approaches to translator and interpreter education, particularly validation issues on testing and assessment of translation and interpreting competence, cognitive aspects of translation process research.

LIU Yi is a PhD candidate in the Department of Chinese and Bilingual Studies at the Hong Kong Polytechnic University. Her research interests include corpus-based translation and interpreting studies, empirical research on interpreting, and interpreting theory and practice. She is also a CATTI-certificated translation and conference interpreting practitioner in China.

LÜ Jie is Associate Professor in the School of English for International Business of Guangdong University of Foreign Studies, where she teaches translation courses to both BA and MA students. She is a professional committee member of the Translation Technology Education Society of World Interpreter and Translator Training Association (WITTA). Her research interests include audiovisual translation, multimodality in translation, and translation teaching.

MU Lei is Professor and PhD Supervisor at Guangdong University of Foreign Studies. She received her PhD in translation and interpreting studies from Hong Kong Baptist University. Her research focuses on theoretical and methodological issues in translation and interpreting studies, translator and interpreter education, and language services.

REN Wen is Professor at the Graduate School of Translation and Interpretation, Beijing Foreign Studies University, China. Her research interests include translator/interpreter ethics, interpreting studies from a sociological perspective, interpreting pedagogy, language policy, etc.

SHANG Xiaoqi is Assistant Professor in the School of Foreign Languages at Shenzhen University. He received his PhD in interpreting studies from the Graduate Institute of Interpretation and Translation at Shanghai International Studies University. His main research interest lies in testing and assessment in interpreting. Shang's works have appeared in *The Interpreter and Translator Trainer*, *Target*, *The Asia Pacific Education Researcher*, *The Chinese Translators' Journal*, and *Foreign Languages*.

WANG Huashu is Associate Professor at the Graduate School of Translation and Interpreting, Beijing Foreign Studies University. He is currently working with governments, research institutions, language service providers, and user associations around China to promote translation technology education. Wang is well recognized as an active researcher and trainer in translation technology in China. His research interests include translation, interpreting, and localization technologies. He is the author, coauthor, or editor of 12 books, including most recently *Interpreting Technology Research, Teaching and Beyond (2021)*, *Insights into Translation Technology Research, Teaching and Developments (2020)*, and *Technology and Computer-Aided Translation: Theory and Practice (2020)*.

XING Jie is Professor of Translation Studies and Vice Dean at the School of Interpreting and Translation Studies of Guangdong University of Foreign Studies, where he teaches courses related to the theory and practice of translation and interpreting at undergraduate and postgraduate levels. He publishes widely on issues related to translation theory, sociology of translation, translation policy, translation pedagogy, and interpreting studies. He obtained his PhD degree at the Hong Kong Polytechnic University and was an academic visitor at Durham University, UK. Currently, he is Vice President of the Socio-Translation Studies Committee of China Association for Comparative Studies of English and Chinese and Expert Member of the Translators Association of China.

YANG Chengshu received her PhD in linguistics from Beijing Foreign Studies University. Her research is focused on interpreting studies, translator studies, and international medical T/I studies. She served as the director of the Graduate Institute of Translation and Interpretation Studies/Cross-Cultural Studies at Fu-Jen Catholic University (FJCU). She also served as a visiting professor at the School of International Studies, Sun Yat-sen University, in Zhuhai from 2016 to 2021. In December 2017, she received an honorary fellowship from the Hong Kong Translation Society. On August 1, 2018, she was named FJCU Tenured Distinguished Research Professor.

ZHAN Cheng is Professor at the School of Foreign Languages, Sun Yat-sen University (Guangzhou, China). He obtained his MA in translation and comparative cultural studies from the University of Warwick, and his PhD in interpreting studies at Guangdong University of Foreign Studies. He is an active member of AIIC whose research interests focus on interpreting practice and interpreter training as well as on translation studies. He has published five monographs and ten interpreting textbooks. Currently, he is the lead investigator of "the effect of audio description training on cognitive processing competence in interpreting," a research project funded by the Chinese national humanities and social sciences council.

ZHANG Han is currently a PhD student at the School of Foreign Languages, Sun Yat-sen University. She obtained her MA in translation and interpreting from Dalian University of Foreign Languages. She taught interpreting at Jiangxi University of Finance and Economics from 2016 to 2021. Her main research interests are related to the sociology of translation and interpreting studies.

ZHANG Wei is Professor of Interpreting and Translation Studies at the School of English and International Studies, Beijing Foreign Studies University (BFSU), China. As a leading researcher of BFSU, he has main research interests that include functional linguistics, text linguistics, cognitive processing in translation, and corpus-based translation. He has published a number of articles in SSCI, A&HCI, CSSCI journals (Chinese Social Science Citation Index), authored several monographs and textbooks, and edited some volumes on cognitive research of interpreting, simultaneous interpreting, working memory, and interpreting corpora.

ZHANG Xiaojun is Assistant Professor in translation and interpreting at Xi'an Jiaotong-Liverpool University and an honorary associate at the University of Liverpool. He is a Professional Conduct Committee member of the Association of Computational Linguistics (ACL) and the deputy chairman of Translation Technology Education Society of World Interpreter and Translator Training Association (WITTA). He is an adjunct professor of Northwestern Polytechnical University. His research interests cover translation technology, natural language processing, computational linguistics, explainable machine translation.

ZHAO Zhuxuan is a PhD candidate at the University of International Business and Economics and a lecturer at the University of Chinese Academy of Sciences. She graduated from the UIBE-SCIC program with a professional diploma in conference interpreting and has worked part-time as a conference interpreter. Her research interests are interpreter education and conference interpreting.

ZHU Yuben is Senior Lecturer at the Graduate School of Translation and Interpretation, Beijing Foreign Studies University, China. He has also been an active conference interpreter since 2011. His field of research is general interpreting studies, with a particular focus on conference interpreting. He has been involved in several research projects on CI and has published various articles and textbooks on interpreting.

ZOU Bin is a lecturer at the College of Foreign Languages, Xinjiang Normal University (Urumqi, China). He was senior visiting scholar to Guangdong University of Foreign Studies, China, and Aberdeen University in Scotland, UK. His research interests focus on interpreting practice and interpreter training. Currently, he is the lead investigator of "Translation Strategies of Political Discourse: A Research on Improvement of the Information Publicity of Xinjiang," funded by the humanities and social sciences department of Xinjiang.

Introduction

Riccardo Moratto and Irene A. Zhang

This volume is part of a larger editorial project concerning conference interpreting in China: the rise and development of a profession. This seminal publication comprises two volumes. This present volume is titled *Conference Interpreting in China: Practice, Training, and Research*.

This two-volume editorial project, published by Routledge in the series Routledge Studies in East Asian Interpreting, is a landmark publication project, spearheaded by the Graduate Institute of Interpretation and Translation (GIIT), Shanghai International Studies University (SISU). The first volume is an effort to piece together how interpreting developed into a profession in China. It is composed of three parts. Part I mainly follows the joint training program between the UN and the Chinese government to train conference interpreters (and translators) that ran from 1979 to 1993. Altogether, 129 colleagues graduated from the program, thus obtaining the qualifications to interpret for/in the UN. Indeed, most of the P4- and P5- interpreters in the UN Chinese booth at present, and some who have landed in management positions in the UN departments or agencies – who have been invited to write a chapter in the first volume – are graduates from the program. They share insider stories that took place while China finally started to liaise with the world. The first book includes a Foreword by Lynette Shi, a trainee in the first batch of the UN program who later worked for the UN in NY and Geneva as interpreter, a member of the International Association of Conference Interpreters (AIIC), and its director of the Asia Pacific Region. Part II, in a similar vein to Part I, is a historical account of the cooperation project between DG Interpretation of the EU and China's Ministry of Commerce. The contributors include senior staff still in service at the Directorate-General for Interpretation, with some post-retirement input from the former EU officials who had been well-trained interpreters and interpreter trainers themselves. Both the longer-standing program of training up conference interpreters from Chinese ministries and agencies (which goes back to 1979, with the formal program starting up in 1985) and the more-specific cooperation with universities in China (University of International Business and Economics started in 2001, Shanghai International Studies University in 2002) are discussed. Part 3 is focused on the growth of the domestic interpreters and

DOI: 10.4324/9781003357629-1

their development with the profession. Interviews are conducted with the first-generation interpreters, that is, the limited few who once interpreted for the first-generation Chinese leaders, including Chairman Mao Zedong, Premier Zhou Enlai, and later, Mr. Deng Xiaoping.

This present volume comprises chapters by leading Chinese scholars with a Foreword by Emeritus Professor and renowned interpreting scholar Daniel Gile. It presents a thoughtful and thorough account of diverse studies on interpreting in China, with a particular focus on conference interpreting, and it introduces readers to a plurality of scholarly voices focusing on different aspects of interpreting training, research, and practice from an interdisciplinary point of view. Given its focus, the book will benefit researchers and students who are interested in different aspects of interpreting and conference interpreting in China. The book offers a unique window on topical issues in the professionalization of interpreting in China.

It is hoped that this book will encourage a multilateral, dynamic, and international approach in a scholarly discussion where, more often than not, approaches tend to be dichotomized. This book aims at bringing together leading Chinese scholars with the same passion, that is, delving into the theoretical and practical issues of interpreting training, research, and practice.

We grouped the chapters for the reader's convenience into two sections, but many of the chapters speak to more than a single aspect. This book consists of 15 chapters, 8 on the professionalization of conference interpreting in China, including historical and pedagogical aspects, and 7 on the professional practice and future trends. Chapter 1 sets the scene for research in the field of conference interpreting. Starting from history, Chapters 2, 3, and 4 are general summarization of professional practice and training. Chapters 5, 6, and 7 are more specific, but they can follow the line from conference interpreting practice to conference interpreting training. Chapter 8 investigates the differences between native and non-native English speakers in assessing Chinese-to-English interpretation. The second section, professional practice and future trends, comprises seven chapters. Again, starting from a general one exploring standards of interpreting services in China, the following Chapters 10, 11, and 12 describe regional situations, namely, Macao, Xinjiang, Gansu, Qinghai, and Ningxia. The last three chapters focus on technology, multimodality, and virtual reality. These final chapters somehow lead the way into future trends. To facilitate reading, the abstracts of the authors will be presented as summary to each chapter.

The first part of this volume is subtitled "Professionalization of conference interpreting in China," and it comprises eight chapters. In Chapter 1, Cheng Zhan and Han Zhang argue that conference interpreting in China has gone through professionalization in a period of 40 years since the late 1970s. Given the increasingly diversified market demand as well as changing institutions, it is of practical importance to approach China's professionalization of conference interpreting from the research community. Based on a review of research and publications, including core journal articles, books, and academic conference proceedings, this chapter describes and summarizes the process and prospects of research on conference interpreting professionalization in China. Through an analysis of the general situation of research, including research evolution, (sub)themes, and methodologies, the chapter concludes that research on conference interpreting professionalization has increased moderately, with limited research topics and adopting homogeneous methods. The chapter suggests that efforts should be made to open wider horizons and strengthen theoretical input so as to provide greater reference for understanding professionalization of conference interpreting in China.

In Chapter 2, Yuben Zhu and Wen Ren contend that the UN Training Program for Interpreters and Translators (UNLTP) jointly initiated by the UN and China in 1979 marks the official debut of professional conference interpreter training in China. In its 14 years of operation, the program had produced a large contingent of high-caliber conference interpreters for the UN headquarters and the various Chinese government agencies. Drawing on the theory of outcome-based education (OBE) model first proposed by Spady, and adopting a historical lens, this chapter looks into the training outcome and principles of UNLTP by combining analysis of firsthand archival evidence with published interviews of former trainers and trainees. Analysis shows that the country's first and highly successful CI program had, in many ways, embodied the principles of OBE, long before the theory itself was even articulated. By calling for attention to the outcome of significance, the research hopes to inspire innovative efforts from all stakeholders involved in interpreter training, now a quickly expanding field in China, in overcoming the challenges they collectively face today.

In Chapter 3, Lei Mu and Xinyuan Liu aim to reveal the interactions between the professionalization of interpreting, professional interpreter education, and the establishment of translation and interpreting studies (TIS) as an independent discipline in the Chinese mainland since its reform and opening-up policy in 1978. The development of China's language service industry and the process of professionalization of interpreting have contributed to establishing a complete professional interpreter education system. After an analysis of professional interpreter education practice and research, including the most recent progress of establishing the doctoral diploma, doctor of translation and interpreting (DTI), external and internal factors of the development of professionalization of interpretation and professional interpreter education are presented, taking the standardized development of interpreting competence scales and interpreter training as examples. It demonstrates how the practice and research of professional interpreter education can meet the needs of national policies and the professionalization of interpreting for the new era. Final remarks are drawn to encourage comparative research on professional interpreter education in China and abroad.

In Chapter 4, Bin Gao and Zhuxuan Zhao argue that institutionalized training of conference interpreting is essential for addressing talent shortage in this most professionalized sector of interpreting. In China, much effort has been made to develop training methods and models for conference interpreting programs, yet little is known about the views of graduates regarding their transition from university to professional employment. To address this less-researched aspect of interpreter training, this chapter investigates the career motivations of 67 graduates from the "UIBE-SCIC" program between 2012 and 2022, as well as their self-perceived employability through a questionnaire survey. As the first CI training program officially supported by SCIC in China, the "UIBE-SCIC" program is held to stringent and profession-oriented training standards, with prestige established in China's interpreting education community and wider society. The career motivations and self-perceived employability of its graduates may shed light on how conference interpreting training has supported students' career development. The authors' research has revealed strong and focused motivations for learning but less-clear career goals during the program, which continue to evolve in the workplace. In contrast to previous research showing the mismatch between master of translation and interpretation (MTI) programs and the industry, the vast majority of conference interpreting graduates in this chapter have built their career profiles largely around the professional know-how developed during training. Although career motivations differ by employment types, with individual career choices seemingly affected by both external and internal factors, interpreting-specific competences have remained central to the formation of career orientations. Interpreting-specific competences have also served as a foundation on which other aspects of employability are further developed in the workplace. In contrast to generally higher levels of satisfaction with the "softer" aspects of employability, the respondents saw practical experience as important to career development but insufficiently developed during the program. Implications for conference interpreting programs are discussed based on the findings, with pedagogical suggestions to better prepare students for successful careers.

In Chapter 5, Wei Zhang and Yu Gao contend that the interpreter's role has been an important but highly debatable issue in interpreting studies, with divergent views concerning neutrality, interpreting performance, and quality. This chapter reports a new survey on the conference interpreters' role perception, intending to contribute more diverse data for a more specific account of the interpreter's role in conference setting. The survey shows that like their colleagues in other settings, conference interpreters tend to see themselves as an active participant in interpreting-mediated communication, playing a visible role in their activities. The survey also represents the first attempt to explore the relation between interpreters' personal factors and their role perception, as well as how interpreters' role identity affects their interpreting behavior. Specifically, the survey finds (1) the interpreter's role perception is greatly influenced by such individual factors as interpreting experience, conference subject familiarity, and working mode; (2) the interpreter's interpreting strategies (namely compression, explanation, correction, and parallel reformulation) and communication pattern (e.g., direct/indirect speech) are evidently conditioned by one's role perception.

Some suggestions for further studies have been made in terms of data size, methodological design (e.g., corpus), and theoretical framework (e.g., CDA, narrative theory, and sociology).

In Chapter 6, Yi Liu and Dechao Li discuss problem-based learning (PBL) and its potential application to conference interpreting training. PBL methods are thought to promote active learning of students, enhance students' performance on complex tasks, and increase knowledge consolidation. Moreover, PBL approach in conference interpreting training is conducive to encouraging interpreting trainees to solve authentic problems during interpreting training. As such, the students can reflect on their interpreting process, which again can be situated in different interpreting contexts. In addition, this chapter proposes seven teaching steps for PBL model in interpreting classrooms and addresses the design and implementation of problems, the role of teachers, and the assessments of students' learning outcomes in problem-based interpreting training. This chapter also provides a case study to demonstrate how PBL can be applied in interpreting classrooms. The article concludes with a discussion of educational benefits brought by applying PBL model in conference interpreter training.

In Chapter 7, Jiqing Dong and Yihui Chen argue that since the launch of the BTI (bachelor of translation and interpreting) and MTI (master of translation and interpreting) programs, translation and interpreting (T&I) education in China has developed rapidly as a response to its surging demand for conference interpreters. However, unlike the teaching activity and student development that have drawn much research attention, studies on the identity of interpreting teachers are relatively small in number. Their expected threefold identity as teachers, practitioners, and researchers, as suggested by scholars including Gile, may be too ideal, especially for those at private colleges with BTI programs alone. This case study targets the interpreting teachers at a private college in a third-tier city in Zhejiang province, hoping to bring to the fore one disadvantaged yet equally important subsector of the national T&I higher education and explore the difficulties experienced by this group of interpreting faculty representing private colleges and universities in China. Through a case study approach, this chapter finds that there is a gap between what the teachers think they should do for career development and what they actually do in teaching, practice, and research. Such a gap results from an interplay of internal and external factors. Explained from the self-discrepancy theory in terms of ideal self, ought self, and actual self, this gap can be regarded as a cause of the teachers' anxiety and crises as well as a driving force for their career pursuit.

In Chapter 8, the last of the first section, Xiaoqi Shang argues that previous literature in language education demonstrates that native English speakers (NES) and non-native English speakers (NNS) exhibit highly divergent assessment patterns in assessing performance-based tests, such as writing and speaking. However, insufficient scholarly attention has been paid to examining their differences in assessing spoken language interpretation. To address this gap, Shang's study adopts a data-driven approach to exploring NES's and NNS's differences in assessing Chinese-to-English (C–E) interpretation, with a special focus on weighting. Eight practicing interpreters who had Chinese as L1 and English as L2 (NNS) and two practicing interpreters who had English as L1 and Chinese as L2 (NES) were recruited to evaluate a total of 50 C–E interpretations, using both analytic and holistic rating scales. Data analyses suggest NES and NNS exhibited significant differences in assigning weights among the three criteria (fidelity, language, and delivery) when assessing interpretation. Specifically, NNS raters assigned the heaviest weight to fidelity (β_1 = .351), followed by delivery (β_3 = .345), and language (β_2 = .325), whereas NES gave the most value to language (β_2 = .396), followed by delivery (β_3 = .343), and fidelity (β_1 = .300). Retrospective interviews were conducted for data triangulation. The implications of the findings are also discussed.

The second section of the book, professional practice and future trends, comprises seven chapters. In Chapter 9, Jie Xing and Yinghua He argue that from 2006 to 2021, standards of interpreting services in China have gone through two stages, the initial and the booming one. The authors collect nine documents of standards that are wholly or at least partially devoted to the discussion of interpreting services issued on the official website of the Translators Association of China (TAC) and further analyze their core contents and typical features. By tracing the aforementioned documents and comparing them with their international counterparts, the authors find that Chinese standards suit the trends of the language service industry in China and are gradually in line with international ones. To promote standardization of the interpreting industry, it is argued that the following measures should be in place in the future: standards should be jointly formulated by all parties involved, targeted to specific domains, focusing on the interpreters' competence and rights, giving full play to technical elements, and strengthening promotion and implementation.

In Chapter 10, Yiqiang Chen, Victoria Lai Cheng Lei, and Defeng Li give a brief account of (conference) interpreting in Macao, a multilingual and multicultural society in the southern part of China. Beginning with a historical and contextual discussion of translation and interpreting in this area, the review looks at interpreting as a practice and profession in Macau, with a focus on its social, political, and economic role in the local society. This review is then followed by an examination of the current interpreting training available at different Macao higher-learning institutions and the accreditation tests administered in this area. Finally, the authors highlight the strengths of interpreting research, with an emphasis on the neurocognitive research conducted at the Centre for Studies of Translation, Interpreting, and Cognition (CSTIC) at the University of Macau, the biggest public university in the Macau Special Administrative Region.

In Chapter 11, Binzou and Xiaoyan Li argue that under the Belt and Road Initiative, Xinjiang is witnessing fast economic development and is in dire need of professional translators, especially high-quality interpreters. To meet the needs of local economic and social development, the teaching institutions in Xinjiang are supposed to adjust their teaching model and adapt to the evolving and rapidly changing market. This chapter reviews the evolution of interpreter training in Xinjiang over the past decade, focusing on two Xinjiang universities for their localization, curriculum design, training methods, scientific research, and trainees' quality control. The chapter then analyzes the challenges faced by interpreter trainers and puts forward some measures to support the development of interpreter training in Xinjiang in the future. The chapter aims to enable trainers to better understand the status quo of interpreter training in Xinjiang and to call for more efforts to develop interpreter training in a scientific and systematic manner.

In Chapter 12, Xuejie Bai argues that due to geopolitical and economical disadvantages, MTI (master of translation and interpreting) education in Gansu, Qinghai, and Ningxia faces major obstacles, especially in conference interpreting education. This chapter discusses some common problems in conference interpreting education in the four higher institutions in the three provinces in terms of curriculum, human resources, theses, and internship program and tries to explore some possible solutions such as enhancing inter-institutional cooperation and sharing resources, taking advantage of opportunities for practice and internship inside and outside of universities, flexibly and effectively encouraging students to participate in conference interpreting–related activities, and making good use of online learning opportunities in the post-pandemic era. It is hoped that this chapter may offer inspirations to universities located in remote places with underdeveloped economy and facilities.

In Chapter 13, Huashu Wang, Zhi Li, and Chengshu Yang argue that in the era of artificial intelligence (AI), conference interpreting has undergone significant technological changes, as big data, deep learning, neural networks, speech recognition, and machine translation quickly advance. Starting with the history of conference interpreting, this chapter clarifies the history of interpreting technology by dividing it into four periods (the preparation, germination, rising, and explosive periods). Drawing on previous research, it defines interpreting technology as a comprehensive technology that is used in practice and training, including in every phase of conference interpreting, such as encoding, outputting, transmitting, inputting, decoding, and storage. It classifies interpreting technology into six categories, specifically, (1) hardware or software, (2) different functions, (3) the degree of automation, (4) the process of interpreting, (5) roles of technology, and (6) different users. In engaging with history and providing definitions and classifications, it predicts that in the future, conference interpreting technology could be characterized by customization, intelligence, ubiquity, platform as a service, and standardization. This chapter also uses a case study to describe the role of technology in the whole process of conference interpreting.

In Chapter 14, Jie Lü and Xiaojun Zhang argue that communication technologies are playing an increasingly important role in interpreting studies, and videoconference interpreting is becoming progressively more multimodal in nature as a result. The authors seek to contribute to the theoretical development of multimodal (interactive) studies, where videoconference interpreting can deal with various forms of data, such as text, audio, video, image, gesture, action, and emotions, in an interactive way between the interpreter on the microphone and the multimodal data. This chapter also adheres to the subfield of meeting content analysis, as this is a convenient way to help interpreters prepare for a meeting and provide a better user experience. The main purpose of the authors is to propose a list of key features and resources that may be used to inform the development of videoconference interpreting technology and applications to support multilingual conferences in the future. Furthermore, the chapter explores the technical issues concerning a prototype computer-aided conference interpreting system (CACIS) between English and Chinese. The automatic multimodal processing and analytic techniques that are employed by this system are key emerging trends in videoconference interpreting and will help shape the future development of this field in China and beyond.

In Chapter 15, the last chapter of the present volume, Yu Jiang and Hui Jia aim to provide a panoramic description of the development of interpreting training and research with the support of virtual reality (VR) in China. The authors find there are two commonly used approaches to embed VR in interpreting training (VR labs and VR-aided interpreting simulation projects) by categorizing different cases in Chinese universities and summarizing the results of VR-supported interpreting research (descriptive research and empirical studies).

We would like to extend our most heartfelt gratitude to the editorial and production team at Routledge, in particular Simon Bates for his patience, and to all the editors at Routledge. Thank you for your support and invaluable guidance. Last but not the least, we are truly indebted to all the contributors to this volume, who provided the erudition and wisdom of each chapter. Thank you for enduring with patience our editorial queries and suggestions. Working with you has been a pleasure, and notwithstanding the names on the spine of the book, this volume is really yours.

Part I

Professionalization of conference interpreting in China

1 Professionalization of conference interpreting in China

Implications from research and publications

Cheng Zhan and Han Zhang

1 Introduction

Professionalization of conference interpreting in China started in the late 1970s with the reform and opening-up policy of the nation. A milestone of conference interpreting becoming a profession was the inauguration of the United Nations Training Program for Interpreters and Translators (UNLTP) in Beijing in 1979. In the mid-1990s, leading T&I schools began to launch programs modeled on AIIC best practice to offer professional diploma in conference interpreting. Graduates of such programs have been active in language service, contributing to China's increasing participation in international governance. With the approval and launch of the brand-new master of translation and interpreting (MTI) program in 2007, professional conference interpreting education in China has been in full swing. Since the founding of the Interpretation Committee in 2016 under the Translators Association of China (TAC), the national-level professional association of translation and interpreting, a number of standards on conference interpreting service have been issued. With increasing value attached to the functions of T&I in national image building and international communication, conference interpreting has become a booming field that attracts greater attention from practitioners and educators alike.

With four decades of professionalization, conference interpreting in China has also become a more popular research subject. In 2004, the 5th National Conference and International Forum on Interpreting was held at Shanghai International Studies University (SISU), with the theme of "Professionalization in Interpreting: International Experience and Developments in China." It was the first time that conference interpreting professionalization had been the focus of a major nationwide academic gathering. The topic has since remained one of the themes in the successive forum series.

China now is home to a large interpreting research community, but the topic of conference interpreting professionalization has not yet been thoroughly explored, with studies so far mostly being general introductions of conference interpreting as a profession or as a particular element in the

DOI: 10.4324/9781003357629-3

broader field of interpreting. When it comes to the question of status quo of research on conference interpreting professionalization in China, the picture is still quite fragmented. As a piece of meta-analysis, this chapter presents a bibliometric study of research publications on China's conference interpreting professionalization, with a view to offer more reliable data for better understanding of this area and analyze the momentum of conference interpreting professionalization as a growing academic (sub)field.

2 Socio-professional theory and conference interpreting research

There have been diversified discussions in social science on professionalization, with the trait model and processual model being the main approaches. The trait model uses an attribute approach to distinguish profession from occupation. Greenwood (1957) suggests five attributes that are typical functional traits of professionalization: (1) systematic theory, (2) authority, (3) community sanction, (4) ethical codes, and (5) a culture. In contrast to the static conception of profession, the processual model stresses the process for achieving the status of a full profession. Wilensky (1964) suggests a prototypical continuum of five stages of professionalization: (1) making the occupation full-time, (2) establishing formal training, (3) developing a professional association, (4) pushing for legalized protection, and (5) adopting a code of ethics. Professional dynamics are explored by Abbott (1988) to further examine the changing nature of profession on how professional groups control expert knowledge and achieve power.

These socio-professional theories have found their way into research on conference interpreting and its professionalization. Most researchers in China have adopted the trait approach to the status quo of different attributes, or one of the attributes, of conference interpreting professionalization. Tseng's (1992) MA thesis, for example, was a demonstration of the dynamic power-attaining process. The development of conference interpreting in Taiwan, China, was divided in his dissertation into four successive phases: (1) market disorder, (2) consensus and commitment, (3) publicity, and (4) professional autonomy.

As research on conference interpreting professionalization in China is still in its preliminary stage, it is necessary to determine the scope and parameters of research for the purpose of a comprehensive review. Researchers' perceptions of the components of conference interpreting professionalization have been quite consistent, with most studies starting off defining the components or important aspects of conference interpreting professionalization. Based on such common practice, summarized and represented in Table 1.1, the research landscape can be mapped on a number of parameters: professional quality, professional association, professional training/education, and professional accreditation.

A major difficulty of conducting a review on this less-charted field lies in the rather-fuzzy research boundaries, which hinders a clear delimitation of its

Table 1.1 Summary of Parameters in Previous Research

Research	Parameters
Bao (2007)	Professional quality, norms, and skills
Pan et al. (2009)	Professional quality and skills; professional market development; accreditation and professional education
Guo et al. (2011)	Professional development; professional qualification and level of education
Chen and Mu (2016)	Professional association; training institutions; accreditation

scope. The previous parameters in conference interpreting professionalization are thus used as keywords for data retrieval for this research. The results are then selected and refined manually to cover research that has a clear orientation toward professionalization and at the same time avoid too specific (sub)topics such as conference interpreting training and competence development.

3   Overview of conference interpreting professionalization research in China

After manual indexing and screening, the final database contains 78 entries, including 55 journal articles, 12 conference papers from three sessions of the National Conference and International Forum on Interpreting, 7 MA dissertations, and 4 monographs, all completed after 1990. Each entry was labelled with author(s), year of publication, type of publication, keywords, research themes, as well as theoretical framework and research methods.

3.1   *Research output*

Hu (1990) expounded the educational resources of interpreting, categories of interpreting, division of labor, and professional challenges in his discussion on the status and development of interpreting in China. His article depicts the circumstances and characteristics of the interpreting profession against China's surging international exchanges in the early 1990s and may be regarded as the beginning of the study of conference interpreting professionalization in China.

Study in this (sub)field had remained dormant until the turn of the century. Figure 1.1 shows the yearly output of conference interpreting professionalization research from 2001 to 2022 (as of August). Publications started to grow moderately during the first decade of the 21st century, making up 39.7% of the total research output. Researchers began to show interest in conference interpreting as a profession, with discussions about regional market development, professional capabilities, and adaptation of training to new professional needs. 2004 alone contributed 16.1% of the research output during this decade. This may partly be due to the publication of a conference

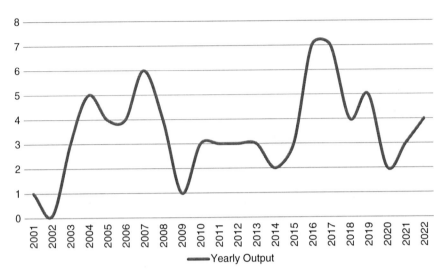

Figure 1.1 Research output by year (2001–2022).

proceeding with the theme "Professionalization in Interpreting: International Experience and Developments in China." Several years after the launching of China Accreditation Test for Translators and Interpreters (CATTI) in 2003, the year 2007, with 19.4% of the total research in the decade, saw the publication of a number of articles on professional accreditation. Two MA dissertations in 2008 analyzed the professionalization of conference interpreting in China from a general perspective.

The significant moves of professional training of conference interpreting were the BATI and MTI programs approved respectively in 2006 and 2007 by the Ministry of Education and the Academic Degree Committee affiliated to the State Council, which gave rise to a surge of research on training in the next decade. Publications in the period from 2011 to 2020 account for approximately 51.3% of the total data, with an average of four publications per year. As the year 2016 and 2017 marked the 10th anniversary of BATI and MTI programs respectively, seven publications, the largest number in a single year, were added each year, including conference proceedings from the 11th National Conference and International Forum on Interpreting, with the theme "Professionalization in Interpreting: Research, Teaching and Development," in 2016, and research on professional training in 2017. Three of the four monographs were also published during this period, which explore interpreters' professional development (Bai 2015), conference interpreting teaching, learning and research (Liu 2017), and interpreting project management (Wang and Li 2019).

In the period of 2001 to 2022, the research output of interpreting studies in China has been in a steady upward trend, and the emergence of new subjects such as CATTI stimulated relevant inquires. It can be argued that research in this period has been able to keep abreast with the socio-professional development of conference interpreting and enriched China's interpreting research. However, compared with research on other topics of interpreting, including process, products, and interpreter training, research on conference interpreting professionalization was relatively marginal. The sluggish growth in publications reflects the fact that professionalization has been somewhat undervalued as a research topic that could have great social and practical significance. The evolution of research on conference interpreting professionalization shows the awakened but still insufficient interest across the academic community.

3.2   *Thematic dimensions*

Despite the relatively small number of research output, research topics of conference interpreting professionalization have been quite diverse. Based on the main parameters mentioned previously, the themes are categorized into professional training, professional practice, professional interpreters, and professional accreditation (see Table 1.2), with each theme subdivided according to research content specificity.

Research on conference interpreting training constitutes nearly one-third of the total. The exploration of professional training has been manifested as the training mode of conference interpreters on the macrolevel, the design of curriculum settings, textbook compilation, as well as training of trainers on mesolevel and the learning motivation of trainees on the microlevel. This category

Table 1.2 Thematic Dimensions of Research

Thematic Labels	(Sub)themes	Number	Proportion
Professional training	Training mode	17	32.1%
	Curriculum design	4	
	Textbook compilation	2	
	Learning motivation	1	
	Training of trainers	1	
Professional practice	Overview of the profession	18	30.8%
	Professional standards	3	
	History of the profession	2	
	Risks in the profession	1	
Professional interpreters	Professional competence	14	24.3%
	Professional emotion	2	
	Professional ethics	1	
	Professional role(s)	1	
	Career development	1	
Professional accreditation	Test design	5	12.8%
	Transnational comparison	3	
	General review	1	
	Washback effect	1	

has thrived since the beginning of professional interpreting education in the late 2000s and has become the dominant research (sub)theme. Educators and researchers have made considerable progress in the essentiality of conference interpreting training, including why to teach, what to teach, and how to teach.

With training mode accounting for 21.8% of the total research output, different models of conference interpreting training oriented toward professionalization have been discussed. Based on local practice and experience, some researchers proposed diversified modes with reference to different means, such as student-centered "post-method" (Wang 2017) and "teaching salon" as a complementary method for professional practice (Jiang 2015). These are attempts to integrate innovative conception into conference interpreting training to meet the practical demand of the profession.

Curriculum setting is crucial to rationalization of the professional nature of BATI and MTI programs. Against the changing labor market, studies in this respect looked into existing problems of program design, like the decoupling between school training and workplace skills, and too much influence from traditional mindset for curriculum design, followed by recommendations. The specific resources and factors involved in professional training also provoked discussions, including textbook compilation (Zhao 2017), learning motivation of students (Zhan 2013), and training of trainers (Liang and Mu 2020), to help mitigate the gap between increasingly professionalized conference interpreting and training approaches. The constant academic input in professional training indicates the progressive improvement of programs and the desire to keep abreast with professionalized conference interpreting practice.

Conference interpreting professionalization has been intertwined with professional practice, and makes up the second largest proportion (30.8%) of data. Occupation surveys on regional level (e.g., Pan et al. 2009; Guo et al. 2011) showed the development of conference interpreting market across China as well as qualifications of conference interpreters perceived and required by stakeholders. The increasing refinement of labor division generated research on professional practice in specific scenarios, such as simultaneous interpreting in focus group discussion settings (Chen 2016), inspired exploration of specified norms, and indicated the direction of conference interpreting training. As for professional standards, investigations have been made from the analysis of professional conference interpreting standards and norms drafted by the TAC Interpretation Committee and comparison with code of conduct elsewhere. These studies present a trend of active adaptation to the growing needs of the language service industry and gradual integration with international standards (Xing and He 2021). Research on professional history and risks has been rare but constructive. Xu and Cheng (2020) summarized the unique experience of conference interpreting practice in China through a historical review. Hong and Hong (2022) analyzed possible risks of remote conference interpreting during the COVID-19 pandemic, and suggested some coping strategies.

As actors of professionalization, conference interpreters have been a (sub) theme of roughly a quarter of the total research publications. Interpreter-centered research revolves around professional competence, role(s), and code of ethics. The professional competence construct of interpreters has received more attention in this category. The widespread use of artificial intelligence has led researchers to introducing the concept of information technology for building a three-dimensional competence model of technology awareness, learning, and utilization (Li and Li 2019). By contrast, the number of studies on the issues of ethics, role, and career is marginal.

Professional accreditation serves the gatekeeping role in conference interpreting professionalization but turns out to be the least-researched area, making up for a small proportion of only 12.8%. Test design is a major topic in this category. After the launch of the Shanghai Interpreting Qualification Certificate Examination in 1995, there were inquiries into its design, the attendees' performance, and its washback role in professional training (Yang 2001). Early researches also cover the introduction of more mature international qualifications, such as a comparison between the interpreting accreditation systems in China and Australia (Ren 2005). As the number of accreditation tests increases, some studies analyzed the consistency and validity of propositions from the perspective of testing theory, with the purpose of ensuring test credibility, protecting the interests of candidates, and maintaining the authority of certificates (Lu et al. 2007).

The previous analysis of thematic dimensions reveals the research foci of conference interpreting professionalization. Substantial research efforts driven by professional training and practice demonstrate growing professional awareness among educators and practitioners alike. Studies on professional conference interpreters center on competence development, overshadowing other social-professional issues.

3.3 Methodological features

Research methodologies for conference interpreting professionalization are categorized according to the methodological division of interpreting research summarized by Zhong and Wang (2010). On the level of basic methodological orientations, research on conference interpreting professionalization is divided into positivist and humanistic research, with quantitative and qualitative methods being the main research approach, respectively. Specific research strategies are further divided and described as follows.

Table 1.3 Summary of Research Methodologies

Methodological Orientation	Methods	Number	Proportion
Humanism	Empirical generalization	44	73.1%
	Literature research	8	
	Theoretical speculation	5	
Positivism	Survey	12	26.9%
	Case study	7	
	Experiment	1	
	Ethnography	1	

Most conference interpreting professionalization researches reviewed (73.1% of the total) adopt humanistic methodology, and over half of them are based on empirical generalization. Pedagogical experience of conference interpreter training has been reflected upon to formulate more profession/market-oriented training models. Archives and publications on conference interpreting professionalization have been the common source of literature for content analysis for transnational comparison or bibliometric study. Accreditation of professional conference interpreters has been studied for better tests design, including comparison among different conference interpreting qualification examinations in China (Huang and Liu 2017). A small number of researchers have also contemplated on the existing problems of conference interpreting professionalization and made theoretical contributions through speculative analysis. For example, Zhong (2003) deduced the formula of interpreter's knowledge structure as KI = KL + EK + S (P + AP) (*KL* refers to knowledge for language; *EK* refers to encyclopedic knowledge; *SP* refers to professional interpreting skills; *SAP* refers to artistic presentation skills), thus updating the old-fashioned mindset of conference interpreter training and providing a new theoretical model for curriculum development. Research with literature methods and theoretical speculation only takes up 16.7% of the total, partly due to the overall limitations of theoretical input.

Positivistic epistemology seems to have been a preferred methodological option of the interpreting studies community but is yet to play an important role in research on conference interpreting professionalization. About 26.9% of the research in the data are conducted with empirical methods, with survey being the major method (15.4%). For the conference interpreting profession, systematic information gathered from different groups of actors is useful for the investigation into the status quo, demand and supply, as well as identity and role issues of conference interpreting. The earliest of such surveys was conducted in Beijing by Wang (2005), who distributed questionnaires to conference interpreters and interpreter users during the 2002–2004 period to study the market scale and qualifications of conference interpreters. Similar surveys were carried out in Southeast and Southwest China (Pan et al. 2009; Guo et al. 2011). Case study has been adopted for research topics such as professional training to illustrate a certain mode or curriculum design. A pilot training model (Zhang and Chai 2022) has been integrated into conference interpreting education to explore more advanced and professionalized ways of training. The only ethnographic research in this category concerns the (sub) theme of interpreter training. Cui (2019) observed the course of "Interpreting Profession and Interpreter Ethics" at Beijing Foreign Studies University and found that students who were exposed to the reality of conference interpreting learned to better cope with ethical issues in the profession. Experimental design was adopted in an MA dissertation to validate the importance of interdisciplinary awareness for professional conference interpreters (Cheng 2010).

Few researches in the data are interdisciplinary in nature or have a solid theoretical framework. In the overall field of interpreting studies, research of conference interpreting professionalization has been lagging behind in terms of methodological solidity and variety. Most studies describe the professional situation and make proposals, based on personal thoughts and experience of the author(s). Experimental and ethnographical attempts in the MA dissertations after 2010 may therefore be seen as a positive sign.

4   Discussion

4.1   Major findings and implications

4.1.1   Slow growth of research publications

Despite continuous study on the T&I profession in general, the scale of conference interpreting professionalization research is still moderate. In the past 40 years, there have been no more than a hundred pieces of core literature on this topic, reflecting the somewhat neglection from academia. Following the first journal discussion on conference interpreting professionalization in 1990, there was no research output on this topic until ten years later, while a total of 112 articles on interpreting in general were published in core foreign languages and translation journals within the same period (Wang 2018).

Despite the actual status of professionalization as being a frontier of the language service industry, it seems to have been perceived as less important by the research community. Technology application in interpreting research has brought about a large number of corpus-based studies, but when it comes to professionalization, it is more difficult to obtain empirical data for verification or analysis due to the characteristics of interpreting activities. The sociological turn in interpreting studies has brought researchers' attention to the social mechanisms of conference interpreting, but such a research perspective still needs to be instantiated by Chinese researchers. In general, there has been a considerable body of research on conference interpreting pedagogy, practice, or interpreters, but few of them were derived from or aimed at the profession or professionalization, resulting in the slow development of this research (sub) field. The mainstream mindset and general trend in interpreting studies have set invisible obstacles for research on conference interpreting professionalization. The volume and growth rate of publications, in turn, affect the weight and presence of this (sub)field in the whole research community of interpreting studies.

4.1.2   Limited dimensions of research themes

The development of the interpreting profession has brought new challenges to interpreting research. The renewal of research themes and methods is imminent. However, most researched topics of conference interpreting professionalization have been limited to the analysis of the composition of professionalization and recommendations for further professionalization with a macroscopic view.

There seems to have been a certain degree of decoupling between academic research and practical issues in the profession. Firstly, the width and depth of conference interpreting professionalization research have not been fully reflected in overall interpreting research. Research themes of conference interpreting professionalization have been quite limited. Studies on practitioners, for example, have still been concentrated on interpreter competence. Other (sub)fields, including social status, self-awareness, stress, gender, and working environment of conference interpreters, are far less explored. Secondly, research has been rather confined to the description of the subject per se from within, depriving professionalization of its dynamic and associated features. For example, research on professional accreditation mainly discusses the inner consistency of test design and reliability, without taking the link-up effect with other stakeholders into consideration. Neither have the published studies sourced much input from different actors in the profession, including conference interpreters, language service companies, and training institutions, whose feedback is thought to represent problems and realities of the profession. Thirdly, academic efforts in conference interpreting professionalization have remained on a rather-general and vague level. The study on professional practice, for instance, is usually presented in the form of introductory and preliminary description. Occupation classifications within the professional community are not clear-cut. As a result, researches targeting at institutional, part-time, or freelance interpreters, respectively, are marginal.

4.1.3   *Homogeneous research methods*

The efficiency and validity of research hinge upon rigorous and appropriate methodology. While positivist methodology has been the preference in interpreting studies in general, humanistic orientation still dominates research on the (sub)field of conference interpreting professionalization in China. Such methodological pattern is partly the result of limited research themes and reflects the epistemological preference of researchers.

It is true that methods such as empirical summarization, theoretical reflection, and literature research are helpful in the early stages of conference interpreting professionalization to draw the general picture and lay a foundation for further theoretical output. However, as professionalization of conference interpreting is intrinsically a process of socialization, positivist research methods can take research in this (sub)field away from subjective deliberation, provide bottom-up evidence for development of the profession, and help discover its unique attributes and mechanisms. Empirical research on the professionalization of conference interpreting emerged as early as 2005 but has so far not been a mainstream method among researchers. The most-used survey tool has remained questionnaires, making survey-based studies insufficient in elaboration on the design rationale and explanation of the results. In addition, given the enormous workload of data collection for individual researchers, such studies usually suffer from a very small sample size, which undermines the validity of research findings.

In a nutshell, existing research on conference interpreting professionalization in general has been homogenous in terms of research (sub)themes and methods. Scholarly awareness and attempts are therefore called for to reorient research to the profession and professionalization of conference interpreting. More efforts need to be made to expand research subjects, diversify research methods for in-depth investigations into professionalization of conference interpreting.

4.2   Future development

It can be argued that existing research publications on conference interpreting professionalization feature a relatively limited and isolated pattern. Based on the overall performance of research publications, the prospects of research turn out to be uncertain, though future research may still be projected and proposed with diversified themes, interdisciplinary frameworks, and different methods.

First, conference interpreting as a profession has been the product of the joint efforts of different actors in the midst of social changes. It would thus be worthwhile to explore the interaction between internal and external stakeholders, human or non-human actors, some of which researchers have already touched upon. An expansive and dynamic vision will help future research move beyond the most-discussed actors, such as conference interpreters and professional training, and open new space for more research (sub)themes. Influencing factors such as technologies, professional associations, and interpreting policies are pervasive across the professionalization of conference interpreting and can either facilitate or impede the development of professionalization. These actors should be investigated individually to discover their functions and collectively to reveal the mechanism of conference interpreting professionalization. When multilayered networks and various actors are investigated, a comprehensive understanding of how the profession has been influenced, recognized, as well as professionalized can be reached.

Second, the relatively underexplored status of conference interpreting professionalization, in theoretical terms, is reflected in a lack of conceptual approaches to ways in which the relationships between social structure and actors underpin and elucidate such phenomenon. To fill the gap, theoretical frameworks from other disciplines are called for. Apart from the frequently discussed frameworks, including Bourdieu's, Latour's, and Luhmann's concepts (see Milani 2022, 239–253), sociological theories such as symbolic interaction can be adopted to investigate issues of professional identity management and role performance (e.g., Yuan 2022). Psychological approaches are valuable conceptual resources on the micro sociopsychological level to explicate interpreters' self-perception, stereotyped attitudes, and social recognition of the general public toward conference interpreting. Conference interpreting is often embedded in institutional settings as a secondary activity and can thus be enriched by organizational and institutional studies. Institutional interpreting can be viewed both as a socialized and professionalized process, and such mechanism can be explained by legislative, normative, and cultural-cognitive institutionalization (e.g., Koskinen 2008). Interdisciplinary research can offer holistic and dynamic approaches to more sophisticated models across a diversified range of research topics.

Third, solid and rigorous research methods are increasingly needed in the study of conference interpreting professionalization. Researchers should be open to various techniques, procedures, and tools. Take the less-researched topic of history of the conference interpreting profession as an example. Oral history with professional conference interpreters of different generations may provide rich evidence to reveal issues of professional disposition and the development of professionalization in specific social context (e.g., Torikai 2014). Thinking portfolios, such as personal logs of conference interpreters, reflect conceptualization of practitioners and can be referred to for examining the formation and evolution of professional awareness, knowledge, and habitus. Network ethnographic approach can be adopted by researchers to observe and record conference interpreting in different settings, such as institutions or virtual communities (see Risku et al. 2022, 324–339), providing new materials for the ecology of the interpreting profession. Digital humanities toolkit can enhance content analysis, discourse analysis, and semantic network analysis of profession-related narratives, interpreting policies, and media representation. These refined methods and undervalued data sources may unveil the profession as well as professionalization in real scenarios. The use of mixed methods is expected to ensure validity, reliability, and representativeness to the best extent.

Diversified research themes with interdisciplinary theoretical frameworks and new research methods help explain the dynamic and complex mechanism of conference interpreting professionalization and shed light on how the profession has been shaped, challenged, and even shifted through a series of social practice and efforts to attain professional autonomy.

5   Conclusion

As a piece of meta-research, this chapter presents an analysis of research and publications on conference interpreting professionalization. With data collected from 1990 to 2022, a review is conducted with the analysis of research evolution, (sub)themes, and methodologies on conference interpreting professionalization. In the past four decades, conference interpreting professionalization in China, though an underexplored area, has seen some developments in a number of ways, including professional training, accreditation, professional associations, and technologies. Relevant research has been on a slow but steady rise, with focus on professional training and practice, especially training modes and professional competence constructs. The extremely uneven distribution across publication types, including journals, monographs, conference papers, and dissertations, may suggest that researchers have not perceived conference interpreting professionalization as a major research topic and have not conducted much investigation. Research methods are mostly found to be congruent with empirical generalization and literature research.

In light of the findings presented previously, future research in this (sub) field may cover more diversified themes, such as legislation and history of the profession, human and machine interaction, and the mechanism of professionalization, to name just a few. With research in such new fronts, conference interpreting professionalization may be further explored with a cross-disciplinary approach and mixed research methods.

Given the lack of research on the important topic of China's conference interpreting professionalization, as this chapter has reflected, the present volume on the professional development of conference interpreting in China is not only timely but also important, as it is expected to bring in a significant piece to complete the puzzle. The multiple and complementary perspectives provided here will hopefully help advance research in this area, which has the potential of development as an actor to demand greater recognition and respect for such a growing profession.

References

Abbott, Andrew. 1988. *The System of Professions: An Essay on the Division of Expert Labor*. Chicago: University of Chicago Press.

Bai Qiumei 白秋梅. 2015. *Kouyi shizhan jineng yu yiyuan zhiye fazhan* 口译实战技能与译员职业发展 [On Interpreting and Interpreter Professional Development]. Beijing: Tsinghua University Press.

Bao Chuanyun 鲍川运. 2007. "Kouyi de zhiyehua" 口译的职业化 [The Professionalization of Interpreting]. *Zhongguo fanyi* 中国翻译 [Chinese Translators Journal] (01): 50–1.

Chen Ruiqing 陈瑞青, and Mu Lei 穆雷. 2016. "Lun kouyi zhiyehua guocheng zhong de kouyi zige renzheng kaoshi" 论口译职业化过程中的口译资格认证考试 [On Interpreting Accreditation Tests in the Process of Interpreting Professionalization]. *Shandong waiyu jiaoxue* 山东外语教学 [Shandong Foreign Language Teaching] (04): 91–100.

Chen Yang. 陈洋. 2016. "Guonei FDG tongchuan hangye shizheng yanjiu: xianzhuang yu wenti – laizi yiyuan yu yonghu de diaocha baogao" 国内FDG同传行业实证研究：现状与问题 – 来自译员与用户的调查报告 [An Empirical Study on the Domestic FGD Simultaneous Interpretation Industry: Current Status and Problems: A Survey Report from Translators and Users]. *Zhongguo fanyi* 中国翻译 [Chinese Translators Journal] (03): 70–7.

Cheng Lin. 程琳. 2010. "Yizhe de kuaxueke yishi yu zhiyehua fazhan" 译者的跨学科意识与职业化发展 [Translator's Interdisciplinary Awareness and Professional Development]. MA Thesis, Shanghai International Studies University.

Cui Enqiao. 崔恩侨. 2019. "'Kouyi zhiye yu lunli' kecheng minzuzhi yanjiu" "口译职业与伦理"课程民族志研究 [Ethnographic Studies in the Course "Professions and Ethics of Interpreting"]. MA Thesis, Beijing Foreign Studies University.

Greenwood, Ernest. 1957. "Attributes of a Profession." *Social Work* 2(3): 45–55.

Guo Lijia 郭力嘉, Zhang Li 张丽, and Li Yanying 李砚颖. 2011. "Kouyi zhiyehua qushixia de xibu kouyi rencai peiyang tanjiu – yixiang jiyu chuan yu liangdi kouyi zhiye diaocha de yanjiu baogao" 口译职业化趋势下的西部口译人才培养探究 – 一项基于川、渝两地口译职业调查的研究报告 [An Inquiry on the Cultivation of Interpreter Talents in Western China under the Trend of Professionalization of Interpreting: A Research Report Based on the Survey of Interpreting Professions in Sichuan and Chongqing]. *Waiyu dianhua jiaoxue* 外语电化教学 [Technology Enhanced Foreign Language Education] (05): 54–9.

Hong Gang 洪岗, and Hong Miao 洪淼. 2022. "Yuancheng huiyi kouyi de fengxian ji fangfan" 远程会议口译的风险及防范 [Risks and Prevention of Remote Conference Interpreting]. *Shanghai fanyi* 上海翻译 [Shanghai Journal of Translators] (04): 40–5.

Hu Gengshen 胡庚申. 1990. "Chuyi woguo kouyi gongzuo de xianzhuang he fazhan" 刍议我国口译工作的现状和发展 [Discussion on the Current Situation and Development of Interpretation Work in China]. *Zhongguo keji fanyi* 中国科技翻译 [Chinese Science & Technology Translators Journal] (02): 41–4.

Huang Min 黄敏, and Liu Junping 刘军平. 2017. "Guonei kouyi zige kaoshi yanjiu de wenxian jiliang fenxi" 国内口译资格考试研究的文献计量分析 [A Bibliometric Analysis of the Research on the Domestic Interpretation Qualification Examination]. *Jiefangjun waigouyu xueyuan xuebao* 解放军外国语学院学报 [Journal of PLA University of Foreign Languages] (05): 119–26.

Jiang Fengxia 蒋凤霞. 2015. "Fanyi shuoshi (MTI) 'kouyi shalong' jiaoxue chutan" 翻译硕士（MTI）"口译沙龙"教学初探 [A Preliminary Study on the Teaching of MTI "Interpreting Salon"]. *Zhongguo fanyi* 中国翻译 [Chinese Translators Journal] (05): 53–9.

Koskinen, Kaisa. 2008. *Translating Institutions: An Ethnographic Study of EU Translation.* Manchester: St. Jerome.

Li Zhi 李智, and Li Defeng 李德凤. 2019. "Rengong zhineng shidai kouyiyuan de xinxi jishu suyang yanjiu" 人工智能时代口译员的信息技术素养研究 [Research on Information Technology Literacy of Interpreters in the Era of Artificial Intelligence]. *Zhongguo fanyi* 中国翻译 [Chinese Translators Journal] (06): 80–7.

Liang Weiling 梁伟玲, and Mu Lei 穆雷. 2020. "'Yi xue wei zhongxin' de fanyi jiaoshi peixun moshi – jiyu rineiwa daxue huiyi kouyi peixun xiangmu de qishi" "以学为中心"的翻译教师培训模式 – 基于日内瓦大学会议口译培训项目的启示 [Learning from University of Geneva's Learning-Centered Training Model for Translation and Interpreting]. *Zhongguo fanyi* 中国翻译 [Chinese Translators Journal] 41(06): 53–60+191–92.

Liu Heping. 刘和平. 2017. *Zhiye kouyi jiaoxue yu yanjiu* 职业口译教学与研究 [*Professional Interpreting: Teaching, Learning and Researching*]. Beijing: Foreign Language Teaching and Research Press.

Lu Min 卢敏, Liu Chen 刘琛, and Gong Xiangfei 巩向飞. 2007. "Quanguo fanyi zhuanye zige (shuiping) kaoshi kouyi shiti mingzhi yizhixing yanjiu baogao" 全国翻译专业资格（水平）考试英语口译试题命制一致性研究报告 [How to Maintain Consistency in CATTI's Interpretation Tests: A Research Report]. *Zhongguo fanyi* 中国翻译 [Chinese Translators Journal] (05): 57–61+96.

Milani, Mila. 2022. "Cultural Sociology." In *The Routledge Handbook of Translation and Methodology*, edited by Federico Zanettin and Chris Rundle, 239–53. London and New York: Routledge.

Pan Jun 潘珺, Sun Zhixiang 孙志祥, and Wang Honghua 王红华. 2009. "Kouyi de zhiyehua yu zhiyehua fazhan – shanghai ji jiangsu diqu kouyi xianzhuang diaocha yanjiu" 口译的职业化与职业化发展 – 上海及江苏地区口译现状调查研究 [The Professionalization and Development of Interpreting: A Survey on the Current Situation of Interpreting in Shanghai and Jiangsu]. *Jiefangjun waiguoyu xueyuan xuebao* 解放军外国语学院学报 [Journal of PLA College of Foreign Languages] (06): 81–5+101.

Ren Wen. 任文. 2005. "Zhong ao kouyi shuiping kaoshi ji zige renzheng duibi tan" 中澳口译水平考试及资格认证对比谈 [A Contrastive Analysis of Aptitude Tests and Accreditation for Interpreters in China and Australia]. *Zhongguo fanyi* 中国翻译 [Chinese Translators Journal] (01): 62–6.

Risku, Hana, Maija Hirvonen, Regina Rogl and Jelena Milosevic. 2022. "Ethnographic Research." In *The Routledge Handbook of Translation and Methodology*, edited by Federico Zanettin and Chris Rundle, 234–39. London and New York: Routledge.

Torikai, Kumiko. 2014. "Oral History as a Research Method to Study Interpreters' Habitus." In *Remapping Habitus in Translation Studies*, edited by Gisela Vorderobermeier, 133–47. Amsterdam: Rodopi.

Tseng, Joseph. 1992. "Interpreting as an Emerging Profession in Taiwan: A Sociological Model." MA Thesis, Fu Jen Catholic University.

Wang Binhua 王斌华. 2018. "Zhongguo kouyi yanjiu 40 nian: licheng, chengjiu he zhanwang" 中国口译研究40年：历程、成就和展望 [40 Years of Chinese Interpreting Research: History, Achievements and Prospects]. *Dangdai waiyu yanjiu* 当代外语研究 [Contemporary Foreign Languages Studies] (03): 48–56+67.

Wang Enmian 王恩冕. 2005. "'Kouyi zai zhongguo' diaocha baogao" "口译在中国"调查报告" [Interpretation as a Profession in China: A Survey]. *Zhongguo fanyi* 中国翻译 [Chinese Translators Journal] (02): 57–60.

Wang Honglin 王洪林. 2017. "Zhiyehua shidai jiyu 'houfangfa' linian de kouyi jiaoyu moshi yanjiu" 职业化时代基于"后方法"理念的口译教育模式研究 [A Study on the Interpretation Education Model Based on the Concept of "Post-Method" in the Era of Professionalization]. *Zhongguo fanyi* 中国翻译 [Chinese Translators Journal] (06): 44–9.

Wang Huashu 王华树, and Li Zhi 李智. 2019. *Kouyi xiangmu guanli* 口译项目管理 [*Interpreting Project Management*]. Beijing: The Commercial Press.

Wilensky, Harold L. 1964. "The Professionalization of Everyone?" *American Journal of Sociology* 70: 137–58.

Xing Jie 邢杰, and He Yinghua 何映桦. 2021. "Zhongguo kouyi fuwu biaozhun tansuo yu zhanwang" 中国口译服务标准探索与展望 [Standards of Interpreting Services in China: Trends and Prospects]. *Shanghai fanyi* 上海翻译 [Shanghai Journal of Translators] (05): 72–8.

Xu Wensheng 许文胜, and Cheng Lulu 程璐璐. 2020. "Huiyi kouyi bainian: huigu yu zhanwang" 会议口译百年：回顾与展望 [100 Years of Conference Interpreting: Review and Prospects]. *Zhongguo fanyi* 中国翻译 [Chinese Translators Journal] (01): 122–29.

Yang Ming 杨明. 2001. "Yingyu kouyi zige zhengshu kaoshi yu fanyi jiaoxue" 英语口译资格证书考试与翻译教学 [English Interpreting Qualification Certificate Examination and Translation Teaching]. *Shanghai fanyi* 上海翻译 [Shanghai Journal of Translators] (03): 32–5.

Yuan, Xiaohui. 2022. "A Symbolic Interactionist Approach to Interpreter's Identity Management." *Interpreting and Society* 2(2): 141–59.

Zhan Cheng 詹成. 2013. "MTI huiyi chuanyi fangxiang xueyuan de xuexi dongji he tiyan – yixiang zhendui guangdong waiyu waimao daxue de shizheng yanjiu" MTI会议传译方向学院的学习动机和体验–一项针对广东外语外贸大学的实证研究 [Study Motives and Experience of Students in the MTI Conference Interpreting Programme]. *Waiyujie* 外语界 [Foreign Language World] (05): 36–44.

Zhang Jiliang 张吉良, and Chai Mingjiong 柴明颎. 2022. "Teseban – benke kouyi rencai peiyang moshi" 特色班 – 本科口译人才培养模式 [Setting up a Special Interpreter Training Program for Undergraduate Students: A New Model]. *Zhongguo fanyi* 中国翻译 [Chinese Translators Journal] (02): 67–74.

Zhao Hanchang 赵汉昌. 2017. "Zhiye daoxiangxing kouyi jiaocai de kaifa yuanze ji duice yanjiu" 职业导向型口译教材的开发原则及对策研究 [Development Principles and Countermeasures of Profession-Oriented Interpreting Textbooks] *Waiyu dianhua jiaoxue* 外语电化教学 [Technology-Enhanced Foreign Language Education] (04): 60–5.

Zhong Weihe 仲伟合. 2003. "Yiyuan de zhishi jiegou yu kouyi kecheng shezhi" 译员的知识结构与口译课程设置 [Knowledge Requirements for Interpreters and Their Implication to Interpreting Course Designing]. *Zhongguo fanyi* 中国翻译 [Chinese Translators Journal] (04): 65–7.

Zhong Weihe 仲伟合, and Wang Binhua 王斌华. 2010. "Kouyi yanjiu fangfalun – kouyi yanjiu de xueke lilun jiangou zhi'er" 口译研究方法论 – 口译研究的学科理论建构之二 [Interpreting Studies as a Discipline: The Methodological Issues]. *Zhongguo fanyi* 中国翻译 [Chinese Translators Journal] (06): 18–24+92.

2 UNLTP as a forerunner of OBE model for conference interpreter training in China

Yuben Zhu and Wen Ren[1]

1 Introduction

China's systematic approach to conference interpreter training may be traced back to the United Nations Language Training Program for Translators and Interpreters in Beijing[2] (hereinafter referred to as UNLTP) launched in 1979 (Dawrant et al. 2021). In its 14 years of operation (1979–1993), the program cultivated some 100-plus top-level conference interpreters for the UN headquarters and key Chinese state agencies (Yao 2019, 446). The program was considered a great success and jump-started China's effort to train conference interpreters at the university level. Since it was reconstituted as the Graduate School of Translation and Interpretation (GSTI) at Beijing Foreign Studies University (BFSU) in 1994, China has witnessed a nationwide expansion of interpreting programs in its higher learning system. With about 120 universities offering professional master's degree in interpreting, China possibly boasts the largest interpreter training market in the world, even if not all of them qualify for conference interpreter training.

In the meantime, the quick expansion has also given rise to a few problems faced by educators. As training is offered at more institutions and in more diverse formats than ever before, the lack of clarity of focus, well-designed training plan, qualified faculty, effective instruction methodology, and sound management approach attracts growing attention from the academic community (Zhong 2014, 40–44). All the aforementioned issues threaten to cause disjunction between interpreting education and the interpreting profession (Zhong 2017, 7–9). However, a scoping review of current research in interpreting education in China indicates that scholars have so far tended to focus on selected aspects of the challenge, that is, enrollment assessment (Xing 2021), specific course design and implementation (Jiang 2021; Zhao et al. 2021), or graduation thesis writing (Han and Hou 2022). A more holistic purview seems in order. The idea that today's interpreting education can benefit from the successful experience of the UN program provides the starting point for this chapter, which aims to reflect on the overall training philosophy and best practices of the program, a forerunner of outcome-based education (OBE) model, long before the term *OBE* was even proposed by

DOI: 10.4324/9781003357629-4

Spady (1994). Through analysis of firsthand archival data on the UNLTP and published interviews of former trainers and trainees, this chapter, through a historical lens, examines how this program had, in reality, if not in name, practiced the philosophy of OBE and, by doing so, successfully produced a sizable group of top-notch conference interpreters. Pedagogical implications are also drawn out for the interpreter training community today.

2   Literature review and conceptual framework

The OBE model was first systematically articulated by Spady (1994) to advise the US's basic education reforms in face of social and economic changes in the contemporary world. As the world shifts from the Industrial Age to the Information Age, Spady (1994, 18) argues that it is no longer sufficient for schools to operate in an Industrial Age–like assembly-line approach, which has largely reduced schools to passive followers of fixed curriculum and timeline preoccupied with covering standardized courses. The consequence of such standardization is that "WHEN and HOW students learn things often take precedence over WHAT is learned and WHETHER it is learned well." To enhance students' chances of success in life, schools should focus on cultivating their abilities in demonstrating observable actions.

This particular emphasis on tangible application, namely, students' ability to do at the end of their learning experience, makes OBE a useful guiding framework for disciplines that are oriented toward professional practice (medicine, law enforcement, engineering, translation and interpreting, etc.). Since its establishment, the model's application has expanded beyond K–12 and has been sought after by higher learning institutes around the globe. For example, a CNKI search using "OBE" as the keyword in November 2022 found 84 CSSCI research papers in China since 2015, with the majority of the papers on engineering education. Although translation and interpreting is considered a practice profession (Dean and Pollard 2011; Setton and Dawrant 2016), only one research (Sun 2020) is directly addressed to T&I education in China from the perspective of OBE, and it stops short at offering fairly general principles on improving the MTI scheme, leaving details on their implementation, such as instruction process and assessment, largely untouched. As interpreters are often compared with doctors and lawyers due to the practicality nature such professions share (Gentile 2017; Xu and You 2021; Pym 2022), there seems to be a lacuna in scholarship that needs to be filled. It is believed that a systematic analysis of the highly successful UNLTP through the lens of OBE could be of benefit to T&I trainers today. However, knowing that this wide-ranging theoretical framework encompasses many subparadigms, "golden rules," and "demonstration pyramids," it is probably very difficult, if not impossible, to reconstruct every aspect of OBE in the present research. Therefore, in what follows, we first tease out the most fundamental concepts and implementation principles of OBE before moving on to the analysis of the program from an OBE perspective.

Key concepts and principles of OBE

In his seminal work on OBE, Spady (1994, 12) defines the term as "focusing and organizing everything in an educational system around what is essential for all students to be able to do successfully at the end of their learning experience." As much as educators may wish for a ready recipe, the broad definition does not offer any set of clearly mapped-out criteria to follow. The seemingly vague definition has also contributed to much of the criticism surrounding OBE in the past years. Opponents dislike it because they think the outcomes' standards "may be too easy, too hard, or wrongly conceived" (Eldeeb 2013, 10).

On second thought, however, it is somewhat unreasonable to expect the model to prescribe what outcomes are and what teaching processes to follow for every school and student, not least because teaching and learning happen in various contexts and for different reasons. Furthermore, education needs to adapt to the demands of ever-evolving society. For this reason, Spady cautions that his work shall not be taken as final interpretation of OBE, as the model will almost certainly continue to develop in the future. He sets out to summate the common attributes possessed by all valid outcomes and the general principles for implementing outcome-based education. The key notions in the following sections shall serve as a springboard from which we investigate the subject matter at hand.

Outcome

The word *outcome*, as in *outcome-based education*, refers to students' ability to demonstrate what they have learned at the end of their learning experience. It refers to actions and performances that can showcase learners' competency in applying information, ideas, and tools successfully. In other words, outcomes involve actual doing, as opposed to just knowing or possessing pure mental processes. The latter should be regarded as goals rather than outcomes. The character of an outcome is that it must involve a demonstration process which should consist of three elements: learners have to KNOW something, be able to DO something with what they know, and BE LIKE a confident, successful performer as they're doing it (Spady 1994, 61).

Outcome of significance

During the process of implementing OBE, educators have come to realize that outcomes that are worth pursuing should embody things that (1) learners would remember and be able to do long after a particular curriculum ends and (2) are truly important to them in their educational and life-career future. To put it in another way, outcome of significance means that educators should always be ready to interrogate themselves with question of "What difference does it make in the long run?" and truly focus on the long-term benefits to their students.

Four principles of implementing OBE

OBE can be practiced at various levels of the educational system and in different ways. According to Spady (1994), practitioners across various contexts should consistently adhere to four fundamental principles, that is, clarity of focus, expanded opportunity, high expectation, and design down. In actual operation, these four principles are often interlinked, and together they essentially say the following: in an authentically outcome-based system, everything educators do, from curriculum design to instruction to assessment, must derive from the culminating outcomes they desire for their students. In other words, schools must first and foremost have a very clear picture of what students need to exhibit upon graduation and make it clear to the students from day one. This implies both teachers and learners, and all other stakeholders alike, need to gain clarity of focus.

To ensure success of learners, the instruction process and assessment should be structured more flexibly to offer them expanded opportunities. Traditional educational systems are often time-based, with procedures, programs, topics, and teaching activities fixated every step of the way through the academic calendar. The weaknesses of such an inflexible approach are obvious. While instructors are led to focus on facts and topics stipulated by the teaching plan rather than students' achievements, learners are rushed through the whole process without much opportunity for personalized growth. Little regard is given to their differences in interest, strengths, learning rate and style, etc. On the contrary, in a system that practices OBE, when achievements clash with the clock, outcomes must always take precedence over the calendar. Moreover, students will be provided with all necessary resources to succeed.

OBE also sets out to counter the practice of competitive grading treasured by traditionalists. Competitive grading follows a forced distribution system, in which students are mapped along a bell curve, with only a small fraction of the class deemed as good performers. Such an appraisal system has drawn strong criticism from the scholarly community for its serious limitations, one of which being the implication that not every student can succeed (Chattopadhayay and Ghosh 2012). Furthermore, grading results are often reduced to permanent records (hence also called "ink" grades) that constantly remind students of their past errors and have little to do with culminating outcomes. On the contrary, OBE differentiates between "pencil" and "ink" grades. "Pencil" grading allows for multiple tests so that students can have opportunities to change past records of errors and continually improve. Thus, it carries a genuine belief that given the time and resources, majority students can do well.

One important feature of the Information Age is the accelerated speed of knowledge expansion, which has made insightful curriculum choices increasingly difficult. The design-down principle championed by OBE holds that in deciding what critical components and building blocks to be selected into the curriculum, educators should start from the significant culminating outcomes desired for the learners and map back from there. Under this principle, educators will be able to better weigh curriculum choices against various external factors, such as deep-rooted traditional beliefs, knowledge explosion in various fields, changing demands in the marketplace, and the total time allowed by the system. If certain short-term, discrete outcomes are of little help to enable attainment of long-term outcomes, they should be replaced or even completely removed from the curriculum.

3   UNLTP as a forerunner of OBE

In the run-up to the celebration of its 40th anniversary in 2019, GSTI commissioned a project to systematically trace the history of its predecessor – the UNLTP. During this process, faculties and students reached out to people who had witnessed the program's story close up, conducting interviews and exchanging correspondence with those who had either directly participated in or have knowledge about the initial negotiations between the three parties (the UN, the Chinese government, and the host university) and UNLTP's subsequent operation. Besides rich oral accounts from university administrators, former trainers, and trainees, a large quantity of photographic and textual evidence was also extracted from the university museum and personal possessions during field visits. Data from different sources were then carefully cross-examined, and information providers were consulted whenever in doubt to ensure accuracy. The project uncovered many previously unknown or forgotten facts, which, together with other open information, formed the basis of the analysis that follows.

Clarity provided by culminating outcome

One key benefit of OBE's "no surprise" philosophy is the clarity it offers not only to educators and students but also to policymakers and employers (Ewell 2008). In the case of UNLTP, the culminating outcome was agreed upon and made known to all stakeholders at a very early stage. The enrollment plan (Figure 2.1) jointly submitted by the Ministry of Foreign Affairs and the Ministry of Education to the State Council on March 26, 1979, stated clearly that after completing the training and meeting the standards set by the UN, graduates would work as conference interpreters or translators at the UN headquarters. Upon approval from the State Council, the subsequent admission brochure (Figure 2.2) released to potential applicants further stated that they would be recruited as conference interpreters or translators and work at the UN headquarters for at least five years. The culminating outcome implied by these documents is clear: at the end of the learning experience, students need to demonstrate that they have the ability to apply the knowledge, skills, and tools as a UN conference interpreter.

The clarity afforded by this culminating outcome created very strong incentives for potential applicants and future students. Previous research

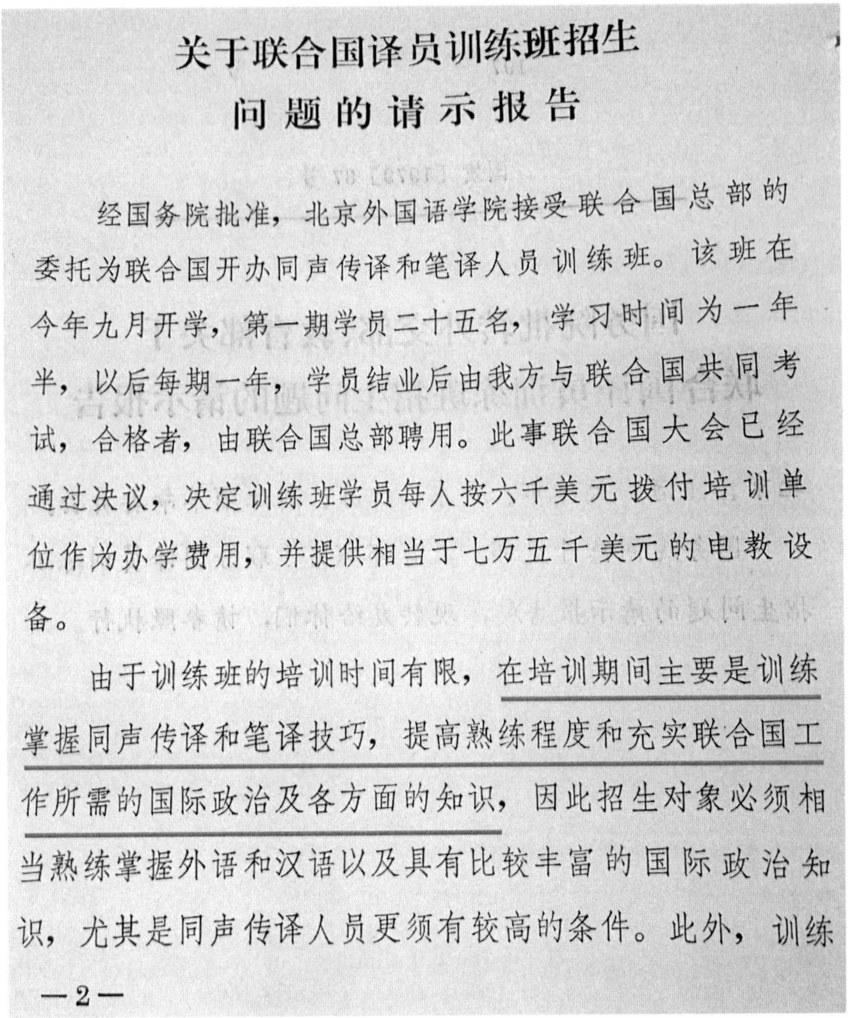

关于联合国译员训练班招生
问题的请示报告

经国务院批准，北京外国语学院接受联合国总部的委托为联合国开办同声传译和笔译人员训练班。该班在今年九月开学，第一期学员二十五名，学习时间为一年半，以后每期一年，学员结业后由我方与联合国共同考试，合格者，由联合国总部聘用。此事联合国大会已经通过决议，决定训练班学员每人按六千美元拨付培训单位作为办学费用，并提供相当于七万五千美元的电教设备。

由于训练班的培训时间有限，在培训期间主要是训练掌握同声传译和笔译技巧，提高熟练程度和充实联合国工作所需的国际政治及各方面的知识，因此招生对象必须相当熟练掌握外语和汉语以及具有比较丰富的国际政治知识，尤其是同声传译人员更须有较高的条件。此外，训练

— 2 —

Figure 2.1 Enrollment plan.

(Lin 2013) has shown that having a clear career prospect is very important in motivating interpreting students to enroll and study. In this case, many applicants were drawn to the program precisely because of the prospect of working at the UN. According to personal accounts by Lynette Shi (2004, 830), also named Shi Xiaojing, who is among the first cohort of trainees under the UNLTP, around 600 applicants registered for the entrance examination in 1979, and only 25 were eventually accepted, out of which only 10 were slated for conference interpreting. After being admitted, every candidate studied diligently. In an interview

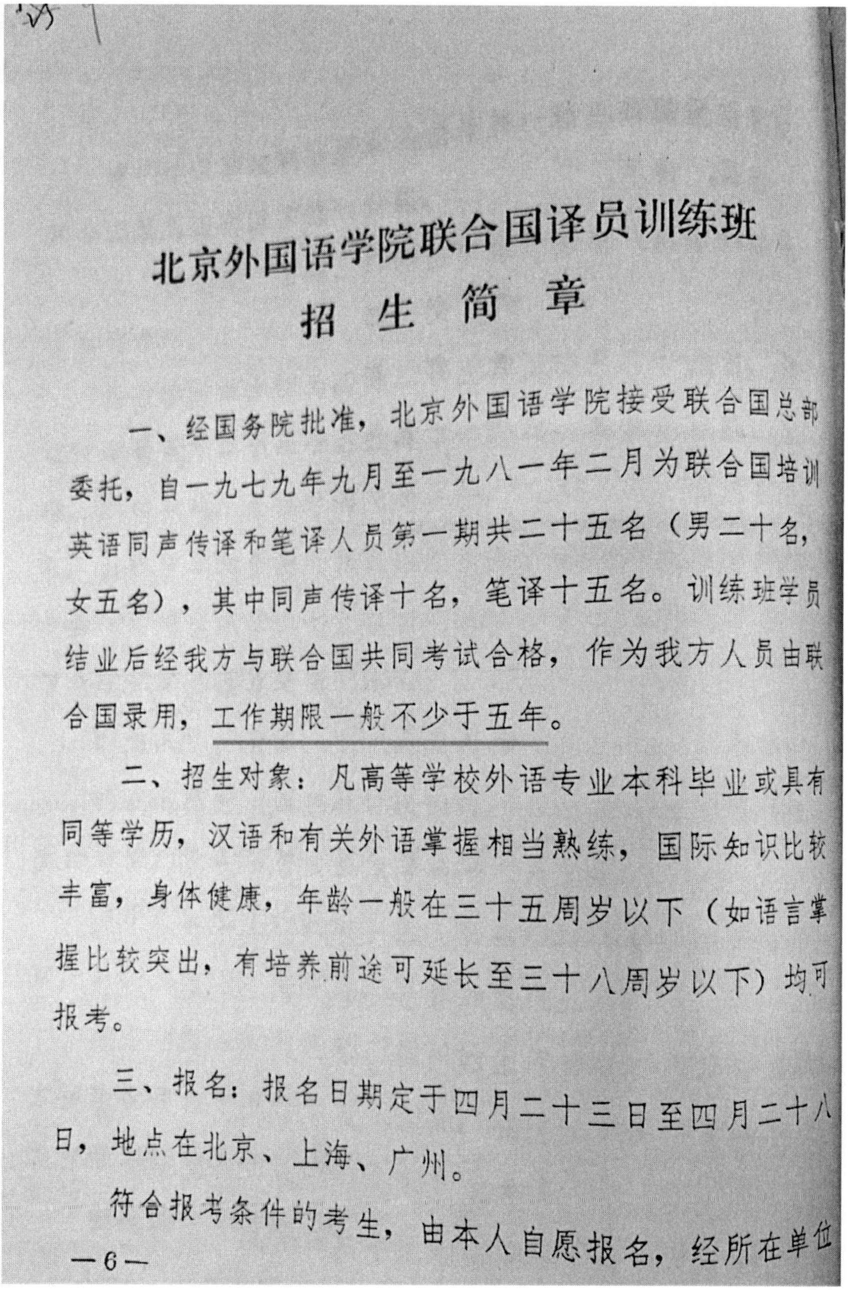

北京外国语学院联合国译员训练班
招 生 简 章

一、经国务院批准，北京外国语学院接受联合国总部委托，自一九七九年九月至一九八一年二月为联合国培训英语同声传译和笔译人员第一期共二十五名（男二十名，女五名），其中同声传译十名，笔译十五名。训练班学员结业后经我方与联合国共同考试合格，作为我方人员由联合国录用，工作期限一般不少于五年。

二、招生对象：凡高等学校外语专业本科毕业或具有同等学历，汉语和有关外语掌握相当熟练，国际知识比较丰富，身体健康，年龄一般在三十五周岁以下（如语言掌握比较突出，有培养前途可延长至三十八周岁以下）均可报考。

三、报名：报名日期定于四月二十三日至四月二十八日，地点在北京、上海、广州。

符合报考条件的考生，由本人自愿报名，经所在单位

— 6 —

Figure 2.2 Admission brochure.

conducted with faculties of GSTI in 2019, Zhang Zailiang, founding director of the UNLTP, recalled that the students were so committed to the program that after the interpreter training lab was closed for the night, they used all possible means to obtain the key from the keeper so that they could spend a few extra hours there to hone their skills (Yao and Deng 2019, 154).

Clarity also means that the instructional process needs to start with the teacher explaining and modeling the outcome from the very beginning and continually thereafter. In an article reviewing the first ten years' operation of the program, former trainer Wu (1990) observed that translation and interpreting techniques were not passed onto the students through abstract instructions but through large amounts of practice on the parts of the students and constant modeling on the part of teachers.

Expanded opportunities

Spady (1994, 24) identifies five dimensions to opportunity, including time, methods and modalities, operational principles, performance standards, and curriculum standards and structuring, but at its most basic level, practitioners of OBE should ensure that students have access to sufficient time and resources to succeed. A system with expanded opportunity can go beyond the traditional system's constraints and expand the duration, frequency, and precise timing of learning opportunities. In the enrollment plan initially submitted to the State Council (Figure 2.1), the duration of the program was set as one year, modeled after a previous program the UN had conducted with the Soviet Union. However, when the admission brochure (Figure 2.2) was formally released to the public, it had been expanded by the host university to one and half years (September 1979–February 1981). According to Zhang (2004, 826), since this was the first SI training program in the university, the decision was made to ensure that the first cohort would have sufficient time to learn and succeed. The strategy paid off. By the end of their learning experience, all 25 students passed the UN examination with flying colors. With the successful experience in running the first cohort, the school decided to shorten it to one year so as to meet the urgent demand for conference interpreters at the UN. However, after the second cohort, the program was extended back to two full years and was kept so for all future cohorts. Zhang (2004, 826–27) explained the rationale behind the adjustment as follows:

> The reason for the extension was that from the third cohort onward, students started to enroll at an increasingly younger age. Whether they will pass the recruitment exam of the UN or not, we felt that we should provide them with more solid training so that they could enjoy better development prospects in their future life.

In the meantime, curriculum was also augmented after the first cohort to include courses on consecutive interpreting. In a 2019 interview, Zhang said:

The first cohort did not take courses on consecutive interpreting. . . . Considering that they will eventually come back and work in China after five years' service at the UN, we decided to add consecutive interpreting to the curriculum so that the students could have better all-around development.

(*Yao and Deng* 2019, 152–53)

According to the agreement signed by the school and the UN, graduates of the program would work as conference interpreters at the UN for at least five years. After that, they would come back to China to either resume their original posts held with former employers or be assigned to Chinese government agencies. Evidence from the preceding text shows that although the culminating outcome of the program was the students' ability to work as UN conference interpreters, educators chose to go after the outcome of significance and focused on the long-term benefits to their students. They were ready to break the convention of existing UN training programs to ensure that the students have what they need to succeed in life.

Moreover, it was implemented in a way that learning opportunities were expanded beyond the duration and locality of the program. According to the agreement (Figure 2.3) between the UN and the students, those who were admitted into the UN would spend the first two years working as "associate interpreters/translators (P-2 contract)" before getting promoted to "(full) interpreters/translators (P-3 contract)," provided that they had demonstrated good performance. During these two years, they would work in collaboration with more senior colleagues and continually learn on the job.

Even before they graduated, students at the program were already provided with opportunities to work as simultaneous interpreters for international conferences organized by the UN. According to Wu (1990, 59), internship constituted an integral component of the curriculum. This is corroborated by Shi's account of her experience working as a simultaneous interpreter for the International Refugees Conference only one month into the program (Yao 2019, 451). By directly working in the booth, oftentimes together with their trainers, students were exposed to ample learning opportunities.

Learning opportunities also existed in abundance when students were left to themselves. According to Shi (2004, 833), after class, students often came together to practice simultaneous interpreting. In such self-directed sessions, they would break for every half hours of practice, during which they would hold discussions on how certain linguistic items in the transcript should be interpreted.

All these expanded opportunities were made available thanks to the resources provided by various stakeholders. On the question of who should be responsible for determining outcomes, Spady (1994) stresses the need for

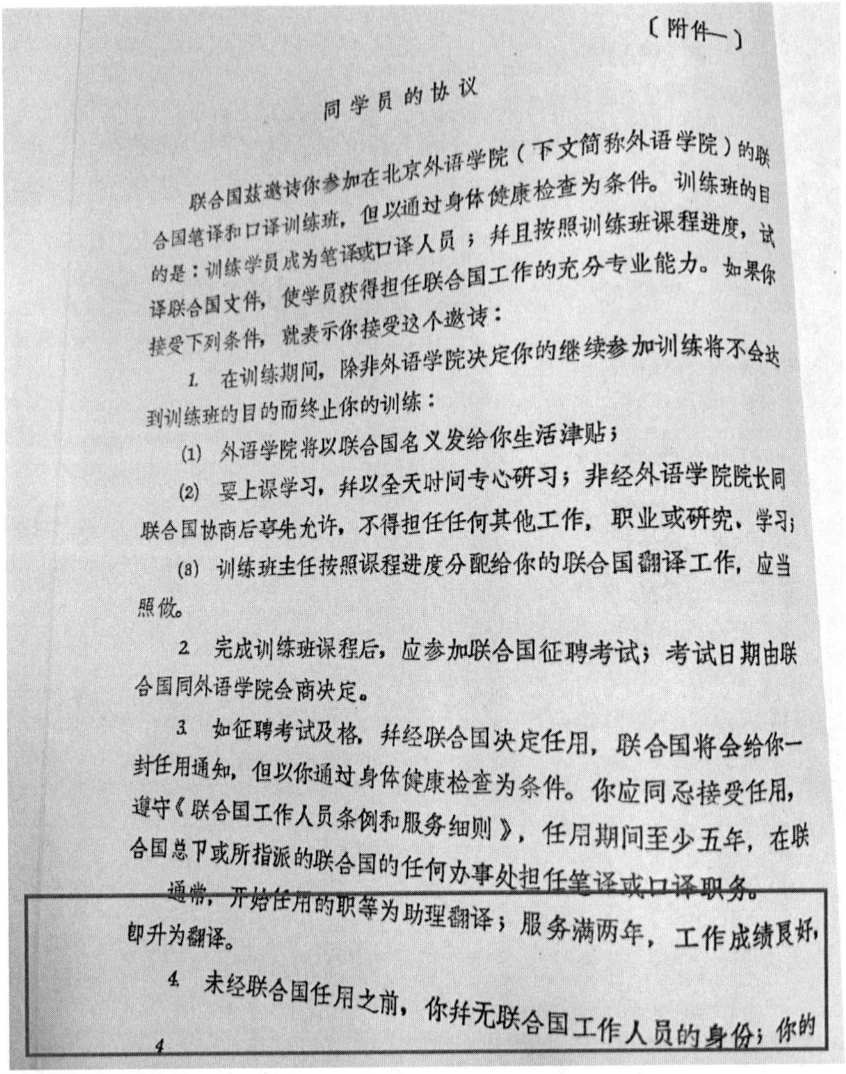

〔附件一〕

同学员的协议

联合国兹邀请你参加在北京外语学院（下文简称外语学院）的联合国笔译和口译训练班，但以通过身体健康检查为条件。训练班的目的是：训练学员成为笔译或口译人员；并且按照训练班课程进度，试译联合国文件，使学员获得担任联合国工作的充分专业能力。如果你接受下列条件，就表示你接受这个邀请：

1. 在训练期间，除非外语学院决定你的继续参加训练将不会达到训练班的目的而终止你的训练：

   (1) 外语学院将以联合国名义发给你生活津贴；

   (2) 要上课学习，并以全天时间专心研习；非经外语学院院长同联合国协商后享先允许，不得担任任何其他工作，职业或研究、学习；

   (8) 训练班主任按照课程进度分配给你的联合国翻译工作，应当照做。

2. 完成训练班课程后，应参加联合国征聘考试；考试日期由联合国同外语学院会商决定。

3. 如征聘考试及格，并经联合国决定任用，联合国将会给你一封任用通知，但以你通过身体健康检查为条件。你应同忍接受任用，遵守《联合国工作人员条例和服务细则》，任用期间至少五年，在联合国总P或所指派的联合国的任何办事处担任笔译或口译职务。通常，开始任用的职等为助理翻译；服务满两年，工作成绩良好，即升为翻译。

4. 未经联合国任用之前，你并无联合国工作人员的身份；你的

4

Figure 2.3 Agreement between the UN and the students.

all stakeholders to be involved so that they can establish one common goal based on consensus. This is essential for the obvious reason that a shared goal would motivate stakeholders to put resources behind it and work together toward its achievement. The UN program was a culmination of several years of negotiation between the UN, the Chinese government, and the host university, during which stakeholders were able to hammer out various aspects of the arrangement with respect to location, facilities, funding, staffing, admission, assessment, and placement of graduates, etc. All the aforementioned arrangements evolved around one central outcome – to cultivate students into capable conference interpreters who can operate across a broad range of situations in the near and distant future. This clear and visible outcome enabled various parties to work closely with each other.

In the agreement signed between the UN and BFSU (Figures 2.4–2.7), the university pledged venues, facilities, maintenance service, staff, etc., whereas the UN agreed to offer training equipment and material (including

Contract PTS/CON/ 5 3 / 88
Page 2 of 8

– 2 –

– Sufficient general knowledge of the structure and activities of the United Nations. The trainees shall sign individual contracts of which Annex I hereto attached is a specimen. These contracts should constitute an integral part of this Agreement and are therefore not subject to change or amendment except by mutual agreement of the Government of China and the United Nations. The programme shall begin on 29 August 1988 and will be completed at the latest on 31 July 1989.

The Head of the University, in consultation with the United Nations, has the right to discharge trainees when such measure is deemed necessary because of protracted illness or failure to comply with scholastic standards. To fill vacancies thus created, the Head of the University may enroll other trainees after consultation with the United Nations.

2. As part of the curriculum of the Training Programme, the University shall arrange for the Translation into Chinese by trainees and the revision and typing by the staff of the Programme, in conformity with the United Nations standards and procedures, of about 1,500 standard pages of English or French official documents which the United Nations will forward for this purpose. A copy of these translations shall be sent to the Director of the Translation Division at the United Nations.

3. The University shall provide premises and facilities for the United Nations Language Training Programme as well as the necessary maintenance and services, as stipulated in Annex II. Documents and reference material, including audio and video tapes, will be provided from time to time by the United Nations as they are needed for training. Upon request of the University, the United Nations will take appropriate measures to enable its

Figure 2.4 Agreement between the UN and the University.

38   *Yuben Zhu and Wen Ren*

Contract PTS/CON/53/88
Page 4 of 8

8.   The United Nations shall allocate an amount of US$6,000 per selected trainee who completes the programme, up to a maximum of 12 trainees as compensation for the expenses incurred by the University. The total amount thus allocated, which shall not exceed US$72,000, shall be paid in three equal installments of up to US$24,000 each on 15 December 1988, 13 February 1989 and 28 July 1989 respectively to the account of the Beijing University of Foreign Studies through the Bank of China in Beijing.

9.   It is understood that the financial contributions specified in paragraph 8 above represent the sole financial burden to be assumed by the United Nations with respect to the arrangements covered by this Agreement which shall be in force from 29 August 1988 to 31 July 1989.

This Agreement has been drawn up in two copies in English and Chinese, both texts being equally authentic.

ON BEHALF OF THE UNITED NATIONS

ON BEHALF OF BEIJING UNIVERSITY OF FOREIGN STUDIES

BY: _____

Allan B. ROBERTSON, Chief
Commercial, Purchase and Transportation Service
Office of General Services

BY: _____

Zhang Xian, First Secretary
Permanent Mission of the
People's Republic of China
to the United Nations

Date: 1 0 JUN 1988

Date: 20 June, 1988

Figure 2.5 Agreement between the UN and the University.

the dual-channel recorders Shi and her classmates used for after-class group practices) and a funding of 6,000 dollars per student. On top of that, the UN also promised job opportunities to future graduates if they succeeded at its examination. Outside of the agreement, the UN also offered internships so that teachers and students could have possibilities to apply what they taught and learned in authentic settings. Furthermore, the Chinese government went to great lengths to ensure the program got the best candidates in the

Contract PTS/CON/ 5-3 /88
Page 7 of 8

ANNEX II

The University, in accordance with paragraph 3 of the Agreement, provides the following premises and training facilities, as well as necessary maintenance and services for the United Nations Language Training Programme in Beijing.

1. Specially equipped classrooms:
   (a) two classrooms for simultaneous interpretation training with appropriate installations (one classroom having ten booths, variable speeds recorder and video projection system, and the other three booths with simulation conference equipment);
   (b) one or two special classrooms fitted out with video training devices (one cinema projector, one video set, one slide projector overhead projector each);
   (c) one classroom fitted out with 15 tape recorders for individual training;
   (d) one classroom fitted with dictating machines;
   (e) one reference library.

2. Classrooms for the Training Programme:
   (a) two classrooms 2
   (b) one reading hall 1

3. Administrative premises:
   (a) director's office 1
   (b) secretary's office 1
   (c) typists' pool room 1
   (d) revisers' room 1

Figure 2.6 Agreement between the UN and the University.

country. The State Council mandated several municipalities to select talents from their foreign service departments. The overall operation of the program clearly embodied the collaborative structure advocated by OBE and directly contributed to its success.

EQUIPMENT AND MATERIAL

- 1 slide projector including accessories
- 1 video set with accessories and 50 blank video cassettes
- 1 video projection system with accessories
- 1 set of movie projection equipment with accessories
- 1 learning laboratory for interpreter
- 1 audio equipment for simulation conference room
- 7 typewriters
- 1 duplicating machine
- 1 ordinary duplicating machine (ditto model)
- 1 overhead projector
- 1 variable speech tape recorder
- 15 dictating machines
- 15 tape recorders with 100 blank audio cassettes
- reference material

Figure 2.7 Agreement between the UN and the University.

High expectation

The high-expectation principle consists of three key dimensions: raising standards of acceptable performance, eliminating success quota, and increasing access to high-level curriculum. For the UNLTP, high standards were set from the very beginning of candidate selection and were upheld throughout the program's duration. In an article to celebrate the tenth anniversary of the UNLTP, former faculty member Wang (1988, 42) said the following when she reflected upon the lessons of running the program:

> *It is important to hold high admission standards. As the proverb goes, a good start is half success. For simultaneous interpreting, whether or not you get good candidates will determine half of the program's success. The candidates we are looking for should have good knowledge of and practical skills in Chinese and English languages, can organize and express their thoughts clearly, and have quick reaction and great eloquence.*

The UN program's admission test comprised two rounds of evaluation. In the first round, applicants would sit for a written examination, during which they were mainly evaluated on their bilingual proficiency. Those who made it to the second round were then examined in an oral interview by a board composed of delegates from the UN, the Chinese government, and the host university. It can be seen here that the test also adopted a collaborative structure involving all key stakeholders. The interview was conducted in English and focused on candidates' ability to organize their thoughts and respond to questions on-site. It is worth pointing out that the principle of high expectation in OBE does not simply mean raising standards so that more applicants would fail and be screened out. Rather, high expectation indicates a strong desire for educators to work with the students continually so that they can eventually achieve high standards. This is why the examination showed a preference for candidates' potential rather than their achievements. When asked about her experience of the interview, Shi (2016) said:

> *The topic I was asked to speak on was Greening. In fact, what they really wanted to see was the logic of the speech, to observe how well candidates can organize and express their views, and whether their pronunciation was good, rather than to test how much expertise they had already mastered. Therefore, the topics were all quite general.*

In her 2019 interview, Shi mentioned how she still got admitted into the program even after what she deemed as unsatisfactory performance in the written Chinese language examination:

> *In fact, when I took the entrance examination, my Chinese was not up to the challenge at all. We were asked to write a Chinese essay on international relations, which I did, but the language was nowhere near elegant. Later I learned from Zhang Zailiang and Dai Xianguang (former trainer) that they accepted me because they knew I would not be working as a translator anyway, and that my strength was not in translating into Chinese, but into English. I was accepted because they thought I could make a good interpreter eventually. This is what a teacher should do, to discover the students' strengths and encourage them to explore it, not to focus on what they can't do, because there is always someone else that can do what they can't.*
>
> (*Yao and Deng 2019, 163*)

The two previous excerpts show how different principles of OBE are interlinked and often work together in actual operation. First, having a clear culminating outcome afforded stakeholders greater rationality and flexibility in assessing candidates' eligibility. As the outcome is the competency to function as conference interpreters who can operate across a broad range of situations, for whom ad hoc knowledge is often acquired on ad hoc basis, the admission test focused on students' potential and avoided subjects that may require specialized knowledge. Second, this clarity of focus also created expanded opportunities to candidates. Since retour interpreting (interpreting from Chinese into English) constitutes an important part of the Chinese booth's responsibility at the UN, candidates like Shi, who had an international upbringing and enjoys native-like command of English, would make a great booth-mate to her Chinese colleagues, whose strengths lie more in interpreting from English into Chinese. The jury accepted her because they consistently maintained a clear picture of this culminating outcome.

With a genuine desire for every student to succeed, the program also eliminated success quota. According to Zhang (2004, 826), most members of the first cohort passed the final UN recruitment test with a score of over 80, against a passing line of 70. Before they sat for the final test, they had already been assessed many times by the school over the entire course of their study. According to Wang (1988, 42), test on regular basis is one of the principles the faculties followed in running the program. Here we see the program embracing "pencil grading" over "ink grading," turning tests into expanded opportunities for students to check for gaps and improve themselves.

Students at the UN program enjoyed access to high-level curriculum as well. Besides courses on interpreting skills, the curriculum also featured courses on UN terminology, economics, and international politics taught by faculties with in-depth knowledge on international affairs or rich hands-on experience working as UN interpreters. Furthermore, guest speakers from the UN or other established interpreting schools were often invited to exchange with the students. For example, Zhang recalled inviting Danica Seleskovitch to share their experience in France (Yao and Deng 2019, 153), and Shi (2004, 832) recalled asking whether they should prioritize words over sense when interpreting UN materials, a pressing question faced by the students at that time, to several active UN conference interpreters visiting the program in Beijing in 1979.

Design down

To implement the first three principles, design down becomes the only sensible and sound approach to follow. UNLTP started with where the students need to ultimately arrive and built back from there. The agreement between the UN and the host university (Figures 2.4–2.7) listed the facilities and materials both parties committed, which included labs, recorders, recordings of authentic UN meetings, transcripts, and a dedicated library where students could read newspapers and keep up with current affairs. Curriculum was also structured in a way to cultivate competencies that matter to their future jobs. For example, the course of sight interpreting and dedicated practice sessions on interpreting numbers were added to the curriculum by founding director

Zhang after he came back from a UNESCO assignment, during which he encountered difficulties keeping up with numeral listings and was frequently asked to conduct sight interpreting with manuscripts provided by the Chinese delegation (Yao and Deng 2019, 151–152).

The instructional process was also mapped out according to the culminating outcome. In interpreting courses, authentic recordings of UN meetings were used as training materials. The way practices were organized means that teachers came to the classroom not knowing the exact errors students would make when interpreting a given material. Instead of covering any predetermined content, they would "continuously diagnose and assess ongoing student practice and performance, offer frequent and focused feedback, and intervene constructively in the learning process in a timely manner" and "model actively successful techniques and behavior" (Spady 1994, 43). Moreover, teachers were able to play the role of a coach precisely because they had good understanding of the culminating outcome and knew from their own experience what were acceptable interpretation performance.

4   Lessons for interpreting schools today

In many aspects, the UNLTP constitutes a unique presence in China's history of conference interpreter training. As is shown in the preceding text, its success is largely attributed to the fact that the program started with a clear and visible culminating outcome shared by all stakeholders and built back its curriculum, instruction, and assessment from there. Many of the conditions the program operated in were created by historical developments outside the interpreting training community. The restoration of PRC's seat at the UN directly triggered the need to train conference interpreters in China's mainland. The UN, obliged to provide quality interpretation to the Chinese delegation, was deeply engaged in the design and operation of the program. Teachers and students regarded it not only as a pathway to new careers but also as an opportunity to serve their country. It is unlikely for any schools today to receive the same level of commitment and attention from external stakeholders. If this is the unfortunate case, the next question that naturally comes to mind is, in the absence of such favorable historical conditions, can interpreting schools still locate a clear culminating outcome and map back its operation from there?

Identifying the outcome in the absence of prearranged employment

According to Spady (1994, 71), the ideal of OBE is to help students attain "life-role functioning," and the responsibility of the educator is to help them grow into that role. Following this line of thinking, having a clear career destination would be essential because both teachers and students will then have a clear picture of the situations in which the students will operate and the functioning role they are required to play. In other words, a clear career destination naturally presents a clear outcome. However, few schools today have the luxury of guaranteed employment by external partners. Nevertheless, we would argue that it is still possible for schools to establish clear outcomes, even without a clear career destination to offer the students.

It has been shown in the earlier text that in the days of the UN program, students were trained to become generalists who can function well across different thematic areas, rather than specialists with narrow expertise. Although the curriculum accentuated on simultaneous interpreting, courses such as consecutive interpreting were added to equip students with broader skills so that they could still function well outside the UN system. Today's graduates face more diverse career options and often need to undertake various tasks apart from conference interpreting. Drawing on Luhmann's sociological framework, Pym (2022, 12) points out that in today's marketplace, it is very difficult for an interpreter system to separate itself from its environment systems. For example, due to the irregularity of interpreting work, interpreters often need to undertake written translation and enjoy "little financial independence from the written." As Daniel Gouadec rightly observed, trainers no longer know what niche students will eventually fit into. However, what they do know is that the marketplace today requires them to be able to translate, interpret, localize, post-edit, and so on with various degrees of specialization (Pym 2000, 223–24). Given this, it makes sense for schools to expand their curriculum so that students are better prepared for the future work. But there is only so much we can fill into a finite time window, and OBE stipulates that the students should develop a certain degree of specialization (outcomes) rather than just some passing knowledge (goals). The key question is then how to be comprehensive without losing the clarity of focus. Again, OBE does not have answers as to what specific courses should be taught, but the previous analysis shows that clarity of focus often stems from a clear culminating outcome, which in turn should be jointly determined by all stakeholders, that is, schools, teachers, students, and most importantly, the community we find ourselves in. For example, a school in Geneva where many international organizations are located may face different skillset demands than a school near the Silicon Valley, where high-tech firms cluster, or a school in Melbourne, where large numbers of new immigrants continually go. Furthermore, an interpreting program run by a university rooted in political sciences might offer different cross-fertilization opportunities than a university specialized in law. OBE's philosophy offers a good starting point for schools to identify their respective culminating outcomes and build back from there every other aspect of their programs.

Preserving flexibility in a less-flexible environment

The UNLTP was able to maintain its flexibility during its operation. Training time was extended, shortened, and then extended again based on practical needs, as were the adjustments made to the curriculum and assessment process. Although academic institutionalization of interpreting education contributes to an enhanced status of the profession and its standing as an independent discipline (Pöchhacker 2016, 30–32), it may risk introducing unwanted constraints, an inherent attribute of almost any forms of social institutionalization (Foucault 2012). In the context of interpreting education, these constraints could take many forms, that is, a fixed calendar, a forced distribution system in grading, an inflexible curriculum, rigid eligibility requirements, or ill-advised appraisal mechanism, both for teachers and students. For example, lack of faculties with interpreting experience has become a major bottleneck for many schools. Yet under the current institutional appraisal climate, schools are reluctant to recruit candidates who are practicing conference interpreters on the ground that they do not hold a PhD. Another example. The current system takes student hour as an important means to measure educational attainment. Therefore, students are usually not allowed to skip classes for an opportunity to work at an authentic task. These problems might be resolved if things are viewed from the perspective of OBE, as was demonstrated by Shi's experience of working at the UN as a student, which provided her with the invaluable expanded opportunity. As the implementation of OBE is always context-based, it is our hope that the key concepts and principles embodied by the UNLTP can provoke thoughts on how interpreting schools today could identify their outcomes and find the best way toward their achievement.

5 Conclusion

China's reintegration into the international system in 1971 not only spawned the country's first systematic training program for conference interpreters but also paved the way for the academic institutionalization of its interpreting profession. However, rapid expansion over the past two decades has created many of the challenges faced by interpreting schools today. Drawing on firsthand archival evidence and published data, this paper conducted a systematic review of the highly successful UNLTP through the perspective of OBE, an educational philosophy widely adopted by disciplines oriented toward cultivating professional practice. Analysis reveals that the UN program's success could be largely attributed to its implementation of key principles advocated by OBE, long before the theory itself was put forward. As China's interpreting education grows more institutionalized, it is the authors' hope that the research can inspire interpreting schools to stay focused on outcomes of significance, as mapping back from there shall guide us toward a better future.

Funding

This work was supported by the National Social Science Fund of China under grant number 18BYY102 and Beijing Foreign Studies University's Double First Class Initiative Fund under grant number 2022SYLA002.

Note

1 Corresponding author.
2 The Program has been referred to elsewhere (e.g., Dawrant et al, 2021 182–96) and in some chapters of this book as the UN Training Programme for Interpreters and Translators or UNTPIT. However, based on our recently discovered historical materials, we adopted UNLTP rather than UNTPIT, throughout the whole chapter.

References

Chattopadhayay, Rachana, and Anil K. Ghosh. 2012. "Performance Appraisal Based on a Forced Distribution System: Its Drawbacks and Remedies." *International Journal of Productivity* 61(8): 881–96.

Dawrant, Andrew C., Binhua Wang, and Hong Jiang. 2021. "Conference Interpreting in China." In *The Routledge Handbook of Conference Interpreting*, edited by Michaela Albl-Mikasa and Elisabet Tiselius, 182–96. Abingdon, UK: Routledge.

Dean, Robyn K., and Robert Q. Pollard Jr. 2011. "Context-Based Ethical Reasoning in Interpreting: A Demand Control Schema Perspective." *The Interpreter and Translator Trainer* 5(1): 155–82.

Eldeeb, Rasha. 2013. "Outcome Based Education (OBE)-Trend Review." *IOSR Journal of Research & Method in Education* (1): 9–11.

Ewell, Peter. 2008. "Building Academic Cultures of Evidence: A Perspective on Learning Outcomes in Higher Education." Paper presented at the Symposium of the Hong Kong University Grants Committee on Quality Education, Quality Outcomes – The Way Forward for Hong Kong, Accessed November 20, 2022 from www.mec.cuny.edu/wp-content/uploads/2018/01/Building-Academic-Cultures-of-Evidence-Peter-Ewell-present_peter.pdf.

Foucault, Michel. 2012. *Discipline and Punish: The Birth of the Prison.* Translated by Alan Sheridan. New York: Vintage.

Gentile, Paola. 2017. "Interpreting as a Postmodern Profession: A Socio-Historical Approach." In *The Changing Role of the Interpreter*, edited by Marta Biagini, Michael S. Boyd and Claudia Monacelli, 32–51. Abingdon, UK: Routledge.

Han Ziman 韩子满, and Hou Xinfei 侯新飞. 2022. "MTI fanyi shijian baogao xiezuo zhong de lilun kuangjia wenti" MTI 翻译实践报告写作中的理论框架问题 [A Study on Theoretical Frameworks in Translation Reports of MTI Theses]. *Waiyu dianhua jiaoxue* 外语电化教学 [Technology Enhanced Foreign Language Education] (05): 25–30+108.

Jiang Qian 姜倩. 2021. "Yixie celue zai hanying biyi shijian yu jiaoxue zhong de yingyong" 译写策略在汉英笔译实践与教学中的应用 – 以MTI笔译实务课为例 [Application of Transwritting Strategy in C-E Translation: With Two Classrooms as Examples]. *Shanghai Fanyi* 上海翻译 [Shanghai Journal of Translators] (04): 74–9.

Lin, Wei. 2013. "Why Do Students Learn Interpreting at the Graduate Level? A Survey on the Interpreting Learning Motives of Chinese Graduate Students in BFSU." *T&I Review* (3): 145–68.

Pöchhacker, Franz. 2016. *Introducing Interpreting Studies.* London and New York: Routledge.

Pym, Anthony. 2000. "Innovation in Translator and Interpreter Training. Report on an On-Line Symposium." *Across Languages and Cultures* 1(2): 209–73.

Pym, Anthony. 2022. "Who Says Who Interprets? On the Possible Existence of an Interpreter System." *The Translator*: 1–16.

Setton, Robin, and Andrew Dawrant. 2016. *Conference Interpreting: A Complete Course*. Amsterdam: John Benjamins.

Shi Xiaojing 施晓菁. 2004. "Beijing lianheguo yixunban xuexi shenghuo sanji 1979 nian qiu zhi 1981 nian chun" 北京联合国译训班学习生活散记 1979 年秋 -1981 年春 [Scattered Memories: Life and Study at the UNTPIT in Beijing between Fall of 1979 and Spring of 1981] In *lianheguo li de zhongguoren* 联合国里的中国人 [Chinese in the United Nations], edited by Li Tiecheng 李铁城, 822–28. Beijing: renmin chubanshe 人民出版社 [People's Publishing House].

Shi, Lynette. 2016. "Interview with Shi Xiaojing, Member of the First Cohort of The UN Training Program for Interpreters and Translators." Accessed May 13, 2016. https://gsti.bfsu.edu.cn/info/1105/1964.htm.

Spady, William G. 1994. *Outcome-Based Education: Critical Issues and Answers*. Arlington VA: American Association of School Administrators.

Sun Lin 孙琳. 2020. "Shi Lun OBE shiyu xia de woguo fanyi rencai peiyang moshi" 试论OBE视域下的我国翻译人才培养模式 [A Pilot Study on the Cultivation Model of Chinese Translation/Interpreting Talents from the OBE Perspective]. *Zhongguo fanyi* 中国翻译 [Chinese Translators Journal] 41(06): 107–11.

Wang Ruojin 王若瑾. 1988. "Fanyi zhanxian shang de Shenglijun" 翻译战线上的生力军 – 庆祝北京外国语学院联合国译员训练部成立十周年 [A Dynamic Force on the Translation Front – Celebrating the 10th Anniversary of the UNTPIT]. *Zhongguo fanyi* 中国翻译 [Chinese Translators Journal] (06): 42+44.

Wu Jiashui 吴嘉水. 1990. "Buyi ze buzhuan, buzhuan ze buneng" 不一则不专,不专则不能 – 北外联合国译员训练部十年 [Expertise Comes from Focus: Reflections upon the Ten-Year Journey of the UNTPIT]. *Waiyu jiaoxue yu yanjiu* 外语教学与研究 [Foreign Language Teaching and Research] (02): 58–61.

Xing Xing 邢星. 2021. "Jiyu MTI ruxue kaoshi de kouyi xueneng ceshi yanjiu" 基于MTI入学考试的口译学能测试研究：调查与反思 [Research on Aptitude Testing for Interpreting: A Survey and Introspection on Chinese MTI Admission Tests]. *Waiyu jiaoxue lilun yu shijian* 外语教学理论与实践 [Foreign Language Learning Theory and Practice] (02): 126–35+161.

Xu, Mianjun, and Xiaoye You. 2021. "Translation Practice of Master of Translation and Interpreting (MTI) Teachers in China: An Interview-Based Study." *The Interpreter and Translator Trainer* 15(3): 343–59.

Yao, Bin. 2019. "The Origins and Early Developments of the UN Training Program for Interpreters and Translators in Beijing." *Babel* 65(3): 445–64.

Yao Bin 姚斌, and Xiaoling Deng 邓小玲. 2019. "Bilu lanlv, yiqi shanlin: Lianheguo yixunban(bu) sishi zhounian fangtanlu" 筚路蓝缕,以启山林 – 联合国译训班(部)四十周年访谈录 [Interviews with Former Faculty Members and Students of the UN Training Program for Interpreters and Translators at Beijing Foreign Studies University]. *Fanyijie* 翻译界 [Translation Horizons] (01): 149–64.

Zhang Zailiang 张载梁. 2004. "Ji Beijing lianheguo yixunban" 记北京联合国译训班 [Recollections of the UNTPIT in Beijing] In *Lianheguo li de zhongguoren* 联合国里的中国人 [Chinese in the United Nations], edited by Li Tiecheng 李铁城, 822–28. Beijing: renmin chubanshe 人民出版社 [People's Publishing House].

Zhao Tianyuan 赵田园, Li Wen 李雯, and Mu Lei 穆雷. 2021. "Fanyi shuoshi 'fanyi zhiye lunli' kecheng goujian yanjiu: Jiyu yuyan fuwu shichang xianzhuang he MTI jiaoxue diaoyan de fansi" 翻译硕士"翻译职业伦理"课程构建研究：基于语言服务市场现状和MTI教学调研的反思 [A Study on Setting an MTI Course 'Professional Translation Ethics' Based on Language Service Market Demands and an MTI

Survey]. *Waiyu jiaoyu yanjiu qianyan* 外语教育研究前沿 [Foreign Language Education in China] 4(01): 26–32+88.

Zhong Weihe 仲伟合. 2014. "Woguo fanyi zhuanye jiaoyu de wenti yu duice" 我国翻译专业教育的问题与对策 [Problems in China's BTI and MTI Education and Suggested Solutions]. *Zhongguo fanyi* 中国翻译 [Chinese Translators Journal] 35(4): 40–4.

Zhong Weihe 仲伟合. 2017. "Shinian yangfan, xushi yuanhang: MTI jiaoyu shinian huigu yu zhanwang" 十年扬帆,蓄势远航:MTI教育十年回顾与展望 [Ten Years' Sailing: Review and prospect on MTI education in the past decade]. *Zhongguo fanyi* 中国翻译 [Chinese Translators Journal] 38(3): 7–9.

3 The professionalization of interpreting and professional interpreter education in the Chinese mainland

Lei Mu and Xinyuan Liu

1 Introduction

Interpreting is one of the longest-standing human activities, and it has an inevitable role in promoting cultural exchange and social development in Chinese history (Li 2002). Nevertheless, its professionalization process started only about four decades ago. Professionalization involves a process of particular types of work that often requires a high-level education to train competent candidates with specific skills and establish their professional identity to be officially recognized by society due to their *credibility* (Rudvin 2007). A new profession needs external and internal factors to facilitate such a process, and important efforts have been made to investigate the professionalization of interpreting so far. External factors include a more considerable extent of analysis of the social and economic background and industry regulations, often region- or nation-specific (Tyulenev et al. 2017; Hoyte-West 2020; Djovčoš and Šveda 2021) and policy-driven, while internal factors relate to professional interpreters' changing role (Dam 2017; René de Cotret et al. 2021) and identity (Setton and Guo 2009; Lázaro Gutiérrez and Gauthier Blasi 2020), disciplinary development manifested in accumulated research (Urpi 2012) and institutionalization (Gambier 2018), interpreter certification (Arocha and Joyce 2013), which are influenced by the knowledge structure presented by individuals, groups, and their relations with the particular domains regarded as professions. In the Chinese context, the most critical factors for the professionalization of interpreting are reflected in the particular industry-based demands (Mu et al. 2017), accreditation of interpreting (Chen and Mu 2016), and institutional development at higher-education level (Mu et al. 2013).

According to the *2022 Report on Development of Translation and Language Service Industry* (Translators Association of China 2022), the number of enterprises with language services as their primary business in the Chinese mainland has reached 9,656, and the output value of the domestic language service industry held an impressive growth trend, up 50.9% compared to 2015. The social and economic developments promote the professionalization of interpreting by means of standardizing the requirements of working conditions, quality evaluation, and managing of interpreting services through

DOI: 10.4324/9781003357629-5

education policies, systems, standards, and industry regulations to effectively control the quality of interpreting and protect the fundamental rights and interests of these professionals in and beyond the workplace.

Interpreter education and research, as the key to talent cultivation for the interpreting profession and language service industry, also play a crucial part in interpreting professionalization. The recognition of translation and interpreting studies (TIS) as an independent academic discipline and the professionalization of translation and interpreting have undoubtedly spurred the increasing numbers of education programs of translation and interpreting from the undergraduate to the doctoral level across the world (Saldanha and O'Brien 2014), particularly in China, "a big nation of interpreting and translation" (Zhong et al. 2020, 883). The professionalization of interpreting provides interpreter education with market demand, talent standards, and practice venues, gradually improving the public's knowledge and understanding of interpreting as a profession.

In the Chinese context, previous research has reported on the status quo of professionalization of interpreting mainly from an industry perspective on the national level (see Wang 2005; Zhong et al. 2020), compared to regional characteristics, such as Shanghai and Jiangsu along the Yangtze River Delta (Pan et al. 2009), Jiangxi (Pan and Liu 2011), Shanghai and Taipei (Setton and Guo 2009), Sichuan and Chongqing (Guo et al. 2011), Beijing-Tianjin-Hebei region (Cui 2021). However, more is needed to know about the external and internal factors that systematically promote the professionalization of interpreting in China regarding the evolving discipline, industry, and educational policies and its relationship with interpreter education and research.

This chapter aims to analyze the dynamic interactions between the professionalization of interpreting, professional interpreter education, and the development of TIS as an independent discipline in the Chinese mainland since its reform and opening-up in 1978. Two research questions are to be addressed:

RQ1: What are the external and internal factors that have facilitated the professionalization of interpreting in the Chinese mainland?
RQ2: How do these factors stimulate the development of professional interpreter education and research?

We first briefly overview the developments of interpreting as a profession, interpreter education practices, and research since 1978, with a focus on the most recent progress in proposing the professional doctoral degree program Doctor of Translation and Interpreting (DTI). The following section analyzes the external and internal factors that have driven the course of the professionalization of interpreting and the development of professional interpreter education in the Chinese mainland. In the next section, we elicit the interactions with two examples: the standardization process of interpreting competence assessment and professional interpreting trainers. A final discussion will be conducted regarding the comparative studies on professional interpreter education in China and abroad.

2 A historical overview of the professionalization of interpreting: past, present, and future

The process of professionalization of interpreting in China began in the 1980s and has entered the fast development track since the new century. In terms of higher education, professional interpreter education has been in the pipeline since 1978. Supported by the Chinese government and the United Nations, the United Nations Training Program for Translators and Interpreters (the predecessor of the Graduate School of Translation and Interpretation at Beijing Foreign Language Institute) was hosted from 1979 to 1993, cultivating more than 200 professional translators and interpreters for the UN (see Yao 2022). After 1995, some universities began to train doctoral students in TIS. In 2006, undergraduate translation and interpreting majors began to enroll candidates. In 2007, a professional translation and interpreting master's degree was established. In September 2022, the Office of the State Council Academic Degrees Committee and Ministry of Education of the People's Republic of China issued the *Catalogue of Subjects and Specialties for Postgraduate Education*, in which translation (including interpreting) as a professional degree can enroll students both at master's and doctoral levels. As the past four decades have witnessed rapid growth in the language service industry and the process of interpreting professionalization, a complete educational system (see Figure 3.1) containing bachelor's (Bachelor of Translation and Interpreting, BTI), master's (Master of Translation and Interpreting, MTI; master of arts in TIS, MA), doctoral (philosophy doctor of TIS), and DTI degrees has been well-established for cultivating professional translators and interpreters for language services as well as researchers for TIS. A recent contribution to reflect on such a process is *The Exploration Road to China's Translation and Interpreting Education* (Mu and Zhao 2022), which documents the historic records from 2006 to 2021 in the Chinese mainland.

For interpreter education research, around 1985, the academic community began to pay attention to the research on the quality of interpreters (i.e., interpreters' ability, see Tang and Zhou 1985). In 1989, research on teaching materials and curricula appeared. In the 1990s, studies on interpreting pedagogy,

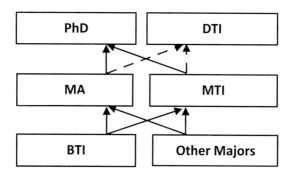

Figure 3.1 The "three horizontals and three verticals" development of the translator and interpreter education system in the Chinese mainland.[1]

testing, and the integration of teaching with computers and networks began. After the new century, the number of articles introducing interpreting teaching and its research has increased. The research focuses on teaching materials, curriculum, personnel training, quality assessment, certification tests, and other aspects concerning interpreting (Mu and Wang 2009). Nowadays, different academic groups across regions have emerged to study interpreting-related empirical research, for example, Xiao's group on sign language interpreting (Han and Xiao 2022), Wang's teams on interpreting assessment (Wang et al. 2020), Dong's work on interpreting competence from a perspective of psycholinguistics (Cai et al. 2023), and Zhang's investigations on learner interpreter corpus (Zhang 2017).

The development process of interpreter education reveals people's evolving understanding of interpreting as a profession and the changing concept of cultivating promising interpreters. Constant needs from the society also have improved the professionalization of interpreting (see Section 3.1), particularly in specialized areas, such as remote conference interpreting and sign language interpreting services (Zheng 2020), which have been neglected before and after the post-COVID-19 pandemic.

3   Factors that have influenced the professionalization of interpreting and interpreter education

This section will demonstrate how interpreter education practice and research cater to the evolving needs of the national policy and professional interpreting services in the ever-changing markets against China's developments for the new era. We analyze two external and two internal factors based on the relevant research and practice in the Chinese context. For assessing the overall landscape of China's interpreting research, we use three self-constructed and theme-annotated databases on TIS to conclude the features of interpreter education research:

1   25,186 research articles in Chinese Social Sciences Citation Index journals from 1978 to 2022
2   1,249 doctoral dissertations from 1992 to 2022
3   2,137 national projects from 1993 to 2022

3.1   *External factors: societal developments and educational policy*

Societal developments generate significant needs for professional interpreting services from the language service industry. After the reform and opening-up, China's political, economic, and cultural development has been on a fast track. The increasing frequency of foreign exchanges has highlighted the demand for translation and interpreting services. Interpreting practice and the workload of interpreters in various fields such as politics and economy, culture and science, military, and diplomacy have increased rapidly. The rapid development of technology has also promoted the process of professionalization of interpreting (see Zhao 2017). The original status of interpreters and talent management are far from being able to adapt to the development of society, which has triggered corresponding theoretical thinking and disciplinary blueprints. The reform and opening-up have not only promoted the rapid development of China's political, economic, and cultural fields but also highlighted interpreting as a profession, which has moved from the backstage to the foreground and become an essential pillar of language services in the tertiary industry of the national economy, with its gross product proliferating.

Over the last decade, the interpreting profession has been included in the national occupational canon and entered the people's vision, becoming a promising employment field. The rapid progress of the interpreting services has given birth to the discipline of TIS. The disciplinary development of TIS serves interpreting practice and puts forward more and higher requirements for interpreting research. As the demand for professional interpreters increased, interpreting training was gradually separated from teaching foreign languages through translation and interpreting and formed into an independent education system.

The educational policy also drives the standardization of professional interpreter education. China has proposed to develop professional degree education in its *Ten-Year Plan for the Modernization of Education in China (2025–2035)* and *Professional Degree Postgraduate Education Plans (2020–2025)*; critical official documents regarding interpreting in higher education, including *The National Criteria of Teaching Quality for Majors in Foreign Language and Literature* (Wang and Zhong 2017) and *Teaching Guide for Undergraduate Translation Major* (Xiao and Feng 2019), have been issued. Over the past decade, the TIS academia and language service industry have become increasingly conscious that the existing translation and interpreting talent training system has not been able to meet the demand for high-level, application-oriented, and specialized interpreting professionals in the language service industry, and the setting of DTI can provide solutions to respond to major national development needs. The training orientation of DTI is to cultivate leading professional interpreters who can fully understand the country's policies in its political, diplomatic, military, legal, communication, economic, and technological systems, better participate in international governance, tell China's story, help Chinese manufacturing and culture go global, and contribute to the global community and civilization protection. It is more than an academic degree with a specific skill, but a correct understanding of interpreting as a profession. National strategic planning, economic and social-cultural development, the language service industry's rapid development, and TIS's continuous disciplinary maturation have all put forward new requirements for interpreter education and brought new opportunities and challenges.

3.2 *Internal factors: disciplinary establishment and theoretical pursuit*

Talent cultivation is the foundation of the **discipline** (Zhong 2016). From the perspective of the education system, the development of a discipline-first requires institutional recognition, that is, a place in the discipline catalog, to be qualified for admission and receiving specific research funding and other resources as a guarantee for future development. As China is home to an enormous education scale, resource allocation is crucial, and more resources can be secured through discipline building. The construction of disciplines can be reflected by the teaching system of undergraduate-master-PhD degrees and its quality research outcomes. Under the influence of the long-term planned economy and the unique social structure of China, the establishment of disciplines and the evaluation of degree programs are subject to unified deployment and arrangement. For a long time, the disciplinary status of TIS was not officially recognized, which greatly affected the development of interpreter education and research in the Chinese mainland. In contrast, the relative backwardness of interpreter education, in turn, restricted the disciplinary construction of TIS.

After the reform and opening-up and the restoration of the college entrance examination system and the postgraduate training system, some schools started to enroll master students in "Translation Theory and Practice" in the 1980s (Mu 1999/2022). At that time, interpreting practice was either part of a course for enhancing foreign language skills or purely an individual preference for more skill-tailored exercises after class. However, specialized interpreting training should be realized by a series of courses that targeted training professionals. In order to cultivate the urgently needed high-level interpreting talents, Beijing Foreign Studies University, Shanghai International Studies University, and Guangdong University of Foreign Studies established one of the earliest translation and interpreting departments. Based on accumulated experience, scholars proposed to the Degree Office of the Ministry of Education in 2005 the setting up of MTI, which was strongly supported by the Office. By now, the number of universities that offer MTI programs has increased from the initial 15 to the current 319, and there are already 301 institutions offering BTI programs in the Chinese mainland.

The most recent establishment of the professional doctorate degree, that is, DTI, is an integral part of the professionalization process of translation and interpreting. The development of industry associations, the promotion of qualification certification, and the optimization of the translator and interpreter education system provides a solid foundation for the setting up of DTI, marking the formation of the "three horizontals and three verticals" development of the translator and interpreter education system (see Figure 3.1).

The interpreting practice and theory in China are at the critical stage of transformation from "input-oriented" to "output-oriented," and the DTI setting is precisely in line with this current national demand, which aims to contribute to the future medium- and long-term development plans of the country. The professional degree of DTI aims to cultivate high-end translation-related talents urgently needed to implement national development strategies. They should have not only high translation and interpreting ability but also in-depth understanding and grasp of national policies, military diplomacy, laws and regulations, economy, and culture and be able to accurately deal with relevant language issues in foreign communication and even directly participate in international governance in related fields.

The requirements of society for interpreters are demanding, and the quality of talents and their standards are also improving. In addition to the requirements of bilingualism and interpreting skills, the cultivation of interpreters gradually adds the construction of interpreters' specific-domain knowledge structure, professional ethics, morality, understanding of workplace and job responsibilities, planning for lifelong learning, and loyalty and honor to the profession. All these requirements need to be satisfied through interpreting service standards at both national and organizational levels, accreditation from state-level tests such as China Accreditation Test for Translators and Interpreters (CATTI),[2] and professional education before the candidates enter the industry.

The inner **theoretical pursuit** to unveil the mystery of how to become a successful professional interpreter has also driven the process of interpreting professionalization. The philosophy of interpreter education is not originated from only teaching means, and the ultimate purpose of education is to nurture people. Interpreter education should not only carry out through the teaching of skills but also through cultivating students' worldviews, family sentiment, social responsibility, and professional ethics through a series of educational approaches. For example, interpreter education should make students understand and recognize the interaction between the language service industry and social development, the history of interpreting as a profession and its changing social role, the social responsibility of interpreters when society urgently needs their professional services and correctly perceive whether their physiological and psychological qualities meet the needs of the work of interpreters.

Although research on interpreting teaching has started late, it has developed rapidly and has better distinguished the critical tasks to be trained in each teaching stage. Due to its solid Chinese characteristics (a large number of students after enrollment), different research groups in China have explored interpreting teaching models to design teaching materials, organize teaching activities, train teachers, and conduct assessments accordingly. For example, the interpreting teaching and research team of Guangdong University of

Table 3.1 The Interpreting-Specific Standards and Regulations at National (N) and Organizational (O) Levels

Year	Title	Type
2006	Specification for Translation Service – Part2 : Interpretation (GB/T 19363.2–2006)	N
2017	Competences of Translator and Interpreter (T/TAC 2–2017)	
2018	Translation Services – Requirements for Interpreting Service (T/TAC 3–2018/ISO 18841)	
2019	Requirements for Translator and Interpreter Training (T/TAC 4–2019)	
2020	Pricing Guidelines on Translation and Interpreting Services (T/TAC 5–2020)	O
2014	Quotation for Interpretation Service (ZYF 003–2014)	
2019	Guidelines on Procurement of Translation Services – Part 2: Interpretation (ZYF 011–2019)	
2019	Code of Professional Ethics for Translators and Interpreters (ZYF 012–2019)	

Foreign Studies has explored its professional teaching system of interpreting or the Guangwai approach (see Zhong 2020), which has become a typical model of professional interpreter education in China.

4   Two examples of the professionalization of interpreting

From earlier observations of interpreter education research in China, there is scant attention on scientific measurements of interpreting competence (Wang et al. 2020) and training professional interpreters. This section introduces the recent outcomes in the Chinese context to demonstrate the practical and theoretical efforts that contributed to the professionalization of interpreting.

4.1   *Facilitating teaching, learning, and assessment: interpreting competence scales*

Interpreting competence is the core of teaching practice and research. The differentiation of education levels and types depends on an accurate assessment of interpreting competence rather than purely on experience. Furthermore, the improvement of teaching objectives, curriculum and teaching methods, assessment of teaching effectiveness, and even the selection of students, preparation of teaching materials, and teacher development all need to be carried out based on a theoretical understanding of professional interpreting competence. Therefore, developing and applying practical standards of interpreting competence play a crucial role in the stepwise and fine-grained assessment for cultivating professional interpreters. As part of the national project for developing China's Standards of English Language Ability (i.e., the CSE project), interpreting competence scales (ICS, see Wang et al. 2020) divides the interpreting competence into descriptive levels under the framework of the comprehensive communicative language ability, with a total of 369 descriptors (see Table 3.4). The scales position interpreting above the fifth level over other language skills (i.e., listening, speaking, reading, writing), indicating interpreting competence needs professional training different from foreign language learning. That also means the term "interpreting" used below level 5 refers only to teaching English by enhancing English proficiency through translation or interpreting practices instead of the professional education of interpreters. The ascending order is from level 5 to level 9 (see the arrow in Table 3.4; the arrowhead directs to the higher level), and each level has corresponding descriptors for what interpreter learners can do. ICS has overturned the traditional and prevailing opinion that "as long as one is good at a foreign language, one can be a capable interpreter." As previous research on job ads (see Mu et al. 2017; Wang and Li 2020) has revealed a conceptual gap regarding interpreters' professionalism between academia and the language service providers in the industry, ICS again proves that only possessing the ability to listen, speak, read, and write is not enough for interpreting for professional purposes. Instead, interpreting competence must be acquired through specialized and systematic training.

ICS describe the overall interpreting ability in four aspects (see level 3 in Table 3.2). Among them, the typical characteristics of the interpreting tasks are mainly related to the types of interpreting, the subject matter of interpreting, and the characteristics of the source language (information density, language speed, segmentation). The interpretation strategy competence, which is regarded as one of the sub-competences, is mainly reflected by the strategies applied before, during, and after interpreting tasks. The criteria (see level 4 in Table 3.2) include content, expression, and interaction. The cognitive processes of simultaneous and consecutive interpreting activities are quite different and considered to be the most important among the interpreting competence. The former requires a certain foundation of consecutive interpreting competence; thus, the initial level of simultaneous interpreting competence is set at level 8. After mastering sufficient consecutive interpreting competence, one can begin to study simultaneous interpreting. In the past, it took much work to obtain a large amount of data to conduct empirical research on interpreting. The CSE project gathered experts in TIS, language testing, and second language acquisition and collected a sampling of around 10,000 participants, including interpreting researchers, professional interpreters, and interpreting students, to obtain firsthand data. Future empirical validation and applied research can be conducted based on the interpreting competence framework.

Table 3.2 The Vertical Descriptor Framework of ICS

Descriptor Framework of ICS			
Level 1 Translation and interpreting			
Level 2 Interpreting competence			
Level 3 Interpreting performance	Interpreting strategies	Interpreting knowledge	Typical interpreting characteristics
Interpreting description Interpreting narration	Planning	Basic concepts and theories	Content
Interpreting exposition	Execution	Practical requirements and techniques	Expression
Level 4 Interpreting argumentation			
Interpreting instruction Interpreting interaction	Appraising/ compensation	Working mechanism and professional norms in the language services industry	Interaction
Level 5 -	-	N/A	Accuracy Completeness Fluency Appropriateness Logical coherence Communication efficiency

Note: To clearly illustrate the outlines of ICS and TICA, the authors use "vertical" and "horizontal" to describe their structures, which are not intentionally proposed by the developers of ICS or TICA.

China's Standards of Translator and Interpreter Competence Assessment[3] (2022) is another latest standard developed jointly by the CICG Academy of Translation and Interpretation, the CICG CATTI Management Center, and the Talent Assessment Committee of Translators Association of China with forces of academia and industry. The standard (TICA), said to have more than 15,000 participants involved, is specialized for describing professional translator and interpreter competence and has a distinct professional, practical, and ability-oriented approach in the definition, classification, and descriptors. In TICA, professional levels are described above (also including) level 3 and the descending order is from S to level 3 (see the arrow in Table 3.4). 51 descriptors are interpreting competence specific, while the whole number is 217 if we assume interpreter competence is measured (see Table 3.3), which includes seven dimensions (linguistic knowledge use, cross-cultural ability, interpreting competence, international communication ability, professional literacy, contribution to industry development, and ability to apply in specific-domain situations).

To a certain extent, ICS and TICA can be a unified body serving the cultivation and assessment of translation and interpreting talents, with some crossover and overlap in competence requirements but slightly different emphasis (Mu et al. forthcoming). In other words, in future research and application practice, interpreting academia and industry will be able to fully explore the relative unity and complementary characteristics of the two, carry out a series of empirical research, and apply them in teaching context and industry practice. In order to assess interpreting or interpreter competence, it is necessary to use the ICS or TICA as a ruler. The graded descriptors of interpreting competence can help position prospective interpreting students of different levels and set up a yardstick for interpreting teaching objectives, contents, effects, material development, teacher training, and other series of educational activities.

4.2 Who are suitable, and how to educate interpreters? Interpreting trainer development

In order to develop quality interpreter education, faculty development is a top priority. What competencies are required of interpreting trainers? What are the similarities and differences between the requirements of different levels of specific positions (including full-time tutors or part-time professionals from the industry) concerning interpreting practice and theory? Scholars constantly seek solutions to solve the dilemma between the professionalization of written translation and teacher professionalization (see Han 2008), yet little concern has been given to interpreting as a profession. Liang and Mu (2020) reflected on their experience of participating in the interpreting training programs in Geneva and suggested more individualized modules to level up interpreting trainers' capabilities, particularly for the visiting scholar programs and annual summer training for translation and interpreting teachers hosted by Translators Association of China since 1997. The growth of interpreting trainers requires standardized and long-term training for younger generations of better quality. Moreover, the contents and methods of interpreting trainers' education should also change with the development of the profession and industry.

Table 3.3 The Horizontal Descriptor Framework of TICA

Descriptor Framework of TICA

Level 1	Level 2	Level 3			
		Phonology	Vocabulary	Grammar	Discourse
Translator and interpreter competence	1 Linguistic knowledge use	Phonology	Vocabulary	Grammar	Discourse
	2 Cross-cultural ability			N/A	
	3 Translation competence			N/A	
	4 Interpreting competence	Consecutive interpreting		Simultaneous interpreting	
	5 Revision competence		N/A	N/A	
	6 International communication ability		N/A	N/A	
	7 Professional literacy	Morality	Career planning	Ethics and norms	
	8 Contribution to industry development		Industrial contribution	Mentoring experiences	
	9 Ability to apply in specific-domain situations ("translation or interpreting" plus)			N/A	

Note: To clearly illustrate the outlines of ICS and TICA, the authors use "vertical" and "horizontal" to describe their structures, which are not intentionally proposed by the developers of ICS or TICA.

Table 3.4 Comparison of Interpreting-Specific Descriptors in ICS and TICA

Levels \ Descriptors	ICS	TICA
S	–	69
Level 1	–	54
Level 2	–	51
Level 3	–	43
Level 4	–	–
Level 5	29	–
Level 6	81	–
Level 7	112	–
Level 8	125	–
Level 9	32	–
Sum	369	217
Maximum	125	69
Minimum	29	43
Mean	75.80	54.24
Std. Deviation	44.35	10.87

The primary faculty team of TIS has improved considerably in terms of indicators such as academic qualifications and professional titles. However, a considerable number of faculty members still need more doctoral-level training, experience in professional interpreting activities, and specialized training in interpreter education; therefore, strengthening faculty development or trainer training is a matter of urgency. The current annual enrollment of PhD candidates of TIS, which is around 110 each year, can hardly satisfy the need in a short period, and the number of doctoral students specialized in interpreting research from international universities is even smaller, and as "returnees" to the Chinese mainland cannot be the mainstream of faculty improvement. Interpreting teachers themselves should also have a sense of urgency and self-improvement in lifelong career planning. In the short term, the interpreting faculty will still be composed of PhDs in TIS as well as practitioners. In the future, teachers with rich practical experience and a DTI degree will be ideal resources to enrich the structure of the faculty team.

5   Conclusion

Professional interpreter education affects the healthy development of interpreting professionalization and vice versa. The reform and opening-up have contributed to establishing the status of TIS as a discipline, promoting the cultivation of professional translators in the Chinese mainland, and initiating the course of professional translator and interpreter education. The translation and interpreting industry and its talents have, in turn, contributed to the national economy and social development. The development of interpreter education practice is inseparable from its scientific research, and both have jointly promoted the process of professionalization of interpreting.

The exchange and mutual appreciation of translator and interpreter education research outcomes between Greater China and foreign countries should be promoted by comparative research. Translator and interpreter education research in China and abroad has commonalities and uniqueness, so we shall strengthen comparative research and promote academic exchanges. In recent years, translator and interpreter education research in China and abroad has shown relatively similar concerns: attaching importance to nurturing people (the concept of cultivating people with moral character in China and the cultivation of global citizenship and otherness in foreign countries (Laviosa and González-Davies 2020)), calling for interdisciplinary research, and paying attention to the influence of sociohistorical and cultural background on the concept of talent cultivation. Regarding the differences in research, in terms of educational systems, the needs for disciplinary development and resource allocation differ between China and abroad. Chinese translator and interpreter education research is mostly macroscopic and speculative, usually good at building comprehensive and complete frameworks. In contrast, international translator and interpreter education research emphasizes microscopic and concrete empirical exploration, and different types of research present distinctive thematic features and focuses (Liang and Mu forthcoming).

Besides the holistic reflection on the professionalization of interpreting and professional interpreter education in the Chinese mainland, we also hope to generate an opportunity for academic exchanges to foster comparative studies on interpreter education research in China and beyond.

Fund

This chapter is supported by the national project of the 2022 National Social Science Foundation in China, titled "Establishing and Developing China's Education System to Cultivate Professional Translators and Interpreters for the New Era" (No. 22AYY006).

Acknowledgments

Sincere gratitude goes to Professor Riccardo Moratto and Professor Irene A. Zhang for giving us this opportunity to assess the professionalization process of interpreting as a profession. We also would like to thank the anonymous reviewers and Dr. Liang Weiling for their valuable suggestions on the early versions of the manuscript.

Notes

1 This diagram was originally adapted by Mu Lei from the figure of American postgraduate education system for professional degree in Zhang and Zhang's (2008,105) article. Figure 1 is different from the previous (Mu et al. 2013, 93; Zhong et al. 2020, 885) because we think graduates from MTI or PhD of TIS are not directly the reserve talents for DTI, with the dotted lines and arrows to show the indirect converted relations (see our arguments in two Chinese articles concerning DTI, namely Mu 2022; Mu and Liu 2022).
2 See the introduction of the tests, www.catticenter.com/en/notices/3291.
3 Translated by the authors.

References

Arocha, Izabel S., and Linda Joyce. 2013. "Patient Safety, Professionalization, and Reimbursement as Primary Drivers for National Medical Interpreter Certification in the United States." In Special Issue on Certification, edited by Alan K. Melby. *The International Journal of Translation and Interpreting Research* 5(1): 127–42. https://doi.org/10.12807/ti.105201.2013.a07.

Cai, Rendong, Jiexuan Lin, and Yanping Dong. 2023. "Psychological Factors and Interpreting Competence in Interpreting Students: A Developmental Study." *The Interpreter and Translator Trainer.* https: //doi.org/ 10.1080/1750399X.2023.2182590.

Chen Ruiqing 陈瑞清, and Mu Lei 穆雷. 2016. "Lun kouyi zhiyehua guohceng zhong de kouyi zige renzheng kaoshi" 论口译职业化过程中的口译资格认证考试 [On Interpreting Accreditation Tests in the Process of Interpreting Professionalization]. *Shandong waiyu jiaoxu* 山东外语教学 [Shandong Foreign Language Teaching] 4: 91–100.

Cui Qiliang 崔启亮. 2021. *Jingjinji xietong fazhan yuyan fuwu diaocha baogao* 京津冀协同发展语言服务调查报告 [*Report on the Beijing-Tianjin-Hebei Region: Collaborative Development of Language Service Enterprises and Its Enlightenment*]. Beijing: Duiwai jingji maoyi daxue chubanshe 北京: 对外经济贸易大学出版社 [Beijing: University of International Business and Economics Press].

Dam, Helle Vrønning. 2017. "Interpreter Role, Ethics and Norms: Linking to Professionalization." In *The Changing Role of the Interpreter: Contextualising Norms, Ethics and Quality Standards* (Routledge Advances in Translation and Interpreting Studies 25), edited by Marta Biagini, Michael S. Boyd and Claudia Monacelli, 228–39. London: Routledge.

Djovčoš, Martin, and Pavol Šveda. 2021. "The Axis of Professionalization: Translators' and Interpreters' Market Behaviour and Its Factors in Slovakia." *Babel* 67(5): 533–52.

Gambier, Yves. 2018. "Institutionalization of Translation Studies." In *A History of Modern Translation Knowledge: Sources, Concepts, Effects* (Benjamins Translation Library 142), edited by Lieven D'hulst and Yves Gambier, 179–94. Amsterdam: John Benjamins.

Guo Lijia 郭力嘉, Zhang Li 张丽, and Li Yanying 李砚颖. 2011. "Kouyi zhiyehua qushi xia de xibu kouyi rencai peiyang tanjiu" 口译职业化趋势下的西部口译人才培养探究 – 一项基于川、渝两地口译职业调查的研究报告 [A Tentative Study on Interpreting Teaching at Universities of Western China under the Trend of Interpreting Professionalization]. *Waiyu dianhua jiaoxue* 外语电化教学 [Technology Enhanced Foreign Language Education] (5): 54–9.

Han, Chao, and Xiaoyan Xiao. 2022. "A Comparative Judgment Approach to Assessing Chinese Sign Language Interpreting." *Language Testing* 39(2): 289–312. https://doi.org/10.1177/02655322211038977.

Han Ziman 韩子满. 2008. "Jiaoshi zhiyehua yu yizhe zhiyehua-Fanyi benke zhuanye jiaoxue shizi jianshe zhong de yidui maodun" 教师职业化与译者职业化 – 翻译本科专业教学师资建设中的一对矛盾 [Teacher Professionalization and Translator Professionalization – Teachers' Qualification in Undergraduate Translator/Interpreter Training]. *Waiyu jie* 外语界 [Foreign Language World] 2: 34–9.

Hoyte-West, Antony. 2020. "The Professional Status of Conference Interpreters in The Republic of Ireland: An Exploratory Study." In Translation in Ireland: Historical and Contemporary Perspectives, edited by Ní Fhrighil Ríóna, Anne O'Connor and Michelle Milan. Special issue of *Translation Studies* 13(2): 183–96. https://doi.org/10.1080/14781700.2020.1745089.

Laviosa, Sara, and Maria González-Davies. 2020. *The Routledge Handbook of Translation and Education*. London and New York: Routledge.

Lázaro Gutiérrez, Raquel, and Laura Gauthier Blasi. 2020. "Vers la professionnalisation de l'interprétation en milieu de soins de santé: quel degré d'(in)visibilité pour l'interprète?" [Towards the Professionalization of Healthcare Interpreting: What About the Interpreter's Degree of (In)Visibility?] *The Interpreters' Newsletter* 25: 81–94.

Li Nanqiu 黎难秋. 2002. *Zhongguo kouyi shi* 中国口译史 [*China Interpretation History*] Shandong: Qiangdao chubanshe 山东: 青岛出版社 [Shandong: Qingdao Publishing Group].

Liang Weiling 梁伟玲, and Mu Lei 穆雷. 2020. "'Yi xue yi zhongxin'" de fanyi jiaoshi peixun moshi – jiyu rineiwa daxue huiyi kouyi shizi peixun xiangmu de qishi "以学为中心"的翻译教师培训模式 – 基于日内瓦大学会议口译师资培训项目的启示 [Learning from University of Geneva's Learning-centered Training Model for Translation and Interpreting]. *Zhongguo fanyi* 中国翻译 [Chinese Translators Journal] 41(6): 53–60+191–92.

Liang Weiling 梁伟玲, and Mu Lei 穆雷. Forthcoming. "Fanyi jiaoxue yanjiu de xianzhuang yu qianlu (2007–2022)" 翻译教学研究的现状与前路 (2007–2022) [China's Translator and Interpreter Education Research: The Present and Future (2007–2022)]. *Zhongguo fanyi*中国翻译 [Chinese Translators Journal].

Mu Lei 穆雷. 1999/2022. *Zhongguo fanyi jiaoxue yanjiu* 中国翻译教学研究 [*Translation Teaching Research in China*]. Shanghai: Shanghai Waiyu waiyu Jiaoyu jiaoyu Chubanshe chubanshe 上海: 上海外语教育出版社 [Shanghai Foreign Language Education Press].

Mu Lei 穆雷. 2022. "Kaishe fanyi boshi zhuanye xuewei de sikao" 开设翻译博士专业学位的思考 [Thoughts on the Establishment of Doctor of Translation and Interpreting]. *Zhongguo fanyi* 中国翻译 [Chinese Translators Journal] 44(6): 21–4.

Mu Lei 穆雷, and Zhao Junfeng赵军峰. November 2022. *Zhongguo fanyi zhuanye xuewei jiaoyu tansuo zhi lu* 中国翻译专业学位教育探索之路 [The Exploration Road to China's Translation and Interpreting Education]. Hangzhou: Hangzhou Zhejiang daxue chubanshe 杭州: 浙江大学出版社 [Hangzhou: Zhejiang University Press].

Mu Lei 穆雷, and Liu Xinyuan刘馨媛. 2022. "Cong zhishi shengchan moshi zhuanxing kan fanyi boshi zhuanye xuewei" 从知识生产模式转型看翻译博士专业学位 [Analyzing Doctor of Translation and Interpreting in the Context of Transformation of Knowledge Production Mode]. *Dangdai waiyu yanjiu*当代外语研究 [Contemporary Foreign Languages Studies] 462(6): 22–9+161.

Mu Lei 穆雷, Shen Huizhi 沈慧芝, and Zou Bing 邹兵. 2017. "Mianxiang guoji yuyan fuwuye de fanyi rencai nengli tezheng yanjiu – Jiyu quanqiu yuyan fuwu gongyingshang 100 qiang de diaoyan fenxi" 面向国际语言服务业的翻译人才能力特征研究 – 基于全球语言服务供应商100强的调研分析 [Practitioner Capabilities and Employment Requirements – A Survey-Based Analysis of Globalizing Language Service Industry]. *Shanghai fanyi*上海翻译 [Shanghai Journal of Translators] 1: 8–16+94.

Mu Lei 穆雷, Liang Weiling 梁伟玲, and Liu Xinyuan 刘馨媛. Forthcoming. "Zhongguo fanyi nengli ceping dengji biaozhun yu CSE fanyi nengli dengji liangbiao" 中国翻译能力测评等级标准与CSE翻译能力等级量表 [China's Standards of Translator and Interpreter Competence Assessment and CSE Translation and Interpreting Competence Scales]. *Zhongguo waiyu*中国外语 [Foreign Languages in China].

Mu Lei 穆雷, and Wang Binhua 王斌华. 2009. "Guonei kouyi yanjiu de fazhan ji yanjiu zouxiang jiyu 30 nian qikan lunwen, zhuzuo he lijie kouyi dahui lunwen de fenxi"

国内口译研究的发展及研究走向——基于30年期刊论文、著作和历届口译大会论文的分析 [Interpreting Studies in China: A Journal Articles-based Analytical Survey]. *Zhongguo fanyi* 中国翻译 [Chinese Translators Journal] 30(4): 19–25+94.

Mu Lei 穆雷, Zhong Weihe 仲伟合, and Wang Weiwei Wang 王巍巍. 2013. "Cong zhiyehua jiaodu kan zhuanye fanyi rencai peiyang jizhi de wanshan" 从职业化角度看专业翻译人才培养机制的完善 [Reflection on Current Translator and Interpreter Education: From the Perspective of Professionalization]. *Zhongguo waiyu* 中国外语 [Foreign Languages in China] 10(1): 89–95.

Pan Hualing 潘华凌, and Liu Bingfei 刘兵飞. 2011. "Fanyi rencai xuqiu zhuangkuang jiqi peiyang duice yanjiu" 翻译人才需求状况调查及其培养对策研究 – 基于江西省的情况 [Translation Talent Requirements and the Strategies of Training the Case of Jiangxi Province]. *Jiefangjun waiguoyu xueyuan xuebao* 解放军外国语学院学报 [Journal of PLA University of Foreign Languages] 34(1): 79–83+90.

Pan Jun 潘珺, Sun Zhixiang 孙志祥, and Wang Honghua 王红华. 2009. "Kouyi de zhiyehua yu zhiyehua fazhan – Shanghai ji Jiangsu diqu kouyi xianzhuang diaocha yanjiu" 口译的职业化与职业化发展 – 上海及江苏地区口译现状调查研究 [Professionalization in Interpreting: Current Development of Interpreting in Shanghai and Jiangsu Province]. *Jiefangjun waiguoyu xueyuan xuebao* 解放军外国语学院学报 [Journal of PLA University of Foreign Languages] 32(6): 81–5+101.

René de Cotret, François, Camille Brisset, and Yvan Leanza. 2021. "A Typology of Healthcare Interpreter Positionings: When 'Neutral' Means 'Proactive'." *Interpreting* 23(1): 103–26.

Rudvin, Mette. 2007. "Professionalism and Ethics in Community Interpreting: The Impact of Individualist Versus Collective Group Identity." *Interpreting* 9(1): 47–69.

Saldanha, Gabriela, and Sharon O'Brien. 2014. *Research Methodologies in Translation Studies*. London and New York: Routledge.

Setton, Robin, and Alice Liangliang Guo. 2009. "Attitudes to Role, Status and Professional Identity in Interpreters and Translators with Chinese in Shanghai and Taipei." In Special issue on Profession, Identity and Status: Translators and Interpreters as an Occupational Group, edited by Rakefet Sela-Sheffy and Miriam Shlesinger. *Translation and Interpreting Studies* 4(2): 210–38. https://doi.org/10.1075/tis.4.2.05set.

Tang Sheng 唐笙, and Zhou Yuliang 周珏良. 1958. "Kouyi gongzuo ji kouyi gongzuozhe de peiyang" 口译工作及口译工作者的培养 [Interpreting Tasks and Cultivating Interpreters]. *Xifang yuwen* 西方语文 [Foreign Language Teaching and Research] 3: 321–327.

Translators Association of China. 2022. "TAC's Reports on Development of China's T&I Industry and Language Professionals Released." *News*. Accessed May 25, 2022. http://en.tac-online.org.cn/2022-05/25/content_41981273.html.

Tyulenev, Sergey, Binghan Zheng, and Penelope Johnson. 2017. "A Comparative Study of Translation or Interpreting as a Profession in Russia, China and Spain." *Toward Comparative Translation and Interpreting Studies* 12(2): 332–54. https://doi.org/10.1075/tis.12.2.07tyu.

Urpi, Mireia Vargas. 2012. "State of the Art in Community Interpreting Research: Mapping the Main Research Topics." *Babel* 58(1): 50–72. https://doi.org/10.1075/babel.58.1.04var.

Wang Enmian 王恩冕. 2005. "'Kouyi zai Zhongguo' diaocha baogao" "口译在中国" 调查报告 [Interpretation as A Profession in China: A Survey]. *Zhongguo fanyi* 中国翻译 [Chinese Translators Journal] 26(2): 57–60.

Wang Weiwei 王巍巍, and Zhong Weihe 仲伟合. 2017. "'Guobiao' zhidao xia de yingyu lei zhuanye kecheng gaige yu jianshe" "国标"指导下的英语类专业课程改革与建设 [*The National Criteria of Teaching Quality* for BA Programs in English Reform and Development]. *Waiyu jie* 外语界 [Foreign Language World] 3: 2–8+15.

Wang, Weiwei, Yi Xu, Binghua Wang, and Lei Mu. 2020. "Developing Interpreting Competence Scales in China." *Frontiers in Psychology* 11(481): 1–16. https://doi.org/10.3389/fpsyg.2020.00481.

Wang, Xiangyu, and Xiangdong Li. 2020. "The Market's Expectations of Interpreters in China: A Content Analysis of Job Ads for In-House Interpreters." *Journal of Specialised Translation* 34: 118–49. https://jostrans.org/issue34/art_wang.php.

Xiao Weiqing 肖维青, and Feng Qinghua 冯庆华. 2019. "*Fanyi zhuanye benke jiaoxue zhinan* jiedu" 《翻译专业本科教学指南》解读 [Interpretation of *Teaching Guide for Undergraduate Translation Major*]. *Waiyu jie* 外语界 [Foreign Language World] 5: 8–13+20.

Yao Bin 姚斌. 2022. "Xin zhongguo gaoji fanyi rencai peiyang de zaoqi tansuo he qishi – yi Beijing waiguoyu daxue fanyiban wei anli" 新中国高级翻译人才培养的早期探索和启示——以北京外国语大学翻译班为案例 [BFSU's Mid-20th Century "Translation Classes" and China's Early Attempt at Training High-Caliber Translators and Interpreters]. *Zhongguo fanyi* 中国翻译 [Chinese Translators Journal] 43(3): 71–80+192.

Zhang Jiangong 张建功, and Zhang Zhengang 张振刚. 2008. "Meiguo zhuanye xuewei yanjiusheng jiaoyu de xuewei jiegou ji qishi" 美国专业学位研究生教育的学位结构及启示 [On Degree Structure of American Postgraduate Education for Professional Degree and Its Enlightenment]. *Gaodeng jiaoyu yanjiu* 高等教育研究 [Journal of Higher Education] 7: 104–9.

Zhang Wei 张威. 2017. "Zhongguo kouyi xuexizhe yuliaoku jianshe yu yanjiu: Lilun yu shijian de ruogan sikao" 中国口译学习者语料库建设与研究：理论与实践的若干思考[J]. *Zhongguo fanyi* 中国翻译 [Chinese Translators Journal] 38(1): 53–60.

Zhao Yihui 赵毅慧. 2017. "Jishu zhexue shiyu xia kouyi jishu de ming yu shi" 技术哲学视域下口译技术的"名"与"实"探析 [Name and Nature of Interpreting Technology: A Technological-Philosophical Perspective]. *Waiyu jiaoxue* 外语教学 [Foreign Language Education] 38(6): 89–94.

Zheng Xuan 郑璇. 2020. "Jiakuai tuijin zhongguo shouyu fanyi de zhiyehua – jiyu xinxing guanzhuang bingdu feiyan yiqing de sikao" 加快推进中国手语翻译的职业化 – 基于新型冠状病毒肺炎疫情的思考 [Promoting the Professionalization of Chinese Sign Language Interpretation: Reflections on the Epidemic Situation of COVID-19]. *Canjiren yanjiu* 残疾人研究 [Disability Research] 1: 24–32.

Zhong Weihe 仲伟合. 2016. "Zhongguo kouyi xueke de weilai fazhan" 中国口译学科的未来发展 [The Future Development of Interpreting Studies in China]. *Zhongguo waiyu* 中国外语 [Foreign Languages in China] 13(5): 4–9.

Zhong Weihe 仲伟合. 2020. *Kouyi jiaoxue – Guangwai moshi de tansuo yu shijian* 口译教学 – 广外模式的探索与实践 [Interpreter Training – The Guangwai Approach] Beijing: waiyu jiaoxue yu yanjiu chubanshe 北京：外语教学与研究出版社 [Beijing: Foreign Language Teaching and Research Press].

Zhong, Weihe, Tianyuan Zhao, and Mianjun Xu. 2020. "Professional Interpreting Translation Education in the Chinese Mainland." *Babel* 66(6): 883–901. https://doi.org/10.1075/babel.00199.zho.

4 Embarking upon careers with a diploma in conference interpreting

Graduates' motivations and self-perceived employability

Bin Gao and Zhuxuan Zhao

1 Introduction

The deepening exchanges between China and the world demand a specialized translation and interpreting (T&I) workforce. However, according to a recent survey by the Translators Association of China (2022, 27), 67.3% of China's industry experts reported the scarcity of high-end T&I talent. In the most professionalized sector of interpreting, conference interpreters, in particular, must meet high professional standards of quality and ethical behavior. Thus, to qualify as conference interpreters, specialized training is required, which, as the International Association of Conference Interpreters (AIIC) recommended, should take place at the graduate level with the active involvement of practicing professionals (AIIC 1999).

Institutionalized training of interpreters began in China in the 1970s as part of the foreign language programs of colleges and universities. Following the launch of Master of Translation and Interpreting (MTI) programs in 2007, Chinese institutions offering MTI degrees have steadily increased in number, amounting to a staggering 316 by the end of 2021. However, there are concerns that MTI enrollments exceed market demand and that the curriculum of MTI programs does not fully match the skills demanded by related industries (e.g., Wu and Jiang 2021). Overall, an urgent need to bridge the gap between MTI teaching and the industry has been identified over the past decade (e.g., Miao and Wang 2010; Wang and Wang 2016; Mu 2020; Wu and Jiang 2021).

Among Chinese colleges and universities offering MTI degrees, only a fraction offers systematic conference interpreting (CI) training, which is often embedded in advanced interpreting programs. The "UIBE-SCIC" program is a collaborative CI training program between the University of International Business and Economics (UIBE) and the Directorate-General for Interpretation of the European Commission (SCIC). As the first CI training program officially supported by SCIC in China, it has trained over 100 highly skilled CI graduates since 2001, with a prestige established in the interpreting education community and wider society. The two-year

DOI: 10.4324/9781003357629-6

program is held to stringent and profession-oriented training standards, each year enrolling around only ten students, after three rounds of aptitude tests, and graduating even fewer after a competitive midterm test and a rigorous professional qualification test at the end of the program. All the trainers are SCIC-accredited practicing professionals, including former SCIC trainers/ interpreters. In an intensive curriculum, classes are taught by native Chinese and English trainers together – a hallmark that has helped to shape the UIBE-SCIC program's image as a top CI program in China.

Like many other institutions, the UIBE adopts a tiered approach to interpreting training. Its MTI degree makes a distinction between "conference interpreting" (UIBE-SCIC program) and "business interpreting" programs. The former aims at training conference interpreters for international organizations and state organs with a small-scale "elitist" approach, while the latter targets the majority of students to prepare them as multilingual talent for careers not limited to interpreting per se (Wang and Wang 2016, 6–7). Compared to the relatively abundant research focusing on the mismatch between industry needs and MTI programs in general, few researchers have looked at the transition of CI students, in particular from the university to the workplace. It would then be interesting to take the UIBE-SCIC program as an example to explore whether similar trends exist in a program with more focused objectives and much smaller enrollment.

With regard to CI pedagogical practices in China, empirical evidence has been provided from the perspective of currently enrolled trainees in terms of their evaluation of teaching strategies (e.g., J. Wang 2012; Zhang 2020) and learning needs (e.g., Ren and Hu 2007), but few attempts have been made from the perspective of graduates. As more Chinese graduates have begun their careers with a diploma in CI, many of whom have years of working experience already, it would be necessary to learn about their career motivations and employability as a means of feedback for the training they have received.

2   Related research

2.1   *Motivations of T&I graduates*

Motivation is what drives human behaviors. Though many studies have proven the significance of motivation as a performance predictor in both academic and professional contexts, motivation has remained an under-researched field in the T&I sphere despite its all-important role in the successful completion of training (Horváth and Kálmán 2020). Attention has been placed on the implications of T&I students' motivations for training (Lung 2005; Timarová and Salaets 2011; Wu 2016; Ameri and Ghahari 2018) and on motivational factors for T&I professionals to engage in volunteer work (Olohan 2012; McDonough Dolmaya, 2012). Less research, however, has been done on the career motivations of T&I graduates. A recent survey conducted by Horváth and Kálmán (2020) investigated the motivational disposition of T&I

graduates of a university in Budapest and found "intrinsic motivation," "ideal self," "mastery," and "significant others" to be the most potent motivators behind learning. Conducted among MA graduates specialized in both translation and interpreting, their research presented enlightening results for T&I programs. However, the focus was more on the implications of motivations for learning effectiveness instead of career development.

In China, there has been growing interest in the careers of MTI graduates (Miao and Wang 2010; Wang and Wang 2016; Wu and Jiang 2021). Through a survey of UIBE's 442 MTI students graduating between 2012 and 2014, Wang and Wang (2016) identified diverse fields of employment and explored the influence of personal backgrounds. Previous research has also depicted similar pictures for job offerings on the market in relation to students' T&I qualifications. For example, consistent with Miao and Wang's (2010) findings about more significant needs for part-time instead of full-time translators and interpreters, Wu and Jiang's (2021) results identified only 13% of graduates working as full-time translators, while 38% work in foreign-language-related jobs, and 49% in jobs not related to a foreign language at all.

Without foregrounding the potentially dynamic nature of careers, these quantitative studies have contributed toward an objective understanding of T&I students' careers after graduation, but the research that addresses interpreting graduates' evolving career goals in a longer time frame has remained lacking. From a career development perspective, Edgar H. Schein (1978) proposed "career anchors," which comprise a cluster of self-perceived values, talents, and motivations underlying an individual's career decisions. As a set of stable orientations one develops over time in the professional journey, career anchors offer a perspective for describing CI graduates' career orientations, as reflected by individual career choices and the motivations behind.

2.2   *Employability of T&I graduates*

Though with various definitions, "employability" is generally seen as the ability to "move self-sufficiently within the labour market to realize potential through sustainable employment" (Hillage and Pollard 1998, 2). As a complex and multidimensional concept, employability is believed to be built upon a number of attributes, including but not limited to knowledge, skills, attitudes, career management, and job search (Hillage and Pollard 1998), capacity for learning (Bagshaw 1996; Lane and Rajan 2000), and professional knowledge (Van der Heijden 2002). It may be examined from a range of perspectives, that is, that of policymakers, universities, employers or employees, and graduates.

Regarding the composition of employability, measurement models have been devised from different angles. For instance, Van der Heijde and Van der Heijden (2006) developed a scale for measuring employability from the dual perspectives of employees and employers, including occupational expertise, anticipation and optimization, personal flexibility, corporate sense, and balance. Such measurement models have made "employability" more operational at the organizational level, as the concept is now widely adopted in employee recruitment, human resource planning and development, and job performance assessment.

Projected into the sphere of education, employability has become an important indicator of the quality of university graduates and training programs. Into the 21st century, universities have placed much emphasis on employability-oriented curriculum design (Cox and King 2006; Ehiyazaryan and Barraclough 2009; Rae 2007; Song and Xie 2006). For graduate employability, Dacre Pool and Sewell (2007) developed a measurement model that comprises career development learning, experience (work and life), degree subject knowledge, understanding and skills, generic skills, and emotional intelligence. For Chinese university graduates, Su and Zhang (2015) developed a competence model reflecting the perspectives of career experts, university career tutors and HR/recruitment managers, and derived five first-level indicators, that is, personal attribute, professional ability, communication and interpersonal ability, practice experiences and ability to solve problems, and career attitude, each comprising several second-level indicators.

The previous studies have emphasized slightly different aspects of employability but have all treated employability as a complex body involving both disciplinary-specific and generic knowledge, understanding and skills required for acquiring or maintaining jobs, as well as individual attitudes, psychological and cognitive features, and personal attributes. As the primary objective of these studies is to establish a measurement model applicable to employers regardless of industries, the role of disciplinary knowledge and specific fields of know-how is minimized.

Regarding the components of employability for T&I graduates, studies have already been done in the Chinese context (Miao and Wang 2010; Wu and Jiang 2021) without specifying students' language combinations. Through an analysis of 434 T&I job descriptions issued by professional language service providers in major cities across China, Miao and Wang (2010) identified 15 professional competences for MTI graduates, among which 4 are directly related to technology application, 7 disciplinary-specific skills, and 4 generic skills. Wu and Jiang (2021) conducted a questionnaire survey among MTI graduates without differentiating between translation and interpreting majors and revealed four core components of employability needed by graduates to work in different sectors, including disciplinary-specific competences, transferable generic competences, personal attributes and practical experience, among which disciplinary-specific competences was regarded as principal by graduates working as full-time translators and in foreign-language-related jobs, while transferable generic competences and personal attributes remain high in rankings regardless of professions.

The employability components identified for MTI graduates may be relevant for CI graduates. But considering the uniqueness of CI in professional requirements and work environment, the employability of CI graduates entails distinctive disciplinary-specific competences and occupational qualities. Zhong and Zhan (2016) distinguished three components of "interpreting competence," that is, bilingual ability, extra-linguistic knowledge, and interpreting skills, with the latter occupying a core position. On top of "interpreting competence," and following Kiraly's (2000) concept of "translator competence," B. Wang (2012) proposed "interpreter competence" that also comprises non-intellectual factors, such as psychological, professional, and physical qualities concerning the distinctive features of interpreting work and professional requirements.

For the purpose of this chapter, we approach graduates' employability with the widely adopted definition given by Yorke (2006, 8) as "a set of achievements – skills, understanding and personal attributes – that makes graduates more likely to gain employment and be successful in their chosen occupations, which benefits themselves, the workforce, the community and the economy." It would be necessary to incorporate the aforementioned scholarly insights in both universal and disciplinary-specific accounts of CI graduates' employability and examine their relevance in the current Chinese workplace.

3 The inquiry

This chapter will answer the following questions:

1 What characterizes the career orientations of CI graduates in China?
2 How do CI graduates perceive their own employability in the workplace in relation with their training?

To answer the two questions, we collected data from 67 graduates from the UIBE-SCIC program between 2012 and 2022 through one online questionnaire in Chinese. The questionnaire was developed based on previous research on motivation and employability, as well as the authors' understandings and personal experiences regarding CI training (one author was formerly a trainer in, and the other a graduate from, the UIBE-SCIC program), and was generated using an online survey tool, *Wenjuanxing* (www.wjx.cn). A pilot test was conducted among 18 CI graduates, who provided suggestions for wording and content. The refined questionnaire consisted of 30 items, of which 4 were biological and background questions. The remaining questions addressed learning motivations, career orientations (as captured by Schein's (1978) five principal career anchors),[1] employability (including interpreting-specific competences, career attitudes, transferable skills, personal attributes, practical experience), and perceptions of CI training, with 23 multiple-choice questions and 6 five-point Likert-scale questions. One open-ended question was also included to elicit views on both the advantages and disadvantages of embarking on a career with a diploma in CI.

The questionnaire was administered online in October 2022 to 67 graduates that completed two-year training in the UIBE-SCIC program

Table 4.1 Information of "UIBE-SCIC" Program Graduates between 2012 and 2022 (n = 67)

Personal Information		Number	Percentage
Gender	Male	21	31.3%
	Female	46	68.7%
Age	≤29	31	46.3%
	30–39	34	50.7%
	≥40	2	3.0%
Year of graduation	2012–2015	22	32.8%
	2016–2019	26	38.8%
	2020–2022	19	28.4%
Type of employment	Governmental agencies	13	19.4%
	Enterprises	18	26.9%
	Public institutions	20	29.9%
	Self-employment (e.g., freelance interpreting)	16	23.9%
Location of workplace	China	57	85.1%
	Overseas	10	14.9%

between 2012 and 2022, with a recovery rate of 100%. Table 4.1 shows the personal information of the respondents, which reflects a relatively young group of professionals whose careers are spread out rather evenly in four types of employment, that is, governmental agencies (19.4%), enterprises (26.9%), public institutions[2] (29.9%), and self-employment (23.9%), most of whom are currently working in China (85.1%). Descriptive statistics were obtained through SPSS 24™, while qualitative data from the open-ended question (with a Chinese character count of 4,066) was analyzed with a thematic approach to identify general trends.

4   Results and analyses

4.1   Formation of career orientations

Career orientations started to take shape even before enrollment and can be partly seen through learning motivations. Notably, over half of the respondents named "becoming a professional interpreter" (50.8%) as their primary motivator before enrollment, followed by "interest in interpreting" (29.9%), "becoming a multi-talented professional with interpreting skills (but not working as a full-time interpreter)" (10.5%), with only 9.0% stating "self-exploration before career goals are identified." These rather-focused and clear patterns of learning motivations, however, did not translate into equally clear career goals. As Table 4.2 shows, 29 or nearly half of the respondents were not clear about their career goals before enrollment. The situation improved at the time of graduation, but still with 12 respondents (17.9%) uncertain about desired jobs. Moreover, there has been a dramatic rise in interest in public-sector jobs,

Table 4.2 Career Goals before Enrollment and upon Graduation (n = 67)

Career Goals	Before Enrollment	Upon Graduation
Freelance interpreter	19	10
Interpreting-related job in governments	6	14
Interpreting-related job in enterprises	8	15
Interpreting-related job in public institutions	5	16
Running one's own business	0	0
Not clear	29	12

as the number of respondents interested in a career in governments more than doubled upon graduation and that in public institutions tripled. Equally noticeable has been a decline in the interest in freelancing. This shows that as students progress through the two-year training, they demonstrate an overall inclination to pursue careers for which interpreting competences are essential, but not all.

Among the key considerations behind career choices, two are dominant, that is, whether the job will help improve interpreting competences (49.3%), and the reputation of the employers (43.3%), which respectively correspond to the career anchors of "technical/functional competence" and "security/stability and organizational identity" (Schein 1978). When compared across different employment types, the top-ranking motivation behind career decisions for those working in the public sector is "security/stability and organizational identity" (36% for those in governmental agencies and 35% for public institutions), "managerial competence" for enterprise employees (33%), and "autonomy and independence" for the self-employed (31%), while "technical/functional competence" features as an important consideration across all employment types (ranging from 24% to 32%); 22 respondents (32.8%) have the experience of changing jobs after graduation, among whom 7 (10.5%) have changed jobs twice or more. The top-ranking driver behind job change was actually to further grow professional competences (40.9%), much higher than the pursuit of greater autonomy (18.2%) and stability (13.6%). This indicates that interpreting-related "technical/functional competence" has always played an essential role in the formation of career orientations.

Current career choices seem to be affected by gender, working years, and market conditions as well. On the whole, male graduates are more inclined to work in governmental agencies (28.6%) and enter into self-employment (28.6%) than their female counterparts (15.2% and 21.7%, respectively), while a higher percentage of female graduates work in enterprises and public institutions (respectively 34.8% and 28.3%, as compared to 19.0% and 23.8% of male graduates). Differences also exist between those with more and fewer working years regarding self-employment, which represents the current employment status of 11 out of the 22 respondents graduating in earlier years (2012–2015), of whom 8 were self-employed immediately upon graduation; in contrast, only

4 out of the 26 respondents graduating between 2016 and 2019 are self-employed, while none is self-employed among the 19 respondents graduating in recent years (2020–2022). Primarily in the form of freelance interpreting, self-employment gradually fell out of favor, probably because of slower growth in salaries due to fiercer market competition. For those graduating in 2020 and after, the shrinking numbers and scales of international conferences and general economic uncertainties under the impact of the COVID-19 pandemic might also be an unfavorable factor for freelancing.

Among the 67 graduates that participated in the survey, nobody wanted to start their own businesses at either the beginning or the end of training (Table 4.2), but three ended up operating their own businesses full-time, with one running new media platforms and two providing online language coaching. But even those who provide language coaching would incorporate interpreting skills into their coaching contents and use their CI qualifications and experiences for successful branding.

Overall, the career orientations of CI graduates were formed under the combined effect of internal and external factors, among which a strong motivation for interpreting-related "technical/functional competence" has remained a centerpiece in evolving career profiles.

4.2   *Employability in diversified careers*

Interpreting-related skills feature prominently in the eyes of CI graduates. Among the 67 respondents, only 3 (4.5%) pursued a career that does not require interpreting competences. In fact, 54 out of the 65 valid answers to the open-ended question mentioned interpreting-specific competences as CI graduates' most distinctive advantage in the job market. Among interpreting-specific competences, there were 32 references to interpreting techniques, followed by 22 references to bilingual competence, 10 to professional ethics, 4 to extra-linguistic knowledge, and 3 to intercultural competence. This shows that interpreting-specific competences, with interpreting techniques at the core, are a cornerstone of CI graduates' employability, either as a quality directly guaranteeing job performance or as something that other aspects of employability are built around, at least at the start of careers.

For CI graduates, a need has been identified to take into account the social context of the workplace. In this chapter, it is first and foremost the Chinese society that should be considered, as almost all graduates work in China or in a foreign country, but in the capacity of a Chinese diplomat or an expatriate employee of a Chinese company. As indicated by survey results, the ability to perform consecutive interpreting (38.8%), simultaneous interpreting without text (32.8%) and with text (19.4%) were regarded as considerably more relevant than liaison interpreting and sight translation in a Chinese context, with the ability to work from Chinese into English and from English into Chinese deemed equally important.

Skills besides interpreting competences gained importance as careers developed. Overall, among the five components of employability in the survey, survey respondents gave the highest ratings to their own career attitudes (M = 4.36, SD = 0.62), followed by transferable skills (M = 3.99, SD = 0.73), personal attributes (M = 3.97, SD = 0.67), and interpreting-specific competences (M = 3.76, SD = 0.72), while the ratings for practical experience (M = 3.22, SD = 1.01) were the lowest and with the greatest divergences. Generally, the respondents demonstrated higher levels of satisfaction with their own "softer" aspects of employability, namely, career attitudes as represented by "responsibility/dedication," transferable skills as by "capacity for learning," and personal attributes as by "moral quality." All three dimensions of softer skills were mentioned in answers to the open-ended question, among which transferable skills in particular were seen as an important contributor to a successful transition from the university to the workplace. Lower ratings of interpreting-specific competences might be associated with the high professional standards that graduates typically impose on themselves, which were actually seen by several respondents in the open-ended questionnaire as a distinct competitive edge. Interestingly, among the dimensions of softer skills, only a minority of respondents regarded career attitudes (M = 1.94, SD = 1.20) and personal attributes (M = 2.47, SD = 1.15) as intrinsic qualities that cannot be effectively improved through training.

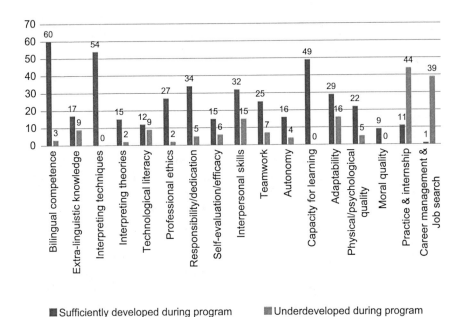

Figure 4.1 Number of references to competences/qualities most relevant to the workplace.

As Figure 4.1 shows, among specific career-relevant competences or qualities developed during the CI program, those mentioned most by survey respondents include bilingual competence (89.6%), interpreting techniques (80.6%), and capacity for learning (73.1%). In contrast, practice and internship (65.7%), career management and job search (58.2%), adaptability (23.9%), and interpersonal skills (22.4%) were seen as important but underdeveloped during the program.

In addition to the five predetermined components of employability, answers to the open-ended question suggest that non-interpreting subject-specific competences should also be given their due place in CI graduates' employability. Aside from the most relevant (written) translation competence, these subject-specific competences may also include teaching and research, project management, and knowledge in other disciplines, depending on the specific requirements of individual career scenes. In fact, the lack of non-interpreting subject-specific competences was seen by a number of respondents as a significant disadvantage for CI graduates venturing into areas less related to interpreting, particularly given the increasing number of skilled bilingual talent in China's workplace today.

4.3 Graduate perspectives on CI program training

The survey also elicited graduates' perspectives on specific CI training contents and found that those regarded as most relevant to professional interpreting work include "improvement of bilingual competence" (91.0%), "memory and retelling" (68.7%), and "note-taking" (52.2%). Among training contents yet to be given more attention, "knowledge of the industry" was mentioned most with a disproportionately high percentage of 70.7%, followed by "extra-linguistic knowledge" (19.4%), "professional norms and ethics" (16.4%), and "T&I technologies" (14.9%), among others. As to the forms of training, mock conference (77.6%), teacher comment (77.6%), and extramural practice (67.2%) were rated as more suitable for building the employability of a professional interpreter.

When evaluated as a whole, the UIBE-SCIC program was seen by the majority of survey respondents as having effectively bridged the university and the workplace (M = 4.40, SD = 0.72). In fact, some mentioned program reputation in the open-ended question as having contributed to graduates' competitiveness in the job market. There was high consensus on the importance of maintaining small enrollments and stringent standards (M = 4.81, SD = 0.43), which promoted greater dedication from both students and teachers. However, opinions diverged regarding the statement that the program must be guided by the overarching objective of training professional interpreters (M = 3.93, SD = 1.15). Lower levels of approval of the statement were observed among the 33 respondents motivated by factors other than "becoming a professional interpreter" (M = 3.67, SD = 1.22) when compared to those who wanted to work full-time as interpreters (M = 4.18, SD = 1.03), though the difference was not statistically significant ($p = 0.069$). The concern that an overly focused objective may constrain career development has also been voiced in answers to the open-ended question. While some mentioned career plateaus for interpreters working in China, others saw a more significant challenge posed by a mindset potentially narrowed by the sole objective of doing interpreting, a condition referred to literally as "tool-person thinking" (a catchphrase on the Chinese Internet) by a number of survey respondents.

While the absolute majority of graduates (95.5%) regarded the program as most suitable for people wanting a career as professional interpreters, only 7 (10.5%) and 2 (3.0%) regarded it as favorable for those seeking higher management positions and wishing to run their own businesses. This imagination of a "standard graduate" following a highly technical career has, perhaps, given the small number of graduates pursuing nontechnical careers, become a self-realizing prophecy to a certain extent.

Another concern is the lack of practice during the program. Nearly half of the respondents (47.8%), despite having passed the SCIC qualification test at the end of the two-year program, believed that a period of real-world practice was needed before they could regard themselves as qualified interpreters. This "transition period" is required after graduation to compensate for the lack of work experience during the program, as the intensive curriculum and the pressure of passing the midterm and final professional tests left limited room for practice and internship. Though an intensive curriculum was part of the program's effort to ensure high training standards, there was a general consensus among survey respondents ($M = 4.67$, $SD = 0.66$) that practice and internship in itself will help build professional expertise.

5   Implications for CI programs

5.1   *Maintaining stringent standards centered on interpreter competence*

Despite the aim of MTI programs to train high-level applied and professional interpreters and translators, only 20.7% of MTI graduates are employed in jobs directly related to their professional know-how (Translators Association of China 2022, 23). This stands in stark contrast with the results of this study, where the absolute majority of CI graduates have built their career profiles largely around interpreting-related competence. While the concept "interpreting competence" (Zhong and Zhan 2016) was developed primarily for building disciplinary-specific knowledge and skills from a trainee perspective, this study has highlighted non-intellectual professional requirements for practitioners in the workplace, as better captured by the term "interpreter competence" (B. Wang 2012). Higher specialization levels centered on "interpreter competence" will help address the shortage of highly skilled T&I talent in China.

In the current workplace filled with an increasing number of bilinguals, stringent training standards must be maintained to ensure sufficient specialization levels of CI graduates. These standards comprise a high teacher–student ratio, the involvement of native-speaking practicing professionals, and tests with rigorous professional criteria, among others. As the case was in this study, after passing the initial aptitude tests, students in the UIBE-SCIC program have to pass a midterm test on consecutive interpreting before they are allowed to enter the second year and study simultaneous interpreting, and a final professional qualification test on both consecutive and simultaneous interpreting at the end of the program. The final professional qualification test has only pass/fail results and thus is different from an achievement test in a typical language course.

To meet these professional standards, students would need to dedicate massive amounts of time and energy to learning and constantly strengthen their learning motivations in the highly specialized, step-by-step training, as fellow classmates with less-stable motivations leave. Such a program orientation has contributed to students' strong motivations for improving interpreting-related competences before enrollment and throughout the program. Meanwhile, highly specialized training with stringent standards will also help establish a distinct image and reputation of the program among employers and prospective students.

5.2   Incorporating employability in CI training

Though the importance of specialized knowledge and skills was recognized in many previous studies (e.g., Van der Heijde and Van der Heijden 2006; Dacre Pool and Sewell 2007; Su and Zhang 2015), its role was often blurred in an attempt to establish generic employability. For highly specialized CI training, it would be essential to incorporate employability specifically needed by CI graduates.

Among the five components of employability identified based on previous literature, interpreting-specific competences, which are qualities necessary for specializing as CI professionals, have occupied a central position. Instead of quickly turning to other sectors after graduation – a trend observed by Wu and Jiang (2021) among MTI graduates – the CI graduates in this study have used interpreting-specific competences developed during the program as their "original capital," on which they further grow professional expertise regardless of career orientations. Under interpreting-specific competences, bilingual competence, interpreting techniques, and professional ethics were well-developed in the program, which speaks volumes for the importance of being trained by experienced practitioners. Though there was no course specifically dedicated to professional ethics, the competence was effectively incorporated into daily training through the trainer's exemplary effect. In contrast, extra-linguistic knowledge and technological literacy are yet to receive more attention. For extra-linguistic knowledge, part of the answer may lie in holding more mock conferences with real-world experts serving as guest speakers, which will allow greater exposure to technical areas. For technological literacy, increased attention to both translation- and interpreting-related technologies is needed to keep abreast of today's technological advances, which may warrant opening a course on T&I technologies in the CI program or encouraging students to enroll in a relevant MTI course. Moreover, intercultural competence is particularly relevant in the Chinese context, where interpreters are expected to work in both directions (e.g., between Chinese and English). In this regard, the collaboration between native Chinese- and English-speaking trainers has become a distinct advantage for developing intercultural competence.

The study also reveals the importance of the softer aspects of employability, including career attitudes, transferable skills, and personal attributes. Though these qualities and skills tend to be forged in the crucible of the workplace, it would be necessary to help students develop the right combination of softer skills during the program so as to enable a smoother transition to professional roles. Adaptability and interpersonal skills among other transferable skills, for instance, were regarded as insufficiently developed during the program. Specific forms of training, particularly extramural practice and mock conference, will help build these qualities by exposing students to the way of how real-world projects or events are organized. Both regarded as desirable for building the employability of a professional interpreter, extramural practice and mock conference should be further institutionalized during CI program training.

Finally, an analysis of the qualitative data shows that despite reliance on interpreting-related skills when entering the workplace, graduates will generally need non-interpreting subject-specific competences as their careers unfold. Relevant optional courses or summer schools are suggested to customize learning for students with different career orientations without affecting the already-intensive CI training agenda.

5.3   *Preparing students for long-term career development*

The present chapter has revealed four major types of employment, corresponding to different key motivations behind career choices. This further shows the controlling effect of career anchors (Schein 1978) on individual career decisions as applicable to CI graduates.

For many CI trainees, career orientations took a longer time to settle compared to more-focused learning motivations and are subject to the joint influence of internal and external factors. However, an earlier start to explore one's own values, talents, and motivations in relation to future careers may benefit graduates by engaging them in the formation of their own career orientations. For the CI program, an approach to preparing students for long-term career development is by acknowledging and helping them recognize their different career motivations through career planning, preferably starting in the early days of the program. Highly valued by graduates, career management and job search currently receive very limited attention in the program but are improvable by guided practice and internship, on-site observations of real interpreting scenarios, as well as by engaging industry experts in workshops or organizing alumni meetings. Such enriched program experiences will address the lack of "knowledge of the industry" for career beginners as identified in this chapter. Career planning will also inform students of the non-interpreting subject-specific competences and the right combination of softer skills they may want to build during the program.

6 Conclusion

The present study depicts a successful CI program for producing highly specialized professionals. Guided by a clear objective and held to rigorous professional standards, the program has helped students establish interpreting-specific competences as an advantageous point of departure, around which other components of employability are further developed in the workplace. The students have demonstrated strong and focused motivations for learning but less-clear career goals during the program. Such understandings have facilitated a re-examination of current CI programs in terms of orientations and pedagogical practices, which include the importance of maintaining stringent training standards and further incorporating employability into CI training. Career planning, guided practice, and generally more connections with the industry are suggested to prepare students for the workplace so that students will be more actively engaged in the formation of their own career orientations.

This chapter has revealed interpreting-specific competences as a core asset for the vast majority of graduates, regardless of how their careers evolve, across all employment types. But since the survey respondents all graduated in the last 11 years, investigations in a longer time frame are required to know whether such tendencies persist. Behind the general trends of CI graduates' career development, future studies would need to explore in more depth the motivations and employability of CI graduates with different types of careers. It is also necessary to check graduates' self-perceived employability against broader social perceptions, such as those represented by employers in a Chinese context.

Notes

1 The five dominant career anchors are security/stability and organizational identity, autonomy and independence, creativity and entrepreneurship, technical/functional competence, and managerial competence (including analytical competence, interpersonal and intergroup competence, and emotional competence).
2 Public institutions in China are organizations offering social services to the public, including public schools, universities, clinics, hospitals, libraries, performing groups, research institutes, and media organizations, which are fully or partly funded by the government.

References

AIIC Training and Professional Development. 1999. "Conference Interpreting Training Programmes Best Practice." Published December 1, 1999. Accessed October 10,

2016. https://aiic.org/document/4498/Conference%20interpreting%20training%20programmes%20best%20practice%20-%20ENG.pdf.

Ameri, Saeed, and Shima Ghahari. 2018. "Developing a Motivational Framework in Translation Training Programs: A Mixed Methods Study Following Self-determination and Social Capital Theories." *The Interpreter and Translator Trainer* 12(2): 227–43.

Bagshaw, Michael. 1996. "Creating Employability: How Can Training and Development Square the Circle Between Individual and Corporate Interest?" *Industrial and Commercial Training* 28(1): 16–8.

Cox, Sharon, and David King. 2006. "Skill Sets: An Approach to Embed Employability in Course Design." *Education+Training* 48(4): 262–74.

Dacre Pool, Lorraine, and Peter Sewell. 2007. "The Key to Employability: Developing a Practical Model of Graduate Employability." *Education+Training* 49(4): 277–89.

Ehiyazaryan, Ester, and Nicola Barraclough. 2009. "Enhancing Employability: Integrating Real World Experience in the Curriculum." *Education+Training* 51(4): 292–308.

Hillage, Jim, and Emma Pollard. 1998. "Employability: Developing a Framework for Policy Analysis." In *Research Brief 85*. London: Department for Education and Employment, Institute for Employment Studies. Accessed March 4, 2023. https://webarchive.nationalarchives.gov.uk/ukgwa/20130401151715/http://www.education.gov.uk/publications/eOrderingDownload/RB85.pdf.

Horváth, Ildikó, and Csaba Kálmán. 2020. "Motivational Disposition of Translation and Interpreting Graduates." *The Interpreter and Translator Trainer* 15(3): 287–305.

Kiraly, Donald. 2000. *A Social Constructivist Approach to Translator Education: Empowerment from Theory to Practice*. Manchester: St. Jerome Publishing.

Lane, David, and Amin Rajan. 2000. *Employability: Bridging the Gap Between Rhetoric and Reality; Second Report: Employee's Perspective*. Tonbridge: Centre for Research in Employment Tech in Europe.

Lung, Rachel. 2005. "Translation Training Needs for Adult Learners." *Babel* (3): 224–37.

McDonough Dolmaya, Julie. 2012. "Analysing the Crowdsourcing Model and Its Impact on Public Perceptions of Translation." *The Translator* 18(2): 167–91.

Miao Ju 苗菊, and Wang Wang 王少爽. 2010. "Fanyi hangye de zhiye quxiang dui fanyi shuoshi zhuanye (MTI) jiaoyu de qishi" 翻译行业的职业趋向对翻译硕士专业 (MTI) 教育的启示 [MTI Education in Light of a Survey on Employment Trend in Translation Industry]. *Waiyu yu waiyu jiaoxue* 外语与外语教学 [Foreign Languages and Their Teaching] (3): 63–7.

Mu Lei 穆雷. 2020. "Woguo fanyi shuoshi zhuanye xuewei xianzhuang yu wenti – jiyu *fanyi shuoshi zhuanye xuewei fazhan baogao de fenxi yanjiu*" 我国翻译硕士专业学位现状与问题－基于《翻译硕士专业学位发展报告》的分析研究 [On China's MTI Programs: Present and Future – An Analysis of the Development Report on Master Degree Programs of Translation and Interpreting]. *Zhongguo fanyi* 中国翻译 [Chinese Translators Journal] (1): 87–96.

Olohan, Maeve. 2012. "Why Do You Translate? Motivation to Volunteer and TED Translation." *Translation Studies* (1): 17–33.

Rae, David. 2007. "Connecting Enterprise and Graduate Employability: Challenges to the Higher Education Culture and Curriculum." *Education+Training* 49(8/9): 605–19.

Ren Wen 任文, and Hu Minxia 胡敏霞. 2007. "Tongsheng chuanyi kecheng sheji de pingjia yu zaisheji" 同声传译课程设计的评价与再设计 [Assessing and Re-Designing Universities' SI Training Course in China]. *Guangdong waiyu waimao daxue xuebao* 广东外语外贸大学学报 [Journal of Guangdong University of Foreign Studies] 18(3): 15–62.

Schein, Edgar H. 1978. *Career Dynamics: Matching Individual and Organizational Needs*. Reading, MA: Addison-Wesley.

Song Guoxue 宋国学, and Xie Jinyu 谢晋宇. 2006. "Keguyongxing jiaoyu moshi: lilun shuping yu shijian yingyong" 可雇佣性教育模式：理论述评与实践应用 [Employability Education Models: Review of Theories and Their Application in Practice]. *Bijiao jiaoyu yanjiu* 比较教育研究 [Comparative Education Review] (2): 62–81.

Su, Wenping, and Miao Zhang. 2015. "An Integrative Model for Measuring Graduates' Employability Skills: A Study in China." *Cogent Business & Management* 2(1): 1060729, doi: 10.1080/23311975.2015.1060729.

Timarová, Sárka, and Heidi Salaets. 2011. "Learning Styles, Motivation and Cognitive Flexibility in Interpreter Training." *Interpreting* 13(1): 31–52.

Translators Association of China. 2022. 中国翻译协会. *Zhongguo fanyi rencai fazhan baogao* 中国翻译人才发展报告 [*Report on Development of Translators and Interpreters*]. Beijing: Zhongguo fanyi xiehui dibaci huiyuan daibiao dahui 中国翻译协会第八次会员代表大会 [8th National Congress of the Translators Association of China].

Van der Heijde, Claudia M., and Beatrice. I. J. M. Van der Heijden. 2006. "A Competence-Based and Multidimensional Operationalization and Measurement of Employability." *Human Resource Management* 45(3): 449–76.

Van der Heijden, Beatrice. 2002. "Pre-Requisites to Guarantee Life-Long Employability." *Personnel Review* 31: 44–61.

Wang Binhua 王斌华. 2012. "Cong kouyi nengli dao yiyuan nengli: zhuanye kouyi jiaoxue linian de tuozhan" 从口译能力到译员能力:专业口译教学理念的拓展 [From Interpreting Competence to Interpreter Competence: Exploring the Conceptual Foundation of Professional Interpreting Training]. *Waiyu yu waiyu jiaoxue* 外语与外语教学 [Foreign Languages and Their Teaching] (6): 75–8.

Wang Jianhua 王建华. 2012. "Yukuai jiaoxue celue dui tigao xuesheng huiyi kouyi zhunquexing de shizheng yanjiu" 语块教学策略对提高学生会议口译准确性的实验研究 [Experimental studies on improving the accuracy of students' conference interpreting performance with a lexical chunk approach]. *Zhongguo fanyi* 中国翻译 [Chinese Translators Journal] (2): 47–51.

Wang Lifei 王立非, and Wang Jing 王婧. 2016. "Fanyi shuoshi zhuanye xuewei yanjiusheng jiuye nengli shizheng yanjiu" 翻译硕士专业学位研究生就业能力实证研究 [An Empirical Study on the Employability of MTI Students]. *Shanghai fanyi* 上海翻译 [Shanghai Journal of Translators] (2): 6–12, 94.

Wu, Yun, and Zhiwei Jiang. 2021. "Educating a Multilingual Workforce in Chinese Universities: Employability of Master of Translation and Interpreting Graduates." *Círculo de Lingüística Aplicada a la Comunicación* 86: 1–15.

Wu, Zhiwei. 2016. "Towards Understanding Interpreter Trainees' (De)motivation: An Exploratory Study." *Translation & Interpreting* 8(2): 13–25.

Yorke, Mantz. 2006. *Employability in Higher Education: What It Is – What It Is Not. (Learning and Employability Series 1)*. New York: Higher Education Academy.

Zhang Lihua 张丽华. 2020. "Yingzi gendu lianxi zai 'guangwai moshi' tongsheng chuanyi kecheng jiaoxue zhong de yingyong" 影子跟读练习在"广外模式"同声传译课程教学中的应用 [Shadowing Exercise in Simultaneous Interpreter Training under the GUANGWAI Approach]. *Dangdai waiyu yanjiu* 当代外语研究 [Contemporary Foreign Languages Studies] (03): 105–19.

Zhong Weihe 仲伟合, and Zhan Cheng 詹成. 2016. "Kouyi zhuanye jiaoxue tixi de goujian – guangwai kouyi zhuanye jiaoxue tixi lilun yu shijian (zhiyi)" 口译专业教学体系的构建 – 广外口译专业教学体系理论与实践(之一) [Constructing a Professional Interpreter Training System – Theory and Practice of the Professional Interpreter Training System at GDUFS (I)]. *Zhongguo fanyi* 中国翻译 [Chinese Translators Journal] 37(6): 39–42.

5 How are they invisibly present? Conference interpreters' role perception

Wei Zhang and Yu Gao

1 Introduction

Since its first presence in the literature of interpreting studies in the 1970s (Anderson 1976; Brislin 1980), the interpreter's role has become "one of the most prominent topics in interpreting studies" (Pöchhacker 2004, 147), yielding diverse and even conflicting ideas or suggestions regarding such issues as the interpreter's identity, power, loyalty, neutrality, invisibility, strategies, etc. What's more notable is that interpreting professionalism has been closely associated with the interpreter's role relating to codes of ethics and practices (Bowen 1995; Wadensjö 1998; Cokely 2000).

1.1 General review

First, the interpreter's role has been prescribed or stated as codes of ethics or professional norms in different directions: some argue the interpreter should work as a "non-person" to maintain neutrality or impartiality, producing as accurate, complete, and faithful rendition as that of channel, conduit, or switching device (Roy 2002; Hale 2007, 126), while others maintain that the interpreter should be allowed or even encouraged to possess some degree of intervention and/or advocacy to facilitate effective communication, working as a communication facilitator, culture agent/broker, or even "conciliator" (Pöchhacker 2015, 356). It is also suggested that the interpreters employed by international organizations are expected to observe complete neutrality and impartiality, displaying equal fidelity and transparency to all participants, while the interpreters recruited by each party (e.g., in diplomatic, business, military settings) may be considered "attached" or affiliated to their clients, whose interests or demands will make the interpreters unable to offer equal services to all parties (Setton and Liangliang 2011; Setton and Dawrant 2016).

It is clear that these norm-oriented prescriptions about the interpreter's role fail to reach uniform conclusion due to various factors: professional and ethical conditions of interpreting settings, the interpreter's practical preference, different parties' expectations, etc. Therefore, empirical data derived from the interpreters and other agents in various situations are needed to present objective features of the interpreter's role.

DOI: 10.4324/9781003357629-7

Second, these empirical data, whether collected from surveys of the interpreters' opinions or by means of observation and description of the interpreters' real interpreting practice, have both led to a similar conclusion: no consistency has been found in the interpreters' role perception or performance, sometimes the interpreters tend to assume more visible role as agents of various kinds (Shlesinger 1991; Wadensjö 2002; Jansen 1995; Roy 2000; Pöchhacker and Kadric 1999; Bolden 2000; Mesa 2000; Zwischenberger 2011; Angelelli 2004; Diriker 2004), while on other occasions they have been found to prefer the "ghost role" over the "intruder role" (Kopczyński 1994) and dislike a cultural mediator role (Setton and Liangliang 2011).

On the one hand, it should be made clear that those different and even conflicting data can be largely attributed to different interpreting settings. It is generally agreed that the interpreters in the community services (hospitals, courts, police stations, etc.) are more likely to be actively/visibly involved in interactions than those in conferences (although some exceptions can be found in Diriker (2004) and Zwischenberger (2011)). Another point deserving attention is that surveys about the interpreter's role are more often made in community settings than in conference environment. So the particularity of the conference interpreters' role perception still remains unclear, and more empirical data are highly needed to look deeper into the interpreter's role recognition in conference settings. On the other hand, it should be argued that the interpreter's role or his power in fulfilling mediating function is not only conditioned by "constraints at the interactional, socio-professional and institutional levels" (Pöchhacker 2004, 153) but ultimately greatly influenced by diverging social and cultural backgrounds (Kent 2007). Therefore, more descriptions of conference interpreters' role performance in more cultural circumstances (especially those beyond the United States and Europe) are needed to reveal the culture-specificity of conference interpreters' role (Angelelli 2004).

1.2   *More reflections*

The aforementioned studies have enabled us to gain a general understanding of the conference interpreter's role, but some key elements have received little or no attention so far.

First, the interpreters normally work in different modes (simultaneous, consecutive, whisper, etc.) in the course of conferences, sometimes due to the conference organizer's specific arrangement, while some other times due to particular demands from the participants (Diriker 2015, 78–82). It is generally agreed that different working modes require the interpreter to shift to corresponding working norms, preparation, strategies allocation, crisis management, among others (Gile 2009). The literature so far on the conference interpreter's role perception or performance largely fails to capture the specific impact possibly produced by the working mode on the interpreter's role understanding, degree of neutrality, communication style, strategy choice, etc. This chapter, therefore, will make the first attempt to describe the relation between the interpreting mode and the interpreter's role perception in conference settings so as to present a more detailed account of the conference interpreters' role.

Second, the interpreter's activity is conditioned by a wide range of factors, and some are beyond his control, namely, those "external factors" (Pöchhacker 2004, 126), for example, topic of the communication, the delivery mode (impromptu speeches or read speeches), speed of delivery, pronunciation, visual access, source-text complexity, etc. (Riccardi 2005), while some are his personal factors, for example, interpreting experience, topic (or theme) familiarity, interpreting mode (simultaneous, consecutive, and whisper interpreting), etc. Despite a lot of research concentrating on the interpreter's role across different settings, the interpreter's own personal factors have not received much attention regarding their possible impact on the interpreter's role perception, so this chapter tries to look at how the conference interpreter's own conditions (e.g., how long he has been working as interpreter, how familiar he is with the conference topic, and what the specific working mode in which he is serving as an interpreter is) will affect his assessment of his own role, thus attempting to reveal some individual features of the interpreter's role.

Third, the interpreter's perception of his own role or identity is believed to have wide-range impact on his behavior, interpreting strategy being one typical case (Pöchhacker 2004, 147–50). It should be noted, however, that no empirical data have been collected so far to verify the relation between interpreters' role perception and their choice of strategies. Four different strategies in two groups will be highlighted in this chapter for the following reasons: compression, explanation, and correction are included in production-based strategies (Pöchhacker 2004, 132), and parallel reformulation serves as an emergency strategy (Gile 2009).

Compression and explanation have been taken as the "most common" strategies adopted by the interpreter to either summarize or simplify some parts of the original speech (also known as "abstracting" (Riccardi 2005; Bartłomiejczyk 2006)) or explain or make explicit to the target audience some terms or expressions in the original speech, alternatively referred to as explicitations, or additions (Shlesinger 1995; Kalina 1999; Gumul 2006; Bartłomiejczyk 2006).

Correction by the interpreter of the original speech is reckoned as one of production-oriented interpreting strategies (Kalina 1999). Although the interpreter has not been found to be ready to correct all those errors when they do occur, his real corrections have been generally seen as a kind of conscious strategy for effective communication, and these corrections can also be taken as a key indicator of the interpreter's active involvement in interpreting-mediated activities (Pöchhacker 2004).

In some cases, the interpreter finds it difficult or even impossible to reconstruct the meaning of the original segment and may resort to "parallel reformulation" (Gile 2009), an effort to utter a message that is more or less plausible in the context so as not to pause or leave a sentence unfinished. Though not perceived as "most common" interpreting strategies (Riccardi 2005), "parallel reformulation" is found to be an emergency "coping tactic" to deal with difficulties in interpreting practice (Al-Khanji et al. 2000; Bartłomiejczyk 2006).

Fourth, another issue worth considering is the interpreter's communicative pattern, or way of addressing the participants involved in interpreting activities, a key indicator of the interpreter's role perception and practical involvement as well as an essential factor relating to interpreting professionalism (Pöchhacker 2004, 152). In community services, interpreters have been shown to follow no consistent communication type, swinging from the first person to the third person in reporting the speakers' utterance (Harris 1990; Shlesinger 1991; Keselman et al. 2010; Merlini 2009). Unlike the community settings featuring multiple rounds of communication between different participants (Hale 2007; Wadensjö 2009), communication in conferences usually follows a one-way model: speaker-to-interpreter-to-listener, with the interpreter seemingly assuming more freedom to govern his own communication pattern (Diriker 2015, 78–82). However, it should be noted that with some case reviews of conference interpreters' choice of first or third person generating inadequate and opposing data (Shlesinger 1991; Diriker 2004), the uniqueness of conference interpreters' role perception in terms of communication pattern is still to be uncovered by more evidence in more diverse cultural backgrounds.

In a word, different from the previous studies on the interpreter's role, this chapter attempts to provide more diverse (in different cultural backgrounds) or not yet collected data in the following two areas: first, the personal factors affecting the interpreter's role perception (e.g., working experience, topic familiarity, working mode); second, the real impact produced by the interpreter's role perception on his behavior (e.g., interpreting strategies, communication pattern).

2   Method

This part will illustrate some methodological features in this chapter, highlighting main research questions, subject description, questionnaire design, and data collection procedure.

2.1   Research questions

This chapter tries to look deeper into the conference interpreter's role perception and its relevant issues, focusing on the following questions:

First, how will the conference interpreter's personal factors influence his role perception?

Second, how will the conference interpreter's role perception affect his interpreting behavior, especially interpreting strategies and communication patterns?

2.2   Subjects

This chapter has managed to obtain permission by 150 Chinese conference interpreters (117 females, 33 males, ranging from 28 to 52 in age) to collect their opinions in their working environment. They have worked as interpreters during 28 international conferences held in seven different cities in China from 2017 to 2019, conference theme ranging from foreign affairs, global economic issues, trade protectionism, to news freedom and others. The interpreters have received interpreting training in their universities but now have different employment backgrounds; some are AIIC members, some are government officials (employed as in-house interpreters), while others are college teachers or freelancers.

2.3   Questionnaire

For the purpose of this chapter, the questionnaire contains two parts (please see the appendix for detailed information). The first part is about the conference interpreter's personal information: (1) interpreting experience as indicated by the number of years devoted to interpreting practice: less than 3 years representing the less experienced, 3–5 years medium experienced, and more than 5 years highly experienced; (2) familiarity with the conference topic; (3) interpreting mode in the conference (consecutive interpreting, simultaneous interpreting, or whispered interpreting). The second part consists of items relating to the interpreter's view on such issues as neutrality (item 1), choice of interpreting strategies (items 2–5), and communication pattern (item 6).

2.4   Data collection procedure

First, opinions are obtained from some questionnaire experts in relation to correlation and internal consistency among all the items in the questionnaire, and some corrections have been made accordingly. Moreover, a preliminary survey is carried out among 20 interpreters, whose feedback and suggestions contribute to further improvement of the questionnaire.

Second, the reliability of the questionnaire is calculated (Cronbach's alpha up to 0.923, standardized Cronbach's alpha reaching 0.931), indicating a high degree of reliability (figure bigger than 0.8 signifying acceptable in statistics), and factor analysis of the validity test shows that all the items are significantly relevant to interpreters' role perception (KMO standing at 0.925, Barlett showing 0.012, <0.05), revealing the questionnaire's conformity with the statistical standards (Qin 2009, 203–32).

Third, after the interpreters finished their interpreting tasks, the researcher and some assistants went to contact the interpreters to distribute and then collect the questionnaires. To be specific, 150 copies of questionnaires were handed out and 141 were returned, of which 6 were invalid (due to incomplete personal information and/or unanswered questions), leaving 135 copies of questionnaires for the subsequent analysis, with an actual return rate up to 90%.

3   Data results and analysis

The collected questionnaires are analyzed in EXCEL for basic percentage description and in SPSS 25.0 for significant difference between the conference interpreter's personal information and the other issues relating to the interpreter's role perception, namely, neutrality, interpreting strategies, and communication pattern.

3.1   *Effects of working experience on the interpreter's role perception*

As shown in Table 5.1, this chapter has identified 135 conference interpreters, 34 of whom can be called novice interpreters, as they have relatively less experience, 46 have accumulated fair amount of experience, while the other 55 have much more experience.

3.1.1   *Neutrality*

It is clear that less-experienced interpreters show the highest degree of self-perceived neutrality (with "high" and "very high" combined amounting to 56%), followed by medium- and highly experienced ones (see Table 5.1.1). And the less-experienced interpreters are significantly more neutral than their very experienced counterparts ($t = 0.836$, $P < 0.05$).

3.1.2   *Interpreting strategy*

The interpreter's working experience has an obvious impact on the interpreting strategies, as shown in the following sections.

Table 5.1 Interpreters' Experience

Interpreting Experience	Number of Interpreters (%)
Less-experienced (less than 3 years)	34 (25%)
Medium-experienced (3–5 years)	46 (34%)
Highly experienced (5 years or more)	55 (41%)

Table 5.1.1 Neutrality

Experience	Very Low (n/%)	Low (n/%)	Ordinary (n/%)	High (n/%)	Very High (n/%)
Less-experienced	5/15%	6/18%	4/11%	6/18%	13/38%
Medium-experienced	12/26%	8/17%	11/25%	4/8%	11/24%
Highly experienced	17/31%	10/18%	13/24%	3/5%	12/22%

a Compression. As displayed in Table 5.1.2, the highly experienced interpreters report compression as the most usual interpreting strategy in their interpreting practice (with "high" and "very high" combined reaching 51%), and they are significantly more likely to choose compression than those less-experienced interpreters ($t = 0.874$, $P < 0.05$).

b Explanation. Whatever their experience, the interpreters have regarded explanation as a highly usual strategy in interpreting, without any significant difference among them ($P > 0.05$), though those highly experienced interpreters show a slightly bigger percentage (see Table 5.1.3).

c Correction. As indicated in Table 5.1.4, the highly experienced interpreters attach more importance to correction than do their less-experienced colleagues, without any significant difference among the three groups ($P > 0.05$). What's notable is that the option of "ordinary" turns out to be the most frequent choice by all groups of interpreters (above 30% each).

d Parallel reformulation. Table 5.1.5 shows that the highly experienced interpreters adopt parallel reformulation most frequently, followed by the medium- and less-experienced ones, with the highly experienced interpreters significantly more frequent in their employment of the strategy than the less-experienced interpreters ($t = 0.912$, $P < 0.05$).

Table 5.1.2 Compression

Experience	Very Low (n/%)	Low (n/%)	Ordinary (n/%)	High (n/%)	Very High (n/%)
Less-experienced	10/29%	7/20%	7/21%	**4/12%**	**6/18%**
Medium-experienced	12/26%	9/19%	10/22%	6/13%	9/20%
Highly experienced	10/18%	8/15%	9/16%	**13/24%**	**15/27%**

Table 5.1.3 Explanation

Experience	Very Low (n/%)	Low (n/%)	Ordinary (n/%)	High (n/%)	Very High (n/%)
Less-experienced	8/24%	7/20%	5/15%	5/15%	9/26%
Medium-experienced	11/24%	8/17%	11/24%	6/13%	10/22%
Highly experienced	10/18%	6/11%	16/29%	8/15%	15/27%

Table 5.1.4 Explanation

Experience	Very Low (n/%)	Low (n/%)	Ordinary (n/%)	High (n/%)	Very High (n/%)
Less-experienced	6/17%	5/14%	**12/34%**	4/12%	7/21%
Medium-experienced	9/20%	7/14%	**15/33%**	6/13%	9/20%
Highly experienced	8/15%	9/16%	**17/31%**	10/18%	11/20%

Table 5.1.5 Parallel Reformulation

Experience	Very Low (n/%)	Low (n/%)	Ordinary (n/%)	High (n/%)	Very High (n/%)
Less-experienced	9/26%	8/24%	8/24%	**4/12%**	**5/15%**
Medium-experienced	13/28%	8/17%	11/24%	5/11%	9/20%
Highly experienced	11/20%	8/15%	10/18%	**12/22%**	**14/25%**

Table 5.1.6 Communication Pattern

Experience	Direct Speech (n/%)	Indirect Speech (n/%)	Neutral Speech (n/%)	Alternative Use of the Previous Three (n/%)
Less-experienced	**4/12%**	10/29%	**12/35%**	8/24%
Medium-experienced	8/17%	10/22%	**16/35%**	12/26%
Highly experienced	**16/29%**	11/20%	**18/33%**	10/18%

Table 5.2 Interpreter's Familiarity with the Conference Theme

Familiarity	Number of Interpreters (%)
Familiar	60 (44%)
Ordinarily familiar	46 (34%)
Unfamiliar	29 (22%)

3.1.3   Communication pattern

The number of the highly experienced interpreters who choose "direct speech" is significantly larger than that of the less-experienced interpreters ($t = 0.826$, $P < 0.05$). The less-experienced interpreters show more tendency to choose "indirect speech," followed by their more-experienced colleagues, but with no significant difference among the three groups ($P > 0.05$) (see Table 5.1.6). Moreover, neutral speech is shown here to be the most usual way of reporting the original speech by all groups of interpreters (above 30% each).

3.2   *Effects of conference theme familiarity on the interpreter's role perception*

As shown in Table 5.2, 66 (44%) of the surveyed interpreters confirm their familiarity with the conference theme, 29 (34%) acknowledge their unfamiliarity, while the remaining 29 interpreters (22%) report no exact knowledge of the conference theme.

3.2.1 Neutrality

As proven in Table 5.2.1, the interpreters who are familiar with the conference theme manifest the highest degree of neutrality ("high" and "very high" put together reaching 47%), followed by those who are ordinarily and not familiar with the theme, without any significant difference among the three groups ($P>0.05$).

3.2.2 Interpreting strategy

The interpreter's familiarity with the conference theme has an apparent effect on the interpreting strategies, as shown in the following parts.

a   Compression. As exhibited in Table 5.2.2, compression is most frequently adopted by the interpreters who are not familiar with the conference theme ("high" and "very high" united amounting to 44%), followed by those who are familiar and ordinarily familiar, without any significant difference among the three groups ($P>0.05$).
b   Explanation. Explanation is most frequently exercised by interpreters who are familiar with the conference theme ("high" and "very high" combined rising to 49%), followed by those who are ordinarily familiar and unfamiliar, with the "familiar" interpreters showing a significantly higher likelihood of explaining those ambiguous elements in the original speech than those "unfamiliar" interpreters ($t = 1.101$, $P<0.05$) (see Table 5.2.3).

Table 5.2.1 Neutrality

Familiarity	Very Low (n/%)	Low (n/%)	Ordinary (n/%)	High (n/%)	Very High (n/%)
Familiar	9/15%	6/10%	17/28%	10/17%	18/30%
Ordinarily familiar	7/15%	9/20%	11/24%	6/13%	13/28%
Unfamiliar	4/14%	6/20%	8/28%	5/17%	6/21%

Table 5.2.2 Compression

Familiarity	Very Low (n/%)	Low (n/%)	Ordinary (n/%)	High (n/%)	Very High (n/%)
Familiar	8/13%	10/17%	18/30%	11/18%	13/22%
Ordinarily familiar	11/24%	8/17%	12/26%	9/20%	6/13%
Unfamiliar	6/21%	6/21%	4/14%	5/17%	8/27%

Table 5.2.3 Explanation

Familiarity	Very Low (n/%)	Low (n/%)	Ordinary (n/%)	High (n/%)	Very High (n/%)
Familiar	10/17%	7/12%	14/22%	**13/22%**	**16/27%**
Ordinarily familiar	10/22%	4/8%	14/30%	7/15%	11/23%
Unfamiliar	8/27%	7/24%	6/21%	**4/14%**	**4/14%**

c　Correction. Correcting is most frequently chosen by the interpreters who are familiar with the conference theme ("high" and "very high" arriving at 43%), followed by those who are ordinarily familiar and unfamiliar, with the "familiar" interpreters carrying out correction significantly more often than those "unfamiliar" interpreters ($t = 0.936$, $P < 0.05$) (see Table 5.2–4).

d　Parallel reformulation. As unveiled in Table 5.2.5, the interpreters who are not familiar with the conference theme resort to parallel reformulation most frequently ("high" and "very high" combined hitting 45%), followed by those who are familiar and ordinarily familiar with the themes, without any significant difference among the three groups ($P > 0.05$).

3.2.3　*Communication pattern*

It can be seen in Table 5.2.6 that the interpreters who are familiar with the conference theme tend to use direct speech most frequently (30%), while those "unfamiliar" interpreters are apt to use indirect speech most frequently (27%), without any significant difference among the three groups ($P > 0.05$).

Table 5.2.4 Correction

Familiarity	Very Low (n/%)	Low (n/%)	Ordinary (n/%)	High (n/%)	Very High (n/%)
Familiar	8/13%	9/15%	17/29%	**11/18%**	**15/25%**
Ordinarily familiar	7/15%	5/11%	16/35%	8/17%	10/22%
Unfamiliar	9/31%	4/14%	10/34%	**4/14%**	2/7%

Table 5.2.5 Parallel reformulation

Familiarity	Very Low (n/%)	Low (n/%)	Ordinary (n/%)	High (n/%)	Very High (n/%)
Familiar	11/18%	7/12%	19/32%	9/15%	14/23%
Ordinarily familiar	9/20%	9/20%	13/28%	5/11%	10/21%
Unfamiliar	5/17%	4/14%	7/24%	6/21%	7/24%

Table 5.2.6 Communication Pattern

Familiarity	Direct Speech (n/%)	Indirect Speech (n/%)	Neutral Speech (n/%)	Alternative Use of the Previous Three (n/%)
Familiar	18/30%	15/25%	16/27%	11/28%
Ordinarily familiar	12/26%	12/26%	7/15%	15/33%
Unfamiliar	7/24%	8/27%	5/18%	9/31%

3.3 Effects of interpreting mode on the interpreter's role perception

As shown in Table 5.3, 50% of the surveyed interpreters answer that they work in simultaneous mode (SI), 40 interpreters (30%) say they work as consecutive interpreters (CI), while the remaining small group (20%) reply that they mainly provide whisper interpreting (WI) to their clients. It should be made clear that 9 interpreters in this survey say that they sometimes shift between different interpreting modes in different sessions of the conference, although one particular mode will take up most of their time.

3.3.1 Neutrality

Table 5.3.1 proves that the interpreters show the highest degree of neutrality in SI ("high" and "very high" combined reaching 45%), followed by WI and CI, without any significant difference among the three interpreting modes ($P>0.05$).

3.3.2 Interpreting strategy

The interpreter's working mode produces an evident impact on the interpreting strategies, as presented in the following parts.

a Compression. As revealed in Table 5.3.2, compression is most frequently adopted in WI ("high" and "very high" combined hitting 61%), followed by SI and CI, with the WI interpreters applying a significantly higher frequency of compression than those SI interpreters ($t = 0.871$, $P <0.05$).
b Explanation. Explanation is most frequently exercised in WI ("high" and "very high" put together arriving at 54%), followed by SI and CI, with WI witnessing a significantly higher frequency of explanation by the interpreters than CI ($t = 0.926$, $P <0.05$) (see Table 5.3.3).

Table 5.3 Interpreting Mode

Interpreting Mode	Number of Interpreters (%)
Consecutive interpreting (CI)	40 (30%)
Simultaneous interpreting (SI)	67 (50%)
Whispering interpreting (WI)	28 (20%)

Table 5.3.1 Neutrality

Interpreting Mode	Very Low (n/%)	Low (n/%)	Ordinary (n/%)	High (n/%)	Very High (n/%)
CI	7/18%	7/18%	11/28%	6/15%	9/21%
SI	8/12%	12/18%	17/25%	12/18%	18/27%
WI	3/11%	4/14%	9/32%	4/14%	8/29%

Table 5.3.2 Compression

Interpreting Mode	Very Low (n/%)	Low (n/%)	Ordinary (n/%)	High (n/%)	Very High (n/%)
CI	7/18%	10/25%	9/22%	**8/20%**	**6/15%**
SI	11/16%	14/21%	13/19%	14/21%	15/23%
WI	3/11%	6/21%	2/7%	7/25%	**10/36%**

Table 5.3.3 Explanation

Interpreting Mode	Very Low (n/%)	Low (n/%)	Ordinary (n/%)	High (n/%)	Very High (n/%)
CI	10/25%	7/18%	12/30%	**5/13%**	**6/15%**
SI	12/18%	15/22%	16/24%	13/19%	11/17%
WI	5/18%	2/7%	6/21%	**8/29%**	7/25%

Table 5.3.4 Correction

Interpreting Mode	Very Low (n/%)	Low (n/%)	Ordinary (n/%)	High (n/%)	Very High (n/%)
CI	10/25%	6/15%	10/25%	6/15%	8/20%
SI	16/24%	18/27%	13/19%	9/13%	11/16%
WI	7/25%	5/18%	5/18%	5/18%	6/21%

Table 5.3.5 Parallel Reformulation

Interpreting Mode	Very Low (n/%)	Low (n/%)	Ordinary (n/%)	High (n/%)	Very High (n/%)
CI	4/10%	9/21%	10/25%	**7/18%**	**10/25%**
SI	13/19%	11/17%	19/28%	10/15%	14/21%
WI	9/32%	3/11%	11/39%	**3/11%**	**2/7%**

c   Correction. Table 5.3.4 shows that correction is most frequently carried out in WI ("high" and "very high" combined amounting to 39%), followed by CI and SI, without any significant difference among the three groups ($P > 0.05$).

d   Parallel reformulation. As exhibited in Table 5.3.5, parallel reformulation is most frequently adopted in CI ("high" and "very high" combined reaching 43%), followed by SI and WI, with the CI interpreters presenting a significantly higher frequency of parallel reformulation than those WI interpreters ($t = 0.814$, $P < 0.05$).

Table 5.3.6 Communication pattern

Interpreting Mode	Direct Speech (n/%)	Indirect Speech (n/%)	Neutral Speech (n/%)	Alternative Use of the Three (n/%)
CI	12/30%	10/25%	8/20%	10/25%
SI	**24/36%**	**12/18%**	17/25%	14/21%
WI	**4/14%**	**11/39%**	10/36%	3/11%

3.3.3 Communication pattern

It is indicated in Table 5.3.6 that indirect speech is most frequently used in WI, significantly more frequently than in SI ($t = 1.015$, $P < 0.05$); direct speech is most frequently implemented in SI, significantly more frequently than in WI ($t = 0.797$, $P < 0.05$).

4 Discussion

As shown in part 3, "Data results and analysis," the conference interpreters in this survey have been greatly influenced by their personal factors in their role perception, which in turn has had noticeable effect on their performance in different aspects.

4.1 Interpreter's neutrality

First, this survey confirms the same idea by previous studies (Wadensjö 1998; Cokely 2000) that the interpreter's neutrality, an essential issue relating to the interpreter's role perception and interpreting professionalism, is not an absolute or static term or notion as rigidly prescribed in some institutional codifications or regulations; rather, it is conditioned by such various factors as interpreting settings; interpreting participants' expectations or even demands; the interpreters' own background, beliefs, and cultural tradition; among others. And it is the normal case that the interpreters often make themselves visible, trying to facilitate the interpreting-mediated communication through various means (Diriker 2004; Zwischenberger 2011)

In this sense, therefore, the interpreter's neutrality, as reflected in role perception and expectation, might be taken as a sort of attitude or disposition (Tipton 2008, 275) or a degree of excellence in the real interpreting practice (Chesterman 2001). What's more, the interpreter should not be described as a "neutral agent" anymore but recognized as an "agent of neutrality," thus reserving some possibilities for the interpreter to exercise his own appropriate judgment according with specific contexts (Pöchhacker 2015, 275).

Second, the interpreter's neutrality is closely related to one's own condition and the working environment:

a Novice interpreters tend to align themselves with a high degree of neutrality, while the more experience the interpreters accumulate, the more likely they are to think it difficult or even impossible to keep completely neutral in rendering the original speech in certain situations (see 3.1.1). The main reason might be that novice interpreters (including interpreting trainees) are still strongly influenced or constrained by translation ethic codes stressing absolute neutrality or fidelity, thus having no much courage or measures to "disobey" the original speaker and his words. Unlike those green hands in interpreting, the well-experienced interpreters usually possess a sharper awareness of particularities of interpreting tasks, consciously and resourcefully adjusting their activities to make possible the effective communication between different interpreting parties (Sunnari 1995; Bajo et al. 2000; Moser-Mercer et al. 2000; Yudes et al. 2013). With a stronger sense of communication, therefore, the highly experienced interpreters seem more likely to set themselves free from those stern requirements on neutrality in both conceptual and practical sense.
b Neutrality seems to be a function of the interpreter's knowledge of the conference theme. Specifically, the more familiar the interpreter is with the conference topic, the more likely he is to remain neutral, keeping his rendering as faithful as possible to the source text, which seems to be compatible with the commonly held idea that the interpreter's experience and preparation for the interpreting task will greatly determine his interpreting performance (neutrality being one key indicator) and ultimate quality (Gile 2009).
c The interpreters show the highest degree of neutrality in SI and the lowest degree of neutrality in CI. That is to say, neutrality appears to be influenced by the interpreter's working mode. It might be explained by the special stress suffered by the SI interpreter: one has to go parallel with the original speaker in translating the latter's words, with no time to make major adjustments, so the interpreter's rendering will more likely be much closer to the original than those in consecutive mode, thus making the SI interpreter seem to be more loyal to the original speaker (Gerver et al. 1989; Shlesinger, 1991; De Bot 2000).

Third, in conference setting (and others), the interpreter's role-related neutrality can still be addressed in different approaches. The interpreter's neutrality can be perceived and determined by different interpreting parties for their (often conflicting) powers and interests, the conference organizer, the client, the speaker, the audience, etc. Much more contrastive examinations of these different participants' expectation or evaluation of the interpreter's neutrality should be conducted to collect more diverse data so as to understand the true nature and workings of the interpreter's neutrality in real interpreting settings (Kopczyński 1994; Pöchhacker 2000, 2001; Kaczmarek 2016).

What's more, the notion of "baseline neutrality" has been proposed that the interpreting parties are advised to use non-emotive language, refraining from offering or asking the interpreter to offer personal opinions, letting the interpreter interpret everything that is said (Pöchhacker 2015, 275), but its relevance to conference interpreting is still to be proven.

4.2   Interpreting strategy

First, the conference interpreters have been actively and visibly involved in interpreting-mediated communication, as all the strategies used by the interpreters in this chapter have been recognized as important tactics or skills to facilitate their target production or to deal with emergencies (Jones 1998; Kalina 1999; Setton 1999; Gile 2009).

Second, the interpreting strategies are closely related to the conference interpreter's personal factors in the following aspects:

a The more experience the interpreters have, the more likely they are to consciously manage their interpreting skills, compression, and parallel reformulation in particular. Moreover, correction is exercised more by the experienced interpreters than those less-experienced ones. This indicates that rich experience in interpreting enables the interpreter to not only improve the quality of interpreting strategies and but also enhance the flexible application of the specific strategies (Zwischenberger 2011). In other words, the experienced interpreter can make more reasonable and reliable choices in their interpreting strategies according to specific communicative contexts.
b The more familiar the interpreters are with the conference theme, the more likely they are to make clear to their audience the original speech (explanation) and to put right those inappropriate or mistaken parts by the original speaker (correction), while they are more inclined to resort to parallel reformulation and cut short or simplify those difficult or controversial contents in the original utterance (compression) if the interpreters do not have much knowledge about the conference theme. The reason could be that adequate background and thematic knowledge provide the interpreters with more resources, even more confidence, so that they can offer explanations or additional information for the benefit of the audience, while insufficient comprehension of the conference topic might usually find the interpreters unable to resolve those unknown terms or expressions, thus leaving more frequent some makeshift strategies (such as parallel reformulation) or compression. It is also a possible though that compression may be serving as the interpreter's purposeful tactic in certain context, with no relation to one's familiarity of the interpreting topic (Yang 2005), and a more-detailed account of the triggers of compression is needed by way of such methods as interview and TAPs (think-aloud protocols) (Lörscher 1991; Kohn and Kalina 1996; Jääskeläinen 2000; Bartłomiejczyk 2006).

c The interpreting strategies seem to be clearly associated with the interpreter's working mode. In whisper interpreting (WI), explanation, correction, and compression stand out as more frequent skills, with the last one reaching as high as 61%. While in consecutive interpreting (CI), parallel reformulation turns out to be more usually applied. In simultaneous interpreting (SI), however, no particular strategy is significantly more favored over the others by the interpreters. Apparently, the WI interpreters attach more importance to the swift comprehension and transmission of key information rather than verbatim translation of the original speech (Hale 2007), and their spatial distance with the (usually one single) listener also makes it more convenient (and necessary) for them to make some needed illustration and simplification (Merlini 2020, 147–52). In CI, the interpreters sometimes are likely to clarify or supply additional information in line with original context or communicative needs (Elghezouani 2007). In SI, by contrast, the huge time pressure usually makes it impossible for the interpreter to make major adjustment of the original speech (especially in linguistic terms). Instead, the SI interpreter is often found to stick close to the original, even to the point of frequent occurrence of word-for-word rendering (Gile 2009), hence other interpreting strategies staying not so prominent (see its relation to the SI interpreter's view of neutrality in 3.3.1).

Third, it should be noted that interpreting strategies (not confined to the conference setting) are conditioned by many other factors, such as translation directionality (i.e., whether the interpreter works into his or her A or B language) (Riccardi 1996; Bartłomiejczyk 2006; Bartłomiejczyk 2015, 108–10), interpreting client's or user's expectation or demands (Kondo 1990; Pöchhacker 1994), or even the possible automatization of interpreting strategy (Kohn and Kalina 1996; Kalina 2000; Riccardi 2005). What's more, methodological reformation is also needed to have a more comprehensive view of interpreting strategies, for instance, more observational studies, possible integration of corpus method, as well as retrospective means (e.g., TAPs) can be a worthwhile way out to gain more insight into the nature and practical use of interpreting strategies (Ivanova 2000; Gumul 2006; Wang 2012).

4.3   Communication pattern

First, conference interpreters have demonstrated manifold discourse patterns in interpreting-mediated communication, out of accord with the provision stated in some prescriptive codes or some suggestions that direct speech or first-person reporting should be a conventional model in the interpreter's recounting of the original speaker's utterance (Wadensjö 1997). Therefore, it can be argued that conference interpreters have proven their role awareness and flexibility in identifying themselves with (or distancing from) the particular interpreting party according to specific communication purpose and context.

Second, the conference interpreter's communication pattern is evidently dependent on one's personal factors, as shown in the following sections:

a   The more experienced the interpreters are, the greater the tendency they show to use direct speech in their reporting; the novice interpreters, in contrast, have been found more likely to resort to indirect speech. The reason might be that the novice interpreters, due to experience shortage, resource inadequacy, among others, will more probably choose indirect speech to maintain a neutral position, endeavoring to keep their interpreting as "faithful" as possible to the source text. On the contrary, the seasoned interpreters (or roughly referred to as professionals) are more likely to take into account the communication context, the specific expectation of given parties in particular, keeping the original perspective of the source text and reducing the influence of intermediate transmission as much as possible to achieve "direct communication" between the speaker and the audience (Wadensjö 1998; Wadensjö 2008).

b   The more familiar the interpreters are with the conference theme, the more possibilities there will be for them to use direct speech, while shortage or even lack of knowledge of the conference subject will leave the interpreters more likely to turn to indirect speech in their reporting. The reason may well be that being familiar with the conference topic and relevant background knowledge can boost the interpreters' confidence, thus empowering them to keep in line with the speaker's speech mode to strike a real or authoritative impression in the audience, whereas insufficient understanding about the conference topic will probably make the interpreters keep themselves apart from the speaker to sound more "objective" in their rendering, thus freeing themselves from the possible responsibility in relation to the original information (Leinonen 2007).

c   The conference interpreters' communication pattern is clearly linked to their working mode. The interpreters tend to use direct speech more often in simultaneous interpreting (SI), while indirect speech will appear more frequently in whisper interpreting (WI). The reason could be that SI usually finds the interpreters difficult or unable to stay too far away from the speaker (especially in linguistic representation, Gile 2009), thus showing more identity with the speaker in his speech pattern, while the intimate spatial distance enjoyed by the WI interpreter with the listener will enable the former to have more possibilities or necessities to shift to third-person pattern in recounting the speaker's utterances (Pöllabauer 2007).

Third, the interpreter's communication pattern (not limited to conference setting) can still be discussed in more domains. For instance, the notion of "footing" can serve as a theoretical framework to conceptualize the interpreter's alignment between speaker and listener in terms of the interpreter's use of the first and third person (Keselman et al. 2010; Merlini 2009). In addition, the real effect produced by the interpreter's choice or even preference of communication pattern on the interpreting activities, especially on the listeners' psychological condition, is to be observed and analyzed across different settings (Diriker 2004).

5   Conclusion

As a long-standing issue, the interpreter's role has been drawing special attention in interpreting studies, either in the form of prescribed profession codes or as manifested in empirical survey data or interpreting performance in the real settings of various kinds. A fact, however, should be kept in mind that no unanimous view has been obtained in the previously mentioned three kinds of research. The interpreter's role, therefore, not only still remains "partially undefined" (Anderson 1976, 216) but also calls for more research in more circumstances.

Given that background, this chapter represents a new attempt to provide survey data in Chinese context to highlight the interpreter's role perception in conference setting. What's more notable is that this survey intends to produce the first gathering of data on how conference interpreters' personal factors affect their role perception and how role identity influences interpreting behavior, for example, interpreting strategies and communication pattern.

With its data, this chapter comes to the following results:

a   Conference interpreters work as an active and visible agent in interpreting activities, consciously adjusting their footing and interpreting behavior to ensure effective communication.
b   Conference interpreters' role perception is obviously affected by interpreter-related factors: the interpreters with more experience tend to take more initiative as an intrusive participant, seemingly giving less attention to neutrality than those less-experienced interpreters; neutrality has more priority when the interpreters are more familiar with the conference theme or when they work under greater working press (e.g., SI).
c   Conference interpreters' role perception has a clear effect on their interpreting strategies: the interpreters with more experience tend to use compression and parallel reformulation; the interpreters with better knowledge of the conference theme will be more likely to apply explanation and correction; and explanation, correction, and compression are more prominent in whisper interpreting, while parallel reformulation is more frequently employed in consecutive interpreting.
d   Conference interpreters' role perception exerts a distinct impact on their communication pattern: direct speech is more likely to be used when the interpreters have more experience or have better knowledge about the conference subject, while indirect speech has more presence in whisper interpreting.

It should be noted that more studies are needed for the following reasons: first, this survey has been conducted among Chinese conference interpreters, its scale is to be further extended to justify more objective description, and the representativeness of the data is yet to be verified against more data from different cultural backgrounds; second, the standard of judging the interpreter's experience is subjective, leaving vulnerable the experience-based account of role perception, though the distinction between the "professional" or expert interpreters and novice interpreters still remains controversial (Moser-Mercer 2015, 155); third, this survey centers on the empirical data about the conference interpreters' role perception, with no particular attention to systematic theoretical analysis, which can be further testified in the following areas: interaction models of prototypical interpreting constellations (Anderson 1976; Gentile et al. 1996; Alexieva 1997; Pöchhacker 2005), critical discourse analysis (CDA) (Pöchhacker 2015, 389), narrative theory (Boéri 2008; Baker 2009), and particularly sociological approaches, such as Goffman's three-level role construct (normative role, typical role, and role performance) (Wadensjö 1998), Gidden's structuration theory (Tipton 2008), Bourdieu's habitus and social construction/reproduction (Inghilleri 2014; Kumiko 2014), and Latour's actor-network theory (ANT) (Serrano 2020, 5–9).

Acknowledgments

This research is funded by the following projects: (1) the National Social Science Fund of China (project no. 18AYY013), (2) the Fundamental Research Funds for Central Universities (project no. 2022JS004), and (3) the Beijing Municipal Social Science Foundation (project no. 19YYB011).

References

Alexieva, Bistra. 1997. "A Typology of Interpreter-Mediated Events." *The Translator* 3(2) (April): 153–74.

Al-Khanji, Raja, Said El-Shiyab, and Riyadh Hussein. 2000. "On the Use of Compensatory Strategies in Simultaneous Interpretation." *META: Journal Des Traducteurs/ META: Translators' Journal* 45(3) (Spring): 548–57.

Anderson, R. Bruce W. and Richard W. Brislin. 1976. *Translation: Applications and Research.* New York: Gardner Press.

Angelelli, Claudia Viviana. 2004. *Revisiting the Interpreter's Role: A Study of Conference, Court, and Medical Interpreters in Canada, Mexico, and the United States.* Amsterdam: John Benjamins.

Bajo, María Teresa, Francisca Padilla, and Presentación Padilla. 2000. "Comprehension Processes in Simultaneous Interpreting." In *Translation in Context*, edited by Andrew Chesterman, Natividad Gallardo San Salvador and Yves Gambier, 127–42. Amsterdam: John Benjamins.

Baker, Mona. 2009. "Resisting State Terror: Theorizing Communities of Activist Translators and Interpreters." In *Globalization, Political Violence and Translation*, edited by Esperanza Bielsa and Christopher W. Hughes, 222–42. Hampshire: Palgrave Macmillan.

Bartłomiejczyk, Magdalena. 2006. "Strategies of Simultaneous Interpreting and Directionality." *Interpreting* 8(2) (February): 149–74.

Bartłomiejczyk, Magdalena. 2015. "Directionality." In *Routledge Encyclopedia of Interpreting Studies*, edited by Franz Pochhacker, 108–10. London: Routledge.

Boéri, Julie. 2008. "A Narrative Account of the Babels vs. Naumann Controversy: Competing Perspectives on Activism in Conference Interpreting." *The Translator* 14(1) (September): 21–50.

Bolden, Galina B. 2000. "Toward Understanding Practices of Medical Interpreting: Interpreters' Involvement in History Taking." *Discourse Studies* 2(4) (May): 387–419.

Bowen, Margareta, David Bowen, Francine Kaufmann, and Ingrid Kurz. 1995. "Interpreters and the Making of History." In *Translators through History*, edited by Jean Delisle and Judith Woodsworth, 245–73. Amsterdam: John Benjamins.

Brislin, Richard W. 1980. "Expanding the Role of the Interpreter to Include Multiple Facets of Intercultural Communication." *International Journal of Intercultural Relations* 4(2) (March): 137–48.

Chesterman, Andrew. 2001. "Proposal for a Hieronymic Oath." *The Translator* 7(2) (September): 139–54.

Cokely, Dennis. 2000. *Exploring Ethics: A Case for Revising the Code of Ethics*. Sheffield: Direct Learn.

De Bot, Kees. 2000. "Simultaneous Interpreting as Language Production." In *Language Processing and Simultaneous Interpreting: Interdisciplinary Perspectives*, edited by Birgitta Englund Dimitrova and Kenneth Hyltenstam, 65–88. Amsterdam: John Benjamins.

Diriker, Ebru. 2004. *De-Re-Contextualizing Conference Interpreting*. Vol. 53. Amsterdam: John Benjamins Publishing Company.

Diriker, Ebru. 2015. "Conference Interpreting." In *The Routledge Handbook of Interpreting*, edited by Holly Mikkelson and Renée Jourdenais, 183–97. London: Routledge.

Elghezouani, Abdelhak. 2007. "Professionalisation of Interpreters." In *The Critical Link 4: Professionalisation of Interpreting in the Community*, edited by Cecilia Wadensjö, Birgitta Englund Dimitrova and Anna-Lena Nilsson, 215–26. Amsterdam: John Benjamins Publishing.

Gentile, Adolfo, Uldis Ozolins, and Mary Vasilakakos. 1996. *Liaison Interpreting: A Handbook*. Melbourne: Melbourne University.

Gerver, David, Patricia Longley, John Long, and Sylvie Lambert. 1989. "Selection Tests for Trainee Conference Interpreters." *META: Journal Des Traducteurs/META: Translators' Journal* 34(4) (March): 724–35.

Gile, Daniel. 2009. *Basic Concepts and Models for Interpreter and Translator Training*. Amsterdam: John Benjamins.

Gumul, Ewa. 2006. "Explicitation in Simultaneous Interpreting: A Strategy or a By-Product of Language Mediation?" *Across Languages and Cultures* 7(2) (June): 171–90.

Hale, Sandra. 2007. *Community Interpreting*. Hampshire: Palgrave Macmillan.

Harris, Brian. 1990. "Norms in Interpretation." *Target* 2(1) (March): 115–19.

Inghilleri, Moira. 2014. "Bourdieu's Habitus and Dewey's Habits: Complementary Views of the Social?" In *Remapping Habitus in Translation Studies*, edited by Margherita Dore, 183–201. Amsterdam: Rodopi.

Ivanova, Adelina. 2000. "The Use of Retrospection in Research on Simultaneous Interpreting." In *Tapping and Mapping the Processes of Translation and Interpreting*, edited by Sonja Tirkkonen-Condit and Riitta Jääskeläinen, 27–52. Amsterdam: John Benjamins.

Jääskeläinen, Riitta. 2000. "Focus on Methodology in Think-Aloud Studies on Translating." In *Tapping and Mapping the Processes of Translation and Interpreting: Outlooks on Empirical Research*, edited by Sonja Tirkkonen-Condit and Riitta Jääskeläinen, 71–82. Amsterdam: John Benjamins.

Jansen, Peter. 1995. "The Role of the Interpreter in Dutch Courtroom Interaction: The Impact of the Situation of Translational Norms." In *Topics in Interpreting Research*, edited by Jorma Tommola, 11–36. Turku: University of Turku.

Jones, Roderick. 1998. *Conference Interpreting Explained*. London: Routledge.

Kaczmarek, Lukasz. 2016. "Towards a Broader Approach to the Community Interpreter'S Role: On Correspondence between Role Perceptions and Interactional Goals." *Interpreting* 18(1) (September): 57–88.

Kalina, Sylvia. 1999. "Strategische Prozesse Beim Dolmetschen: Theoretische Grundlagen, Empirische Fallstudien, Didaktische Konsequenzen." *Interpreting* 4(2) (May): 225–30.

Kalina, Sylvia, and Fachhochschule Köln. 2000. " Interpreting Competences as a Basis and a Goal for Teaching." *The Interpreters' Newsletter* 10 (July): 3–32.

Kent, Stephanie Jo. 2007. "Why Bother?: Institutionalization, Interpreter Decisions, and Power Relations." In *The Critical Link 4: Professionalisation of Interpreting in the Community*, edited by Cecilia Wadensjö, Anna-Lena Nilsson and Birgitta Englund Dimitrova, 193–204. Amsterdam: John Benjamins.

Keselman, Olga, Ann-Christin Cederborg, and Per Linell. 2010. ""That Is Not Necessary for You to Know!": Negotiation of Participation Status of Unaccompanied Children in Interpreter-Mediated Asylum Hearings." *Interpreting* 12(1) (July): 83–104.

Kohn, Kurt, and Sylvia Kalina. 1996. "The Strategic Dimension of Interpreting." *META: Journal Des Traducteurs/META: Translators' Journal* 41(1) (September): 118–38.

Kondo, Mi. 1990. "What Conference Interpreters Should Not Be Expected to Do." *The Interpreters' Newsletter* 3 (June): 59–65.

Kopczyński, Andrzej. 1994. "Quality in Conference Interpreting: Some Pragmatic Problems." In *Translation Studies: An Interdiscipline: Selected Papers from the Translation Studies Congress, Vienna*, edited by Mary Snell-Hornby, Franz Pochhacker and Klaus Kaindl, 189–98. Amsterdam: John Benjamins.

Kumiko, Torikai. 2014. "Oral History as a Research Method to Study Interpreters' Habitus." In *Remapping Habitus in Translation Studies*, edited by Gisella Maria Vorderobermeier, 133–47. Amsterdam: Rodopi.

Leinonen, Satu. 2007. "Professional Stocks of Interactional Knowledge in the Interpreter's Profession." In *The Critical Link 4: Professionalisation of Interpreting in the Community*, edited by Cecilia Wadensjö, Birgitta Englund Dimitrova and Anna-Lena Nilsson, 227–40. Amsterdam: John Benjamins.

Lörscher, Wolfgang. 1991. *Translation Performance, Translation Process, and Translation Strategies: A Psycholinguistic Investigation*. Tübingen: Gunter Narr.

Merlini, Raffaela. 2009. "Seeking Asylum and Seeking Identity in a Mediated Encounter: The Projection of Selves Through Discursive Practices." *Interpreting* 11(1) (May): 57–93.

Merlini, Raffaela. 2020. "Dialogue Interpreting." In *Routledge Encyclopedia of Translation Studies*, edited by Mona Baker and Gabriela Saldanha, 147–52. London: Routledge.

Mesa, Anne-Marie. 2000. "The Cultural Interpreter: An Appreciated Professional." In *The Critical Link 2: Interpreters in the Community*, edited by Roda Roberts, Silvana E. Carr, Diana Abraham and Aideen Dufour, 67–79. Amsterdam: John Benjamins.

Moser-Mercer, Barbara. 2015. "Expert-Novice Paradigm." In *Routledge Encyclopedia of Translation Studies*, edited by Mona Baker and Gabriela Saldanha, 155. London: Routledge.

Moser-Mercer, Barbara, Ulrich H Frauenfelder, Beatriz Casado, and Alexander Künzli. 2000. "Searching to Define Expertise in Interpreting." In *Language Processing and Simultaneous Interpreting: Interdisciplinary Perspective*, edited by Birgitta Englund Dimitrova and Kenneth Hyltenstam, 107–31. Amsterdam: John Benjamins.

Pöchhacker, Franz. 1994. "Simultaneous Interpretation: 'Cultural Transfer'or 'Voice-over Text'." In *Translation Studies: An Interdiscipline*, edited by Mary Snell-Hornby, Franz Pochhacker and Klaus Kaindl, 169–78. Amsterdam: John Benjamins.

Pöchhacker, Franz. 2000. "The Community Interpreter's Task: Self-Perception and Provider's Views." In *The Critical Link 2: Interpreters in the Community*, edited by Roda Roberts, Silvana E. Carr, Diana Abraham and Aideen Dufour, 49–65. Amsterdam: John Beniamins.

Pöchhacker, Franz. 2001. "Quality Assessment in Conference and Community Interpreting." *META: Journal Des Traducteurs/META: Translators' Journal* 46(2) (March): 410–25.

Pöchhacker, Franz. 2004. *Introducing Interpreting Studies*. London: Routledge.

Pöchhacker, Franz. 2005. "From Operation to Action: Process-Orientation in Interpreting Studies." *META: Journal Des Traducteurs/META: Translators' Journal* 50(2) (June): 682–95.

Pöchhacker, Franz. 2015. *Routledge Encyclopedia of Interpreting Studies*. London: Routledge.

Pöchhacker, Franz, and Mira Kadric. 1999. "The Hospital Cleaner as Healthcare Interpreter: A Case Study." *The Translator* 5(2) (May): 161–78.

Pöllabauer, Sonja. 2007. "Interpreting in Asylum Hearings: Issues of Saving Face." In *The Critical Link 4: Professionalisation of Interpreting in the Community*, edited by Cecilia Wadensjö, Birgitta Englund Dimitrova and Anna-Lena Nilsson, 39–52. Amsterdam: John Benjamins.

Qin Xiaoqing. 秦晓晴. 2009. *Waiyu jiaoxue wenjuan diaocha fa* 外语教学问卷调查法 [The Method of Questionnaire in Foreign Language Teaching]. Beijing: Waiyu jiaoxue yu yanjiu chuban she 外语教学与研究出版社 [Foreign Language Teaching and Researching Press].

Riccardi, Alessandra. 1996. "Language-Specific Strategies in Simultaneous Interpreting." In *Teaching Translation and Interpreting*, edited by Cay Dollerup and Vibeke Appel, 213–22. Amsterdam: John Benjamins.

Riccardi, Alessandra. 2005. "On the Evolution of Interpreting Strategies in Simultaneous Interpreting." *META: journal des traducteurs/META: Translators' Journal* 50(2) (April): 753–67.

Roy, Cynthia B. 2000. *Interpreting as a Discourse Process*. New York: Oxford University Press.

Roy, Cynthia B. 2002. "The Problem with Definitions, Descriptions, and the Role Metaphors of Interpreters." In *The Interpreting Studies Reader*, edited by Franz Pochhacker and Miriam Schlesinger, 344–53. London: Routledge.

Serrano, Manuel. 2020. "Actor-Network Theory (ANT)." In *Routledge Encyclopedia of Translation Studies*, edited by Mona Baker and Gabriela Saldanha, 5–10. London: Routledge.

Setton, Robin. 1999. *Simultaneous Interpretation: A Cognitive-Pragmatic Analysis*. Amsterdam: John Benjamins.

Setton, Robin, and Alice Guo Liangliang. 2011. "Attitudes to Role, Status and Professional Identity in Interpreters and Translators with Chinese in Shanghai and Taipei." In *Identity and Status in the Translational Professions*, edited by Rakefet Sela-sheffy and Miriam Shlesinger, 89–117. Amsterdam: John Benjamins.

Setton, Robin, and Andrew Dawrant. 2016. *Conference Interpreting: A Complete Course and Trainer's Guide*. Amsterdam: John Benjamins.

Shlesinger, Miriam. 1991. "Interpreter Latitude Vs. Due Process. Simultaneous and Consecutive Interpretation in Multilingual Trials." In *Empirical Research in Translation and Intercultural Studies*, edited by Sonja Tirkkonen-Condit, 147–55. Tübingen: Gunter Narr.

Shlesinger, Miriam. 1995. "Shifts in Cohesion in Simultaneous Interpreting." *The Translator* 1(2) (October): 193–214.

Sunnari, Marianna. 1995. "Processing Strategies in Simultaneous Interpreting: Experts Vs. Novices." In *Proceedings of the 36th Annual Conference of the American Translators Association*, edited by Peter W. Krawutschke, 157–64. Medford: Information Today.

Tipton, Rebecca. 2008. "Reflexivity and the Social Construction of Identity in Interpreter-Mediated Asylum Interviews." *The Translator* 14(1) (March): 1–19.

Wadensjö, Cecilia. 1997. "Recycled Information as a Questioning Strategy: Pitfalls in Interpreted-Mediated Talk." In *The Critical Link 2: Interpreters in the Community*, edited by Roda Roberts, Silvana E. Carr, Diana Abraham and Aideen Dufour, 35–54. Amsterdam: John Benjamins.

Wadensjö, Cecilia. 1998. *Interpreting as Interaction*. London: Longman.

Wadensjö, Cecilia. 2002. "The Double Role of a Dialogue Interpreter." In *The Interpreting Studies Reader*, edited by Franz Pochhacker and Miriam Schlesinger, 355–70. London: Routledge.

Wadensjö, Cecilia. 2008. "In And off the Show: Co-Constructing 'Invisibility' In an Interpreter-Mediated Talk Show Interview." *META: Journal Des Traducteurs/ META: Translators' Journal* 53(1) (February): 184–203.

Wadensjö, Cecilia. 2009. "Community Interpreting." In *Routledge Encyclopedia of Translation Studies*, edited by Mona Baker and Gabriela Saldanha, 43–48. London: Routledge.

Wang, Binhua. 2012. "Interpreting Strategies in Real-Life Interpreting: Corpus-Based Description of Seven Professional Interpreters' Performance." *Translation Journal* 16(2). https://translationjournal.net/journal/60interpreting.htm.

Yang Chengshu 楊承淑. 2005. "Tongbu kouyi de jianhua leixing yu guilü" 同步口譯的簡化類型與規律 [The Types and Principles of Simplification in Simultaneous Interpreting]. *Guoli bianyi guan guankan* 國立編譯館館刊 [Journal of the National Institute for Compilation and Translation] 16(1): 20–39.

Yudes, Carolina, Pedro Macizo, Luis Morales, and M Teresa Bajo. 2013. "Comprehension and Error Monitoring in Simultaneous Interpreters." *Applied Psycholinguistics* 34(5) (March): 1039–57.

Zwischenberger, Cornelia. 2011. "Conference Interpreters and Their Self-Representation: A Worldwide Web-Based Survey." In *Identity and Status in the Translational Professions*, edited by Rakefet Sela-sheffy and Miriam Shlesinger, 119–33. Amsterdam: John Benjamins.

Appendices

Appendix 1

Part 1: personal information

(1) Your sex is _____.

    1. Male   2. Female

(2) Your age is _____.

    1. Under 25   2. 25–30   3. 31–40   4. 41 and older

(3) Your interpreting experience is _____.

    1. Less-experienced (less than 3 years of interpreting experience)
    2. Medium-experienced (3–5 years of interpreting experience)
    3. Highly experienced (more than 5 years of interpreting experience)

(4) As for the conference theme or topic, you are _____.

    1. Familiar   2. Generally familiar   3. Unfamiliar

(5) You major interpreting mode in this conference is _____.

    1. Consecutive interpreting   2. Simultaneous interpreting   3. whisper Interpreting

Part 2: questions

(1) In your interpreting practice, the interpreter's neutrality should be _____.

    1. Very low   2. Low   3. Ordinary   4. High   5. Very high

(2) In your interpreting practice, to summarize or simplify some parts of the original speech (known as compression or "abstracting") is _____.

    1. Very unusual   2. Unusual   3. Ordinary   4. Usual   5. Very usual

(3) In your interpreting practice, to explain or make explicit to the target audience some terms or expressions in the original speech (also known as explicitation or addition) is _____.

    1. Very unusual   2. Unusual   3. Ordinary   4. Usual   5. Very usual

(4) In your interpreting practice, to correct some mistakes in the original speech is _____.

    1. Very unusual   2. Unusual   3. Ordinary   4. Usual   5. Very usual

(5) In your interpreting practice, to exercise "parallel reformulation" (to utter a message that is more or less plausible in the context so as not to pause or leave a sentence unfinished) is _____.

    1. Very unusual   2. Unusual   3. Ordinary   4. Usual   5. Very usual

6 Problem-based learning (PBL) in conference interpreting pedagogy

A holistic approach

Yi Liu and Dechao Li

1 Introduction

In his seminal paper "The name and nature of translation studies" (Holmes 1972/1988), Holmes outlined the scope of translation studies and used the name "translation studies" (TS) for the first time to describe his envisaged discipline, which consists of two broad branches of pure translation studies and applied translation studies. His programmatic vision of the specificities of this new discipline has gradually crystalized since the early 1980s (Hermans 1991; Baker 1995; O'Hagan 2013). Compared to theoretical and descriptive research which belong to the pure studies branch within Holmes's blueprint, translator training, a subbranch of applied research, in which sharing of personal experience and teaching techniques still predominates, has developed more slowly. Although interpreting is not mentioned in Holmes's original research framework, it is generally believed that the term *translation studies* he used is of nature, which also embraces interpreting studies (Colina and Angelelli 2015). Thus, it is reasonable to assume that translator training in the map also includes interpreting pedagogy.

Meanwhile, there has been considerable progress in approaches to educational and technological teaching and learning activities over the last decades. The focus of education has gradually shifted away from traditional student-teacher instructivism toward constructivism, a philosophy of how we learn (Sánchez-Gijón et al. 2011; Colina and Angelelli 2015). A constructivist approach to learning assumes that knowledge, which does not pre-exist and cannot be assimilated by learners, could only be constructed by learners themselves (Sánchez-Gijón et al. 2011).

However, in the field of translation studies, the development of translation teaching research seems to lag behind as it is still widely believed that translation teaching is "an application of principles and strategies work out in theory first" (Hmelo-Silver 2004, 190). One possible way out of this stagnation, at least to us, is to take stock of the recent developments in the field of education and apply some well-established pedagogical approach to the field of interpreting studies. Problem-based learning (PBL), a learner-centered method which has already been widely adopted in the education of various fields and proven

DOI: 10.4324/9781003357629-8

effective since the 1970s, is one of such possible candidates. It is believed that the application of PBL to translation and interpreting teaching helps to reach the goal of developing not only professional knowledge and skills in the field but also the general ability to deal with various translation and interpreting challenges (Tan 2008).

2   Problem-based learning: a brief review

Problem-based learning (PBL) is an instructional approach as well as an educational philosophy which was first seen in the health sciences curricula in the 1960s at McMaster University in Canada (Boud and Feletti 1997). According to Savery (2015, 5), "it is an instructional learner-centred approach that empowers learners to conduct research, integrate theory and practice, and apply knowledge and skills to develop a viable solution to a defined problem." In medical education, the traditional approaches were based on the bucket theory (Wood 1994) of teaching multiple discipline-specific contents separately in lectures, which did little help for learners to solve realistic problems in a clinical application (Savery 2015). However, in a PBL environment, students actively analyze, discuss, and solve problems through self-directed and collaborative learning under the guidance of a facilitator.

Several researchers have described the features that are necessary for a successful PBL approach (Barrows 1996; Boud and Feletti 1997; Duch et al. 2001; Torp and Sage 2002; Hmelo-Silver 2004). Summarized by Savery (2015), some of the key features of PBL include:

- Students must have responsibility for their own learning.
- The problem simulations used in problem-based learning must be ill-structured and allow for free inquiry.
- Learning should be integrated from a wide range of disciplines or subjects.
- Collaboration is essential.
- What students learn during their self-directed learning must be applied back to the problem with reanalysis and resolution.
- Assessment is carried out after each problem is solved.

These criteria for PBL require facilitators to shift "from presenter of information to facilitator of a problem-solving process" (Allen et al. 2011, 23) and to play the role of scaffolding in students' active learning and knowledge construction (Amador et al. 2006). Although PBL stresses the active role of students during the learning process, facilitators are still responsible for providing guidance by observing students' discussion, raising questions when appropriate, bringing up new topics for closer attention, and boosting active participation (Mayo et al. 1995).

It is also important to note that PBL supports the development of a variety of "soft" skills. Specifically, students are found to consistently retain knowledge, especially more principled knowledge, for longer periods of time than students in a traditional curriculum (Shahabudin 1987; Norman and Schmidt 1992). Moreover, PBL students can apply basic science knowledge and transfer problem-solving skills in real-world professional or personal situations more effectively. They become more self-regulated lifelong learners (Vernon and Blake 1993).

In general, PBL methods are thought to promote active learning of students, boost students' performance on complex tasks, and increase knowledge consolidation. This effective teaching pedagogy was first widely used in health-care-related education, such as medical, dental, and nursing fields, ever since the 1960s and was then adopted by different disciplines of humanities and social sciences (Duch et al. 2001; Allen et al. 2011) and expanded into elementary schools, middle schools, high schools, universities, and professional schools (Torp and Sage 2002).

3   Previous studies on PBL in translation and interpreting pedagogy

Whereas PBL has widely been used in a number of disciplines such as medical science, business, mathematics, or even literary studies over the last several decades, the application of PBL to translation and interpreting didactics to date has only been made "sporadically and in a piecemeal fashion" (Hatim 2014, 191). The interpreting teaching, which has evolved from topic/content-based training to skills-based training (Wang 2018), remains to be trainer-centered rather than trainee-centered. The teaching philosophy for translation and interpreting pedagogy have only recently begun to change from behaviorism to constructivism (Tao 2019).

In China's mainland, the application of PBL in translation teaching is still in the exploratory stage, mainly involving the application of PBL in different translation courses (Li 2021), such as Chinese medicine translation (Zhang 2012), cultural translation (Yang 2012), and business English translation (Zhao 2013; Yang 2015). There are also studies that introduce the epistemological basis of PBL (Yang 2012; Zhao 2013) and explore the PBL translation teaching model (Yang 2012; Zhao 2013; Yang 2015; Liu 2017), all of which concluded that PBL is an effective tool for teaching translation. However, most of these conclusions about the effectiveness of PBL are based on intuitive experiences and not supported by empirical analysis (Liu and Li 2019).

Among few exceptions of empirical studies on PBL in translation classrooms, Liu and Li (2019) applied empirical methods of think-aloud protocols, problem templates, and reflection reports to analyze the effectiveness of using PBL mode in translation classrooms. Their study indicates that collaborative learning is conducive to the development of students' independent judgment and creativity, which leads to a high quality of their translation. In 2021, the journal of Shandong Foreign Language Teaching published a special column of "PBL in translation teaching," consisting of three papers discussing the challenges and difficulties of applying PBL in translation classrooms from the perspectives of macro-curriculum development and micro-case analysis. Specifically, Li (2021) conducted a large-scale questionnaire survey regarding the challenges of applying PBL to translation teaching and learning in universities in China's mainland and in Hong Kong. The survey showed that the learning environment for PBL mode in translation classrooms is not satisfactory, as translation teachers reported the shortage of extracurriculum resources and opportunities to conduct cooperative learning. In addition, authentic translation questions are rarely used in translation classrooms. Liu (2021) analyzed the application of PBL in a computer-assisted translation (CAT) environment, showing that CAT is suitable for PBL teaching, in which instructors should also play the role of scaffold to guide students in recognizing and solving problems and using external resources. Yang (2021) proposed that self-directed learning (SDL) in PBL learning can be a pedagogy to innovate the teaching practice. Through applying SDL in the PBL approach in a translation course, she suggested that the learner-based approach has facilitated the learning process and helped to develop learners' lifelong learning skills.

Based on case studies, Inoue (2005) discussed the problems of teacher-centered translation teaching and then proposed the feasibility of PBL for translator teaching to promote novices' autonomy and self-reflective actions. In addition, Kerkkä (2009) performed an experiment to test the application of PBL in actual translation courses, summarizing seven effective steps of PBL teaching for translation students to follow. Sánchez-Gijón et al. (2011) argued that teaching activities in translation classrooms should reflect the changes in European higher education and allow students to work in groups to find solutions to real-world problems in an active manner. Through PBL teaching approaches, translation trainees can develop the skills to solve the problems posed by terminology in translation practice. Hatim (2014) pointed out that the application of the learner-centered PBL model in translation teaching was only at the beginning stage and far left behind compared to the adjacent discipline of applied linguistics. Ertmer and Glazewski (2015) summarized the three main challenges of applying PBL in the context of classroom practice, namely, creating an environment of collaboration, adapting to changing roles, and facilitating students' learning process. Mellinger (2018) discussed the potential of PBL application to computer-assisted translation (CAT), suggesting that the PBL approach is conducive to fostering students' professional behavior and identity and to developing their intentionality in self-directed learning.

In a nutshell, research on PBL teaching in translation classrooms at home and abroad is still at an early stage, at which theoretical concepts were proposed and preliminary attempts to incorporate these concepts in translator training were used. There is still a lack of systematic discussion on the factors affecting the application of PBL in translation teaching. In addition, further empirical studies are needed to testify to the effectiveness of PBL in translation classrooms.

Comparatively speaking, the PBL mode is even less explored in interpreting training. Only several general introductions to how PBL mode can be applied in interpreting classrooms (Zhang 2009; Wang and Zhang 2019) can be found as of today. However, the findings of all these studies are based on their personal experience rather than on empirical studies conducted in Chinese context. In terms of interpreting education in China, practice-oriented conference interpreting training programs in China's mainland are offered at both bachelor and the postgraduate level, also known as bachelor in translation and interpreting (BTI) and master in translation and interpreting (MTI). Similar to the pedagogy development trajectory in the West, interpreting training programs in China's mainland have also evolved from an apprenticeship approach focusing on "know-how and professional knowledge" taught by modeling real-life tasks to a more "scientific, theory-driven approach" (Pöchhacker 2016, 191–192). Although interpreting training in China has developed from a topic-based paradigm to a skill-based paradigm during the last three decades (Wang and Mu 2011; Wang 2018), interpreting training pedagogy is still largely dominated by teacher-centered approach. The current research proposes a student-centered method to interpreting education integrating PBL into interpreter training curriculum.

4   Integration of PBL into interpreting teaching

While the earlier state of conference interpreting pedagogy features a strong focus on specific simultaneous interpreting (SI) techniques of segmentation and linear rendering in sight translation exercise (Dawrant 1996; Dawrant et al. 2021), the interpreting training program has gradually evolved to aim at enhancing "students' language competence, encyclopedia knowledge and interpreting skills" and to enable them to function on the professional interpreting practice (Chen et al. 2019, 91). In this case, the interpreting pedagogy seems well positioned to adopt PBL as the interpreting training which aims at encouraging interpreting trainees to solve authentic problems during interpreting practice. As such, the students can reflect on their interpreting process, which again can be situated in different interpreting contexts.

4.1   *PBL process in interpreting teaching*

To effectively apply PBL in interpreting teaching, the course design and teaching steps should be well planned beforehand. It should be noted that PBL is not as an instructional method but a well-knitted educational philosophy. To apply PBL to interpreter training is to actively involve students to complete a learning loop. Each step involved is indispensable and linked to the next one. Only when one stage has been duly completed can we move on to the next stage.

According to Schmidt (1983), PBL teaching can be divided into seven steps, namely, clarifying terms, defining the problem, analyzing the problem, drawing explanations, formation of learning objectives, collecting additional information, and synthesis and testing new information. Moreover, the Republic

Polytechnic of Singapore has designed a five-phrase PBL approach including problem analysis, first self-directed learning (SDL), group discussion, second SDL, and group debriefing (Yew and Schmidt 2012). In PBL translation teaching, Liu and Li (2019) put forward seven specific steps concerning the process of problem identification, discussion, and problem-solving.

Based on the aforementioned PBL teaching steps, we propose that PBL in interpreting teaching can be subdivided into the following seven steps.

1 The first step in a PBL environment is to assign students an authentic interpreting task. Designing interpreting problems and choosing optimal ones are essential. This task could be an interpreting exercise modeled on authentic conferences or a specific problem relating to interpreting practice.

2 The second step is to provide a definition of the interpreting problem by students when working in small groups.

3 When the problem is identified, students should conduct the first round of self-directed learning (SDL) to brainstorm possible solutions to the problem guided by the facilitator. They may use their existing knowledge and also look for outside resources to solve the problem. They are also encouraged to consult with the facilitator.

4 The fourth step requires students to discuss with their group members and the facilitator about their understanding of the problem. Students may reflect on their own interpreting process or share opinions on the problem.

5 In the fifth step, the second round of SDL is conducted for providing solutions to the problem. Students are asked to present their interpreting exercise individually and their reflections on the interpreting task or their solutions to the interpreting problem. Other group members and the facilitator should give feedback based on students' performance and opinions.

6 In the sixth step, each learning group should report their solutions to the problem as a group and answer questions from other groups and the facilitator.

7 The last step is to give a similar interpreting task to students in order to consolidate what they have learned.

The PBL methods proposed here are designed specifically for interpreting training and meet the core features of PBL introduced previously. When applying PBL to interpreting teaching classrooms, we need to pay special attention to the following issues.

4.2 *Key issues on applying PBL in interpreting training*

4.2.1 *General principles for PBL problems*

In general, there are specific requirements concerning PBL problems. Firstly, the PBL problem should be open-ended and ill-structured, the latter of which refers to problems without a single correct answer (Hmelo-Silver 2004). Secondly, PBL problems should be complex. Meanwhile, the degree of complexity should be challenging and motivating enough to the extent of engaging students' interests. Moreover, these problems should provide opportunities for students to examine the problem from multiple perspectives or disciplines. In addition, PBL problems should be adapted to students' prior knowledge and students' cognitive development and readiness. Finally, PBL problems should be authentic, namely, contextualized as to students' future or potential workplaces. Under these general principles for designing PBL problems, we advocate to adapt the five broad categories of problem types put forward by Jonassen and Hung (2015) to be applied in interpreting training.

The first category is diagnosis–solution problems, which involve identifying the cause(s) of symptoms and prescribing treatment (patient management). In medical education, diagnosis–solution problems usually begin with symptoms of a sick person or a system in medical training classrooms. In interpreting teaching classes, examples of diagnosis–solution problems could be analyzing an interpreter's different performances under the various source speech rate or discussing frequent pitfalls for interpreters. This type of problem focuses more on the cognitive aspects of interpreting activities.

The second category is decision-making problems, which require a decision to be made among a number of competing alternatives. While diagnosis–solution problems focus on identifying the causes of the problem, decision problems concentrate more on identifying the most viable solution to the problem under the circumstances in which the problem occurs. The options usually have a variety of interpretations that require interdisciplinary thinking, and each option may have an equal level of legitimacy. In interpreting classrooms, the discussion could center on the specific strategies used by interpreters. Some of the possible questions include: How to interpret complex numbers in SI? How to interpret source speeches with a very fast speaking rate? What are the relevant parties in an interpreting assignment, and how to work with them celebratedly? The decision-making problems aim to encourage students to use interdisciplinary thinking, paying more attention to procedural, textual aspects of interpreting activities.

The third category is situated case/policy problems, which refer to typically complex, multifaceted situations. The initial state of the problem is vague, and the problem space is more ambiguous and highly untransparent. The difference between case problems and diagnosis–solution or decision-making problems is that the first may have a known worked (or failed) reasoning path and solution, while the latter two do not. The purpose of policy-making problems is to create a set of rules to regulate situations that usually involve multiple parties with conflicting interests. In order to solve these problems successfully, a deep level of understanding of all these perspectives and variables must be addressed in some way in order to balance the perspectives of all parties involved. (e.g., translator/interpreter's stance or positioning). The problem-solving process would have to take into account the perspectives of all parties involved, addressing more social, political, cultural, and policy issues related to interpreting practice.

The fourth category is troubleshooting problems. Troubleshooting shares many characteristics with diagnosis–solution problems. Troubleshooting is predominately a cognitive task that includes the search for likely causes of faults through a potentially enormous problem space of possible causes (Schaafstal et al. 2000). The scope for troubleshooting problems correlates with the scale of the system where the faults occur. Problems of this category can be formulated as what interpreters should do when they make errors or when they identify errors made by speakers. For example, what are the available interpreting technologies, and will they facilitate the interpreting process?

The last category refers to design problems, which are usually in the most complex and ill-structured category of all problem types (Jonassen 2000). Design problems possess all the common attributes of ill-structured problems, such as vaguely defined goals, multiple solutions, multiple solution paths, and unstated constraints. There are usually multiple criteria for evaluating design solutions. Many inquiry-based and project-based curricula focus on design problems, using a method known as learning by design (Hmelo et al. 2000; Kolodner 2002). This type of problem focuses more on innovative, dynamic, and subjective aspects of interpreting activity. The classes can be designed as mock court trials or mock conferences, in which students should play the roles of different participants involved.

4.2.2   *Teacher as facilitator in the PBL model*

Teachers should play the role of providing scaffolding for students throughout the PBL process and act as facilitators of the learning process (Sánchez-Gijón et al. 2011; Ertmer and Glazewski 2019; Hmelo-Silver et al. 2019). In each step of the PBL teaching environment, the function of facilitators is to engage students in a self-directed learning process, assisting them to discover the solutions to the posed problem (McCaughan 2015). According to Barrows (1986), the role of the facilitator is to move students through various stages of the learning process through discussion, monitor students' learning processes, and manage productive group work. It is the facilitators' responsibility to ensure that all students are involved and encourage them to externalize their opinions and give comments on each other's thoughts (Koschmann et al. 1994). Moreover, Azer (2005) provided 12 tips for PBL facilitators during tutorials, including situating students in the PBL learning model, assisting group work by helping build trust and encouraging the bonding of group members, fostering critical thinking, and providing feedback.

In the context of interpreting classes, one of the responsibilities of facilitators is to set up the instructional situation in which interpreting trainees can conduct complex tasks without feeling overwhelmingly frustrated. In this sense, interpreting facilitators are required to have solid interpreting skills, preferably interpreting experience, so as to provide guidance to solve problems that may occur in the interpreting occupation, promoting students' learning by monitoring, and raising questions. The facilitator should be able to "model good strategies for learning and thinking instead of being an expert in the content itself" (Hmelo-Silver 2004). When scaffolding students' learning via posing open questions, facilitators may gradually adjust their participation during the learning process as students are becoming more experienced with PBL. The goal of teaching is to encourage students to become independent learners, preparing them to be capable of tackling various challenges in their future career. Moreover, the PBL model requires a commitment to the change from didactic learning, which is familiar to students and teachers, to student-centered approach. Familiarity with the PBL teaching philosophy will help in this regard.

4.2.3   Assessment in PBL model

After PBL process, it is important to evaluate students' attainment of the intended learning outcomes sought in problem-based interpreting subjects/programs by seeking empirical evidence. In addition, it is recommended to assess how students' assessment results can feed into the next cycle of PBL and how students' assessment results can inform future PBL curriculum design/updates. It is expected that evaluating how students' assessment results can inspire the problem(s) to be used in the next cycle of PBL interpreter training.

In the traditional teacher-centered teaching model, evaluation of the learning process may include exams, peer assessment, self-assessment, teaching assistant/instructor evaluation, oral presentations, and reports, which can reflect students' learning results but cannot effectively promote students' learning process. However, the assessment of the student-centered PBL model should also focus on the learning process, personality traits, and coordination among groups, with the goal of reflecting students' learning abilities and promoting good learning habits. The assessment should help students understand "the relationships between their learning and problem-solving goals" (Hmelo-Silver 2004, 247). Therefore, the assessments in PBL have generally been categorized into formative and summative ones. The *formative assessments* contain a wide range of methods that facilitators use to evaluate "student comprehension, learning needs, and academic progress" in each course or unit, with the aim to "inform in-process teaching and learning modifications" (Albanese and Hinman 2019, 389). In interpreting courses, the assessment may include individual learning logs, group reflection sheets, activity reports, surveys and interviews of students, project plans, etc. Students can reflect on the process of their learning through the self-evaluation of the contents of the file. On the other hand, *summative assessments* refer to the evaluation of students' learning progress and outcomes when a teaching session is concluded.

5 Example: what are the ethical principles in court interpreting based on the Postville case study?

As discussed previously, the problems posed in PBL teaching should be ill-structured and authentic. It would be best if they are directly borrowed from actual interpreting events. The example that follows is a case study on how to apply PBL in interpreting classrooms. The following central problem is proposed to facilitate the students' learning: What are the ethical principles in court interpreting based on the Postville case study? This problem fits the criteria of PBL learning as it is based on an authentic scenario and does not have a straightforward answer. In addition, this problem involves multiple undefined variables relating to the ethical codes of interpreters and could occur in the professional practice of different contexts, such as political debates and business negotiations.

The posed problem is based on a real-life case of a court interpreter, Dr. Camayd-Freixas (Camayd-Freixas 2008, 2013), who is a federally certified interpreter and was one of 16 court interpreters working at the hearing following the Postville immigration raid and criminal prosecutions in May 2008. This was one of the largest worksite regional raids on illegal immigrants in U.S. history (Goodman 2008). The interpreter in the case played the roles of a court officer and expert witness at the same time. The "divergent ethical duties of the interpreter, officer of the court, and citizen" had problematized the interpreting task as the case was facing ethical challenges complicated by the issues of "social conflict, ethnic prejudice, and human rights" (Camayd-Freixas 2013, 16). The unveiling of the court trial to the public was also controversial, as interpreters might have the obligation to maintain the confidentiality of the process. The conflicting roles that the interpreter played in this particular case posed great stress for the interpreter (Zhu and Gao 2015).

According to the seven steps of PBL teaching in interpreting classrooms proposed in this chapter, the facilitator should first provide related materials for the student to understand the task. Then, students should work in groups and try to identify what the possible ethical codes are in this case study. To solve the problem, students need to apply their existing knowledge of the ethical issues of interpreters and also look for other materials to help them present their solutions. These materials may include but are not limited to research papers relating to court interpreter ethics, relevant legal documents and regulation, and news reports of the event. Students may find out the multiple roles the interpreter is taking on in the case, and each role may bear different ethical conducts which can be conflicting with each other. This complicated issue may help stir discussion among the group members. Apparently, there is no clear-cut solution to the posed problem. Through the learning process, students may acquire a better understanding of interpreters' roles and responsibilities during interpreting practice as well as the general or specific ethical principles that regulate interpreters in their future careers. Moreover, this problem can be extended to other scenarios, such as business negotiations and political debates, for students to further reflect on their role as interpreters in different working settings.

As noted earlier, solving the posed problem requires students to first identify the problem by recognizing the roles and responsibilities of being an interpreter in the court setting. This task goes beyond a straightforward answer to the problem but stimulates critical thinking about the complicated ethical issues that interpreters are facing. Additionally, this problem requests students to find outside resources of different disciplines and synthesize the information together to formulate their solutions to the problem. It is important to mention that solving the specific problem is not the end, but rather a means to provoke students' thinking about the complicated relations between all parties involved during the interpreting practice, as well as to remind them the possible ethical challenges ahead in their future careers. The knowledge and skills acquired throughout the PBL process could be further consolidated via the discussion of similar problems.

6   Discussion

The example provided previously will be able to engage students to acquire knowledge and skills through active learning and guide students to explore interdisciplinary resources. As there is no single answer to the problem, students are encouraged to find various solutions and attain ample insights of knowledge concerning the ethical conduct of interpreters.

A holistic model for PBL-based interpreting training could bring a number of educational benefits. Firstly, the PBL teaching model could benefit students more than the traditional model of transmission because it engages students in a more active learning context. In PBL teaching, students are required to develop their learning abilities through self-directed learning and collaborative learning, where they learn by themselves and from their peers and the facilitator. Their learning becomes more personalized. Throughout their learning process, students grow as interpreters with acquired abilities and skills. Instead of closing in on a predetermined ideal outcome, they are encouraged to "evolve as unique, yet interconnected emergent selves" (Aguilar 2015, 13).

Secondly, it allows students to develop inquiry-based learning strategies. The authentic translation problems in PBL are often ill-structured and related to real-life contexts. These problems could engage students in more active participation in the learning of translation. In order to solve authentic translation problems, students need to identify both linguistic and extra-linguistic problems. The complexity of problems often drives students to go beyond the linguistic horizons and search for detailed contextual information, to make independent judgments and to give a comprehensive evaluation of the communicative function of translation products.

Thirdly, PBL learning promotes students' communication skills. In the interactive PBL model for interpreting teaching, students' interaction with each other and with the facilitator takes place throughout the learning process.

More importantly, the facilitator's feedback is often timely and personalized. For instance, the facilitator could scaffold each student in the search for external resources and the coordination of group discussion.

Fourthly, the PBL model helps develop a holistic assessment of students' performances. PBL practitioners generally "consider the learning process to be equally important as the understanding and application of concepts in assessing the student's performance" (Yew and O'Grady 2012, 12). Therefore, in translation assessment, teachers will not judge students' performance in the final test. Instead, they will make a holistic assessment of students' performances by observing students' performances in self-directed learning, collaborative learning, their final products, and their reflections throughout the PBL process.

Lastly, the PBL process expands the goal of interpreter education. Under the impact of the interactive PBL model of interpreting teaching, the goal of a PBL model of interpreting teaching is consequently expanded from producing professional interpreters to cultivating critical thinkers, efficient communicators, skilled inquirers, and lifelong learners, namely, social beings who develop in an all-around way. Furthermore, the interactive PBL model helps develop a holistic assessment of students' performances.

7 Conclusion

This chapter serves as a proposal for incorporating PBL in interpreter training. In the PBL model, students are no longer seen as passive recipients of knowledge but as autonomous, active, and collaborative learners in the construction of knowledge, critical thinking, and reflection. By discussing the benefits of applying PBL in translation and interpreting pedagogy, the chapter puts forward a PBL framework for interpreting training which is exemplified with a case study on alerting students' ethical awareness in interpreting. Moreover, this chapter addresses the principle of designing and implementing problems in the interpreting classroom. Further research on PBL application in translation and interpreting training is needed to examine the effectiveness of this student-centered approach on developing students' knowledge and skills.

Acknowledgments

This work was supported by LTC Projects CBS LTG19–22/SS/CBS3, "Applying Problem-based Learning to Translation Classrooms: A holistic approach" (project code: 49KZ), and Departmental Projects (CBS) CBS/1718/LD, "Applying Problem-based Learning (PBL) to Translator Training: A holistic approach" (project code: 88DX).

References

Aguilar, Raquel P. 2015. "The Question of Authenticity in Translator Education from the Perspective of Educational Philosophy." In *Towards Authentic Experiential*

Learning in Translator Education, edited by Don Kiraly, 13–32. Newcastle upon Tyne: Mainz University Press.

Albanese, Mark A., and Georgia L. Hinman. 2019. "Types and Design of Assessment in PBL." In *The Wiley Handbook of Problem-Based Learning*, edited by Mahnaz Moallem, Woei Hung and Nada Dabbagh, 389–409. Hoboken, NJ: John Wiley & Sons, Inc.

Allen, Deborah E., Richard S. Donham, and Stephen A. Bernhardt. 2011. "Problem-Based Learning." *New DirectSrefjions for Teaching and Learning* (128): 21–9.

Amador, José A., Libbt Miles, and Calvin B. Peters. 2006. *The Practice of Problem-Based Learning: A Guide to Implementing PBL in the College Classroom*. Bolton, MA: Anker Publishing Company.

Azer, Samy A. 2005. "Challenges Facing PBL Tutors: 12 Tips for Successful Group. Facilitation." *Medical Teacher* 27(8): 676–81.

Baker, Mona. 1995. "Corpora in Translation Studies: An Overview and Some Suggestions for Future Research." *Target: International Journal of Translation Studies* 7(2): 223–43.

Barrows, Howard. S. 1986. "A Taxonomy of Problem-Based Learning Methods." *Medical. Education* 20(6): 481–86.

Barrows, Howard S. 1996. "Problem-Based Learning in Medicine and Beyond: A Brief. Overview." *New Directions for Teaching and Learning* 1996(68): 3–12.

Boud, David, and Grahame Feletti. 1997. *The Challenge of Problem-Based Learning*. 2nd ed. London: Kogan Page.

Camayd-Freixas, Erik. 2008. "Raids, Rights and Reform: The Postville Case and the Immigration Crisis." *DePaul J. Soc. Just.* 2: 1.

Camayd-Freixas, Erik. 2013. "Court Interpreter Ethics and the Role of Professional. Organizations." In *Interpreting in a Changing Landscape*, edited by C. Schäffner, K. and Y. Fowler. Amsterdam and Philadelphia: John Benjamins.

Chen, Jing, Rongrui Yu, and Xiao Zhao. 2019. "Interpreting Training in China: Practice and Research." In *Translation Studies in China: The State of the Art*, edited by Ziman Han and Defeng Li, 87–109. Singapore: Springer.

Colina, Sonia, and Claudia V. Angelelli. 2015. "Translation and Interpreting Pedagogy." In *Researching Translation and Interpreting*, edited by C. V. Angelelli and B. J. Baer, 126–35. Abingdon, UK: Routledge.

Dawrant, Andrew C. 1996. "Word Order in Chinese-English Simultaneous Interpretation: An Initial Exploration." Unpublished MA Thesis, Fu Jen University.

Dawrant, Andrew C., Binhua Wang, and Hong Jiang. 2021. *Conference Interpreting in China: The Routledge Handbook of Conference Interpreting*. Abingdon, UK: Routledge.

Duch, Barbara J., Susan E. Groh, and Deborah E. Allen. 2001. *The Power of Problem-Based Learning: A Practical "How to" for Teaching Undergraduate Courses in Any Discipline*. Sterling, VA: Stylus Publishing, LLC.

Ertmer, Peggy A., and Krista D. Glazewski. 2015. "Essentials for PBL Implementation: Fostering Collaboration, Transforming Roles, and Scaffolding Learning." In *Essential Readings in Problem-Based Learning*, edited by Andrew Walker, Heather Leary, Cindy Hmelo-silver and Peggy A. Ertmer, 58: 89–106. West Lafayette, Indiana: Purdu Univerisy Press.

Ertmer, Peggy A., and Krista D. Glazewski. 2019. "Scaffolding in PBL Environments: Structuring and Problematizing Relevant Task Features." In *The Wiley Handbook of*

Problem-Based Learning, edited by Mahnaz Moallem, Woei Hung and Nada Dabbagh, 321–42. Hoboken, NJ: John Wiley & Sons, Inc.

Goodman, Amy. 2008. "Court Interpreter Breaks Confidentiality Code to Speak Out for Workers Rounded up in Largest Immigration Raid in US History." *Democracy Now*. Accessed July 14, 2008. www.democracynow.org/2008/7/14/court_interpreter_for_workers_rounded_up.

Hatim, Basil. A. 2014. *Teaching and Researching Translation*. London: Routledge.

Hermans, Theo. 1991. "Translational Norms and Correct Translations." In *Translation Studies: The State of the Art*, edited by Kitty M. Leuven-Zwart and Ton Naaijkens, 155–69. Amsterdam: Rodopi.

Hmelo, Cindy E., Douglas L. Holton, and Janet L. Kolodner. 2000. "Designing to Learn About Complex Systems." *The Journal of the Learning Sciences* 9(3): 247–98.

Hmelo-Silver, Cindy E. 2004. "Problem-Based Learning: What and How Do Students Learn?" *Educational Psychology Review* 16(3): 235–66.

Hmelo-Silver, Cindy E., Susan. M. Bridges, and Jessica. M. McKeown. 2019. "Facilitating Problem-Based Learning." In *The Wiley Handbook of Problem-Based Learning*, edited by Mahnaz Moallem, Woei Hung and Nada Dabbagh, 297–319. Hoboken, NJ: John Wiley & Sons, Inc.

Holmes, James S. 1972/1988. "The Name and Nature of Translation Studies. Translated!" In *Papers on Literary Translation and Translation Studies*, edited by J. Holmes, 67–80. Amsterdam: Rodopi.

Inoue, Izumi. 2005. "PBL as a New Pedagogical Approach for Translator Education." *Meta: Translators' Journal* 50(4).

Jonassen, David H. 2000. "Toward a Design Theory of Problem Solving." *Educational. Technology Research and Development* 48(4): 63–85.

Jonassen, D. H., and Woei Hung. 2015. "All Problems Are Not Equal: Implication for Problem-Based Learning." In *Essential readings in Problem-Based Learning: Exploring and Extending the Legacy of Howard S. Barrows*, 9(2): 5–15. West Lafayette, IN: Purdu Univerisy Press.

Kerkkä, Karita. 2009. "Experiment in the Application of Problem-Based Learning to a Translation Course." *Vakki: n julkaisut* 36: 216–27.

Kolodner, Janet. L. 2002. "Facilitating the Learning of Design Practices: Lessons learned From an Inquiry into Science Education." *Journal of Industrial Teacher Education* 39(3): 9–40.

Koschmann, Timothy. D., A. C. Myers, Paul J. Feltovich, and Howard S. Barrows. 1994. "Using. Technology to Assist in Realizing Effective Learning and Instruction: A Principled Approach to the se of Computers in Collaborative Learning." *The Journal of the Learning Sciences* 3(3): 227–64.

Li Dechao 李德超. 2021. "PBL zai fanyi jiaoxue zhong de yingyong: tiaozhan yu duice". PBL 在翻译教学中的应用: 挑战与对策 [Applying Problem-Based Learning to Translation Classrooms: Challenges and Solutions]. *Shandong waiyu jiaoxue* 山東外語教學 |Shandong Foreign Language Teaching] 42(6): 101–11.

Liu Jing 刘晶. 2017. "Shuang PBL jiaoxue moshi zai MTI biyi jiaoxue zhong de shijian yanjiu" 双PBL 教学模式在MTI笔译教学中的实践研究 [A Practical Research on the Application of Double-PBL Mode in the MTI Translation Teaching]. *Jiaoyu jiaoxue luntan* 教育教学论坛 [Education and Teaching Forum] 50: 164–65.

Liu Lixiang 刘立香. 2021. "CAT huanjingxia PBL fanyi jiaoxue moshi yingyong gean yanjiu" CAT 环境下 PBL 翻译教学模式应用个案研究. [Applying Problem-Based

Learning to CAT Course: A Case Study]. *Shandong waiyu jiaoxue* 山東外語教學 [Shandong Foreign Language Teaching] 42(6): 112–22.

Liu Lixiang 刘立香, and Li Dechao 李德超. 2019. "PBL yu fanyi jaoxue: amli fenxi yu qishi" "PBL 与翻译教学: 案例分析与启示" [Applying Problem-Based Learning to Translation Classrooms: A Case Study and Its Pedagogical Implications]. *Waiyu yu fanyi* 外语与翻译. [Journal of Foreign Languages and Translation] (4): 73–9.

Mayo, W. Porter, Michael. B. Donnelly, and R. W. Schwartz. 1995. "Characteristics of the Ideal. Problem-Based Learning Tutor in Clinical Medicine." *Evaluation & the Health Professions* 18(2): 124–36.

McCaughan, Kareen. 2015. "Theoretical Anchors for Barrows' PBL Tutor Guidelines." In *Essential Readings in Problem-Based Learning*, edited by Andrew Elbert Walker, Heather Leary, Cindy E. Hmelo-Silver and Peggy A. Ertmer, 57–68. West Lafayette, IN: Purdu Univerisy Press.

Mellinger, Christopher. D. 2018. "Problem-Based Learning in Computer-Assisted Translation. Pedagogy." *HERMES-Journal of Language and Communication in Business* (57): 195–208.

Norman, Geoffery. R., and Henk. G. Schmidt. 1992. "The Psychological Basis of Problem-Based. Learning: A Review of the Evidence." *Academic Medicine* 67(9): 557–65.

O'Hagan, Minako. 2013. "The Impact of New Technologies on Translation Studies: A Technological Turn?" In *The Routledge Handbook of Translation Studies*, edited by Carmen Millan-Varela and Francesca Bartrina, 521–36. London and New York: Routledge.

Pöchhacker, Franz. 2016. *Introducing Interpreting Studies*. London: Routledge.

Sánchez-Gijón, Pilar., Anna Aguilar-Amat, Bartolomé Mesa-Lao, and Marta Pahisa Solé. 2011. "Applying Terminology Knowledge to Translation: Proplem-Based Learning for a Degree in Translation and Interpreting." In *Teaching and Learning Terminology: New Strategies and Methods*, edited by Amparo Alcina, 107–19. Amsterdam: John Benjamins Publishing Company.

Savery, John R. 2015. "Overview of Problem-Based Learning: Definitions and Distinctions." In *Essential Readings in Problem-Based Learning: Exploring and Extending the Legacy of Howard S. Barrows*, 9(2): 5–15. West Lafayette, IN: Purdue Univerisy Press.

Schaafstal, Alma, Jan Maarten Schraagen, and Marcel Van Berl. 2000. "Cognitive Task Analysis and Innovation of Training: The Case of Structured Troubleshooting." *Human Factors* 42(1): 75–86.

Schmidt, Hendricus Gerard. 1983. "Problem-Based Learning: Rationale and Description." *Medical. Education* 17(1): 11–6.

Shahabudin, S. H. 1987. "Content Coverage in Problem-Based Learning." *Medical Education* 21(4): 310–13.

Tan, Zanxi. 2008. "Towards a Whole-Person Translator Education Approach in Translation. Teaching on University Degree Programmes." *Meta: Translators' Journal* 53(3): 589–608.

Tao, Youlan. 2019. "The Development of Translation and Interpreting Curriculum in China's Mainland: A Historical Overview". In *Translation Studies in China*, edited by Han Ziman and Li Defeng, 111–33. Singapore: Springer.

Torp, Linda, and Sara Sage. 2002. *Problem as Possibilities: Problem-Based Learning for K-16 Education*. Alexandria, VA: Association for Supervision and Curriculum Development.

Vernon, David. T., and Robert. L. Blake. 1993. "Does Problem-Based Learning Work? A Meta-Analysis of Evaluative Research." *Academic Medicine* 68(7): 550–63.

Wang, Binhua, and Lei Mu. 2011. "Interpreter Training and Research in Mainland China." In *Interpreting Chinese, Interpreting China*, edited by R. Setton. 157–74. Amsterdam and Philadelphia: John Benjamins Publishing Company.

Wang Binhua 王斌华. 2018. "Zhongguo kouyi yanjiu 40 nian" 中国口译研究 40年: 历程, 成就和展望 [Interpreting Studies in China in the Past 40 Years: Progress and Prospects] *Dangdai waiyu yanjiu* 当代外语研究 [Contemporary Foreign Languages Studies] 18(03): 48.

Wang Yang 王洋, and Zhang Yin 张印. 2019. "Yingyong benke yuanxiao PBL moshi xia yingyu kouyi kecheng tansuo yu fanse" 应用本科院校 PBL 模式下的英语口译课程探索与反思 [The Probe and Reflection of Problem-Based Learning English Interpreting Class in Application-Oriented Universities] *Hubei kaifang zhiye xueyuan xuebao* 湖北开放职业学院学报 [Journal of Hubei Open Vocational College] 32(05): 156–57.

Wood, E. 1994. "The Problems of Problem-Based Learning." *Biochemical Education* 22(2): 78–82.

Yang Qiaonan 杨巧南. 2015. "Minzu diqu shangwu fanyi rencai peiyang de PBL moshi yanjiu" 民族地区商务翻译人才培养的 PBL 模式研究. [Research on the PBL Model for Training Business Translators in Ethnic Minorgity Regions]. *Neimenggu shifan daxue xuebao: jiaoyu kexue ban* 内蒙古师范大学学报: 教育科学版 [Journal of Inner Mongolia Normal University (Educational Science)] (8): 145–47.

Yang Xiaohua 杨晓华. 2012. "Jiyu wenti xuexi de fanyi jiaoxue yanjiu: yi MTI wenhua fanyi kecheng weili" 基于问题学习的翻译教学研究 – 以 MTI 文化翻译课程为例 [Study on PBL in Teaching Translation – Taking MTI Cultural Translation Course as an Example] *Zhongguo fanyi* 中国翻译 [Chinese Translators Journal] 33(01): 35–9.

Yang Xiaohua 杨晓华. 2021. "Jiyu wenti xuexi huanjingzhong de yizhe ziwo. daoxiang xuexi nengli peiyang yangjiu" 基于问题学习环境中的译者自我导向学习能力培养研究. [Fostering Translators' SDL Competence in PBL Environments] *Shandong waiyu jiaoxue* 山東外語教學 [Shandong Foreign Language Teaching] 42(6): 123–33.

Yew, Elaine. H. J., and G. O'Grady. 2012. "One-Day, One-Problem at Republic Polytechnic." In *One-Day, One-Problem: An Approach to Problem-Based Learning*, edited by G O'Grady, Elaine H. J. Yew, Karen P. L. Goh and Henk G. Schmidt. 3–19. Singapore: Springer.

Yew, Elaine. H. J., and Henk. G. Schmidt. 2012. "The Process of Student Learning in One-day, One Problem". In *One-Day, One-Problem: An Approach to Problem-Based Learning*, edited by G O'Grady, Elaine H. J. Yew, Karen P. L. Goh and Henk G. Schmidt, 63–83. Singapore: Springer.

Zhang Jing 张晶. 2012. "Jiyu Blackboard wangluo pingtaixia de zhongyi yingyu. fanyi jiaoxue moshi yanjiu" 基于 Blackboard 网络平台下的中医英语翻译教学模式探究." [Study on Teaching Mode of English Translation of TCM Based on Blackboard Network Platform] *Xibu Zhongyiyao* 西部中医药 [Western Journal of Traditional Chinese Medicine] 25(3): 39–40.

Zhang Yucui 张玉翠. 2009. "PBL moshi zai yingyu kouyi jiaoxuezhong de yingying". PBL 模式在英语口译教学中的应 [The Application of PBL in English Interpreting] *Yancheng Gongxueyuan xuebao: shhui kexue ban* 盐城工学院学报: 社会科学版 [Journal of Yancheng Institute of Technology (Social Science Edition)] 22(4): 80–3.

Zhao Jun 赵军. 2013. "PBL moshi zai shangwu yingyu fanyi jiaoxue zhong de yingyong shijian yanjiu" PBL 模式在商务英语翻译教学中的应用实践研究 [Practical Study on the Application of PBL Model in Teaching Business English Translatio] *Changchun jiaoyu xueyuan xuebao* 长春教育学院学报 [Journal of Changchun Education Institute] (21): 86–7.

Zhu Bo 朱波, and Gao Hong 高虹. 2015. "Fating kouyizhong de juese chongtu" 法庭口译中的角色冲突 – 以 Camayd-Freixas "声明为例 [Role Conflicts in Court Interpreting – Using the Camayd-Freixas' Statement]." *Waiyu yu waiyu jiaoxue* 外语与外语教学 [Foreign Languages and Their Teaching] (5): 75–9.

7 Exploring the identity and crisis of interpreting teachers in China

A case study of a private college in Zhejiang province

Jiqing Dong and Yihui Chen

1 Introduction

China's BTI program was launched in 2005, followed by the MTI program in 2007, with an aim to prepare top linguistic talents for formal international conferences and diplomatic occasions. Since then, an increasing number of colleges and universities have begun to recruit students for these programs, with some of them offering one program alone while others offering both. The latest figures suggest that the number of colleges and universities that are qualified to enroll BTI students reaches 301 (China National Committee for BTI Education 2022), and that of MTI reaches 316 (China National Committee for Translation and Interpreting Education n.d.). The booming of professional T&I training at undergraduate and postgraduate levels has substantially invigorated the market for language services, such as conference interpreting in China and worldwide, as Pöchhacker (2016, 46) observes that "the number of institutions engaged in interpreter education and interpreting research throughout the world has continued to rise, not least as a result of the enormous expansion of this field in China." In Zhejiang province alone, seven institutions offer MTI programs, and ten offer BTI programs, among which three are private colleges.

However, such rapid development does not entail a problem-free industry of T&I education that is meant to nurture future conference interpreters and other professionals, especially in the recruitment and career development of qualified faculty in less-developed areas. For example, many T&I teachers are traditional EFL (English as a foreign language) teachers with no or little professional experience in T&I, some of whom switched from neighboring disciplines (Chai 2017, 6–7), such as linguistics, literature, or intercultural studies, constituting an obvious weak link in local T&I education. This contravenes the mainstream belief that T&I should be instructed by practitioners and that learning activities should simulate real-life conference or community situations (Orlando 2019, 219).

Unfortunately, much research on T&I education focuses on the pedagogical design and student development, without considering one of the

DOI: 10.4324/9781003357629-9

most important participants in T&I class – the teachers (Lü 2018, 48). In the limited body of research mentioning interpreting faculty, BTI teachers are either mostly neglected or considered indiscriminately as T&I teachers, not to mention those working in less-prestigious or private institutions.[1] Since MTI and BTI programs aim to train application-oriented talents who are familiar with fundamental theories and practical skills, the requirements of the interpreting teachers and the path of their career development may be different from those of other EFL teachers in Chinese universities, which deserves to be further explored.

2   Status quo of T&I teachers

Several quantitative studies investigated the background of the frontline T&I teachers and revealed their unique characteristics and problems, which have greatly informed this chapter. In a pioneering survey on the status quo of T&I teachers in 145 colleges and universities in China, Zhang and Chen (2012, 67) found that the average age of T&I teachers is 37.34 years, while in an earlier survey conducted by Mu (1999, 52), those aged 45 years and above account for more than 60%. This indicates that young and middle-aged teachers constitute the majority in T&I education, most of whom have lecturers and associate professors as their professional titles (42.99% and 34.45%, respectively). About 71.04% of them have master's degrees, and only 23.78% have doctoral degrees. Upon expanding the sample scope, Liu and Xu (2020, 30) recently identified a reasonable age structure of T&I faculty with more details: teachers aged 36 to 45 account for 41.63%, and those aged 46 to 55 years account for 34.82%. Teachers who have a doctoral degree in relevant fields have increased 16% after almost ten years of development in China, compared to those in Zhang's study (2012, 83). However, they still face the same problem regarding the acquisition of professional titles, many of whom confessed to "being unable to care for both family and work, both academic studies and practical work at the same time" (Liu and Xu 2020, 31).

As for interpreting teachers, the situation seems direr. Hua (2016, 37) used stratified sampling and focused on 43 interpreting teachers of MTI programs in the east, middle, and west regions of China. Findings show that 76.74% of them are lecturers or assistant lecturers, and nearly 80% do not have a doctoral degree. Around 72% of these teachers are not originally interpreting majors. Even more alarming is that these teachers lack experience in teaching interpreting, with 93.02% of them having teaching experience of less than five years. In terms of qualifications, unlike MA programs, MTI and BTI programs pay more attention to the application of theories and T&I skills in teaching and training, thus bringing requirements that are different from research-focused majors. Chai (2017, 6–7) acknowledges that although T&I education in China has progressed dramatically over the years, many T&I teachers are traditional EFL teachers with limited professional experience. Some may have published one or two literary translation works, but their working procedure is poles apart from the T&I industrial standard. Some switched to T&I from other majors and disciplines, such as linguistics and literature, with no T&I experience at all. These problems are flagged up by the students as well, given only 31.33% of 399 first-year postgraduates believe their undergraduate T&I teachers to have rich experience in practice, and only 35.59% students deem these teachers as "well familiar with the current T&I market" (Zhang and Chen 2012, 70).

For those who *have* actual practical experience of T&I, Xu and You (2021, 14) found that their own practice is often passive, random, and "somewhat utilitarian rather than well-planned, regular, and systemic." While translation assignments do help them in having abundant teaching materials and better understanding difficulties encountered by students, the main purpose of their own translation practice is to "satisfy others' requests and their own research quotas" (*ibid.*). One of the reasons behind this reluctance is that apart from teaching, university teachers have to undertake research, administrative, and other responsibilities, leaving them little time and energy for anything else. This is also true of interpreting teachers who have to balance the high demands on their mobility and flexibility in class schedules in order to attend conference sessions. Hua (2016, 38) found that although 98.92% of surveyed interpreting teachers acknowledge the importance of practice, only 6.72% of them practice interpreting for more than five hours on a monthly basis, and only 9.03% of them practice for more than one hour monthly. It can thus be concluded that the vast majority of teachers lack the opportunities to practice advanced interpreting outside the classroom. However, teachers who can manage both are not trouble-free either. Due to the shortage of proper pedagogical training, many interpreting classes are conducted in a rigid "audio-playing" mode in which the teacher plays auditory conference speeches for students to practice and then gives out so-called correct interpretations previously prepared (Lu 2016, 61). The importance of mastering pedagogical knowledge and integrating methods and means that are in accordance with students' cognitive behaviors in interpreting classes is often neglected (Chai 2017, 5).

3 Career development of T&I teachers

Based on a survey of 147 teachers of English interpreting in 116 Chinese universities, Wang (2014, 108) suggests that interpreting teachers have stronger extrinsic motivation (the fact that teaching helps them do better in interpreting and thus enables them to earn more monetary benefits) than intrinsic motivation (preference and interest). However, in order to gain higher professional titles, interpreting teachers, especially young and middle-aged ones, need to take on yet another role – academic researcher, an identity of which they usually feel short. Since the general context in most Chinese universities sets promotion standards, most of which focus on their academic achievements, interpreting teachers are, more often than not, faced with a "glass ceiling" in their career development (Liu 2011, 106; Liu and Xu 2020, 31).

Many interpreting teachers have realized such kind of barriers in their career development and expressed their anxiety on different occasions. In Hua's survey (2016, 38), the most craved topics of training by interpreting teachers are pedagogy (42.7%), quality assessment (33.2%), and theories (18.2%). The urgent needs for training in interpreting theories and research methodology are in bleak contrast to their inadequate number of published research works. Among them, only 12.8% have published two or more articles regarding interpreting theories and education on a yearly basis; only 17.4% have published one such article annually, leaving the majority of them publishing nothing whatsoever every year. This may explain why academic research, instead of teaching, is widely regarded as the "bloodline" of a teacher's career path, which gives birth to the necessity of training the interpreting teachers.

Having explored the multifaceted role of interpreting teachers, including that of a teacher, a practitioner, and a researcher, a few scholars begin to probe into the integration among these three identities. The threefold identity of an interpreting teacher at the university level can be traced back to Gile (1994, 150), who introduced the concept of "practisearcher" to describe "practitioners cum researchers . . . most of whom were also interpretation teachers" (*ibid.*). His remarks emphasized that the identity of an interpreting trainer has truly been multifaceted since the birth of this profession. Similar terms that appeared in the literature include "practeasearcher" (Lu 2016, 62), "practitioners-researchers-teachers" (Orlando 2019, 220), and the PTR (practice-teaching-research) model (Kang and Shi 2020, 604), to name a few. Orlando's article (2019, 216) advocates the presence of both the vocational and the academic in T&I classrooms and the necessity of any practitioner, academic, or "practisearcher" to take part in TOT (training of trainers) programs in order to "properly guide and advise future T&I professionals" (*ibid.*). Unlike Lu's idea of "practeasearcher" (2016, 62), which is used to refer to the multiple roles undertaken by one teacher, Orlando's proposal (2019, 220) can be regarded as the diversity and inclusiveness of higher education institutions when assembling faculty teams of T&I education, since "practitioners-researchers-teachers" actually refers to the recruitment of "practisearchers" who need to acquire didactic knowledge before taking on the role of teaching.

In the same vein, Kang and Shi (2020, 604) focused on the unbalanced factors among the interpreting practice (IP), interpreting teaching (IT), and interpreting research (IR) of interpreting teachers in Chinese universities. Based on the investigation of interpreting teachers at five universities in Shanghai, they put forward a "practice-teaching-research" (PTR) model as a "three-in-one approach" (*ibid.*). According to this PTR model, a teacher's overall interpreting (OI) is a combination of these three factors (OI = IP + IT + IR). Contrasting that of Lu (2016, 62) and Orlando (2019, 220), the purpose of Kang and Shi's (2020, 604) model is not to place requirements on one single interpreting teacher in achieving all three roles but to help assemble *teams* of interpreting teachers with each member realizing his or her multi-tasks and shouldering differentiated responsibilities, making the whole team stronger and sustainable.

The situation of interpreting teachers may be worsened in private colleges that offer BTI programs alone. For one thing, private colleges are usually considered to be inferior to public universities in terms of social status, financial support, research facilities, students' qualifications, etc. As private institutions tend to be away from urban centers of intercultural and commercial exchanges, the opportunities to take conference assignments remain rather scarce. For another, colleges that are only qualified to enroll BTI students are less likely to assemble a team of high-quality faculty consisting professionally of teachers, practitioners, and researchers, meaning, that the interpreting teachers in these institutions are more often than not confronted with inadequacy in these aspects. Yet existing research on interpreting teachers only aims at MTI teachers or those in first-tier cities, such as Shanghai, leaving BTI teachers, especially those in private colleges in second- and third-tier cities, an uncharted territory. In fact, there are 64 private colleges across China currently offering BTI programs, which account for over 20% of the total BTI-inclusive institutions (China National Committee for BTI Education 2022), a number and scale that can no longer be underestimated. To address this gap, and drawing on the existing debate on the multiple roles of interpreting teachers in China, this chapter conducts a case analysis focusing on the entire team of English–Chinese interpreting teachers at a private college which offers a BTI program alone, by probing into their alliance with the threefold identity of a teacher, a practitioner, and a researcher and exposing the challenges they are faced with in their career development with the following research questions:

1 To what extent do BTI teachers in private colleges identify themselves as teachers, practitioners, and/or researchers?
2 What are the major causes of crises concerning the teachers when taking on these identities?

4   Context and methods

This case focuses on full-time BTI teachers at XYZ College (pseudonym), a private institution located in a third-tier city in Zhejiang province. The School of English Language offers undergraduate degree programs in three majors: English, business English, and translation and interpreting (BTI). Each year, approximately 100 students are enrolled in the BTI program and are allowed to choose translation or interpreting as their major orientation. A comprehensive interpreting curriculum including liaison, business, consecutive, and simultaneous interpreting is offered to students of all three majors, although some courses are limited to BTI students or interpreting students only.

Participants who met the following criteria were invited to take part in this case study: (1) full-time faculty members of the school; (2) teaching interpreting as part of or all their job responsibilities within the last school year. Using a convenience sampling approach, the authors managed to recruit six participants who met the aforementioned criteria (and coincidently constituted the entire team of English–Chinese interpreting teachers at XYZ College). Since one of the authors worked in this college for several years and has built personal relations with these participants, their opinions are expected to be honest and unreserved. All the participants in this study act on a voluntary basis and are asked for consent before having their opinions published anonymously. A random number is assigned to each participant when making references in this chapter.

Data was collected from two sources: a questionnaire and follow-up semistructured interviews. Both were conducted in Chinese, the A language of the participants. The authors contacted each participant regarding the purpose of this study and promised their anonymity, clearly stating their right to decide on the use of the data. The online questionnaire covers participants' demographic data, their teaching, practice, and research experience, and probes into their alliance with the three identities by using a five-point Likert scale. The one-on-one semistructured interviews were also conducted online due to the different geographic locations between the authors and the two participants who were recruited on a voluntary basis. Their desensitized profiles are provided in Table 7.1, which follows. An outline was sent to each participant prior to the interview. Each session of the interview, which lasted about 30 minutes, began with an exchange of pleasantry to lighten up the mood and then moved on to the questions listed in the outline. Since the interviews were semistructured in nature, the authors did not follow the outline strictly but improvised so as to facilitate more natural interactions and shed light on factors unaddressed in their feedback to section III of the questionnaires.

The audio recordings were fully transcribed. Factors related to these teachers' alliance with the threefold identity of teacher, practitioner, and/or researcher

Table 7.1 Desensitized Profiles of the Participants in the Semistructured Interviews

Participant	Desensitized Profile
No. 1	Master of translation (MT) degree; has worked as an interpreting teacher for nine years (immediately after graduation) at XYZ; relatively active in interpreting practice.
No. 2	Master of interpreting (MI) degree; has worked at XYZ University (immediately after graduation) for nine years; first employed as an English-language teacher, later as an interpreting teacher; relatively active in T&I practice; engaging in administrative work at the time of the interview.

and their problems in taking on this identity were codified and then sent to each participant for revision to ensure the validity of the findings of this paper.

5   Findings

5.1   Quantitative data

Before analyzing the quantitative data, it should be pointed out that the numeric values generated by the first two sections of the questionnaire should be regarded not as results with general reliability but as an overall picture of the interpreting faculty of XYZ College.

As is shown in Figure 7.1, the most senior interpreting teacher is 50 years old (female), while the youngest is only 28 (also female). The age structure shows a lack of teachers aged from the 36-to-40 group and the 41-to-45 group. As for

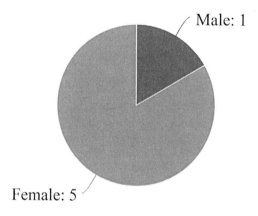

1.1 Gender.

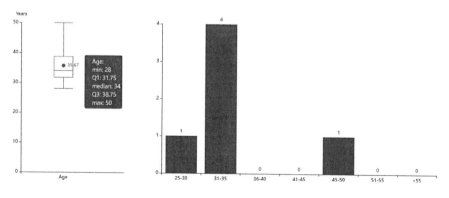

1.2 Age structure.

Figure 7.1 Desensitized demographic data.

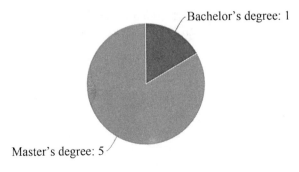

1.3 Degree of education.

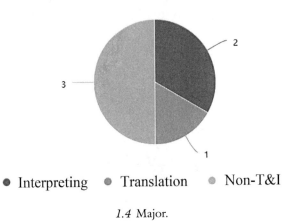

● Interpreting   ● Translation   ● Non-T&I

1.4 Major.

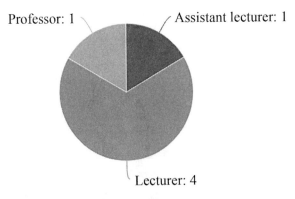

1.5 Professional title.

Figure 7.1 (Continued)

the educational background, three of them graduated with interpreting-related majors (such as MI), two with translation-related majors (such as MT), and one with a non-T&I major (applied linguistics). Only one of them is a professor, and no one in the faculty team owns the professional title of associate professor.

Figure 7.2 reveals data related to the identity of "teacher" among these six participants. The median value of their teaching experience in total is

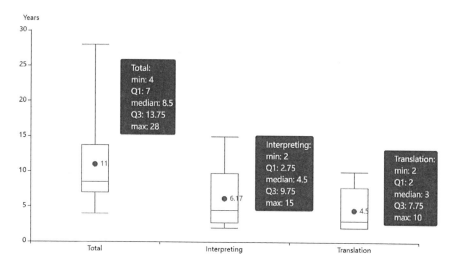

2.1 Teaching experience.

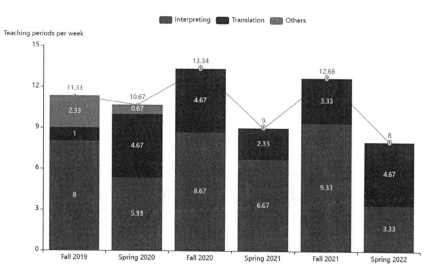

2.2 Teaching workload.

Figure 7.2 Teaching-related data.

8.5 years, and that of interpreting teaching is 4.5 years. The one with the most experience has been teaching interpreting for 15 years, while the one with the least has merely two years of experience in training student interpreters. They also conduct teaching in translation-related and other non-T&I courses. The average workload of fall semesters is 12.44 teaching periods per week, which is higher than the 9.22 weekly teaching periods of spring semesters, suggesting an unbalanced workload for these interpreting teachers in different school semesters.

Figure 7.3 shows data related to the identity of "practitioner." Average simultaneous conference, consecutive conference, and liaison interpreting assignment hours reach 1.33, 4.67, and 12, respectively. The teachers' practice in liaison/escort interpreting is more frequent, with an average of 6 hours; the maximum value is 20 hours, and the median value is 2 hours. In terms of their translation practice, the maximum number of translated words reaches 600,000, with the average and the median value being 124,183.33 and 22,500, respectively.

Figure 7.4 reveals data related to the identity of "researcher" among these six participants. Three of them choose interpreting as their main research field, while two of them choose translation, and the remaining one chooses a non-T&I field (applied linguistics, to be more exact). They are generally more prolific in translation studies, including translation pedagogy and practice and corpus-based translation studies, than studies in interpreting and other fields. In the recent three school years, the average number of published articles in translation studies reaches 1.33, with the maximum value of 5 and the median value of 0.5.

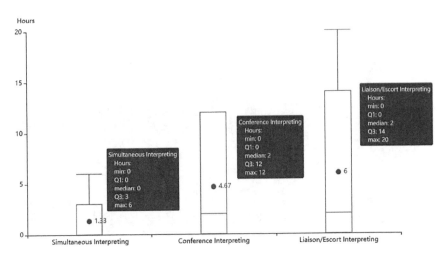

3.1 Hours of interpreting practice in recent three school years.

Figure 7.3 Practice-related data.

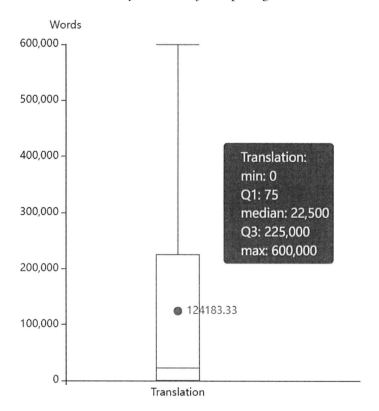

3.2 Words of translation practice in recent three school years.

Figure 7.3 (Continued)

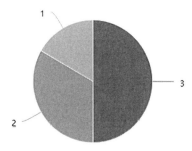

4.1 Research fields.

Figure 7.4 Research-related data.

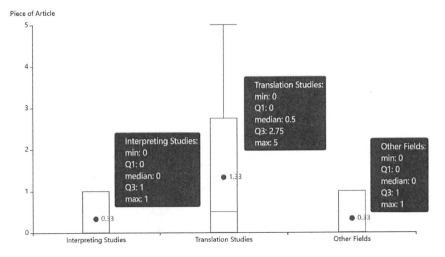

4.2 Number of published articles in recent three school years.

Figure 7.4 (Continued)

5.2 *Qualitative data*

When asked about their options toward teaching, practice, and research, all six of them rate teaching and practice as "relatively important" and "very important"; in ordering the significance of these three facets in their own career development, research ranks first as the most important part, followed by teaching. Practice, including conference and other settings, can be seen as evidently less important than the remaining two. It should be pointed out that due to the limited sample size, Figure 7.5 can only be regarded as qualitative results showing not absolute value but relative importance.

In the interviews, the two participants do acknowledge the gap between what they think they should do in their pursuit of career development and what they actually do as reflected by quantitative data generated by the questionnaire. They then share their opinions regarding the factors leading to such a gap, which are summarized into internal and external factors in the following Table 7.2.

Internal factors are those caused by the participants themselves, and external factors are those imposed by others or the larger context of the surrounding environment. It should be pointed out that many of the factors are interconnected, and therefore, such a dichotomy may not be scientific enough in distinguishing factors caused by the participants themselves and those by others. Nevertheless, Table 7.2 does provide an overview of the crises encountered by participants in teaching, practice, and research.

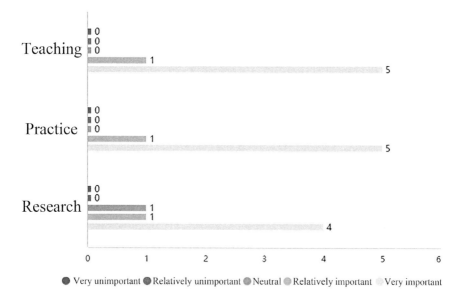

5.1 Importance of teaching, practice, and research for BTI teachers.

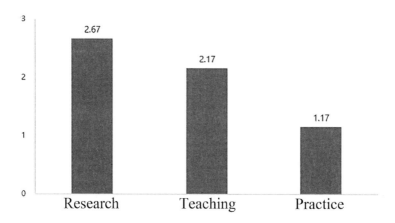

5.2 Order of significance among research, teaching, and practice for career development.

Figure 7.5 Alliance with the threefold identity.

6 Discussion

6.1 The teachers' threefold identity

The feedback provided by the six participants, though limited in number, in both the questionnaire and the following semistructured interviews, offers a glimpse into the interpreting faculty of XYZ College in Zhejiang province.

Table 7.2 Factors Leading to the Gap in the Participants' Threefold Identities

Identity	Factors	
Teacher	Internal	• Limited time and energy in class preparation and evaluation of students' performance (audio recordings) • Large consumption of time in class preparation and homework assessment • Lack of theoretical guidance in teaching skills and training students
	External	• Out-of-date/unpractical textbooks and teaching materials • Students' weak foundation in both language skills and cultural knowledge • Students' lack of initiative to learn interpreting well • Lack of online platforms for the latest teaching materials, AI-assisted homework assessment, and communication among teachers at different universities • Similar courses in different semesters
Practitioner	Internal	• Lack of interpreting skills for professional settings • Lack of knowledge and in-depth understanding of other fields and industries
	External	• Lack of opportunities partly due to geographic constraints of a third-tier city • Clients' poor understanding of the profession: • Unwillingness in handing out materials for in-advance preparation • Improper venue arrangement and lack of specialized equipment • Ignorance of the type of interpreting suitable for the tasks • Low payment
Researcher	Internal	• Lack of systematic training in academic research, partly due to their own MTI backgrounds • Difficulty in collecting data for interpreting studies, such as discourses for corpus-based interpreting studies • Lack of proper skills for empirical interpreting studies, including using certain computer programs and even writing computer programs for data processing and analysis • Lack of motivation, time, and energy due to heavy workload in teaching
	External	• Lack of positive atmosphere for academic research and models and examples to follow • Lack of guidance and channels when applying for research programs and publishing articles

The desensitized demographic data in Figure 7.1 suggests that the interpreting faculty is young in age, less than ideal in educational background, and low in professional titles, the situation of which is similar but direr than that of Zhang and Chen (2012, 67–69), Liu and Xu (2020, 30–33), and Hua (2016, 38). Clearly, the interpreting faculty is mainly comprised of young teachers, with five of them aged younger than 35 years. In addition, the fact that only half of them graduated with interpreting-related degrees corroborates the observations of Chai (2017, 6–7) and Hua (2016, 38) that many interpreting teachers do not major in interpreting-related fields or they switched from translation-related fields. It can be argued that the recruitment of someone with a doctoral degree in interpreting studies and the professional title of associate professor, preferably aged between 36 and 45 years, should be considered as one of the directions for sharing of the teaching workload and sustainable development of the faculty team.

As Figure 7.2 shows, the participants' interpreting teaching experience reaches 6.17 years, with a median value of 4.5 years. This is a slight improvement compared with Hua's observations (2016, 38) that more than 90% of his surveyed teachers have less than five years of teaching experience. Noticeably, their teaching workload is exceptionally high in the fall semesters, because not only BTI students but also junior and senior students of the English major and business English major are required by the curriculum to take interpreting courses. In order to meet the minimum workload requirement, they need to teach other non-interpreting-related courses, preferably translation-related ones. Such a kind of workload, although seems lighter in spring semesters, does constantly require interpreting teachers to prepare for other courses and update their knowledge base while limiting their time and energy for other research and practice.

Apart from these reasons, the deficiency of updated, relevant, and practical textbooks and teaching materials also contribute to the disproportional allocation of time in class preparation. Teachers often face the dilemma of using the textbook, which is required by the employer but often outdated and not specifically tailored for their student levels. Most prefer to use their own materials in conference and community settings, which are more interesting for the students but require large amount of time and energy in selecting and editing.

In addition, the participants have to deal with students' lack of motivation in interpreting training. Currently, Zhejiang province is witnessing a decline in the number of candidate students for the National College Entrance Examination (*gao kao*), which impacts private colleges more severely than public ones in terms of student recruitment. Although not publicly acknowledged, the financial interest in school-running is one of the driving forces, if not the most important one, for private colleges as well as the enterprises, institutions, and social groups behind them to start a school in the first place. As a result, private colleges with a BTI program intend to enroll as many students as permitted by relevant government departments. Moreover, when choosing their major orientations, students are not required to undergo a selection process, at least not at XYZ College. Subsequently, those with a weak foundation in language skills and a lack of both cultural knowledge and learning motivations can still be enrolled in the BTI program, thus posing greater challenges to these teachers in classroom settings.

Last but not the least, the participants' lack of pedagogical knowledge and skills is also one of the reasons for their crisis in taking on the identity of a teacher. To make matters worse, administrators at the college and department levels often try to follow the examples set by first-tier universities in the field, especially in curriculum offerings. As a result, the participants have to teach courses such as simultaneous conference interpreting to these BTI students who certainly are less equipped for the course. As a matter of fact, few of these participants have rich experience in simultaneous conference interpreting practice (which shall be discussed in the following paragraphs), let alone pedagogical knowledge in this regard. The unpreparedness of both the teachers and the students in courses of this kind contributes jointly to the teachers' career crises.

In terms of their professional practice, although the participants do acknowledge its positive effect on teaching, which corroborates Xu and You's observations of experienced MTI teachers (2021, 14), they all are quite limited in this regard, especially in more advanced interpreting tasks, as is shown in Figure 7.3. The reasons behind this are partly due to the geographic location of XYZ College and the strict regulations imposed by the college authorities. As it is located in a third-tier city in Zhejiang province, there is not a well-developed market for interpreting services. Most of the interpreting tasks for these teachers are assigned by the college for internal affairs with minimum pay or requested occasionally by departments in the municipal government. Some of these clients are ignorant of the requirements and standards for successful interpreting service, including handing out materials for in-advance preparation, choosing the appropriate form of interpreting for different tasks, and booking the proper venue and standardized equipment for each task. This situation is worsened by the tight and strict management of the college's Department of Academic Affairs, whose regulations clearly forbid teachers to reschedule their classes simply for the reason of professional practice.

Moreover, the participants do acknowledge their lack of advanced skills in interpreting practice (such as simultaneous interpreting) and the need for further training in this regard. On some occasions, the fear of their inability to successfully perform certain interpreting tasks, especially those requiring in-depth knowledge and understanding of other fields and industries, is also one of the factors resulting in their unwillingness or reluctance to conduct practice. Translation practice, on the other hand, is affected to a less extent by geographic constraints or inflexible time schedules. With the assistance of online tools, the participants are, therefore, more willingly and frequently engaged in the practice of written translation.

As for their research output, the situation, shown in Figure 7.4, is far worse than their performance in teaching and professional practice, which is once again consistent with Hua's observation (2016, 38) in terms of interpreting teachers' inadequate number of published research works. What is of interest is that the participants in this case study seem to be more prolific in translation studies than in interpreting studies. After further investigation, this is actually caused by one particularly productive teacher who is applying for a doctoral program in corpus-based translation studies. Nevertheless, the participants confirm their inadequacy in academic achievements, especially in high-quality outputs, their lack of theoretical knowledge, and their urgent need for systematic academic training in such areas as empirical interpreting studies, which validates the necessity of TOT programs that include a module for academic research as envisioned by Ren (2009, 51). Participants also acknowledge the existence of other internal factors, such as the heavy workload in teaching, administrative work, and family life, as well as external factors, including the lack of research culture and incentives and their disadvantaged position in applying for research programs, resulted from the college's status as a private one in a third-tier city.

6.2   *The teachers' crises in career development*

The interpreting teachers' gap between their ideal perception of the threefold identity and their actual performance in taking on such roles can be viewed from the perspective of the self-discrepancy theory.

According to Higgins (1987, 320–21), the three basic domains of the self include the actual self, the ideal self, and the ought self, referring to "the attributes that someone (yourself or another) believes you actually possess," "the attributes that someone (yourself or another) would like you, ideally, to possess," and "the attributes that someone (yourself or another) believes you should or ought to possess" (*ibid.*). Although the discrepancy between these domains might be related to disappointment, dissatisfaction, fear, or restlessness (for example, Higgins 1987, 321), some acknowledge the motivational function of such discrepancies (for example, Higgins 1989, 130). Some scholars have examined the self-discrepancies of EFL teachers in China and subsequent motivation for their efforts, examples of which include Gao and Xu (2014), who investigated the dilemma of being English-language teachers in rural secondary schools in China's hinterland regions, and Ruan et al. (2020), who examined the agency of English department teachers in the context of curriculum reform in a Chinese university.

In this chapter, the discrepancy among the interpreting teachers' ideal self (what they and others think of BTI teachers as teachers, practitioners, and researchers), ought self (what they and others think they should possess for career pursuit and development in the context of Chinese universities), and actual self (what they have actually done as reflected by quantitative results) does exist.

The fact that they are teachers of an application-oriented discipline requires them to actively engage in professional practice, especially conference interpreting. The image of a successful conference interpreter will not only supply intriguing materials for classroom teaching but also inspire students to embark on a similar career path, possibly leading to further pursuing of MTI degrees and becoming professionals. In a sense, interpreting teachers at the BTI level can be regarded as "gatekeepers" in the current education system who may either offer firsthand field experience to budding conference interpreters or dishearten them with unprofessionalism and even annihilate any possible attempts. Therefore, for the sake of the ideal self perceived by others as well as themselves, interpreting teachers should attach greater importance to professional practice in conference and other high-end settings. However, when they try to pursue career development in the greater context of Chinese universities, research becomes the factor that must be given priority to. Policies at the university level and even the state level give preference to research-oriented faculty and are more likely to promote them as associate professors and professors in China. Therefore, the image of a researcher constitutes a larger proportion of the ought self of these interpreting teachers at the BTI level. Contrasted with what their actual self (higher performance in teaching, although not free of problems, than in research or practice) is, a discrepancy does occur as a cause of their anxiety, crises, and other negative emotions when taking on this three-faceted identity.

Nevertheless, such a kind of discrepancy could also function as driving forces for them to work harder and aim higher (see Figure 7.6).

For example, participant no. 1 is currently involved in a provincial-level curriculum reform project to incorporate online teaching platforms into classroom teaching and excavate training materials specifically tailored for the students. Participant no. 2 is currently applying for a doctoral program while consolidating theoretical foundations for both student training and empirical interpreting studies. Although sometimes frustrated and even thwarted by the discrepancies in their threefold identity of teacher, practitioner, and researcher, these interpreting teachers, regardless of the so-called disadvantaged position of being employed by a private college in a third-tier city in Zhejiang province, are exercising their agency in making decisions, shouldering responsibilities, and pursuing career development.

Importantly, it should also be pointed out that the ideal role of interpreting faculty as teachers, practitioners, and researchers integrated into

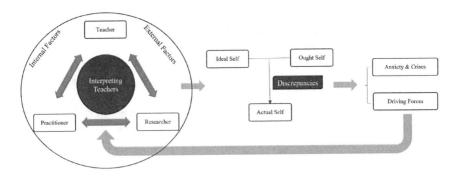

Figure 7.6 Discrepancies as both anxiety and crises and driving forces.

one may not be practical or even realistic for most of these teachers. As suggested by Kang and Shi (2020, 604), such identities as the PTR model are proposed as indicators of diversity among interpreting teachers, with some of them focusing more on teaching while others more on practice or research. The requirements of possessing skills in teaching, practice, and research simultaneously should be posed not on one single teacher but on the team of interpreting faculty as a whole. Regretfully, the preferential policies of most Chinese universities focus on academic achievements when promoting teachers, regardless of their backgrounds, which results in the discrepancy between interpreting teachers' ought self and actual self and constitutes a major part of their anxiety and crises. Therefore, it is suggested that university and college administrators should take into consideration the differentiated requirements for teachers with different orientations and encourage diversity instead of seeking uniformity among these teachers, just as what has been advocated in the diversified cultivation and development of our students.

7   Concluding remarks

Although an interpreting teacher is supposed in many studies to be a teacher (as stipulated by the profession), a practitioner (as required of professional training), and a researcher (as a prerequisite for career development in Chinese universities), this chapter, as corroborated by a few others, finds that such a threefold identity may be too ideal and even unrealistic for interpreting teachers of BTI programs, especially for the case of a private college in a third-tier city in Zhejiang province. A huge gap exists between what the teachers think they should do in professional development and career pursuit and what they actually do in terms of teaching, practice, and research. Qualitative data shows an interplay of internal factors and external factors in causing such a gap. The discrepancies among their ideal self, ought self, and actual self, as in the self-discrepancy theory, can be used to explain the causes of their anxiety and crises. Such discrepancies, if properly channeled, could also be regarded as driving forces for them to exercise agency and pursue career development. In addition, it should be pointed out that current preferential policies for recruiting and promoting teachers in many Chinese universities, which are mostly research-oriented, should be tailored for differentiated, diversified, and sustainable development of not only interpreting teachers but also those with similar dilemmas.

Due to its nature as a case study and the small size of the sample, the findings of this paper are relatively limited in terms of generalizability. Moreover, the complex interplay between internal factors and external factors is not properly addressed due to the scope of this paper. Nevertheless, it is hoped that the findings would possibly enlighten prospective BTI teachers in their career development and inform university administrators when recruiting and promoting these teachers.

Note

1 Top universities in China are unanimously public institutions and mostly located in more-developed areas, for example, first-tier cities, coastal cities, in contrast to private colleges (*min ban*), which can only attract average students or those who fail to be admitted to public universities.

References

Chai Mingjiong 柴明颎. 2017. "Renshi xianzhuang tisheng zhiliang kaituo qianxing – fanyi zhuanye de weilai fazhan" 认识现状 提升质量 开拓前行 – 翻译专业的未来发展 [Understanding the Status Quo, Upgrading Quality and Pioneering Forward – the Future Development of Translation Programmes]. *Dongfang fanyi* 东方翻译 [East Journal of Translation] 06: 4–8.

China National Committee for BTI Education 教育部高等学校翻译专业教学协作组. 2022. "Quanguo fanyi benke zhuanye peiyang yuanxiao minglu" 全国翻译本科专业培养院校名录 [Directory of BTI Institutions]. https://cnbti.gdufs.edu.cn/info/1006/1595.htm.

China National Committee for Translation and Interpreting Education 全国翻译专业学位研究生教育指导委员会. n.d. "Quanguo fanyi shuoshi peiyang yuanxiao minglu" 全国翻译硕士培养院校名录 [Directory of MTI Institutions]. Accessed November 22, 2021. https://cnti.gdufs.edu.cn/info/1017/1955.htm.

Gao, Xuesong (Andy), and Hao Xu. 2014. "The Dilemma of Being English Language Teachers: Interpreting Teachers' Motivation to Teach, and Professional Commitment in China's Hinterland Regions." *Language Teaching Research* 18(2): 152–68. https://doi.org/10.1177/1362168813505938.

Gile, Daniel. 1994. "Opening up in Interpretation Studies." In *Translation Studies: An Interdiscipline*, edited by Mary Snell-Hornby, Franz Pöchhacker, and Klaus Kaindl, 149–58. Amsterdam and Philadelphia: John Benjamins.

Higgins, E. Tory. 1987. "Self-Discrepancy: A Theory Relating Self and Affect." *Psychological Review* 94(3): 319–40. https://doi.org/10.1037/0033-295X.94.3.319.

Higgins, E. Tory. 1989. "Self-Discrepancy Theory: What Patterns of Self-Beliefs Cause People to Suffer?" In *Advances in Experimental Social Psychology*, edited by Leonard Berkowitz, 22: 93–136. Elsevier. https://doi.org/10.1016/S0065-2601(08)60306-8.

Hua Liang 花亮. 2016. "Fanyi zhuanye jiaoshi fazhan yanjiu: yixiang jiyu kouyi jiaoshi de diaocha" 翻译专业教师发展研究：一项基于口译教师的调查 [Research on the Professional Development of Teachers with Master of Translation: A Survey Based on Teachers of Interpretation]. *Jiaoyu lilun yu shijian* 教育理论与实践 [Theory and Practice of Education] 36(06): 37–9.

Kang, Zhifeng, and Ying Shi. 2020. "The Construction of a Practice-Teaching-Research (PTR) Model for the Accomplishments of College Interpreting Teachers in China." *Babel. Revue Internationale de La Traduction/International Journal of Translation* 66(4–5): 604–18. https://doi.org/10.1075/babel.00173.kan.

Liu Yi 刘熠. 2011. *Xushi shijiao xia de daxue gonggong yingyu jiaoshi zhiye rentong jiangou yanjiu* 叙事视角下的大学公共英语教师职业认同建构研究 [Professional Identity Construction of College English Teachers: A Narrative Perspective]. Beijing: Waiyu jiaoxue yu yanjiu chubanshe 外语教学与研究出版社 [Foreign Language Teaching and Research Press].

Liu Yi 刘熠, and Xu Hongchen 许宏晨. 2020. "Gaoxiao MTI jiaoshi de zhiye fazhan xianzhuang ji kunjing" 高校MTI教师的职业发展现状及困境 [A Study on Current Situation and Barriers of MTI Teachers' Professional Development]. *Waiyu jiaoxue lilun yu shijian* 外语教学理论与实践 [Foreign Language Learning Theory and Practice] 03: 29–35+9.

Lu Xinchao 卢信朝. 2016. "Zhongguo kouyi jiaoxue 4.0: Practeasearcher moshi" 中国口译教学 4.0: Practeasearcher 模式 [Interpreting Teaching 4.0 in China: Practeasearcher Model]. *Shanghai fanyi* 上海翻译 [Shanghai Journal of Translators] 04: 60–7+94.

Lü Bing 吕冰. 2018. "Jin ershi nian guoneiwai fanyi jiaoshi yanjiu zongshu" 近二十年国内外翻译教师研究综述 [A Literature Review on Translation Teacher Research at Home and Abroad in the Past Two Decades]. *Shanghai fanyi* 上海翻译 [Shanghai Journal of Translators] 02: 48–53.

Mu Lei 穆雷. 1999. "*Zhongguo fanyi jiaoxue yanjiu*" 中国翻译教学研究 [Translation Teaching in China]. Shanghai: Shanghai waiyu jiaoyu chubanshe 上海外语教育出版社 [Shanghai Foreign Language Education Press].

Orlando, Marc. 2019. "Training and Educating Interpreter and Translator Trainers as Practitioners-Researchers-Teachers." *The Interpreter and Translator Trainer* 13(3): 216–32. https://doi.org/10.1080/1750399X.2019.1656407.

Pöchhacker, Franz. 2016. *Introducing Interpreting Studies*. Second Edition. London and New York: Routledge.

Ren Wen 任文. 2009. "Fanyi jiaoxue de fazhan yu TOT jihua de shishi" 翻译教学的发展与 TOT 计划的实施 [Development of Professional Translation/ Interpreting Teaching and Implementation of the TOT Project]. *Zhongguo fanyi* 中国翻译 [China Translators Journal] 30(02): 48–52+95.

Ruan, Xiaolei, Xinmin Zheng, and Auli Toom. 2020. "From Perceived Discrepancies to Intentional Efforts: Understanding English Department Teachers' Agency in Classroom Instruction in a Changing Curricular Landscape." *Teaching and Teacher Education* 92 (June): 103074. https://doi.org/10.1016/j.tate.2020.103074.

Wang Yong 王永. 2014. "Zhongguo gaoxiao kouyi ke jiaoshi jiaoxue dongji shizheng yanjiu" 中国高校口译课教师教学动机实证研究 [An Empirical Study on Teaching Motivation of Teachers of Interpretation in Chinese Universities]. *Waiyu jiaoxue* 外语教学 [Foreign Language Education] 35(02): 108–12.

Xu, Mianjun, and Xiaoye You. 2021. "Translation Practice of Master of Translation and Interpreting (MTI) Teachers in China: An Interview-Based Study." *The Interpreter and Translator Trainer* 15(3): 343–59. https://doi.org/10.1080/1750399X.2021.1900711.

Zhang Ruie 张瑞娥. 2012. "Zhongguo fanyi shizi xianzhuang yu juese shixian" 中国翻译师资现状与角色实现 [Current Situation and Role Realization of Translation Teachers in China]. *Jiefangjun waiguoyu xueyuan xuebao* 解放军外国语学院学报 [Journal of PLA University of Foreign Languages] 35(04): 82–5.

Zhang Ruie 张瑞娥, and Chen Deyong 陈德用. 2012. "Zhongguo fanyi shizi jiben zhuangkuang bianhua fenxi" 中国翻译师资基本状况变化分析 [Analysis of Changes in the Basic Situation of Translation Teachers in China]. *Waiyu yanjiu* 外语研究 [Foreign Languages Research] 02: 67–71.

8 Investigating the differences between native and non-native English speakers in assessing Chinese-to-English interpretation

Xiaoqi Shang

1 Introduction

Exploring the differences between native English speakers (NES) and non-native English speakers (NNS) in assessing language performance has been a contested topic in the broader context of language education (e.g., Brown 1991; Chalhoub-Deville 1995; Fayer and Krasinski 1987; Sheorey 1986; Shi 2001). NES and NNS are found to exhibit markedly different patterns in assessing both written and spoken language performance (e.g., Galloway 1980; Gui 2012; Rao and Li 2017; Shi 2001; Zhang and Elder 2011). For instance, NNS were identified as more severe raters than NES toward "grammatical forms" (Galloway 1980) or "error gravity" (Rao and Li 2017), whereas NES tended to be more concerned about non-verbal delivery (Gui 2012) when assessing spoken language performance.

In contrast with the plethora of pertinent studies in language education, there is still a paucity of research exploring the differences between NES and NNS in assessing spoken language interpretation, with the exception of a few works (e.g., Su 2019; Author Year). Despite their efforts to identify the similarities and differences between NES and NNS in teaching and assessing interpretation, these few existing studies have fallen short of identifying the patterns by each rater group in attending to different criteria when assessing interpretation. Furthermore, despite the appeal of a few interpreting researchers such as Setton and Dawrant (2016) to include at least one (preferably two) NES in the panel for the candidate's B language (i.e., less-dominant language) when assessing spoken language interpretation, NES remains largely underrepresented in the current assessment practice due to various personal and institutional reasons, such as lack of candidates with the demanding credentials and qualifications (should have English as L1 and Chinese as L2 and be conference interpreters themselves) or funding constraints (ibid.). Yet considering that previous research in language education has demonstrated that NES and NNS differed significantly in their assessments, it would be thus meaningful to investigate whether NES and NNS attend to assessment criteria differently when assessing spoken language interpretation. The reasons for investigating this topic are twofold.

DOI: 10.4324/9781003357629-10

Firstly, investigation on the assessment of spoken language interpretation could offer new insights to the research on NES's and NNS's assessment differences in the broader context of language education. Unlike general spoken language performance, interpretation is a higher-order cognitive activity, requiring the interpreter to undertake a wider range of cognitive efforts, including memory, note-taking, production, and coordination (Gile 2009). In addition, the quality of interpretation is considered "essentially relative and multi-dimensional" (Pöchhacker 2004). The findings of the present chapter are therefore expected to further validate the research findings concerning the NES and NNS dichotomy in language assessment by providing more empirical evidence through a different lens.

Secondly, the study of NES and NNS differences in assessment could also be of practical significance. As the number of interpreter training institutions is rising exponentially across the world, particularly in China, where more than 300 schools are now offering the program of master of translation and interpretation (MTI) assessment of interpretation is playing an increasingly important role in pre-selection of interpreter candidates, midstreaming, and certification (Sawyer 2004). The investigation of the potential differences between NES and NNS when assessing interpretation could inform policymakers and interpreter trainers to optimize training practices by improving the reliability of assessment.

Against this background, this chapter adopts a data-driven approach to exploring the differences between NES and NNS raters (who were all conference interpreters) in their assessments of Chinese-to-English (C–E) spoken language interpretation, with a particular focus on weighting assignment among assessment criteria. It seeks to address the following two research questions (**RQ**):

RQ 1: Do NES and NNS raters exhibit different patterns in assigning weights among the criteria for assessing C–E interpretation?
RQ 2: What might be the underlying factors behind these divergent assessment patterns?

2   Literature review

2.1   *NES and NNS assessment in language education*

Studies comparing the differences between NES and NNS in their assessments have been primarily focused on performance-based tests, such as writing (e.g., Connor-Linton 1995; Sheorey 1986; Shi 2001) and speaking (e.g., Barnwell 1989; Fayer and Krasinski 1987; Galloway 1980; Kim 2009), which require examinees to "demonstrate their knowledge and skills by engaging in a process or constructing a product" (Roberts 2009). Previous research has yielded highly mixed findings. For example, with regard to assessing writing performance, a number of studies indicated that NNS were more severe raters than NES toward errors (e.g., Hughes and Lascaratou 1982), whereas other studies found the opposite to be true (e.g., Kobayashi 1992). Since this chapter mainly concentrates on comparing NES's and NNS's differences in assessing spoken language interpretation, I will primarily focus on an overview of studies pertaining to differences between NES and NNS when assessing spoken language performance in the following.

Differences between NES and NNS raters in assessing spoken language performance were largely examined by focusing on the impact of professional background (e.g., Chalhoub-Deville 1995; Hadden 1991), linguistic background (e.g., Brown 1995; Fayer and Krasinski 1987), or social and cultural background (e.g., Carless and Walker 2006; Dafouz and Hibler 2013; McConnell 2000).

As regards the impact of raters' professional background on assessment, previous studies have also produced ambiguous findings. For example, Hadden (1991) compared 25 ESL teachers' and 32 non-teachers' assessments of second-language communication and found that teachers were more severe than non-teachers when rating the linguistic elements of an oral performance. In contrast, Chalhoub-Deville (1995) compared three native Arabic-speaking rater groups with different professional background when assessing learners' L2 oral ability and found that teachers were more tolerant of linguistic features than non-teachers.

With respect to the influence of raters' language background on assessment, no significant differences were found among NES and NNS in terms of their overall quantitative scores, but noticeable disparities existed among the two rater groups when attending to individual criteria (e.g., Brown 1995; Kim 2009; Zhang and Elder 2011). For instance, Zhang and Elder's study (2011), comparing NES and NNS raters' differences in assessing China's national College English Test – Spoken English Test (CET-SET), found that the two rater groups drew on highly different constructs of oral proficiency despite their broadly similar holistic gradings. More specifically, NNS raters were found to be more "form focused," paying more attention to such criteria as accuracy and grammar, whereas their NES peers were more "communication focused," emphasizing strategies such as interaction and compensation in communication. In contrast, Gui's (2012) mixed-methods research, comparing three Chinese and three American EFL teachers in assessing learners' speech performance, indicated that in spite of their consensus on the holistic scoring of the examinees' spoken language performance, NES and NNS raters differed in their qualitative comments on criteria including pronunciation, usage of English expressions, and non-verbal delivery. It appeared that NES raters placed more emphasis on both the form and communication aspects of the spoken performance than do their NNS peers.

Differences in assessment were also ascribed to raters' social and cultural differences. For example, Dafouz and Hibler (2013), drawing on theories from systemic functional linguistics and discourse analysis, found qualitative differences between local Spanish teachers of English and their NES peers in their comments on students' spoken language performance. Findings suggested that NES teachers attached more importance to the social-pragmatic and interpersonal dimensions of the speech performance than do their NNS peers.

In sum, the existing literature on differences in NES's and NNS's assessments in language education has yielded highly inspiring yet controversial results, which could be due to different research methodologies, language specificity, and rater samples (Brown 1995).

2.2 NES and NNS assessment in interpretation

Compared with the previous abundant literature in language education, studies pertaining to the assessment differences between NES and NNS in the field of interpreting studies remain rather scant, with the exception of works by a highly limited number of interpreting scholars (e.g., Su 2019; Su and Shang 2020). The study by Su (2019), exploring three NES's and three NNS's assessments of spoken language interpretation, found discrepant assessment behavior between the two rater groups. Results indicated that NNS teachers employed more "notating" (i.e., note-writing on the source sentence to indicate the nature of the translation problem), while NES teachers preferred "post hoc marking" (i.e., adding underlines or notations to preceding sentences to complement earlier judgments), among the four major marking patterns the author had identified. Drawing on the initiation-response-follow-up-talk analysis, a recent endeavor was made by Su and Shang (2020), who compared the assessments of one NES teacher and one native Chinese-speaking teacher (NNS) in a co-taught interpretation class at the graduate level. The study identified a complementary pattern between the NES and NNS teachers, where NNS tended to diagnose students' translation pitfalls whereas NES tended to monitor students' English use.

Overall, these studies have pointed out some similarities and dissimilarities between NES and NNS in teaching and assessing interpretation. Nevertheless, they have fallen short of identifying the patterns by each group in attending to different criteria when assessing interpretation. Furthermore, though the NES raters recruited in these studies had English as their L1 and some experience of co-teaching interpretation-related courses, they had not trained in conference interpreting. The present study fills this gap by recruiting NES raters who were not only native English speakers but also practicing conference interpreters and comparing how they differ in attending to different criteria with their NNS peers when assessing interpretation.

In the following section, a brief overview of the literature on quality criteria and weighting for assessing spoken language interpretation will be presented.

2.3 Quality criteria and weighting schemes for assessing interpretation

Quality assessment has been a central concern in all domains of interpretation (Pöchhacker 2001). The perception of quality hinges to a large extent on the viewpoint of each participant in communication, including the speakers, clients, colleagues, and the interpreter (Gile 2009).

Over the years, interpreting scholars have sought to look into the quality components of interpretation using a wide range of approaches, such as conceptual analysis (e.g., Pöchhacker 2001; Roberts 2000; Schjoldager 1995; Setton and Dawrant 2016; Skaaden 2013), experimental studies (e.g., Choi 2013; Clifford 2005; J. Lee 2008; S-B. Lee 2015; Wu 2013), and questionnaire surveys (e.g., Bühler 1986; Kurz 1993; Gile 1991). The number of assessment criteria varies significantly due to different interpreting modes and domains, research methodologies, as well as other "environmental variables" and "socially constituted norms" (Collados and Becerra 2015). However, there is a general consensus among researchers on a set of criteria that remains central to the assessment of quality independent of various contexts, namely, fidelity, target language quality (hereinafter referred to as "language"), and delivery (see the *Rating Criteria* section for definitions).

Relative to the abundant literature on assessment criteria for interpretation, there is a dearth of research on exploring the proper weights that should be assigned to different criteria when assessing interpretation. Research methodologies primarily include theoretical explorations (e.g., Choi 2013; J. Lee 2008; Roberts 2000; Setton and Dawrant 2016; Skaaden 2013), experimental studies (e.g., S-B Lee 2015; Wu 2013), and questionnaire-based surveys (e.g., Bühler 1986; Kurz 2001; Pöchhacker 2012).

As regards theoretical exploration, for instance, Setton and Dawrant (2016) argued that fidelity should be always regarded as the primary factor for assessing interpretation, provided that the overall expression and delivery are acceptable, regardless of interpreting direction. Similarly, in exploring the impact of text length on English-to-Korean consecutive interpretation, Choi (2013) conceptually assigned 10 (50%) to accuracy (fidelity), followed by 6 (30%) for expression (language), and 4 (20%) for presentation (delivery), out of a total weight value of 20.

Other scholars have sought to address the issue of weighting based on empirical interpretation of assessment data. The empirical study by Wu (2013) identified five categories of assessment criteria by raters, including fidelity and completeness (FC), audience point of view (APV), interpreting skills and strategies (ISS), presentation and delivery (PD), and foundation abilities for interpreting (FAI). FC (i.e., fidelity) and PD (i.e., delivery) were found to account for 86% of 300 decisions made, indicating their predominant weighting among the five assessment criteria. S-B Lee (2015) analyzed two interpreter trainers' assessments of 33 English-to-Korean consecutive interpretations by undergraduate students and found that the criterion of content (fidelity) was assigned 50% of the total weight, whereas form (language) and delivery were assigned 25% of the total weight, respectively.

Questionnaire-based surveys were also used to elucidate user expectations on interpretation quality. Bühler (1986), for example, asked 47 AIIC interpreters to rate the relative importance of 15 linguistic and extra-linguistic criteria and found that sense consistency was rated as the most important criterion, followed by terminology, fluency, and completeness, whereas accent was deemed as the least important criterion. Similarly, Pöchhacker (2012) elicited opinions from 704 AIIC interpreters on the importance of the assessment criteria for interpretation and found that sense consistency, logical cohesion, and delivery ranked as the top three criteria, respectively.

A few gaps can be identified from the previous research pertaining to weight assignment among the criteria for assessing spoken language interpretation. Firstly, despite the differences in the specific ratio of weighting assigned to the assessment criteria, research findings have suggested a general consensus where content-related criteria were regarded as the predominant property and thus given the heaviest weight among all assessment criteria. Nevertheless, insufficient scholarly attention has been paid to exploring the potentially essential roles of other criteria, such as language and delivery. Divergent views still exist among interpreting scholars with regard to their weighting in assessment. Secondly, most of the previous research on weighting for assessing spoken language interpretation has merely focused on interpreting from English, where raters were largely non-native speakers of English (e.g., J. Lee 2008; S-B. Lee 2015; Wu 2013). Interpreting into English has barely been touched upon, and NES raters have been insufficiently examined. Thirdly, rater training was not specified in most of the research, with only a few exceptions, such as the studies by J. Lee (2008) and Han (2015; 2018). As rater variability is a big source of construct-irrelevant variance, rater training should be provided to improve rating reliability (Lumley and McNamara 1995; Weigle 2002).

Against this background, this study seeks to empirically investigate how weights are assigned by both NES and NNS rater groups when assessing Chinese-to-English interpretation. In the following, the research design, results, and discussion of the current study will be presented in turn. Implications of the findings of this study for interpreting assessment, interpreter training, and assessment in language education at large will be discussed at the end of the paper.

3   Methods

3.1   Examinees and rater participants

A total of 50 first-year interpreter trainees enrolled in the master program of translation and interpreting (MTI) at four Chinese universities participated in the C–E interpreting test; 43 of them were female, and 7 were male, aged between 23 and 25. All participants had Chinese as their L1 and English as their L2. Prior to this study, they had all trained in consecutive interpreting for almost a year, capable of interpreting speeches on a wide range of domains using acquired interpreting skills.

Eight raters with Chinese as their L1 and English as their L2 and two raters who had English as their L1 and Chinese as their L2 were recruited to evaluate a total of 50 C–E audio recordings of interpretation by trainee interpreters. The eight Chinese raters were all practicing conference interpreters. Three of them were male, and five were female, aged between 28 and 36. They all had more than four years of interpreting experience and prior experience of evaluating interpreting performance on multiple occasions. The two native English speakers were also practicing conference interpreters. One was male, aged 34, and the other female, aged 30. Both had more than six years of interpreting experience and prior experience of assessing interpreting performance.

3.2   *Material*

The material for the C–E interpretation test was a five-minute Chinese speech. The topic of the speech was China's efforts on tobacco control. It was a live video pre-recorded by a Chinese native speaker who was a conference interpreter himself. The speech was well structured and delivered at the rate of approximately 170 words per minute.

3.3   *Procedures*

The interpreting test was held at the language labs of the participants' respective universities. Participants were required to interpret the Chinese speech in three separate segments on a consecutive mode. Prior to the tests, the participants were provided with relevant topical knowledge and a glossary pertinent to the speech 15 minutes in advance to help them prepare for the interpretation. During the tests, participants were required to interpret the speech into the target language on the consecutive mode. Note-taking was allowed during the test. After the tests, their interpretations were audio-recorded, and each was assigned a unique code for subsequent data analysis.

3.4   *Data collection*

3.4.1   *Rating criteria*

Each interpreting performance in this study was evaluated based on the three criteria of fidelity, target language quality (language), and fluency of delivery (delivery) using both an analytic rating scale and a holistic rating scale, drawing inspirations from the evaluation rubrics designed in previous studies (J. Lee 2008; S-B Lee 2015; Schjoldager 1995; Setton and Dawrant 2016). *Fidelity* in the present study refers to the full, faithful, and accurate rendering of all the message elements in the source speech without unjustified additions, changes, or omissions. *Language* concerns target language quality, which mainly concerns a strong command of the target language, including terminology, word choice, register, style, and appropriateness. *Delivery* focuses on comprehensibility and communicability of the output, such as liveliness and expressiveness, being free from backtracking, fillers, and pauses.

For each recording, raters were required to assign a numerical score to each of the three criteria using a ten-point analytic rating scale and to the overall performance using a ten-point holistic rating scale (see Appendices 1–2: 'Band descriptions' and 'Sample marking sheet'). In addition, raters were also required to comment on the strengths and weaknesses of each candidate's performance so as to elicit more qualitative data for triangulation of the research findings.

3.4.2   Rater training

It has been widely recognized that rater training is necessary to enhance the reliability and validity of scoring in language performance tests (Fulcher 2007). Rater training was thus carried out separately among the two rater groups prior to formal rating for the present study, with a view to improving inter-rater and intra-rater reliability (IRR).

Each rater group was asked to evaluate a total of ten C–E interpretations based on the three assessment criteria of fidelity, language, and delivery, using both an analytic and a holistic rating scales. They all underwent a rigorous rater training session, ranging from an orientation and overview, familiarization with scoring rubrics, reviewing benchmark performances, and anchoring (Johnson et al. 2009; Setton and Dawrant 2016).

3.4.3   Retrospective interview

After the formal ratings, semistructured retrospective interviews were conducted with the two NES and eight NNS raters individually to look into their decision-making process during interpreting assessment for data triangulation (see Appendix 3: 'Interview questions').

3.5   Data analysis

During the rater training session, the many-facet Rasch measurement (MFRM), using facets (3.57.0) (Linacre 2005), was applied to investigate their severity/leniency level (as measured by logits) and internal consistency (as measured by infits). Inter-rater reliability was also measured by Cronbach alpha, using SPSS 22.

After all formal ratings had been received, Pearson's correlation analysis using SPSS 22 was conducted to investigate the intercorrelations between the scores of the three assessment criteria and the overall interpretation scores. Subsequently, based on the correlation coefficients, multiple linear regression analysis, using the default "enter" method, was conducted to examine to what extent each of the three assessment criteria could predict the candidate's interpreting performance.

All the interview data with the raters were transcribed manually by both the author and an independent researcher based on the audio recordings. Transcripts were also double-checked with the two rater groups so as to ensure the accuracy and consistency of these data.

Table 8.1 Pilot Rating for the C–E Interpretation (NNS): Rater Report

	Severity (Logits)	Error	Infit (Mean Square)
Rater 1	0.38	0.19	1.04
Rater 2	−0.30	0.20	0.82
Rater 3	−0.30	0.20	1.06
Rater 4	0.38	0.19	0.96
Rater 5	−.67	0.20	0.77
Rater 6	0.98	0.19	0.56
Rater 7	0.67	0.19	0.71
Rater 8	−1.13	0.21	1.98

Notes: Reliability of separation index = .91; fixed (all same) chi-square: 91.7; df: 7; significance: $p = 0.00$.

Table 8.2 Inter-Rater Reliability for the C–E Interpretation (NNS)

Assessment Criteria	Fidelity	Language	Delivery	Holistic
Cronbach's alpha	0.90	0.94	0.95	0.92

4 Results

4.1 Reliability for pilot rating by NNS raters

According to MFRM analysis, a logit value between -1 and +1 indicates an acceptable severity/leniency level, and an infit value of 0.6–1.4 means acceptable internal consistency (Linacre 2005). Results show that all NNS raters except rater 8 exhibited acceptable leniency and severity and self-consistency (logits: -1 to +0.92; infits: 0.81–0.91). Rater 8 was found to be overly lenient compared to others and was retrained accordingly later.

As seen in Table 8.2, with respect to C–E interpretation, Cronbach's alphas for the analytic scoring with regard to the criteria of fidelity, language, delivery, and the holistic scoring were 0.90, 0.94, 0.95, and 0.92, respectively. As an inter-rater reliability of 0.7 and over is generally regarded as acceptable (Shohamy 1985), it could be said that there was a high level of inter-rater reliability among the eight raters in this study in evaluating C–E interpretation.

4.2 Reliability for pilot rating by NES raters

As seen in Table 8.3, the two raters both fall within the range of logits -1 to +1, indicating that there was an acceptable inter-rater variability among them. The infits for rater 1 and rater 2 were 0.90 and 0.84, respectively, indicating that each individual rater displayed a sufficient degree of self-consistency.

As seen in Table 8.4, Cronbach's alphas for the analytic ratings (i.e., fidelity, language, and delivery) were 0.75, 0.67, and 0.75, and that for the holistic ratings was 0.81. It can be claimed that the inter-rater reliability in the

Table 8.3 Pilot Rating for C–E Interpreting (NES): Rater Report

	Severity (Logits)	Error	Infit (Mean Square)
Rater 1	0.20	0.13	0.90
Rater 2	0.13	0.13	0.84
Mean	0.00	0.13	0.87
SD	0.23	0.00	0.13

Notes: Reliability of separation index = 1. 87; fixed (all same) chi-square: 8.7; df: 2; significance: p = 0.01.

Table 8.4 Inter-Rater Reliability for the C–E Interpreting (NES)

Assessment Criteria	Fidelity	Language	Delivery	Holistic
Cronbach's alpha	0.75	0.67	0.75	0.81

present study was acceptable on the whole except on the criterion of language (Cronbach's alpha: 0.67). Raters' retraining, particularly on assessing the criterion of language use, was conducted accordingly.

After obtaining the formal ratings, Pearson's correlation analysis was performed to examine the intercorrelations between the analytic scores and the holistic scores by each rater group. And multiple linear regression analysis, using the default "enter" method, was conducted to examine to what extent each of the three assessment criteria could predict the candidate's interpreting performance.

4.3   NNS rater group

4.3.1   Correlation analysis

As is seen in Table 8.5 that follows, with regard to Chinese–English interpretation, the correlation coefficients between the scores of fidelity, language, delivery, and the holistic score were r_1 = .940, r_2 = .964, and r_3 = .957, respectively. As a correlation coefficient of above 0.7 indicates significant correlation between variables (Xu 2013, 64), it can be claimed that the scores of all the three assessment criteria were significantly correlated with the holistic score.

4.3.2   Linear regression analysis

As can be seen in Table 8.6, the three assessment criteria as a whole could explain 97.2% of the variance in the holistic score in Chinese–English interpreting (adjusted R^2 = .972). More specifically, fidelity, language, and delivery contributed to 35.1% (β_1 = .351), 32.5% (β_2 = .325), and 34.5% (β_3 = .345) of the variance of the holistic score, respectively (p < .05).

Table 8.5 Descriptive Statistics and Correlation Matrix for Ratings by NNS (C–E) (n = 50)

Variables		Descriptive Statistics		Correlation Matrix		
		M	SD	1	2	3
	Holistic	6.482	1.141	.940	.964	.957
	1. Fidelity	6.759	.942	–	.891	.867
	2. Language	6.463	1.106		–	.943
	3. Delivery	6.318	1.170			–

* $p < .05$.

Table 8.6 Summary of Linear Regression Statistics for Ratings by NNS (C–E) (n = 50)

Variable		R	R^2	Adjusted R^2	F	Beta	t	Sig.	Tolerance	VIF
Dependent variable	Holistic score	.987[a]	.974	.972	562.577		–3.376	.002		
Independent	1. Fidelity					.351	6.528	.000	.199	5.013
	2. Language					.325	4.032	.000	.089	11.273
	3. Delivery					.345	4.704	.000	.107	9.340

* $p < .05$.

4.4   NES rater group

4.4.1   Correlation analysis

Table 8.7 shows that the correlation coefficients between the scores of fidelity, language, and delivery and the holistic score were $r_1 = .914$, $r_2 = .932$, and $r_3 = .927$, respectively, suggesting that the scores of all the three assessment criteria were significantly correlated with the holistic score.

4.4.2   Linear regression analysis

As can be seen in Table 8.8, the three assessment criteria as a whole could explain 95.9% of the variance in the holistic score in Chinese–English interpretation (adjusted $R^2 = .959$). More specifically, fidelity, language, and delivery contributed to 30.0% ($\beta_1 = .300$), 39.6% ($\beta_2 = .396$), and 34.3% ($\beta_3 = .343$) of the variance of the holistic score, respectively ($p < .05$).

5   Discussion

As can be seen in the results section, the scores for fidelity, language, and delivery were all significantly correlated with the overall interpreting scores for both the NES and the NNS rater groups. As regards the predictive powers of specific

Table 8.7 Descriptive Statistics and Correlation Matrix for Ratings by NES (C–E) (n = 50)

Variables		Descriptive Statistics		Correlation Matrix		
		M	SD	1	2	3
	Holistic	5.745	1.545	.914	.932	.927
1. Fidelity		6.418	1.276	–	.826	.835
2. Language		5.694	1.384		–	.841
3. Delivery		5.174	1.694			–

* $p < .05$.

Table 8.8 Summary of Linear Regression Statistics for Ratings by NES (C–E) (n = 50)

Variable		R	R^2	Adjusted R^2	F	Beta	T	Sig.	Tolerance	VIF
Dependent variable	Holistic score	.981ª	.961	.959	373.712		-2.833	.004		
Independent variable	Fidelity					.300	5.120	.000	.250	4.002
	Language					.396	6.660	.000	.242	4.124
	Delivery					.343	5.623	.000	.231	4.333

* $p < .05$.

assessment criteria to the interpretation performance, a number of trends can be identified: (1) For NNS, fidelity was assigned the heaviest weight ($\beta_1 = 0.351$) among all assessment criteria, whereas it was accorded the smallest weight by NES ($\beta_1 = 0.300$). (2) Delivery was ranked at second in terms of weighting by both NNS ($\beta_3 = 0.345$) and NES ($\beta_3 = 0.343$) rater groups. (3) Language was given top priority among all assessment criteria by NES raters ($\beta_2 = 0.396$), while it was considered the least important by NNS raters ($\beta_3 = 0.325$).

5.1 Fidelity

The fact that NNS assigned the heaviest weight to fidelity when assessing C–E interpretation is consistent with the long-held view of interpreting researchers that fidelity constitutes the predominant property of interpretation (e.g., Gile 2009; Hale 2007; Jones 1998; Kurz 2001; J. Lee 2008; S-B. Lee 2015; Setton and Dawrant 2016). Interpretation should aim to maintain the correspondence between the source text and the target text and present a "faithful image" of the original (Gile 1991, 198) and be an "exact and faithful reproduction" (Jones 1998, 5). Similarly, the empirical study by S-B

Lee (2015) found that raters assigned 50% of the total weight to fidelity and 25% of the weight to language and delivery, respectively, when assessing student interpreters' English-to-Korean interpretations. The importance of fidelity for assessing interpretation was also echoed by the eight NNS raters who participated in the present study, with the illustrative remarks from two of them as follows:

Interview excerpt by NNS rater 2:

Fidelity comes on the top when it comes to weight distribution regardless of the number of criteria. Personally, how I would go about evaluating interpretation performance is that I'll first check if the intended message of the original speaker is conveyed before touching upon other aspects of the assessment.

Interview excerpt by NNS rater 5:

I regard content as the most important assessment criterion for interpretation, followed by delivery. For instance, if candidate A performs very well on delivery but averagely on content and candidate B performs averagely on delivery but excels in content, I'll not hesitate to choose the latter.

Notwithstanding the crucial importance of fidelity in assessing C–E interpretation deemed by all NNS raters, NES raters, nevertheless, seemed to have divergent views, as evidenced in the statistical analysis of the present study (see Table 8.8). As the data suggest, fidelity was assigned the least weight among the three criteria by NES when assessing C–E interpreting, though it remained a powerful predictor ($\beta_1 = 0.300$). This discrepancy may be explained by the differences between NES and NNS in defining and assessing fidelity due to their different linguistic and sociocultural competence. Traditionally, fidelity primarily refers to the accuracy and completeness of the interpreter's utterance (Gile 2009). While assessing interpretation in the present study, the NNS raters may have concentrated on the correspondence between the elements of the source and target texts more at the semantic and syntactic levels due to their linguistic and sociocultural constraints. Conversely, NES raters may have focused more on whether the interpreter has conveyed the intent of a communication through the use of "linguistic and paralinguistic choices made for their impact in a particular context and situation" (Setton 2015, 162), thus assigning more weight to the criteria of language and delivery while giving less weight to fidelity in their assessment.

5.2   *Delivery*

With regard to delivery, there was a consensus among both NES and NNS raters that it should take the second place in terms of its weight contribution to the overall interpreting performance. For NNS raters, delivery was given 34.5% ($\beta_2 = 0.345$) of the total weight, comparable to fidelity, which was assigned 35.9% ($\beta_1 = 0.359$). Similarly, NES raters assigned 34.3% ($\beta_2 = 0.343$) of the total weight to delivery, making it the second most important assessment criterion after language.

The essential role of delivery in assessment has long been recognized in a large number of studies in language education. Goffman (1981) argued that avoiding "linguistically detectable faults" can "keep the curtain drawn on any production problems backstage." In a similar vein, Brennan and Williams (1995) contended that sometimes *how* speakers say something may be as critical as *what* they actually say. Furthermore, fluency has been regarded as one of the central criteria since the early days of second language speaking assessment and has recurred in the scoring rubrics of various standardized tests, such as TOEFL iBT and IELTS.

The finding about the essential role of delivery for assessing interpretation is in line with those reported in previous interpretation literature (e.g., Bühler 1986; Gile 2009; Pöchhacker 2012; Wu 2013). Gile (2009), for example, argued that while "accurate rendition" remains essential for assessing interpretation quality, trainee interpreters should also be made aware of the weight of the "packaging" of their utterance, as an assertive delivery usually exerts a "confidence-inspiring effect." Furthermore, the importance of delivery has been highly valued by different end users in a number of survey-based studies in interpretation literature (e.g., Bühler 1986; Pöchhacker 2012). In a survey with conference interpreters, Bühler (1986) found that fluency was ranked at the third place among all the assessment criteria for interpretation, only after content-related criteria, including sense consistency and terminology. Similarly, Pöchhacker (2012) also found that fluency was rated as the third most important criterion after sense consistency and logical cohesion by AIIC (International Association for Conference Interpreters) interpreters.

The importance of delivery for assessing interpreting was also echoed by most of the NES and NNS raters. Following are two illustrative remarks from two of the raters:

Interview excerpt by NNS rater 3:

I prefer to evaluate interpreting performance from the perspective of listeners. You usually feel comfortable when you hear an interpretation which is quite comprehensible and has a good flow; therefore, you would want to trust the interpreter. On the contrary, you tend not to trust the interpreter if he or she renders hesitant, choppy utterances in spite of his or her good performance on other criteria.

Interview excerpt by NES rater 2:

Most of the time, the audience tend to judge the quality of an interpreting performance based on the overall fluency of the utterance. Fluency of delivery usually makes the interpretation sound trustworthy.

5.3   *Language*

Though coinciding with the finding of Gui's (2012) study, where NES attended more to "form and communication," the finding about the differences of weighting regarding the criterion of language between NES and NNS raters is at odds with the findings reported in most of the studies in the broader context of language education. As stated previously in the literature review section, compared with NES raters, NNS raters tend to focus more on "grammatical form" (Galloway 1980), "linguistic form" (Fayer and Krasinski 1987), or "rule infringement" (Hyland and Anan 2006) when assessing spoken language output. Nevertheless, the results of the present study suggested that NES accorded the heaviest weight (β_2 = .396) to the criterion of language among the three criteria for assessing spoken language interpretation, whereas NNS assigned the least weight (β_2 = .325) to language. This discrepancy might further foreground the differences between interpretation and general spoken language performance and thus necessitate the need to bridge the disconnect between scholars in interpreting studies and language education experts.

The finding about language being given the largest weight by NES raters also conflicts with the argument made by Setton and Dawrant (2016) that fidelity should be the primary factor for assessing interpretation, provided that the overall expression and delivery are acceptable, irrespective of language direction. One possible explanation for the discrepancies between these findings could be due to the influence of directionality. The main challenge for interpreters when interpreting from L1 to L2 lies in production, and the main challenge for them when interpreting from L2 to L1 lies in comprehension (Setton and Dawrant 2016). In the course of interpreting from L1 to L2, the interpreter had a "comprehension bonus" but experienced a "production deficit" (ibid). Therefore, the interpreter's performance on language while performing C–E interpretation might have helped raters more to distinguish better interpreters from poorer ones. Accordingly, raters might have assigned more weight to the criterion of language than to other criteria.

The primary importance of language among the three assessment criteria was also supported by the two NES raters who made the following remarks in the retrospective interview:

Interview excerpt by NES rater 1:

I think they should be weighed differently. I'd put them in this order: Language > fidelity > delivery. Although in two distinctive cases, I remember that one student had great fidelity but not so great delivery, which made his/her overall score lower than it could be, and another student who had wonderful delivery also had glaring meaning errors, so his overall score suffered.

Interview excerpt by NES rater 2:

I mostly agree with the findings – when interpreting into their L2, those who demonstrated excellent language control were more often than not better interpreters than their peers who struggled with grammar, pronunciation, etc.

6   Conclusions and implications

This study adopted an evidence-based and data-driven approach to exploring the weighting schemes for assessing C–E interpretation by recruiting eight NNS and two NES raters to evaluate a total of 50 interpretations by student interpreters. Research findings suggested that NES and NNS rater groups adopted highly divergent weighting schemes when assessing C–E interpretation. More specifically, NNS raters assigned the heaviest weight to fidelity (β_1 = .351), followed by delivery (β_3 = .345) and language (β_2 = .325), whereas NES gave the most value to language (β_2 = .396), followed by delivery (β_3 = .343) and fidelity (β_1 = .300). Though remaining tentative, these findings could be of theoretical and practical significance.

Theoretically, the discrepant findings with respect to the weightings of assessment criteria for interpretation and general spoken language education testify the need for the dialogue between scholars in these two fields, which has been consistently voiced by a number of interpreting scholars (e.g., Sawyer 2004; Setton and Dawrant 2016). The current practice in interpreting testing is still characterized by a lack of consistent and systematic standards ranging from test development, administration, to assessment (Liu, 2015; Setton and Dawrant 2016). Yet despite the many advances in language testing and measurement, there has not been any movement by interpreting scholars toward seeking expertise from language testing and assessment specialists. Meanwhile, given that interpretation is a "complex cognitive, linguistic, cultural and social process" (Grbić 2015), scholars in language testing should also conduct research in interpretation so as to inform their assessment theory and practice through a different lens. The wider field of measurement represents a solid source of knowledge interpreting scholars can draw on to improve their assessment practice.

Pedagogically, it is worth noting that despite the intriguing findings of this study regarding the fidelity and language weight comparison, interpreter training cannot afford to underestimate the role of fidelity. This factor should still be deemed as one of the essential quality assessment criteria for interpretation, as agreed by all the eight NNS raters and also demonstrated by its comparable though lower weighting (β_1 = 0.300) derived from the ratings by NES raters. Any embellishment or distortion of the message of the original in pursuit of flowery language should therefore, by no means, be encouraged in the course of interpreting.

Furthermore, as indicated in this study through both quantitative and qualitative data and supported by a number of previous studies, delivery should be given its due attention in interpreter training. As disfluency in the interpreter's delivery tends to strain comprehension and affect listeners' overall assessment of the quality of interpreting, interpreter trainees should be trained to optimize the "packaging" effect of the interpreting output. This emphasis on the dimension of "listener orientation" or "target text comprehensibility" (Pöchhacker 2001) should run through the process of interpreter training.

162   *Xiaoqi Shang*

However, this study is not without limitations. On one hand, due to the Chinese-to-English language specificity, the findings of this study should not be overgeneralized to other linguistic and cultural contexts. On the other hand, given the high demanding credentials and qualifications required of NES raters in this study (should be both professional interpreters and with English as their L1 and Chinese as their L2), the rather-small sample size of the NES raters might render the research exploratory and its findings tentative. Future studies could employ a larger sample of NES raters so as to further validate the findings of the present study.

In sum, considering the differences in their assessment behavior, a combination of NES and NNS raters in the panel is suggested so as to make more informed decisions for quality assessment for interpretation. Further communication between scholars in interpreting studies and language education needs to be facilitated so as to optimize the assessment and training practices of spoken language interpretation and illuminate the research in the field of language education.

References

Barnwell, David. 1989. "Naive Native Speakers and Judgements of Oral Proficiency in Spanish." *Language Testing* 6(2): 152–163. https://doi.org/10.1177/026553228900600203.

Brennan, Susan, and Maurice Williams. 1995. "The Feeling of Another's Knowing: Prosody and Filled Pauses as Cues to Listeners about the Metacognitive States of Speakers." *Journal of Memory & Language* 34(3): 383–98.

Brown, Anne. 1995. "The Effect of Rater Variables in the Development of an Occupation-Specific Language Performance Test." *Language Testing* 12(1): 1–15. https://doi.org/10.1177/0265532295.

Brown, James. 1991. "Do English and ESL Faculties Rate Writing Samples Differently?." *TESOL Quarterly* 25(4): 587–603. https://doi.org/10.2307/3587078.

Bühler, Hildegund. 1986. "Linguistic (Semantic) and Extralinguistic (Pragmatic) Criteria for the Evaluation of Conference Interpretation and Interpreters." *Multilingua* 5(4): 231–35.

Carless, David, and Elizabeth Walker. 2006. "Effective Team Teaching between Local and Native-Speaking English Teachers." *Language and Education* 20(6): 463–77. https://doi.org/10.2167/le627.0.

Chalhoub-Deville, Michel. 1995. "Deriving Oral Assessment Scales Across Different Tests and Rater Groups." *Language Testing* 12(1): 16–33. https://doi.org/0.1177/026553229501200102.

Choi, Jungyoon. 2013. "Assessing the Impact of Text Length on Consecutive Interpreting." In *Assessment Issues in Language Translation and Interpreting*, edited by Dina Tsagari and Roelof van Deemter, 85–96. Frankfurt am Main: Peter Lang.

Clifford, Andrew. 2005. "Putting the Exam to the Test: Psychometric Validation and Interpreter Certification." *Interpreting* 7(1): 97–131. https://doi.org/ doi:10.1075/intp.7.1.06cli.

Collados, Angela, and Olalla Garcia Becerra. 2015. "Quality Criteria." In *Routledge Encyclopedia of Interpreting Studies*, edited by Franz Pöchhacker, 337–8. London: Routledge.

Connor-Linton, Jeff. 1995. "Cross-Cultural Comparison of Writing Standards: American ESL and Japanese EFL." *World Englishes*, 14(1): 99–115. https://doi.org/10.1111/j.1467–971x.1995.tb00343.x.

Dafouz, Emma, and Abbie Hibler. 2013. "Zip Your Lips" or "Keep Quiet": Main Teachers' and Language Assistants' Classroom Discourse in CLIL Settings." *Modern Language Journal* 97(3): 655–69. https://doi.org/10.1111/j.1540-4781.2013.12026.x.

Fayer, Joan, and Emily Krasinski. 1987. "Native and Non-Native Judgments of Intelligibility and Irritation." *Language Learning*, 37(3): 313–27. https://doi.org/10.1111/j.1467-1770.1987.

Fulcher, Glenn, and Fred Davidson. 2007. *Language Testing and Assessment: An Advanced Resource Book*. London and New York: Routledge.

Galloway, Vicki. 1980. "Perceptions of the Communicative Efforts of American Students of Spanish." *Modern Language Journal*, 64(4): 428–33. https://doi.org/10.2307/325864.

Gile, Daniel. 1991. "A Communication-Oriented Analysis of Quality in Nonliterary Translation and Interpretation." In *Translation: Theory and Practice*, edited by Mildred Larson, 188–200. Binghamton NY: SUNY.

Gile, Daniel. 2009. *Basic Concepts and Models for Interpreter and Translator Training*. Revised Edition. Amsterdam: John Benjamins.

Goffman, Erving. 1981. *Forms of Talk*. Philadelphia: University of Pennsylvania Press.

Grbić, Nadja. 2015. "Quality." In *Routledge Encyclopedia of Interpreting Studies*, edited by Franz Pöchhacker, 333–6. London: Routledge.

Gui, Min. 2012. "Exploring Differences between Chinese and American EFL Teachers' Evaluation of Speech Performance." *Language Assessment Quarterly* 9(2): 186–203. https://doi.org/ 10.1080/15434303.2011.614030.

Hadden, Betsy. 1991. "Teacher and Nonteacher Perceptions of Second-Language Communication." *Language Learning* 41(1): 1–24. https://doi.org/10.1111/j.1467-1770.1991.tb00674.x.

Hale, Sandra. 2007. *Community Interpreting*. Basingstoke: Palgrave Macmillan.

Han, Chao. 2015. "Investigating Rater Severity/Leniency in Interpreter Performance Testing: A Multifaceted Rasch Measurement Approach." *Interpreting* 17(2): 255–83. https://doi.org/ 10.1075/intp.17.2.05han.

Han, Chao. 2018. "Using Rating Scales to Assess Interpretation: Practices, Problems and Prospects." *Interpreting* 20(1): 59–93. https://doi.org/10.1075/intp.00003.han.

Hughes, Arthur, and Chryssoula Lascaratou. 1982. "Competing Criteria for Error Gravity." *ELT Journal* 36(3): 175–182. https://doi.org/10.1093/elt/36.3.175.

Hyland, Ken, and Eri Anan. 2006. "Teachers' Perceptions of Error: The Effects of First Language and Experience." *System* 34(4): 509–19. https://doi.org/10.1016/j.system.2006.09.001.

Jones, Roderick. 1998. *Conference Interpreting Explained*. Manchester: St. Jerome Publishing.

Johnson, Robert, James Penny, and Belita Gordon. 2009. *Assessing Performance: Designing, Scoring and Validating Performance Tasks*. New York: The Guilford Press.

Kim, Youn-Hee. 2009. "An Investigation into Native and Non-Native Teachers' Judgments of Oral English Performance: A Mixed Methods Approach." *Language Testing* 26(2): 187–217. https://doi.org/10.1177/0265532208101010.

Kobayashi, Toshihiko. 1992. "Native and Non-Native Reactions to ESL Compositions." *TESOL Quarterly* 26(1): 81–112. https://doi.org/10.2307/3587370.

Kurz, Ingrid. 1993. "Conference Interpretation: Expectations of Different User Groups." *The Interpreters' Newsletter* (5): 13–21.

Kurz, Ingrid. 2001. "Conference Interpreting: Quality in the Ears of the User." *Meta* 46(2): 394–409. https://doi.org/10.7202/003364ar.

Lee, Jieun. 2008. "Rating Scales for Interpreting Performance Assessment." *The Interpreter and Translator Trainer* 2(2): 165–84. https://doi.org/10.1080/1750399X.2008.10798772.

Lee, Sang-Bin. 2015. "Developing an Analytic Scale for Assessing Undergraduate Students' Consecutive Interpreting Performance." *Interpreting* 17(2): 226–54. https://doi.org/10.1075/intp.17.2.04lee.

Linacre, J. M. 2005. *A User's Guide to Facets: Rasch-Model Computer Programs.* [Computer software and manual]. Accessed April 10, 2005 from www.winsteps.com.

Liu, Minhua. 2015. "Assessment." In *Routledge Encyclopedia of Interpreting Studies*, edited by Franz Pöchhacker, 20–23. London: Routledge.

Lumley, Tom, and Tim McNamara. 1995. "Rater Characteristics and Rater Bias: Implications for Training." *Language Testing* 12(1): 54–71. https://doi.org/10.1177/026553229501200104.

McConnell, David. 2000. *Importing Diversity: Inside Japan's JET Program.* Berkeley: University of California Press.

Pöchhacker, Franz. 2001. "Quality Assessment in Conference and Community Interpreting." *Meta* 46(2): 410–25. https://doi.org/10.7202/003847ar.

Pöchhacker, Franz. 2004. *Introducing Interpreting Studies.* London and New York: Routledge.

Pöchhacker, Franz. 2012. "Interpreting Quality: Global Professional Standards?." In *Interpreting in the Age of Globalization: Proceedings of the 8th National Conference and International Forum on Interpreting*, edited by Wen Ren, 305–18. Beijing: Foreign Language Teaching and Research Press.

Rao, Zhenhui, and Xin Li. 2017. "Native and Non-native Teachers' Perceptions of Error Gravity: The Effects of Cultural and Educational Factors." *The Asia-Pacific Education Researcher* 26(1): 51–9. https://doi.org/10.1007/s40299-017-0326-5.

Roberts, Johnson. 2009. *Assessing Performance: Designing, Scoring, and Validating Performance Tasks.* New York: The Guilford Press.

Roberts, Roda. 2000. "Interpreter Assessment Tools for Different Settings." In *Critical link 2*, edited by Roda Roberts, Silvana Carr, Diana Abraham and Aideen Dufour, 103–30. Amsterdam: John Benjamins.

Sawyer, David. 2004. *Fundamental Aspects of Interpreter Education: Curriculum and Assessment.* Amsterdam: John Benjamins.

Schjoldager, Ane. 1995. "Assessment of Simultaneous Interpreting." In *Teaching Translation and Interpreting 3: New Horizons*, edited by Cay Dollerup and Vibeke Appel, 187–95. Amsterdam: John Benjamins.

Setton, Robin. 2015. "Fidelity." In *Routledge Encyclopedia of Interpreting Studies*, edited by Franz Pöchhacker, 161–63. London: Routledge.

Setton, Robin, and Andrew Dawrant. 2016. *Conference Interpreting: A Trainer's Guide.* Amsterdam: John Benjamins.

Sheorey, Ravi. 1986. "Error Perceptions of Native Speaking and Non-Native Speaking Teachers of ESL." *ELT Journal* 40(4): 306–312. https://doi.org/10.1093/elt/40.4.306.

Shi, Ling. 2001. "Native and Nonnative-Speaking EFL Teachers' Evaluation of Chinese Students' English Writing." *Language Testing* 18(3): 303–25. https://doi.org/10.1177/026553220101800303.

Shohamy, Elana. 1985. *A Practical Handbook in Language Testing.* Tel Aviv: Tel Aviv University.

Skaaden, Hanne. 2013. "Assessing Interpreter Aptitude in a Variety of Languages." In *Assessment Issues in Language Translation and Interpreting,* edited by Dina Tsagari and Roelof van Deemter, 35–50. Frankfurt am Main: Peter Lang.

Su, Wei. 2019. "Exploring Native English Teachers' and Native Chinese Teachers' Assessment of Interpreting." *Language and Education* 33(6): 577–94. https://doi.org/10.1080/09500782.2019.1596121.

Su, Wei, and Xiaoqi Shang. 2020. "NNS and NES Teachers' Co-teaching of Interpretation Class: A Case Study." *The Asia Pacific Education Researcher* 29(4): 353–64. https://doi.org/10.1007/s40299-019-00489-7.

Weigle, Sara. 2002. *Assessing Writing.* Cambridge: Cambridge University Press.

Wu, Fred. 2013. "How Do We Assess Students in the Interpreting Examinations?" *Assessment Issues in Language Translation and Interpreting,* edited by Dina Tsagari and Roelof van Deemter, 15–33. Frankfurt am Main: Peter Lang.

Xu Hongchen 许宏晨. 2013. *Di'er yuyan yanjiu zhongde tongji anli fenxi* 第二语言研究中的统计案例分析 [Learning Statistics from Examples of Second Language Research]. Beijing 北京 Beijing: Waiyu jiaoxue yu yanjiu chuban she 外语教学与研究出版社 [Foreign Language Teaching and Research Press].

Zhang, Yin, and Cathie Elder. 2011. "Judgments of Oral Proficiency by Non-Native and Native English Speaking Teacher Raters: Competing or Complementary Constructs?" *Language Testing,* 28(1): 31–50. https://doi.org/ 10.1177/0265532209360671.

Appendix 1
Band descriptions

1 The band descriptions that follow are provided for the reference of jury members at the exam.
2 They are intended to provide a structured framework for grading the performances of candidates in each test, taking into account:

- Fidelity
- Target language quality
- Delivery

3 After each candidate has completed each test, jury members are invited to fill in the marking sheet provided, as follows:

a Assign a score in each of these three areas, having regard to the band descriptions provided in this document for distinction, good, fair, weak, and poor, respectively.
b Assign an overall grade of distinction, pass, discussion, or fail.
c Make detailed comments on the strengths and weaknesses of the interpretation.

Fidelity

Scale	Descriptors
Distinction (9–10)	Full, faithful, and accurate rendering of all message elements in the passage, including all or nearly all details, nuances, mood, and tone.
Good (7–8)	Faithful and accurate rendering of all important message elements and most details in the passage, with no significant meaning errors.
Fair (5–6)	Despite generally clear rendering of all important message elements and most details, there exist isolated and infrequent minor meaning errors on details (but NOT on key messages) that will not fundamentally mislead the audience or embarrass the speaker.

Scale	Descriptors
Weak (3–4)	There exist more serious isolated meaning errors that might mislead listeners, or a pattern of minor distortions. Non-trivial omission or incompleteness.
Poor (1–2)	Serious misinterpretation of important message elements, resulting in major meaning error that would mislead the audience or embarrass the speaker. Serious omission of important message elements.

Language

Scale	Descriptors
Distinction (9–10)	Strong and impressive command of the target language, including register, terminology, word choice, and style.
Good (7–8)	Solid command of the target language at required standard for A or B, with appropriate register and terminology.
Fair (5–6)	Appropriate, acceptable. For the most part, idiomatic and clear. Occasional problems with register and idiomatic usage (but not with basic grammar and pronunciation).
Weak (3–4)	Inadequate command of register, technical terms not rendered accurately. Output is clearly understandable but contains too many distracting errors of grammar, usage, or pronunciation.
Poor (1–2)	Inadequate language skills: for example, pattern of awkward, faulty expression, strong foreign accent, poor grammar and usage, inadequate vocabulary.

Delivery

Scale	Descriptors
Distinction (9–10)	Very clear, with expressive and lively delivery. The candidate is very communicative, as though giving his or her own speech with momentum and conviction.
Good (7–8)	Fluent and effective delivery: minimum hesitations or voiced pausing (um-er), intelligent prosody.
Fair (5–6)	Some recurrent delivery problems, such as hesitation, backtracking, voiced pausing (uh, um) – tolerable for audience but not quite as polished as expected in a trained interpreter.
Weak (3–4)	Delivery exhibits patterns of hesitation and backtracking.
Poor (1–2)	a. Stammering, halting delivery.

Appendix 2
Sample marking sheet

Examinee No. 4

	Distinction (9–10)	Good (7–8)	Fair (5–6)	Weak (3–4)	Poor (1–2)	Score
Holistic score						7
Fidelity						8
Language						7
Delivery						6

Please tick the one that best represents your view of the candidate's performance.

Overall performance: Distinction   Pass√   Discussion   Fail

Strengths

Generally accurate meaning.
Successfully used generalization to circumvent vocabulary issues/meaning loss.
Voice is calm, no fillers.
Accurate numbers, though switched sales for consumption, which is a minor inaccuracy.

Weaknesses

Awkward expressions: to hold this media press? Audition? Ordinary people?
Misuse of/missing conjunctions and prepositions.
Backtracking
Very long pauses during interpretation that show gaps in memory.
The interpreter sacrificed the whole picture for details, for example, the first sentence of segment 3.

Appendix 3
Questions for retrospective interviews

1 Do you find the two rating scales provided in this study easy to operate?
2 What were the major problems you encountered in the process of evaluating the interpreting recordings while using the ratings scales?
3 Could you distinguish between different proficiency levels of the students' interpreting performance using the descriptors listed in the rating scales?
4 Do you think all three criteria should be weighted differentially? If so, how would you assign the weights?
5 What do you think of the weighting schemes based on the data derived from this study?
6 Do you think we should adopt different weighting schemes accordingly, taking into the factor of directionality? Why?

Part II

Professional practice and future trends

9 Exploring standards of interpreting services in China (2006–2021)

History and prospects

Jie Xing and Yinghua He

1 Introduction

Over the past dozens of years, the interpreting service industry has developed vigorously, resulting in increasing demands for industry standardization and regulation. The formulation of standards serves as an important measure to improve the industry's overall quality and stability. In retrospect, China's interpreting service standards have demonstrated their features and gradually aligned themselves with their international counterparts, providing substantial support for the professional development of the Chinese interpreting industry. The Translators Association of China (TAC), the only national association of language services in China, regularly drafts and publishes standards or specifications of translation and/or interpreting. From 2006 to 2021, nine documents of standards that are wholly or at least partially devoted to the discussion of interpreting services have been released in China, the contents of which reflect the focus and requirements of the industry's regulation in different periods.

From an overarching perspective, standards for the language service industry in China can be classified into three categories: national standards issued by the General Administration of Quality Supervision, Inspection, and Quarantine of the People's Republic of China (AQSIQ) and the Standardization Administration of the People's Republic of China (SAC), and sector specifications and association standards both released by TAC. Among all the aforementioned nine documents, one national standard, which is the first of the interpreting services, was released in 2006, namely, GB/T 19363.2–2006 *Specification for Translation Service – Part 2: Interpretation*. From then on, the TAC issued four sector specifications, which are ZYF 003–2014 *Quotation for Interpretation Service*, ZYF 011–2019 *Guidelines on Procurement of Translation Services – Part 2: Interpretation*, ZYF 012–2019 *Code of Professional Ethics for Translators and Interpreters*, and ZYF 013–2020 *Specifications for Judicial Translation and Interpreting Services*, respectively, and four association standards, which are T/TAC 2–2017 *Competences of Translator and Interpreter*, T/TAC 3–2018 *Translation Services – Requirements for Interpreting Services*, T/TAC 4–2019 *Requirements for Translator and Interpreter*

DOI: 10.4324/9781003357629-12

Training, and T/TAC 5–2020 *Pricing Guidelines on Translation and Interpreting Services*, respectively.

This chapter traces the development of the nine aforementioned interpreting service standards, paying attention to their interconnections and comparing them with some of their international counterparts. In this connection, it could be observed that despite their late start in China, interpreting service standards have been developing rapidly with strong momentum. Their focus, taking fully into consideration the notion of project management, has gradually shifted to all the different factors and components of the social process of interpreting, which covers not only interpreting service providers and interpreters but also other related stakeholders, such as requesters, clients, users, project managers, technical staff, policymakers, and training institutions. Therefore, this study is to discuss the history and trends of the interpreting service standards in China, to take stock of their future development and, as a result, to provide a reference for the prospective formulation of standards.

2   Interpreting service standards in China: history and development

2.1   An overview

According to the *China Language Service Industry Development Report 2018*, the development of standards in the language service industry, which include both translation and interpretation, can be divided into three stages: the first one (2001–2008) when preliminary exploration of national standards started, the second one (2009–2015) when an increasing number of sector specifications were promoted to regulate the language service industry, and the third one (2015–2018) when association standards were the focus and the standards grew gradually in line with their international counterparts (TAC 2018a, 35–41).

In light of the TAC's classification, this paper divides the development of interpreting service standards into two stages, namely, the initial one (2006–2014) and the booming one (2015–2021), based on the release date and the number of interpreting standards. It takes the year of 2014 as a dividing line because there were only two basic and unspecific standards released before it, even with a gap of up to eight years between them. Since the year of 2015, a total of seven interpreting service standards have been introduced, notably indicating that standards of interpreting services have gradually entered a booming stage. The release year and the corresponding types of existing standards are shown in Figure 9.1.

Table 9.1 shows the topics discussed in these standards. Generally speaking, it could be seen that the focus ranges from the overall process of interpreting services to specific elements, such as procurement and quotation, and to certain verticals, such as judicial interpreting. As for the agents involved, the standards are not only targeted at interpreters and service providers but also at purchasers, trainers, and educators increasingly.

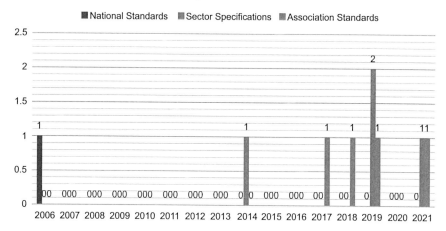

Figure 9.1 Interpreting service standards.

Table 9.1 Topics of Interpreting Standard Documents

Year	Topics	Interpreting Service standards
2006, 2018	Interpreting services	GB/T 19363.2–2006 *Specification for Translation Service – Part 2: Interpretation* T/TAC 3–2018 *Translation Services – Requirements for Interpreting Services*
2014, 2021	Quotation	ZYF 003–2014 *Quotation for Interpretation Service* T/TAC 5–2020 *Pricing Guidelines on Translation and Interpreting Services*
2017	Interpreter competence	T/TAC 2–2017 *Competences of Translator and Interpreter*
2019	Professional code of ethics	ZYF 012–2019 *Code of Professional Ethics for Translators and Interpreters*
2019	Procurement	ZYF 011–2019 *Guidelines on Procurement of Translation Services – Part 2: Interpretation*
2019	Interpreter training	T/TAC 4–2019 *Requirements for Translator and Interpreter Training*
2021	Interpreting services in verticals	ZYF 013–2020 *Specifications for Judicial Translation and Interpreting Services*

2.2   Initial stage: 2006–2014

Since 2002, the Translation Service Committee of TAC has organized relevant departments and companies to formulate national standards for the translation service industry (Zhang 2006, 78). But it was not until 2006 that the first standard for interpreting services, GB/T 19363.2–2006 *Specification for Translation Service – Part 2: Interpretation*, was released by AQSIQ and SAC.

Compared with its global counterparts, China is a latecomer to developing interpreting service standards. For example, Italy issued its national standard UNI 10547 *Definizione dei servizi e delle attività delle imprese di traduzione ed interpretariato (Definition of Services and Activities of Translation and Interpreting Enterprises)* in 1996, and the American Society for Testing and Materials (ASTM) released ASTM F2089–01 *Standard Guide for Language Interpretation Services* in 2001. Nevertheless, the Chinese national standard marks a new and fresh start in the promulgation of interpreting service standards in China. Specifically speaking, it contributes to the preliminary regulation of interpreting services by listing the definitions of key terms, such as different types of interpretation, the qualifications of interpreters and interpreting service providers, the requirements for signing business contracts, and the process control of interpreting services (AQSIQ and SAC 2006, 1–4). All the items, to some extent, reflect that the interpreting service industry was developing rapidly at that time in China, and relevant standards thus should be in place as a reference for all stakeholders, who, accordingly, need to act responsibly in managing a process or delivering a service.

Despite its symbolic meaning in the history of interpreting service industry in China, the first standard indeed still has some room for improvement. If compared with the ASTM F2089–01 *Standard Guide for Language Interpretation Services* in the United States, its definitions of some terms are vaguer and lack precise parameters. First, the definition of *interpreting* is not comprehensive enough. The ASTM counterpart defines "interpretation" as "the process of understanding and analyzing a spoken or signed message and re-expressing that message faithfully, accurately and objectively in another language, taking the cultural and social context into account" (ASTM 2001, 1). However, the definition of *interpretation* in the 2006 version is simply "the oral translation of the source language into the target language" (AQSIQ and SAC 2006, 1), neglecting the possibility of signed messages, which is later included in the definition of *interpretation* in the 2017 standard T/TAC 2–2017 *Competences of Translator and Interpreter*. Moreover, the ASTM version catches up with the newest developments in translation studies by pointing out the cultural and social nature of interpreting. Being able to view interpreting as a socially governed activity at that point is pretty forward-looking. Second, the requirements for interpreter qualifications are not specific enough. The ASTM standard guide classifies working languages into active languages, which could be "A" language or "B" language, and passive language, that is, "C" language, divides speaking and listening proficiency into multiple levels from 0 to 5 with detailed descriptions and also specifies interpreting qualifications, needs analysis, technological requirements, code of ethics and professional conduct, and responsibilities of providers and clients (ASTM 2001, 1–14). In contrast, the 2006 standard stipulates that interpreters must "have an interpreter qualification certificate issued by a nationally recognized authority or have the appropriate competence" and "have the professional ethics" (AQSIQ and SAC 2006, 3), without explanation in detail of the specific requirements for certificates, competence, and professional code of ethics.

It is proper to say that the release of GB/T 19363.2–2006 *Specification for Translation Service – Part 2: Interpretation* in 2006 set certain rules for the interpreting service market to follow; the standardization of interpreting services in China, however, was still in its infancy, which showed observable disconnection from the industry's rapidly growing scale. For example, there existed unfair competition in interpreting service quotations, and thus it demanded new and appropriate standards in place to tackle market problems. TAC shouldered its responsibility of taking the lead in drawing up new standards and, as a result, releasing the sector specification ZYF 003–2014 *Quotation for Interpretation Service* in 2014, which proves to be an effective and practical measure in response to market demands for orderly development. The 2014 standard stipulates the scope and methods of quotation for interpretation, which is a detailed supplement to "charging methods" in the 2006 national standard. It embodies at least two major characteristics as compared with the previous one. First, the new standard provides cost composition, charging methods, and pricing formulae, as well as corresponding quotation formulae for different modes of interpretation, be it liaison, consecutive, or simultaneous interpreting. Second, notwithstanding its retainment of the prior standard's definitions of "consecutive interpreting" and "simultaneous interpreting," its categorization reaches a certain degree of refinement by subdividing the former into three modes, including liaison interpreting, conference consecutive interpreting, and remote consecutive interpreting, and the latter into whispering, conference simultaneous interpreting, and remote simultaneous interpreting (TAC 2014, 2–4).

From what has been discussed earlier, we could see that the release of the two standards in 2006 and in 2014, respectively, symbolizes a shift in the focus of interpreting service standards in China from a general discussion of the entire interpreting service process to specific elements of interpreting service provisions. However, the interpreting service industry was still in its early stage of standardization, barely touching upon issues in specific vertical fields, such as medical, legal, or military interpreting. In contrast, interpreting service standards in other parts of the world have already expanded to various vertical sectors, such as the *Court Interpreters Act* enacted in the United States in 1978, the *California Standards for Healthcare Interpreters* by the California Healthcare Interpreting Association (CHIA) in 2002, and the *National Standard Guide for Community Interpreting Services* by the Canadian Language Industry Association (AILIA) in 2007.

2.3 *Booming stage: 2015–2021*

The pilot work of association standards in the field of translation and interpretation began in 2015 in China, following the successive introduction of several national standards and sector specifications (TAC 2018a, 39). As could be seen from Figure 9.1, the TAC released several standards, such as T/TAC 2–2017 *Competences of Translator and Interpreter*. Altogether, a total of three sector specifications and four association standards have been released since 2015. The increasing frequency of releasing new standards indicates substantive progress in the development of interpreting service standards in China.

The T/TAC 2–2017 *Competences of Translator and Interpreter* supplements the "Interpreter Qualification" in GB/T 19363.2–2006 *Specification for Translation Service – Part 2: Interpretation* by providing details of basic competence and assessment methods for interpreters and translators. It defines "interpret" as "transferring spoken or gestural information from one language to another by means of oral or gestural means." Compared to the 2006 national standard, it broadens the concept of interpreting and enriches the ways of transferring meaning in interpretation. It also includes five core areas of competence, that is, "ability to process spoken and written language in source and target languages," "research, information mining and processing ability," "cultural ability," "technical ability," and "ability to acquire domain-specific knowledge." Moreover, seven specific parameters are offered for language service providers to use in guiding interpretation qualification assessment and gauging the competence of interpreters in terms of work experience, frequency of interpreting practice, and so on. For example, one of the suggested parameters is as follows:

> [An interpreter should] obtain documented evidence equivalent to five years of full-time professional experience in interpreting, or equivalent to no less than 60 conference sessions of interpreting and 200 hours of telephone interpreting or 100 days of liaison interpreting, or equivalent to no less than 800 tape hours of interpreting practice or 60 hours of audio-visual interpreting practice.
>
> (TAC 2017, 1–5)

In 2018, the TAC released an association standard, T/TAC 3–2018 *Translation Services – Requirements for Interpreting Services*, which is a Chinese version of the international standard ISO 18841:2018 *Interpreting Services – General Requirements and Recommendations*. The introduction of this association standard indicates that the interpreting service standards in China are catching up to their international counterparts. It specifies the general requirements for interpreting services, covering the terms and definitions, basic principles of interpreting, basic conditions governing interpreting assignments, qualifications and competences related to interpreting, a non-exhaustive list of settings and specializations, and responsibilities of all participants in interpreting services, which can provide practical guidelines for all agents involved (TAC 2018b, 1–12). Furthermore, it has three main features. First, it elaborates on the differences of A, B, and C languages, where A language is a primary language of which the interpreter has complete command, B language is one in which the interpreter is proficient but is not his/her primary language, and C language is one from which the interpreter interprets into his/her A language(s) or B language(s). This distinction, as could be seen, is in line with the 2001 ASTM standard guide. Second, it incorporates the concept of project management. The basic conditions governing interpreting assignments consisted of four parts: request and offer, accepting assignments, during assignments, and after assignments. Third, the self-care responsibilities of interpreters are emphasized, which means that interpreters should be aware of the importance of ensuring appropriate working conditions and avoid vicarious trauma (TAC 2018b, 1–15).

By the end of 2018, four interpreting service standard documents had been released in China, with their emphasis shifting from contract signing to quotation, competence, qualifications, and so on, reflecting the progress that has been made. However, challenges still exist. For example, the lack of authoritative accreditation and specific requirements for service providers poses challenges to potential interpreting service requesters. Some small companies didn't fully understand the system and mechanism of the industry, and its structure as well as features, all of which also make it hard for the interpreting service industry to operate in a standard way. Moreover, a rising number of training institutions springs up to suit the rapidly growing need for interpreters in China, but partly because of the limited number of standards, some of them haven't attached great importance to the function and value of industry service standards in their teaching programs yet, resulting in a fact that some university graduates or postgraduates have little knowledge of professional standards and tend to work in unprofessional ways in the market, which, to our disappointment, constitutes a detriment to the public image of interpreters as well as the interpreting industry as a whole. In response to such circumstances and market demands, the TAC continued to release three sets of standards in 2019, that is, ZYF 011–2019 *Guidelines on Procurement of Translation Services – Part 2: Interpretation*, ZYF 012–2019 *Code of Professional Ethics for Translators and Interpreters*, and T/TAC 4–2019 *Requirements for Translator and Interpreter Training*.

The ZYF 011–2019 *Guidelines on Procurement of Translation Services – Part 2: Interpretation* outlines the procurement of interpreting services, the resources and capabilities of service providers, contracts, and templates that can be referred to by the interpreting service purchasers as well as providers to safeguard the interests of both parties (TAC 2019a, 1–18). The ZYF 012–2019 *Code of Professional Ethics for Translators and Interpreters* specifies the professional ethics and behavioral norms for interpreters to follow. This forward-looking standard first establishes technical ethics for interpreters and translators, who, as stated in it, should always reject any technical arrangements that would mislead or even do harm to clients and other stakeholders (TAC 2019b, 1–6). The T/TAC 4–2019 *Requirements for Translator and Interpreter Training* outlines the requirements for faculty, courses, resources, and training environment of institutions (TAC 2019c, 1–7). It is constructive in strengthening training management and improving training quality by emphasizing different forms of training, such as face-to-face training, online training or blended training, and assessments at the different stages of training.

Furthermore, interpreting service standards are gradually focused on various domains to address issues involved in vertical fields. For example, with the ongoing opening-up and international exchanges, judicial issues concerning foreign nationals have grown more prominent than ever before. Oral and written language communication plays an important role in addressing these issues. To further regulate judicial translation and interpreting services, the TAC released ZYF 013–2020 *Specifications for Judicial Translation and Interpreting Services* in March 2021. It specifies the professional guidelines, basic competence, and practice requirements for judicial translators and interpreters, the qualifications of whom are expressed in terms of specific amount of practice, and timely correction of errors, as a practitioner, in or after the interpreting process, and his/her exemption from liability for judicial interpreting services are also proposed (TAC 2021a, 1–9). In addition, the price of translation and interpreting services, constrained by many factors with regard to the different types of services, is another issue that has plagued the language service industry unremittingly. To regulate scientific and reasonable pricing methods of both translation and interpreting services, the TAC released an association standard, T/TAC 5–2020 *Pricing Guidelines on Translation and Interpreting Services*, in 2021 as a replacement for ZYF 003–2014 *Quotation for Interpretation Service* issued in 2014. The new standard highlights contents such as interpreter qualifications, task difficulties, and core service procedures, provides quantitative methods for pricing of interpreting services, and designs a visualized model of pricing with nine parameters, such as working hours, base price, task difficulties, interpreter qualifications, and service types, to assist service purchasers and providers in determining appropriate price of interpreting services (TAC 2021b, 1–22).

Altogether, seven standards that involved interpreting services were issued from 2017 to 2021, symbolizing substantial progress in the standardization of the interpreting service industry. The standards in this stage present no less than five features. First, the terminology used in interpreting services becomes more specific and detailed. The definition of *interpreting* includes gesture information in addition to the oral one and covers all different modes of whispered, consecutive, and simultaneous interpreting. Second, more parties in the whole process of interpreting services are included, and relevant description could be seen in various standards, which make requirements for not only service providers and interpreters but also purchasers and clients, or even training institutions. Third, the rights and duties of different roles in interpreting services become increasingly clearer. Many existing standards incorporate the notion of project management and clarify the responsibilities of all parties involved before, during, and after interpreting services. Fourth, the requirements for interpreter qualifications are being optimized. Qualified interpreters are selected based on their acquired certificates and the amount of practice. The techniques for assessing interpreters are more diverse, which provide a useful reference for both purchasers and service providers. Last but not the least, the standards develop from general to specific domains, such as judicial translation and interpreting. The introduction of ZYF 013–2020 *Specifications for Judicial Translation and Interpreting Services* indicates the specialization of language service standards in China. In general, the standards issued at this stage are no longer limited to regulating the elements of the interpreting process in a narrow sense but are more aimed at all sections in the broad "social" process. The standards are thus constantly improved and developed to guarantee the sound growth of the industry.

3 Prospects of interpreting service standards in China

Reviewing the history and development of interpreting service standards in China, some scholars argue that "interpreting service standards have less pertinence to the market," and "different interpreting service standards are generally isolated and have not formed a cohesive system" (Cui and Sun 2019, 81). However, the previous situation has been improved by the newly released standards, especially those issued since 2019. Interpreting service standards in China apply to a wide range of stakeholders, such as purchasers, providers, interpreters, and translation institutions. The new standards supplement the old ones, and they are linked to one another, which helps build a sound system of interpreting service standards in China. As the standardization of the industry advances, new challenges emerge, such as insufficient standards in specific verticals and inadequate promotion and application of standards. Based on the previous analysis of published standards, the authors would like to put forward the following five suggestions.

3.1 Involving more parties in formulating standards led by the TAC

TAC, the only national translation association in China, plays a leading role in fostering the orderly development of the interpreting service industry. In 2019, nine language service experts from the TAC joined the China National Technical Committee for Standardization of Language and Terminology, where they will be directly involved in organizing and formulating national interpreting, translation, and technical standards. The TAC has 15 branches, including the Translation Services Committee, the Interpreting Committee, and the Translators and Interpreters Appraisal Committee. The Translation Services Committee is responsible for developing standards for interpreting and translation services and hosting a national seminar on translation management each year to promote the standardization of the language service industry. Despite its short history in academia and the marketplace, the Interpreting Committee, established in 2016, actively participates in the development of standards in the field of interpreting and promotes their implementation.

The formulation of interpreting service standards in China is spearheaded by the TAC, which organizes language service companies, training institutions, and standardization research organizations to participate in the formulation with concerted efforts. However, the peer experience of experts from other countries, as well as the needs and feedbacks of stakeholders such as foreign clients, have not been fully incorporated into China's interpreting service standards. The TAC can continue to play a leading role in the future by hosting forums on the standardization of language services in the Asia-Pacific region and throughout the world, boosting exchanges between Chinese standardization authorities and their counterparts elsewhere in the world, and building a bridge for future collaboration on a solid ground. Based on a thorough investigation of the current stage of development, the TAC could absorb the cutting-edge international experience in standardization, encourage domestic and foreign language service users to provide feedbacks on their experiences, and subsequently incorporate them into the Chinese standards, so as to keep up with the newest trends of international standards.

3.2 *Promoting standards in vertical areas and multilingual versions*

Interpreting service standards in China are mainly divided into two types: general ones targeted at the entire process of interpreting services and specific ones aimed at certain themes of interpreting services. The former includes GB/T 19363.2–2006 *Specification for Translation Service – Part 2: Interpretation* and T/TAC 3–2018 *Translation Services – Requirements for Interpreting Services*, while the latter contains ZYF 011–2019 *Guidelines on Procurement of Translation Services – Part 2: Interpretation*, T/TAC 2–2017 *Competences of Translator and Interpreter*, T/TAC 4–2019 *Requirements for Translator and Interpreter Training*, and so on. However, there is still room for improvement in standards aimed at specific verticals, such as medical interpreting, healthcare interpreting, and other kinds of public service interpreting, as well as in specific modes, such as remote interpreting and telephone interpreting. More interpreting standards for specific domains could be formulated by drawing on the experience of existing international standards in vertical fields and taking into account the actual growth of the interpreting service industry in China, thereby promoting the internationalization of interpreting service standards in China. Be that as it may, there is indeed one thing that shall be borne in mind that new standards must be consistent with the old ones, and especially, the ones that are applied to specific domains must not contradict the general ones, so that new standards could serve as effective supplements to earlier ones, rather than cause confusion among clients or practitioners because of unclear or even opposite ways of description.

Despite a growing number of foreign nationals and corporations doing business in China, the Chinese interpreting service standards are still only available in Chinese, posing obstacles for international clients trying to understand relevant contents. In contrast, the standard *Interpreting: Getting It Right – A Guide to Buying Interpreting Services* released in 2011 by American Translators Association (ATA) offers five language versions: English, Brazilian

Portuguese, French, Spanish, and Galician. *Code of Ethics and Code of Conduct* released in 2012 by the Australian Institute of Interpreters and Translators (AUSIT) provides eight language versions: English, Chinese, German, French, Japanese, Italian, Korean, and Polish. The *Guidelines for Distance Interpreting* published in 2019 by the International Association of Conference Interpreters (AIIC) is available in English, German, and Spanish. Against the backdrop of the Belt and Road Initiative, demands for language services soar due to the frequent bilateral or multilateral trade relations between China and other countries or regions along the route. When seeking interpreting services, foreign companies and clients also need to be familiar with essential contents of relevant standards. Therefore, existing standards, if provided in multilingual versions, could be handy references for them in finding language service companies that they need.

3.3 *Refining interpreter competence, duties, and rights*

The definition of *interpreting competence* today differs greatly from previous ones, with components ranging from language and cultural competence to professional conduct and code of ethics. Interpreter competence, according to Wang, should encompass "bilingual competence, extra-linguistic knowledge, interpreting skills, psychological quality, professionalism, and physical quality" (Wang 2012, 75). As early as 2001, the *Standard Guide for Language Interpretation Services* issued by ASTM lists "ability to cope with stress" as one of the criteria for interpreter qualifications (ASTM 2001, 4), suggesting that the psychological trait is essential for a qualified interpreter. Although many competences, such as information mining ability and cultural ability, are covered in the T/TAC 2–2017 *Competences of Translator and Interpreter*, the parameters, such as professional ethics and behavioral norms, are not elaborated. In addition, in-depth analysis of certain competence is still insufficient, and the current way of assessment, relying on evidence of degree, certificate, or past working hours, though practically feasible and convenient, is still called into question if considering whether it is well-equipped theoretically and pedagogically. With further advancement of interpreter competence research and the increasingly diverse roles played by the interpreters in various settings, the standards for interpreting competence should keep pace with the times, updating and upgrading to redefine its definition and constituents.

The ZYF 012–2019 *Code of Professional Ethics for Translators and Interpreters* outlines the ethical qualities and requirements for interpreters and translators. In fact, countries such as the UK and Australia implemented a variety of rules pertaining to the obligations and rights of interpreters and translators. To be more specific, the *Disciplinary Framework and Procedures* issued in 2016 by the National Register of Public Service Interpreters (NRPSI) in the UK clarifies the procedures for client complaints and interpreter appeals, which could play a supervisory role in urging interpreters to comply with code of ethics and protect their rights at the same time (NRPSI 2016, 1–16). In the era of professionalization of interpreting services, the interpreters' rights are occasionally violated, which is unfavorable for establishing the status and professional identity of interpreters. To foster a healthy procurement environment, the ZYF 011–2019 *Guidelines on Procurement of Translation Services – Part 2: Interpretation* in 2019 makes statements about the interpreter's transportation, accommodation, safety, and protection (including helmets, masks, and other protective equipment when applicable), admission documents, interpreting equipment and technical support for interpreting services, and resting place (TAC 2019a, 3). However, standards for interpreters' rights in China remain inadequate, such as the lack of explicit regulations on economic and social security, salary, and insurance. Given this circumstance, the following standards could focus on helping interpreters secure their rights in disputes of service and strengthening the protection system for their rights, thereby reducing their occupational risks. In order to achieve this goal, relevant institutions and working mechanisms must be in place to facilitate communication among interpreters, clients, and companies and help to settle conflicts of interest.

3.4   Formulating standards that cater to the trend of interpreting technologies

Nowadays, interpreting technologies abound, with computer-assisted translation (CAT) helping translators and interpreters complete their tasks with quality and efficiency. On the one hand, the rapid development of interpreting technologies has expanded the modes of interpreting services from purely human interpreting to human–machine cooperation. On the other hand, convenient and inexpensive services provided by machine interpreting will inevitably affect the market price of interpreting services and even revolutionize the career development of interpreters. To cater to the development of interpreting technologies, the International Organization for Standardization (ISO) released ISO 20109:2016 *Simultaneous Interpreting – Equipment – Requirements*, which serves as a practical technical guideline for service providers and on-site management. So far, there are still participants in the language service industry who only have limited knowledge of interpreting technologies. In a continued effort to fill the gap, the ISO further promoted the terminology standard ISO 20539:2019 *Translation, Interpreting, and Related Technology – Vocabulary* to give all industry practitioners a general view of the involvement of technology in both translation and interpreting. Drawing on these extant standards and to guide Chinese service providers and interpreters to view interpreting technologies rationally and accurately, similar ones for interpreting technologies could also be developed in China to highlight the requirements for interpreting equipment, systems, and tools. Furthermore, as translation education at the postgraduate level is thriving in China, "postgraduate programs of translation and interpreting should keep track of the development of translation and interpreting technology and seize the opportunity of human-machine interactive translation and interpreting" (Xing and Jin 2020, 49), and translation departments in more than 300 Chinese universities could build teaching modules integrating technological standards, thus guiding novice interpreters to understand the technical resources of interpreting and apply technology in practice from the very beginning of their training.

Since web streaming technology develops rapidly and severe public health emergencies arise, remote interpreting is increasingly favored by the language service industry to facilitate international communication. It can be conducted anytime and anywhere, which increases the efficiency of interpreting services and resource utilization. It requires interpreters to master the operating skills of relevant software and platforms, which poses additional hurdles to interpreters so that their performance might be compromised to some extent. Interpreters should "understand the innovative mode of interpreting technology and follow the trend of interpreting technology" (Wang and Yang 2019, 77). The T/TAC 2–2017 *Competences of Translator and Interpreter* includes technical competence as the basic competence of translators and interpreters, accentuating the importance of translation and interpreting technology. Standards for technological modes of interpreting, such as remote interpreting, could be formulated to help companies and interpreters better understand technical resources and interpreter competence.

3.5   Facilitating accreditation of interpreting service and implementation of standards

Standards provide a foundation on which the interpreting service industry can rely, and strict market access is a significant guarantee for regulating the industry and enhancing its reputation. Accreditation for language service companies is an important means of establishing the entry threshold to the translation market and ensuring its healthy and orderly operation. In 2018, the TAC, in collaboration with professional accreditation bodies, started the accreditation work of the translation service industry, which is one of the vital measures to apply standards. Until 2019, a great number of translation service companies had completed the accreditation process. In contrast, the work of accreditation for interpreting service companies has lagged far behind, probably due to the difficulty of quantifying the accreditation criteria for interpreting services. Besides, interpreting boasts simultaneity and on-site service, which, in one way or another, also complicates the accreditation work. Notwithstanding the accreditation for translation service companies has taken the lead but is still in its very early stages, its working mechanisms and procedures are yet to be perfected. In contrast, to improve the quality and stability of the interpreting service industry, it is necessary to start the interpreting service accreditation as soon as possible to ensure companies have effective workflow management systems and quality assurance systems in place. Experience from other countries could serve as reference. For example, the Canadian Language Industry Association set up a certification program for interpreting service providers under the National Standard Guide for Community Interpreting Services (NSGCIS) in early 2010.

Although the formulation and promotion of interpreting service standards have made substantial progress over the years, the implementation of these standards still requires improvement. Many government offices, agencies, companies, training institutions, interpreters, and clients are unclear about the contents of interpreting service standards in China, and their awareness of referring to the standards at work has not been firmly established. To ensure that the standards are in place, translation associations at all levels across the country could recommend that all parties involved in the language service industry use the standards more actively, and universities could also design courses in the sociology and professionalization of the translation and interpreting industry, helping their students learn standard-related knowledge and act in the market accordingly. Even if the standards are not mandatory and don't have a strictly binding force for the industry, certification and implementation of standards are doubtlessly conducive to a healthy growth of the interpreting industry, and with them, the rights of both the agencies and interpreters could be guaranteed. Therefore, many scholars have advocated for translation legislation (Huang 2011, 29–30; Jiang et al. 2012, 49–52; Zhao and Dong 2019, 24–30) and a strict regulatory mechanism for the industry. Indeed, the rapidly changing market and the newly emerging features of interpreting services pose some challenges for translation legislation, but some contents in previous standards that have been repeatedly tested and widely accepted in practice could be codified as laws, thus facilitating the healthy and orderly regulation of the industry.

4   Conclusion

The development of the Chinese interpreting service standards has gone hand in hand with that of translation and interpreting education in China. It can be divided into two stages from 2006 to 2021: the initial one and the booming one, respectively, with each stage presenting a different focus on regulating the interpreting industry. The aforementioned standards cover topics ranging from the general interpreting service process to various components throughout the whole social process of service. They incorporate the notion of project management which classifies service requirements before, during, and after the interpreting. They gradually involve more parties, such as purchasers, providers, interpreters, and translation training institutions, and become more in line with their international counterparts. To further improve the robust growth of the industry, it is hoped that the future standards would be jointly formulated by all parties involved, targeted to specific domains, focusing on the interpreters' competence and rights, giving full play to technical elements, and strengthening promotion, thus upgrading the interpreting service industry's structure to help it enter a new stage of self-discipline and healthy development.

References

AQSIQ (General Administration of Quality Supervision, Inspection and Quarantine of the People's Republic of China) and SAC (Standardization Administration of the People's Republic of China) 中华人民共和国国家质量监督检验检疫总局、中国国家标准化管理委员会. 2006. *Fanyi fuwu guifan dier bufen: kouyi* 翻译服务规范 第2部分：口译 [Specification for Translation Service – Part 2: Interpretation]. GB/T 19363.2–2006. Beijing: AQSIO and SAC.

ASTM (American Society for Testing and Materials). 2001. *Standard Guide for Language Interpretation Service*. ASTM F2089–01. West Conshohocken: ASTM International.

Cui Qiliang 崔启亮, and Sun Jin 孙谨. 2019. "Zhongwai kouyi fuwu biaozhun yu guifan duibi yanjiu yu qishi" 中外口译服务标准与规范对比研究与启示 [A Comparative Study of Chinese and Foreign Interpretation Service Standards and Norms]. *Shanghai fanyi* 上海翻译 [Shanghai Journal of Translators] (2): 78–82.

Huang Youyi 黄友义. 2011. "Tuidong fanyi lifa, cujin fanyi hangye de jiankang fazhan" 推动翻译立法，促进翻译行业的健康发展 [Promote Translation Legislation and the Healthy Development of the Translation Industry]. *Zhongguo fanyi* 中国翻译 [Chinese Translators Journal] 32(3): 29–30.

Jiang Lihua 蒋莉华, Wang Huaping 王化平, and Yan Li 严荔. 2012. "Zhongguo fanyi hangye lifa zhi lu: laizi deguo de jiejian" 中国翻译行业立法之路：来自德国的借鉴 [The Way to Legislation of China's Translation Industry: Lessons from Germany]. *Zhongguo fanyi* 中国翻译 [Chinese Translators Journal] 33(4): 49–52.

NRPSI (National Register of Public Service Interpreters). 2016. *Disciplinary Framework and Procedures*. Accessed www.nrpsi.org.uk/downloads/NRPSI_Disciplinary_Framework_and_Procedures_22.01.16.pdf.

TAC (Translators Association of China) 中国翻译协会. 2014. *Kouyi fuwu baojia guifan* 口译服务报价规范 [Quotation for Interpretation Service]. ZYF 003–2014. Beijing: TAC.

TAC (Translators Association of China) 中国翻译协会. 2017. *Koubiyi renyuan jiben nengli yaoqiu* 口笔译人员基本能力要求 [Competences of Translator and Interpreter]. T/TAC 2–2017. Beijing: TAC.

TAC (Translators Association of China) 中国翻译协会. 2018a. *2018 Zhongguo yuyan fuwu hangye fazhan baogao* 2018 中国语言服务行业发展报告 [*China Language Service Industry Development Report 2018*]. Beijing: waiwen chubanshe 北京：外文出版社 [Beijing: Foreign Language Press].

TAC (Translators Association of China) 中国翻译协会. 2018b. *Fanyi fuwu kouyi fuwu yaoqiu* 翻译服务 口译服务要求 [Translation Services – Requirements for Interpreting Services]. T/TAC 3–2018. Beijing: TAC.

TAC (Translators Association of China) 中国翻译协会. 2019a. *Fanyi fuwu caigou zhinan di'er bufen: kouyi* 翻译服务采购指南 第2部分：口译 [Guidelines on Procurement of Translation Services – Part 2: Interpretation]. ZYF 011–2019. Beijing: TAC.

TAC (Translators Association of China) 中国翻译协会. 2019b. *Yiyuan zhiye daode zhunze yu xingwei guifan* 译员职业道德准则与行为规范 [Code of Professional Ethics for Translators and Interpreters]. ZYF 012–2019. Beijing: TAC.

TAC (Translators Association of China) 中国翻译协会. 2019c. *Fanyi peixun fuwu yaoqiu* 翻译培训服务要求 [Requirements for Translator and Interpreter Training]. T/TAC 4–2019. Beijing: TAC.

TAC (Translators Association of China) 中国翻译协会. 2021a. *Sifa fanyi fuwu guifan* 司法翻译服务规范 [Specifications for Judicial Translation and Interpreting Services]. ZYF 013–2020. Beijing: TAC.

TAC (Translators Association of China) 中国翻译协会. 2021b. *Koubiyi fuwu jijia zhinan* 口笔译服务计价指南 [Pricing Guidelines on Translation and Interpreting Services]. T/TAC 5–2020. Beijing: TAC.

Wang Binhua 王斌华. 2012. "Cong kouyi nengli dao yiyuan nengli: zhuanye kouyi jiaoxue linian de tuozhan" 从口译能力到译员能力：专业口译教学理念的拓展 [From Interpreting Competence to Interpreter Competence: Exploring the Conceptual Foundation of Professional Interpreting Training]. Waiyu yu waiyu jiaoxue 外语与外语教学 [Foreign Languages and Their Teaching] (6): 75–8.

Wang Huashu 王华树, and Yang Chengshu 杨承淑. 2019. "Rengong Zhineng Shidai de kouyi jishu fazhan: gainian yingxiang yu qushi" 人工智能时代的口译技术发展：概念、影响与趋势 [Interpreting Technologies in the Era of Artificial Intelligence: Concepts, Influences and Trends]. *Zhongguo fanyi* 中国翻译 [Chinese Translators Journal] 40(6): 69–79.

Xing Jie 邢杰, and Jin Li 金力. 2020. "Xinban ouzhou fanyi shuoshi nengli fanyi kuangjia de sikao yu qishi" 新版欧洲翻译硕士能力框架的思考与启示 [Reflections on and Implications of European Master's Translation Competence Framework 2017]. *Shanghai fanyi* 上海翻译 [Shanghai Journal of Translators] (2): 46–50.

Zhang Nanjun 张南军. 2006. "Fanyi fuwu biaozhunhua dui chanye fazhan de yiyi ji qushi" 翻译服务标准化对产业发展的意义及趋势 [The Significance and Trend of Translation Service Standardization for Industrial Development]. *Shanghai fanyi* 上海翻译 [Shanghai Journal of Translators] (4): 78–80.

Zhao Junfeng 赵军峰, and Yan Dong 董燕. 2019. "Meiguo Fating Kouyiyuan fa ji qi xiuzheng'an dui woguo fating kouyi lifa de qishi" 美国《法庭口译员法》及其修正案对我国法庭口译立法的启示 [Implications of US Court Interpreters Act and Its 1988 Amendment for China's Court Interpreting Legislation]. *Shanghai fanyi* 上海翻译 [Shanghai Journal of Translators] (3): 24–30.

10 Interpreting in Macao

Practice, training, and research

Yiqiang Chen, Victoria Lai Cheng Lei, and Defeng Li

1 Introduction

1.1 Macao as a multilingual society

Macao is a multilingual and multicultural society, with Portuguese and Chinese being the two official languages and English widely used in commerce and tourism. Cantonese, Putonghua, and Hokkien dialects are commonly spoken in the region among residents of Chinese origin (Sheng 2004). Tracing back to 1553, the Portuguese first settled in Macao, which gradually was developed later into a trading center, with multiple foreign languages and cultures mingling with the local Chinese language and culture. When China resumed sovereignty over Macao in 1999, both Chinese and Portuguese were adopted as official languages. There have been extensive studies into the development of the various languages and translation policies in Macao as the region serves as a bridge for international communications between China and the rest of the world, in particular, the Portuguese-speaking countries (see Li 2022; Han and Yang 2022).

Chinese, English, and Portuguese are now the main languages in Macao. Lam and Ieong (2022) reviewed census data (1991–2016) (Table 10.1) for population aged 3 and above and their primary language choice in Macao over time. Cantonese is the most-used dialect of the Chinese language. Since the liberalization of the gaming industry in 2002, more and more Putonghua speakers have come to Macao for work and leisure activities in addition to an English-speaking cohort. The Portuguese-speaking population is relatively small in the last 20 years. In general, Chinese is the primary language of communication in Macao and has gradually gained importance in its official status, while English, as a major language for the business world today, is used mostly in finance, modern technology, international trade, and university education, where a significant proportion of programs in Macao's tertiary institutions are offered in English.

1.2 Development of relevant sectors in Macao

The coexistence of multiple languages and cultures in Macao, the government's language policies, and the economic development have significant impact on the development of Macao's language industry, which includes translation

DOI: 10.4324/9781003357629-13

Table 10.1 Population Aged 3 and Above and Their Primary Language Choice in Macao (1991–2016)

	1991 (%)	1996 (%)	2001 (%)	2006 (%)	2011 (%)	2016 (%)
Cantonese	85.8	87.1	87.9	85.7	83.3	80.1
Putonghua	1.2	1.2	1.6	3.2	5	5.5
Other Chinese dialects (including Hokkien/ Minnan)	9.6	7.8	7.6	6.7	5.7	5.3
Portuguese	1.8	1.8	0.7	0.6	0.7	0.6
English	0.5	0.8	0.7	1.5	2.3	2.8
Others	1.1	1.3	1.7	2.3	3	5.8

Source: Adapted from DSEC, 2002, 2007, 2012, 2017 (Lam and Ieong, 2022).

and interpreting services. Since Macao returned to China in 1999, the Macao Special Administrative Region government has implemented a corresponding language education policy to cater for the current needs.[1] At the same time, all the pillars of Macao's economy, namely, tourism, MICE (convention and exhibition industry), and gaming, are sectors that can benefit immensely from language services. According to the Statistics and Census Service of the Macao SAR, before the COVID-19 pandemic, principal indicators, such as visitor arrivals, available guest rooms, total and per-capita spending of visitors, as well as the tourist price index, were generally on the rise. For instance, the hotel occupancy rates by classification of establishments (five-star, four-star, three-star, two-star, and guesthouse) were above 70% from 2002 to 2018 on average.[2] For example, it was predicted that the demand for human resources in the gaming industry would reach 67,949 by the end of 2020. Language competence, including English language proficiency, was identified as one of the most important of the pillar industries' employee competency requirements (Zeng et al. 2018). The Macao Government Tourism Office (MGTO) estimated that the number of people employed in the tourism industry in Macao would be as high as 258,000 in 2025. As Macao aspires to become a center for major international events, such as the Macao International Tourism (Industry) Expo, the Macao International Trade and Investment Fair, the Macao Grand Prix, the Macao International Film Festival and Awards, among others, it is reasonable to anticipate a growing need for language services, including translation and interpreting.

2   Interpreting in Macao: an industry overview

2.1   *Language industry market nationwide*

According to statistics from the Chinese Translators Association and the Intelligence Research Group,[3] by 2021, there were 423,547 enterprises providing relevant language services business in China, an increase of 20,452 from the end of 2019, including 9,656 enterprises with language services as their main business. The total output value of these language service enterprises amounted to RMB 55,448 million in 2021, an increase of RMB 8,524 million from 2019, representing an average annual growth rate of 11.1%. The language industry has contributed to as well as benefited from China's economic development.

2.2 Translation and interpreting service in the private sector in Macao

However, to date there is no specific information provided by the Statistics and Census Service about the total number of private businesses and revenue figures in the language service industry, which includes translation and interpreting. The translation industry in Macao is relatively small in terms of the number of registered translation companies.

There are currently around a dozen of translation and interpreting service agencies in Macao: Ponte-Língua Macao, Palavas Acertadas Traduções Lda Macao, Beruf Translation (Macao) Company, C&C Translation Centre Macao, Macao Translations Limited, Gold Harvest Translation Ltd Macao, Poema Language Services (PLS) Macao, Boss Translation Macao, Universal Translation and Consultancy Macao, Companhia de Tradução Macao Mega Limitada. The list is by no means exhaustive due to changing market activities. Most of these agencies provide general language services and cover many languages at the client's request. In general, interpreting assignments in the local market mostly involve Portuguese, Chinese, and English. Take Boss Translation Macao as an example: translation, CAT (computer-aided translation) consultancy, certificate translation, interpretation (including simultaneous interpretation), and equipment leasing are among the services provided. The agency also provides CPA (Chinese–Portuguese assistant), CPL (Chinese–Portuguese laws), CPN (Cantonese–Pinyin names), CEP (Chinese–English–Portuguese terms) translation and translation for social media users, such as WeChat FREE Translation, which provides "free query/translation services for Chinese, English and Portuguese information about Macao."[4] Other translation companies mentioned also provide a similar range of services, including written translation (official government documents, materials related to economy and trade, statistics, medical reports, laws and regulations, notarization and authentication papers, academic papers, drivers' licenses, etc.), oral interpreting (international conferences, business negotiations, on-site services, tours and visits), audiovisual translation and dubbing, website translation, and so on.

2.3 Translation and interpreting service in Macao SAR government

As for translation and interpreting in the public sector, in particular between Portuguese and Chinese, which are the official languages of Macao, the Public

Administration and Civil Service Bureau, which is known locally as SAFP – the acronym for Direcção dos Serviços de Administração e Função Pública – provides relevant service to both the general public and various government units upon request.

SAFP is a public unit responsible for researching, coordinating, and providing technical support for the improvement and modernization of the public administration and personnel policies of the civil service as well as the centralized management of public servants. One of the services provided upon request is translation and interpreting service, including (1) for the general public, Chinese–Portuguese translation, Chinese–Portuguese interpretation (in consecutive and simultaneous modes), and certification of private translations, and (2) for government departments, Chinese–Portuguese translation, Chinese–Portuguese interpretation (in consecutive and simultaneous modes). According to information on the official government website,[5] the Chinese–Portuguese translation service is provided to citizens and private entities as well as public units. On-site Chinese–Portuguese interpretation service in simultaneous and consecutive modes is provided to private entities as well as public units. For interpretation service, requests for interpretation services should be submitted at least ten days in advance of the event to the Language Services Department of SAFP in order to have sufficient time for the unit to deploy interpreters and prepare for the event. Currently, language combinations of the interpretation service from SAFP, for simultaneous interpretation, include Cantonese/Portuguese, Putonghua/Portuguese, and Cantonese/Putonghua, and for consecutive interpretation include Cantonese/Portuguese, Putonghua/Portuguese, and Cantonese/Putonghua. Detailed request procedure, location and office hours, rates, and time needed for approval can be found on the official website of SAFP.

Manuela Teresa Sousa Aguiar, former director of the Language Services Department, provides details regarding the history and evolution of the translation and interpreting service at SAFP shortly after the establishment of the Macao SAR (Aguiar 2003), including the different positions and levels of translators and interpreters, requirements for promotion, the number of translators and interpreters working in the department over time, and the number of requests received and the amount of completed translation and interpreting work for both the general public and public units.

2.4   *Translation and interpreting service in other institutions*

Besides SAPF, public entities such as the Legislative Assembly, the Public Prosecution Office, the Security Forces, the Health Bureau, and the University of Macau also have their own teams of in-house interpreters. As Macao becomes increasingly cosmopolitan after the liberalization of the gaming industry, English/Cantonese and English/Putonghua as language combinations quickly gain importance alongside the Portuguese/Cantonese language pair in the public sector.

3 Interpreting training in Macao

3.1 Interpreting-related programs provided by universities

Institutions of higher learning are the main providers of translation and interpreting degree programs in Macao. There are not many programs directly related to oral interpreting, and most of the oral interpreting courses are open to students from different academic fields rather than being offered exclusively to students of an interpretation major. There are ten higher-learning institutions (public and private) in Macao,[6] but only three (University of Macau, Macao Polytechnic University, University of Saint Joseph) offer translation/interpreting degree programs.

3.1.1 BA programs

Undergraduate degree programs in translation and interpretation are offered by three institutions in Macao, namely, Macao Polytechnic University, University of Saint Joseph, and the University of Macau. These programs are offered in English, Portuguese, and Chinese. Designated courses on oral interpretation are listed in the following under program specifications (see Table 10.2).

It is worth noting that the University of Macau used to have a minor in translation program for students admitted before the 2018/2019 academic year. It was a 2–4 year program offering translation and interpretation courses: Introduction to Interpretation (ENGL2006), Consecutive Interpretation (ENGL2007), Conference Interpretation (ENGL3046), and Simultaneous Interpretation (ENGL4005).

3.1.2 MA programs

Postgraduate programs related to translation and interpretation are offered by two institutions in Macao, namely, the University of Macau and the Macao Polytechnic University. These programs are offered in English, Portuguese, and Chinese for a two-year duration. For these programs, translation and interpretation courses are offered alongside other courses on linguistics and literary study. Table 10.3 lists the program specifications of the MA programs.

3.1.3 PhD programs

PhD programs offered in Macao's higher-learning institutions related to translation and interpreting are offered at the University of Macau and the Macao Polytechnic University. At the University of Macau, translation studies is a four-year program taught in English offered under PhD in linguistics (English). Currently, about half of the enrolled students are doing interpreting-related research. It requires 27 credits to graduate.

At the Macao Polytechnic University, doctor of philosophy in Portuguese is offered as a three-year program taught in both Portuguese and Chinese, which

Table 10.2 Specifications of BA Programs in Translation and Interpretation in Macao

Institution	Program Title	Medium of Instruction	Duration	Credit Requirement	Mode	Oral Interpretation Courses
Macao Polytechnic University	Bachelor of Arts in Chinese–Portuguese/Portuguese–Chinese Translation and Interpretation (for students from Portuguese education systems)	Chinese and Portuguese	4 years	166 credits	Day/evening	Consecutive Interpreting (TRAN4103; Introduction to Simultaneous Interpreting (TRAN4104)
	Bachelor of Arts in Chinese–Portuguese/Portuguese–Chinese Translation and Interpretation (for students from Chinese/English education systems)	Chinese and Portuguese	4 years	166 credits	Day/evening	Consecutive Interpreting (TRAN4103; Introduction to Simultaneous Interpreting (TRAN4104)
	Bachelor of Arts in Chinese–English Translation and Interpretation	Chinese and English	4 years	154 credits	Day/evening	Introduction to Interpreting (TRAN2101; Consecutive Interpreting (E–C) (TRAN3105; Consecutive Interpreting (C–E) (TRAN3106; Simultaneous Interpreting (TRAN4109)
University of Saint Joseph	Portuguese–Chinese Translation Studies	English, Chinese, Portuguese	4 years	127 credits	Evening	Portuguese–Chinese Interpretation (Year 2); Consecutive Portuguese–Chinese Interpretatio, Simultaneous Portuguese–Chinese Interpretation (Year 4)
	Portuguese–Chinese Translation (Associate Diploma)	English, Chinese, Portuguese	2 years	74 credits	Evening	Portuguese–Chinese Interpretation (Year 2)

Table 10.3 Specifications of MA Programs in Translation and Interpretation in Macao

Institution	Program Title	Medium of Teaching	Duration	Credit Requirement	Oral Interpretation Courses
University of Macau	MA in Translation Studies (Portuguese–Chinese)	Chinese and Portuguese	2 years	30 credits	Interpreting I – Chinese/Portuguese; Interpreting II – Chinese/Portuguese
	MA in Translation Studies (English–Chinese)	Chinese and English	2 years	30 credits	Theories and Practice of Interpreting; Consecutive Interpreting; Simultaneous Interpreting; Conference Interpreting
Macao Polytechnic University	Master of Chinese–Portuguese Translation and Interpreting	Chinese and Portuguese	2 years	36 credits	Sight Translation (TICP6131); Consecutive Interpretation (TICP6132); Advanced Consecutive Interpretation (TICP6133); Simultaneous Interpretation (TICP6134); Consecutive Interpretation Practice (TICP6104); Simultaneous Interpretation Practice (TICP6105)

covers related areas of Portuguese studies, including translation. It requires 30 credits to graduate.

In short, degree programs of translation/interpreting are only available at several institutions, providing training in interpreting in the consecutive and simultaneous modes with preliminary or introductory modules of interpreting. Graduate students also conduct research in translation/interpreting under the supervision of their advisers. As mentioned earlier, Portuguese is the prominent language for most of the curricula for its status as the official language of the region. Most of the oral interpreting courses are provided in the senior years of the programs, and students are required to take other courses to enhance their language proficiency, culture sensitivity, and encyclopedia knowledge, which indicates that the curricula have addressed the importance of the philosophy of integrated learning for interpreter training. However, it is a pity that, looking at the current curricula, the more recent trend in technology-assisted interpreting and interpreting in remote and hybrid modes in the context of the pandemic have not yet been reflected in these programs.

3.2 Other interpreter training programs

Besides universities, there are also training programs offered by organizations outside Macao or collaborative programs for interpreter training. These programs, which are specifically designed to cultivate professional interpreters, are necessary supplements to the existing university-led degree programs. Most of the trainees from these programs have become active professional interpreters in Macao at different organizations.

3.2.1 EU–China Interpreter Training Project (EUCITP)

The EU–China Interpreter Training Project (EUCITP) (Dawrant et al. 2021) started in 1985 by the European Commission's Directorate-General for Interpretation (SCIC). It has been recruiting civil servants from government ministries as well as staff from other public institutions and state-owned enterprises in China from different language backgrounds, including Chinese–Portuguese and Chinese–English, for an intensive session at the headquarters of the European institutions in Brussels, Belgium. It is an ongoing program offering a half-year introductory conference interpreting course in Brussels for selected trainees from China, including the Macao SAR. The selection process is administered by the Ministry of Commerce of PRC, with 8–10 trainees admitted to each course cycle. During the two cycles offered annually in spring and autumn, respectively, interpreters work between Chinese and a European language, such as Portuguese, French, German, Spanish, and so on. The course is taught by EU staff interpreters who do not have Chinese as a working language. During each cycle, a visiting scholar from China joins the program and co-teaches for the last three months.

3.2.2 *MPU-DG SCIC collaboration*

Another milestone of international collaboration in Macao's interpreter training, also with European Union's Directorate-General for Interpretation (DG-SCIC), is the effort made by Macao Polytechnic University (MPU). MPU has maintained friendly relationship with DG-SCIC since 2006. Faculty members of MPU, interpreters from Macao government agencies, and international radio stations have since then benefited from the Chinese–Portuguese interpretation and translation program and conference interpretation training assisted by DG-SCIC since 2010. By 2018, eight professional conference interpretation training sessions had been held.[7] MPU officially opened the International Portuguese Training Centre for Conference Interpreting on December 5, 2019, aiming to

> further consolidate Macao's role as a service platform for business cooperation between China and Portuguese-speaking countries, improve the training effectiveness of both local and overseas Portuguese-speaking talents, strengthen the cooperation between Macao and other regions in cultivation of Portuguese-speaking talents, and raise the quality of the related human resources.[8]

3.3 *Professional associations of translation and interpreting*

Due to the comparatively small number of professional interpreters and translators, there are very few professional associations in Macao. The current review has found to date two such associations, namely, the Federation of Translators and Interpreters of Macao (FTIM) and the Translation Society of Legal Public Administration of Macao.

3.3.1 *Federation of Translators and Interpreters of Macao*

The Federation of Translators and Interpreters of Macao (FTIM) was officially registered in Macao in 2007 and became a member of the International Federation of Translators (FIT) in 2008. It has made remarkable achievements in translation and interpreting practice, teaching, and research since then. The FTIM has hosted the Macao Special Administrative Region Youth Translation Competition (2009), organized the 6th Asian Translators' Forum of FIT in 2010, participated in the National Interpreting Contests, and organized the National Contests' regional selection sessions in 2012, 2014, 2016, and 2018. FTM has also been actively taking part in the Cross-Strait Interpreting Contest since 2016. In 2023, the Grand Final of the 9th Cross-Strait Interpreting Contest will be hosted by FTIM at the University of Macau.

3.3.2 *The Translation Society of Legal Public Administration of Macao*

The Translation Society of Legal Public Administration of Macao was established in 1994. It has been dedicated to the research and translation related to law and public administration. It has organized activities in the aforementioned areas and cooperated with local or non-local organizations since its establishment. In 1996, there were more than 70 individual members, all of whom were professionals in the fields of law, public administration, and translation in Macao. The association's accomplishments include the publication of the *Annotations to the Code of Administrative Procedure* in 1995 and the *Documentation of Macao Constitution History* (1820–1974) jointly published in 1997 with the Legal Translation Office. In 1997, the Society hosted the Seminar on Macao's Administration towards the Ninth Five-Year Plan, joined by invited experts and scholars from the Chinese mainland, Macao SAR, and Portugal.[9]

3.4   *Interpreting accreditation test*

A key milestone in the professionalization of Macao's conference interpreting sector is the introduction of the China Accreditation Test for Translators and Interpreters (CATTI). Organized under the auspices of the Ministry of Human Resources and Social Security (MHRSS), it is the best-known accreditation test in China. Currently, for oral interpreting, CATTI certification is available at three levels in the consecutive mode – levels 1, 2, and 3, and one level in the simultaneous mode. The Macao Polytechnic University (MPU) is the first institute in both Hong Kong and Macao to offer CATTI tests to eligible participants. The MPU test site administered its first English–Chinese and Portuguese–Chinese translation and interpreting tests on June 18 and 19, 2021, concurrently with test sites on the Chinese mainland.

4   Interpreting research in Macao

Previous accounts of translation and interpreting in Macao have not given much attention to the research of interpreting, obviously due to the small number of research outputs in the area. However, in the last decade or so, research related to interpreting studies (IS) has been picking up as new research institutions and scholars are making headways in many related areas of interest using cutting-edge technologies in collaboration with scholars from other areas of expertise.

On the one hand, data from publications on IS in China's mainland, Hong Kong, Macao and Taiwan show that research work by scholars from Macao makes up only a very small proportion of the total amount. A recent review by Ren et al. (2020) borrows the categorization standard of IS from Wang and Liu (2015) and roughly divides research topics of IS into the following seven classifications: interpreting process, interpreting practice and interpreting profession, interpreting products, interpreters, interpreting pedagogy, interpreting theories, and meta-research. Results from Ren's review show that the volume of IS research is obviously small from 1978 to 2018, especially for Macao (see Table 10.4). Altogether, only 22 works have been identified within the aforementioned categories.

Table 10.4 Topics by Period from 1978 to 2018 as Found in the Journals of Hong Kong, Macao, and Taiwan

Period	Interpreting Product			Meta-Research			Interpreters			Interpreting Pedagogy			Interpreting Practice and Profession			Interpreting Theories			Interpreting Process		
	T	HK	M	T	HK	M	T	HK	M	T	HK	M	T	HK	M	T	HK	M	T	HK	M
1978–1995	0	0	0	0	0	0	0	0	0	0	5	0	0	5	0	3	0	0	2	1	0
1996–2005	4	1	4	2	1	1	0	0	0	31	4	6	5	5	1	9	0	1	4	1	3
2006–2018	5	1	0	6	3	1	2	0	1	29	2	1	12	2	1	11	0	1	10	1	0

Source: Ren et al. (2020).
* Taiwan is abbreviated as *T*, Hong Kong as *HK*, and Macao as *M*.

On the other hand, scholars from Macao studying translation and interpreting are expanding presence in the international community. Among them, the team from the University of Macau, in particular the Centre for Studies of Translation, Interpretation, and Cognition (CSTIC), has been making headways in research related to IS in recent years (see 4.2).

4.2   Centers and representative research

A systematic investigation into IS in Macao began in 2014 when the Centre for Studies of Translation, Interpretation, and Cognition (CSTIC) of the University of Macao was established and headed by Prof. Defeng Li and has since then been one of the most prominent research centers for translation, interpretation, and cognition studies internationally. The recent collaboration between CSTIC and the Centre for Cognitive and Brain Sciences (CCBS) of the University of Macau using state-of-the-art technologies to conduct cognitive interpreting research has attracted much attention in the research community both at home and abroad.

4.2.1   CSTIC and its research team

CSTIC aims to provide a platform for promoting and conducting original frontline research, promoting regional and international collaboration and cooperation. It includes an international advisory team of renowned scholars, scientists, and practitioner researchers as well as faculty members from multiple disciplines. CSTIC also includes graduate students conducting thesis projects under their supervisors who are affiliated to the research center. CSTIC has been working closely with CCBS, a brand-new multidisciplinary research and educational center at the University of Macau, for the study of cognition and brain sciences. CSTIC is now collaborating with scientists and experts from disciplines such as psychology, education, and neuroimaging to investigate the neurocognitive mechanism inside the "black box" – the interpreter's brain. Members of CSTIC are using technologies such as eye trackers, EEG/ERP, fNIRS, fMRI, BIOPAC physiology system, as well as behavioral methods, corpus, survey, and interview, to carry out empirical studies in IS with publications mostly in international journals.

4.2.2   The New Frontiers in Translation Studies series

The New Frontiers in Translation Studies series, with Prof. Defeng Li as the series editor, aims to capture the newest developments in translation studies, with a focus on (1) translation studies research methodology, an area of growing interest among translation students and teachers; (2) data-based empirical translation studies, a strong point of growth for the discipline because of the scientific nature of the quantitative and/or qualitative methods adopted in the investigations; and (3) Asian translation thoughts and theories, to complement the current Eurocentric translation studies. Started in 2016, the series now includes 34 edited volumes (the latest of which will come out in early 2023) covering a wide range of topics in translation and interpreting studies. Several of the edited volumes have chapters particularly dedicated to interpreting studies: *Advances in Cognitive Translation Studies* (Martín et al. 2021), *Cognitive Processing Routes in Consecutive Interpreting* (Liu 2021), *Eye-Tracking Processes and Styles in Sight Translation* (Su 2020), and *Researching Cognitive Processes of Translation* (Li et al. 2019), among the latest productions.

4.2.3 CSTIC research and publications

Since its establishment, CSTIC members have been active in interpreting research, and their work have appeared in international peer-reviewed journals. Since 2014, CSTIC has published dozens of items, including journal articles, monographs, and book chapters related to cognitive IS, corpus-based IS, interpreting education, among others. There are also PhD dissertations investigating IS from different research perspectives. Some adopted the corpus-assisted or corpus-based approach to look at questions related to cognitive processes in oral interpreting, such as memory-pairing in simultaneous interpreting (Lang 2017; Lang et al. 2018) and processing routes in consecutive interpreting (Liu 2018). Others made use of laboratory equipment to conduct experiments. For example, functional near-infrared spectroscopy (fNIRS) has been used to investigate brain activation associated with the use of different translation strategies during Chinese–English simultaneous interpretation (Lin et al. 2018) and to map the brain activation underlying translation asymmetry during Chinese–English sight translation (He et al. 2017). Eye-tracking has been deployed to investigate the interplay between speech rate, cognitive load, and performance in simultaneous interpreting with text (Yang 2019; Yang et al. 2020). More recent development with the CSTIC team involves using functional magnetic resonance imaging (fMRI) and eye-tracking to look at the relationship between simultaneous interpreting, an extreme form of bilingualism, and executive functions (Li et al. 2021).

5 Summary of the chapter

A multilingual and multicultural metropolis, Macao has been a unique testimony to the first and longest-lasting encounter between Western and Chinese cultures (Zhang 2012). With its booming economy and cultural interchange and the attractive diversity of languages used among its population, we can expect further achievements in the future for conference interpreting–related practice, training, and research.

A region rich in language resources, Macao enjoys unique advantages to develop its language industry, interpreting services included, in synergy with the development of the tourism industry as laid out in the SAR government's plan for the next decade. Macao can also make full use of the strengths of its status as the Sino-Portuguese platform to create a regional chain of language industries in the Greater Bay Area. It will not only contribute to the healthy and stable development of Macao's pillar industries but also meet the needs of Macao's "moderate economic diversification."[10] Incentive policies should be created to encourage more private translation and interpreting entities to join the market.

As mentioned in the discussion of Macao's interpreting training, more programs need to be established, covering more language combinations and inviting more institutions to develop new curricula, especially in the era of technology-driven language service. A good example, however, in translation rather than in interpreting, is the development of the world's first intelligent Chinese–Portuguese–English translation platform, "Online Chinese-Portuguese-English Computer Aided Translation platform" (UM-CAT), at the University of Macao.[11] In the future, technology in computer-aided interpreting is expected to emerge and be put into application, which should not only provide professional training to would-be interpreters and students at various levels but also become potential tools to professional interpreters providing services to clients in both the public and the private sectors in the region. Another issue is to develop technology and expertise in the context of distance interpreting (DI) to meet the challenges we face in the post-COVID era.

Finally, research on IS should also expand its scope to cover more topics of interest and methodologies. Apart from looking into the professional practice of interpreting, more work can be done to investigate "big questions" in relation to cognition and brain sciences in response to national initiatives. The communities for interpreting teaching, practice, and research in Macao should work in coordination with the government, industry, and academia to further strengthen interdisciplinary and cross-regional collaboration.

Notes

1 Retrieved November 24, 2022, from www.dsedj.gov.mo/~webdsej/www/grp_db/policy/lang_policy_e.pdf?timeis=Fri%20Sep%202017:21:55%20GMT+08:00%202019&&.
2 Retrieved November 24, 2022, from www.dsec.gov.mo/ts/#!/step2/PredefinedReport/en-US/19.
3 Retrieved November 24, 2022, from www.chyxx.com/industry/1111782.html.
4 Retrieved November 24, 2022, from www.boss.mo/en/products/wechat/.
5 Retrieved November 24, 2022, from www.safp.gov.mo/safptc/ur/index.htm.
6 Retrieved November 24, 2022, from https://es.dsedj.gov.mo/cees/en/colleges.html.
7 Retrieved November 24, 2022, from www.mpu.edu.mo/eslt/en/cwtdgiec.php.
8 Retrieved November 24, 2022, from www.gov.mo/en/news/120646/.
9 Retrieved November 27, 2022, from www.adat.org.mo/about.html.
10 Retrieved November 27, 2022, from www.dsec.gov.mo/en-US/Home/Publication/SIED.
11 Retrieved November 24, 2022, from http://nlp2ct.cis.umac.mo/views/news/2020041601.html.

References

Aguiar, Manuela Teresa Sousa 施佩玲. 2003. "Aomen de fanyi yu chuanyi" 澳門的翻譯與傳譯. [Translation and Interpretation in Macau]. *Gangao tequ xingzheng yu shehui* 港澳特区行政与社会 [Administration and Society in Hong Kong and Macao SAR] 1: 32–48.

Dawrant, Andrew, Binhua Wang, and Hong Jiang. 2021. "Conference Interpreting in China." In *The Routledge Handbook of Conference Interpreting*, edited by Michaela Albl-Mikasa and Elisabet Tiselius, 182–96. Abingdon, UK: Routledge.

Han, Lili, and Nan Yang. 2022. "Remapping the Translation Policies in China: Contributions from Macau." *Asian-Pacific Journal of Second and Foreign Language Education* 7(1): 1–17.

He, Yan, Wang Mengyun, Li Defeng, and Yuan Zhen. 2017. "Optical Mapping of Brain Activation during the English to Chinese and Chinese to English Sight Translation." *Biomedical Optics Express* 8(12): 5399–5411. https://doi.org/10.1364/BOE.8.005399.

Lam, Johnny F. I., and Wai In Ieong. 2022. "Translanguaging and Multilingual Society of Macau: Past, Present and Future." *Asian-Pacific Journal of Second and Foreign Language Education* 7(1). https://doi.org/10.1186/s40862-022-00169-y.

Lang, Yue. 2017. "A Corpus-Assisted Case Study of Memory-Pairing in English-Chinese and Chinese-English Simultaneous Interpreting." PhD diss., University of Macao.

Lang Yue 朗悦, Hou Linping 侯林平, and He Yuanjian 何元建. 2018. "Tongsheng chuanyi zhongjiyi peidui de renzhi yanjiu" 同声传译中记忆配对的认知研究 [A Cognitive Study on Memory Pairing in Simultaneous Interpreting]. *Xiandai waiyu* 现代外语 [Modern Foreign Languages] 41(6): 1–11.

Li, Defeng, Victoria Lai Cheng Lei, and Yuanjian He, eds. 2019. *Researching Cognitive Processes of Translation*. Singapore: Springer.

Li, Defeng, Victoria Lai Cheng Lei, and Ruey-Song Huang. "Executive Functions in Translation/Interpreting Process: Seeking Neurocognitive Evidence for Bilingual Advantages" *Keynote, 7th International Conference on Cognitive Research on Translation and Interpreting* Wuhan, China, June 12, 2021.

Li, Wei. 2022. "Translanguaging as a Political Stance: Implications for English Language Education." *ELT Journal* 76(2): 172–82. https://doi.org/10.1093/elt/ccab083.

Lin, Xiaohong, Victoria Lai Cheng Lei, Defeng Li, and Zhen Yuan. 2018. "Which Is More Costly in Chinese to English Simultaneous Interpreting, 'Pairing' or 'Transphrasing'? Evidence from an fNIRS Neuroimaging Study." *Neurophotonics* 5(2): 025010.

Liu, Xiaodong. 2018. "How Do Interpreting Patterns Implicate Neurocognitive Processing Routes? Evidence from English Vs Chinese Consecutive Interpreting." PhD diss., University of Macao.

Liu, Xiaodong. 2021. *Cognitive Processing Routes in Consecutive Interpreting*. Singapore: Springer.

Muñoz, Martín Ricardo, Sanjun Sun, and Defeng Li, eds. 2021. *Advances in Cognitive Translation Studies*. Singapore: Springer.

Ren, Wen, Guo Cong, and Huang Juan. 2020. "A Review of 40 Years of Interpreting Research in China (1978–2018)." *Babel. Revue internationale de la traduction/International Journal of Translation* 66(1): 1–28. https://doi.org/10.1075/babel.00137.ren.

Sheng, Yan. 2004. *Languages in Macao: Past, Present and Future*. Macao: Macao Polytechnic Institute.

Su, Wenchao. 2020. *Eye-Tracking Processes and Styles in Sight Translation*. Singapore: Springer.

Wang Qian 王茜, and Liu Heping 刘和平. 2015. "2004–2013 zhongguo kouyi yanjiu de fazhan yu zouxiang" 2004–2013 中国口译研究的发展与走向 [New Developments of Interpreting Studies in China (2004–2013)]. *Shanghai fanyi* 上海翻译 [Shanghai Journal of Translators] 1: 77–83.

Yang, Shanshan. 2019. "Investigating the Effect of Speech Rate on the Cognitive Load in Simultaneous Interpreting with Text." PhD diss., University of Macau.

Yang, Shanshan, Defeng Li, and Victoria Lai Cheng Lei. 2020. "The Impact of Source Text Presence on Simultaneous Interpreting Performance in Fast Speeches: Will It Help Trainees or Not?" *Babel* 66(4–5): 588–603.

Zeng Zhonglu 曾忠禄, Xiao Jinxiong 萧锦雄, Ji Chunli 纪春礼, and Xue Wen 薛文. 2018. "Aomen bocaiye weilai rencai xuqiu diaoyan (jianbao)" 澳门博彩业未来人才需求调研(简报). [Research on Future Talent Needs of Macau Gaming Industry (Briefing)][EB/OL]. Accessed November 23, 2022. www.scdt. gov.mo/wpcontent/uploads/2017/03/2018%E6%BE%B3%E9%96%80%E5%8D %9A%E5%BD%A9%E6%A5%AD%E6%9C%AA%E4%BE%86%E4%BA%BA%E6%89% 8D%E8%B3%87%E6%BA%90%E9%9C%80%E6%B1%82%E8%AA%BF%E7%A0%94- %E7%B0%A1%E5%A0%B1.pdf.

Zhang Meifang. 2012. "Reading Different Cultures through Cultural Translation: On Translation of Site Names in Macao Historic Centre." *Babel* 58(2), 205–19.

11 Interpreter training in Xinjiang

Challenges and solutions

Bin Zou and Xiaoyan Li

1 Introduction

With the progressive advancement of China's opening-up, the Western development, and the joint construction of the Belt and Road Initiative, Xinjiang, located in the hinterlands of the Eurasian continent, is moving from a relatively closed inland region to the forefront of openness. Based on its position as the core area of the Silk Road Economic Belt, Xinjiang is making efforts to enhance its international influence and popularity and strengthen close ties with neighboring countries. Against this background, important exhibitions, such as China–Eurasia Expo and China Asia–Europe Commodity Trade Fair, are held one after another, which calls for the cultivation of high-level foreign language talents. At the same time, the Outline of the Medium- and Long-Term Talent Development Plan of Xinjiang Uygur Autonomous Region (2010–2020) points out that the cultivation of export-oriented publicity as well as cultural and bilingual talents should be vigorously strengthened. The training of bilingual talents, especially translation talents, is high on the agenda for Xinjiang higher education. The training units for MTI in Xinjiang shoulder the responsibility of training translators and interpreters.

Up to now, there are four universities in Xinjiang enrolling MTI students, namely, Xinjiang University, Xinjiang Normal University, Shihezi University, and Kashi (Kashgar) University; the latter two were approved for enrollment in 2022. This chapter elaborates on the problems in the training of interpreters, taking Xinjiang University and Xinjiang Normal University as examples, which were approved for enrolling MTI students in 2011. This chapter introduces the localization, curriculum design, teaching methods, scientific research, and trainees' quality control of the interpreter training programs of these two universities and analyzes the challenges faced by interpreter trainers. It puts forward some measures for overcoming these challenges and then explores a localized interpreter training model, providing reference for local interpreter training.

2 Interpreter training in Xinjiang

The formal interpreter training program in Xinjiang started in 2011 in two universities: Xinjiang University and Xinjiang Normal University. Toward

DOI: 10.4324/9781003357629-14

Table 11.1 MTI and Its Training Programs in Xinjiang Universities

University	MTI	
Xinjiang University	CE Translation Program	
	CR Translation Program	
Xinjiang Normal University	CE Translation Program	CE Interpreter Training Program
	RE Translation Program	RE Interpreter Training Program
Shihezi University	CE Translation Program	CE Interpreter Training Program
Kashi (Kashgar) University	Translation Program	

the end of 2022, two other universities were newly approved by the Chinese Ministry of Education to offer MTI programs: Shihezi University and Kashi (Kashgar) University. So among the 55 universities and colleges in Xinjiang, only four are authorized to offer MTI programs. To be more specific, three also offer interpreter training programs and diplomatic training. Among all the MTI programs, two language pairs are covered, namely, English to Chinese and Russian to Chinese. Xinjiang Normal University is the only one that offers interpreter programs for both language pairs.

The annual enrollment number of MTI students for all the four universities in Xinjiang adds up to 120, among which students for the interpreter training program are only 17, or less than 15%. The majority of the students are enrolled in the translation program instead. Although the actual number of students for the interpreter training program could be more than 17, because Shihezi University does not distinguish students between translation and interpreter training programs at enrollment, generally speaking, MTI in Xinjiang prioritizes translation more than interpreter training.

Among the four universities, Xinjiang University and Shihezi University are both included in the Double First-Class Initiative, Xinjiang Normal University is the key university at the provincial level, and Kashi (Kashgar) University has been newly upgraded to a comprehensive university since 2015 due to its unique geographic location in the Kashi (Kashgar) Special Economic Development Zone (the other three universities are located in northern Xinjiang, where the economy and industry have developed faster).

Because both Shihezi University and Kashi (Kashgar) University were only recently approved to offer the MTI program, their first group of students will not be enrolled until 2023. Thus, Xinjiang University and Xinjiang Normal University are the focus of our research. Xinjiang University is the largest university in scale and traces its origins from the former Russian Law and Politics Institute in 1924 and is considered the most prestigious university in Xinjiang. Its MTI covers two language pairs, Chinese to English and Chinese to

Russian, with 80 students annually enrolled. It only offers interpreter training program of Chinese to Russian.

Compared with Xinjiang University, Xinjiang Normal University is much younger, as it was founded in 1978 from the Urumqi No. 1 Teachers' College and Xinjiang Teacher Training Department. Comparatively speaking, XJNU's strength lies in the study of the arts; its journal is recognized for exclusive comprehensive CSSCI in Xinjiang and even ranks among the top of all Chinese university journals for philosophy and social sciences with an IF of 6.593. Xinjiang Normal University offers both translator and interpreter training programs for Chinese to English as well as Chinese to Russian (although these are comparatively small). From 2020, Xinjiang Normal University was approved by the Chinese Ministry of Education to offer bachelor's degree for translation. Thus, it is the only university with translation programs for both bachelor's and master's degrees. According to BFSU Research Center for Country-Specific Translation Competence, Xinjiang Normal University ranked 74 among all the universities in China in 2019. Even though its rank dropped out of the top 100 in 2021, many teachers and students are still active in various local translation and interpreting practices.

3 Curricula of interpreter training in Xinjiang

By reviewing the MTI curricula of Xinjiang University and Xinjiang Normal University, it was discovered that both universities are experimenting with some localized training programs even if they are not particularly impressive. Generally speaking, the training programs do not present distinguishing characteristics compared with other universities, yet local demands for interpreters cannot be fully met and reflected in the curriculum.

The interpreter training in Xinjiang will be analyzed from the following five aspects: training purposes, training targets, training curriculum, training methods, and dissertation.

3.1 Training purpose

For the majority of the universities offering MTI in China, the training program is either translation-oriented or interpretation-oriented, but none of the universities have integrated translation and interpreter training into one program (Shi and Niu 2020). However, both Xinjiang University and Xinjiang Normal University are making positive efforts by sharing some of the core courses for their interpreter training programs.

It is noted that both universities share one of the fundamental courses: translation theory and practice for interpreter training program candidates; however, Xinjiang University attaches more importance to the language proficiency courses, while Xinjiang Normal University believes CAT courses are more helpful for trainees.

Table 11.2 Shared Courses in the Interpreter Training Programs of XJNU and XJU

Interpreter Training Program and University	CE Interpreter Training Program at XJNU	CR Interpreter Training Program at XJU
Shared compulsory courses	Translation Theory and Skills	Translation Theory and Practice
	Introduction of Central Asian Countries	
Shared optional courses	Computer-Aided Translation	Russian Lexical and Rhetorical Studies
	Translation and Technology	Advanced Russian

Table 11.3 Training Targets of Interpreter Training at XJNU and XJU

Interpreter Training Program and University	CE Interpreter Training Program at XJNU	CR Interpreter Training Program at XJU
Morality	Patriotism and Adherence to the Leadership of the CPC	Guided by Marxism
	Safeguarding National Unity, Social Stability, and Ethnic Solidarity	Overall Development in Morality, Intelligence, and Stamina
	Understanding the Basic Tenets of Marxism	Entrepreneurial, Innovation, and Adaptation
	Law-Abidance and Discipline	
	Prudent Attitude in Scientific Research, Diligence in Working, Entrepreneurism, and Innovation	
Knowledge	Solid Linguistic Knowledge	High Language Proficiency
	Solid Translation Theory	Cross-Cultural Communication Knowledge
Capacity	Translation Capacity in Culture, Science, and Business Language	Translation Competence in Economic Globalization, BRI Trade, Cultural Exchanges
	Instrumental Capacity by Using Corpus and CAT	Instrumental Capacity by Using Big Data, Translation Software, and Corpus

3.2 *Training targets*

The training targets for both Xinjiang University and Xinjiang Normal University are designed to train localized high-level translators and interpreters with professional skills with political reliability.

Compared with the norm of defining training targets in a broad and macroscopic perspective at the majority of Chinese universities, both Xinjiang University and Xinjiang Normal University share the consensus of political reliability, especially strengthening training with the theory of socialism with Chinese characteristics. Linguistic competence is prioritized by both universities due to the consideration of candidates' language proficiency. Even though both universities agree to train localized interpreters, Xinjiang University develops more of a candidate's business interpreting capacity, while Xinjiang Normal University develops more comprehensive interpreting capacities.

3.3 Training curriculum

The training curriculum for MTI can be divided into three categories: language courses, interpreter training courses, and related courses.

Table 11.4 Curriculum Design at XJNU and XJU

Interpreter Training Program and University	CE Interpreter Training Program at XJNU	CR Interpreter Training Program at XJU
Language courses	Chinese Language and Culture Dissertation Writing	Chinese Language and Culture Advanced Russian Russian Advanced Listening Russian Language and Culture Russian Lexical and Rhetorical Studies Comparison of Russian and Chinese Writing in Russian Russian Literature
Interpretation courses	Introduction of Translation Translation Theory and Skills Interpreting Theory and Skills Consecutive Interpretation Simultaneous Interpretation Comparison of English and Chinese for Translation Virtual Conference Interpretation Interpretation Practice Computer-Aided Translation Sight Interpretation (Sight Translation) Themed Interpretation History of Translation in the World Translation and Technology	Introduction of Translation Translation Theory and Skills Interpreting Theory and Skills Consecutive Interpretation Simultaneous Interpretation Translation History in China and the World Interpretation Workshop Updated Russian News Translation
Related courses	Introduction to Central Asia Second Foreign Language (Russian or Japanese) Cross-Cultural Communication	Second Foreign Language (English) Foreign Trade Negotiation and Writing

In the language courses for MTI, both Xinjiang University and Xinjiang Normal University regard the Chinese language and culture as fundamental courses for the further development of the mother language. As is shown in the list, Xinjiang University provides more language courses for its MTI candidates mostly due to the consideration that even students with a BA in Russian language and literature have only four years to consolidate the language foundation, that is, more time to internalize a foreign language is required.

The interpretation courses normally consist of three types: interpretation knowledge, interpretation skills, and professional development. Generally speaking, Xinjiang Normal University has more diversified interpretation courses than Xinjiang University. To be more specific, Xinjiang University only has four interpretation courses because more credits are given to language courses as being discussed earlier.

In the related courses, Introduction to Central Asia is included in the courses for EC interpretation candidates, even though the official language for this area is Russian. Through further investigation, it was found that since Xinjiang neighbors most of the Central Asian countries and has close cooperation and exchanges with those countries in business and trade, Central Asia is one of the favorite research topics for Xinjiang scholars and think tanks. Having background knowledge of Central Asia is necessary for MTI candidates.

3.4 *Training methods*

The training methods of MTI are mainly composed of three parts: classroom instruction, internship, and tutoring from instructors (Wang and Cheng 2020). Traditional classroom instruction is still prevalent in the interpreter training program of both universities. However, this is usually conducted in a multimedia classroom or simultaneous interpretation laboratory. The courses of Xinjiang Normal University are more practice-oriented.

Both universities acknowledge the importance of internship and require no less than one semester of social practice and at least 400 hours of interpretation practice. Both universities have an instructor team which is composed of professors as well as experienced interpreters from government, companies, etc.

3.5 *Dissertations*

Dissertations for MTI usually take the form of an internship report, a translation practice report, a translation experiment report, an investigation report, and a research paper (Mu and Li 2019). According to Xinjiang University and Xinjiang Normal University, MTI candidates must submit dissertations of no less than 15,000 words before graduation, including an investigation report.

4 Challenges facing interpreter training in Xinjiang

Even though the interpreter training program at both universities targets localized interpreters, the localization cannot be reflected from curriculum design or teaching. It even deviates from the practice-orientated purpose of MTI. Due to a lack of a quality control mechanism, especially for interpretation capacity, trainees can seldom be found in the local interpreter market (which has been gradually diminishing in the past three years because quarantine policy canceled offline meetings). Interpreter training is faced with multiple challenges in Xinjiang.

4.1 Challenges in localization

Localization is the process of adapting a product or content to a specific locale or market (LISA 2007). While the localized curriculum of MTI is a whole training plan and procedure for localized translators and interpreters – including courses, software, and technology as well as project management, etc. – which aim to develop the localized technological capacity for translators and interpreters (Leng 2012). Both Xinjiang University and Xinjiang Normal University are making proactive efforts to localize their curricula regardless of how trivial they are. According to an investigation into MTI in China, only 30 universities and colleges except for foreign-languages universities have localized programs for the training of translators and interpreters in a specific field, such as trade and business, medicine, science and technology, etc., which accounts for 11.9% of all the MTI schools (Wang and Cheng 2020).

The major challenges for both Xinjiang University and Xinjiang Normal University are, first, how to further localize the curriculum in order to concentrate on specific fields of translation and interpretation and develop specialty as well as strength and, second, how to integrate translation technology into the curriculum.

4.2 Challenges in faculty building

There is a serious shortage of high-quality interpreting trainers. Most interpreting trainers have an academic background in English, not in interpretation. These interpreting trainers usually lack field interpretation practice and have difficulties in providing professional guidance to students. Lack of systematic knowledge of interpreter training teaching methods makes their classes ineffective. With the rapid development of Internet technology and big data, trainers have insufficient technology application and learning ability, which disqualifies them from helping students keep up with the development of new interpretation technologies.

Although students have part-time practice supervisors, they have limited exchanges with each other, and these supervisors do not fully participate in educating students.

Training resources for interpreting trainers are insufficient. The annually held Training of Trainers for Translation and Interpreting program is the only official training program in China. Not all the interpreting trainers have the opportunity to attend the intensive training program each year. Meanwhile, there is limited communication among MTI colleges in Xinjiang and outside Xinjiang.

The awareness of conducting scientific research among interpreting trainers in Xinjiang is also weak, and so is the quality of their papers. Their academic achievements are also not closely connected with teaching and the translation industry in Xinjiang.

4.3   Challenges in curriculum design

The interpreter training curriculum is basically designed according to the National Talent Education Plan, with no distinctive and local characteristics. Courses are not fully adapted to the needs of students and their abilities and to the demands of the local translation industry.

The curriculum design for consecutive interpreter training teaching only lasts for one semester, and students may not have established a solid foundation for CI study before they convert to SI. Courses on interpretation technology application are not included in the interpreter training curriculum. Courses for interpretation and translation students are not integrated effectively, and interpretation students are not encouraged to select courses that are designed for translation students.

4.4   Challenges in training

Training methods are relatively traditional and unsystematic, without innovation in terms of training means and materials. Training content is not closely related to the local translation industry. There are few localized interpreter training and translation textbooks.

4.5   Challenges in quality control

Until 2022, 316 universities and colleges in China are entitled to offer MTI programs and degrees. Concurrently, the research interests for quality MTI training rest on the assessment of MTI universities and the evaluation of MTI training quality (Lü 2019). To be more specific, the quality control for interpreter training programs is at least decided by the three dimensions of training quality, study quality, as well as professionalization quality. Through a comprehensive survey with graduates from interpreter training in both universities, it was discovered that a great gap exists between training quality and the expectations of trainees. Through interviews with interpreter trainers in both universities, it was also found that study quality is far below the average level. As far as professionalization quality is concerned, a minority of graduates are still doing interpretation-related jobs, while the majority of graduates failed to enter the interpretation job market or quit halfway. Thus, the major challenge for interpreter training in Xinjiang is the quality control mechanism.

5 Measures for improving interpreter training in Xinjiang

5.1 Enhancing localization

Professionalization is what distinguishes MTI from a traditional MA or MS, which is based on career-oriented training and translation capacity that meets the actual market demands in various fields (Huang and Bo 2016). The first step of localization for XJNU and XJU is to assess the disciplinary advantages in order to better integrate them into the interpreter training program. XJU has its strength in scientific and technological research, while XJNU prioritizes the humanities and social sciences, which both lay a solid foundation for the cross-disciplinary development of the interpreter training program, gradually developing into a specialty of their interpreter training. Since both universities attach great importance to the political reliance of the MTI candidates, political interpretation could also be considered as a potential direction for professionalization.

Compared with traditional translation services which focus only on the transition of codes, localization focuses more on the integration of scientific project management, procedures, information technology, and quality control (Cui 2012). Computer-aided translation should gain more weight in the curriculum design, and the translation kit must at least include Alchemy Catalyst, Passolo, Trados, and WorldServer in order to reuse translation resources, online translations, translation corpus constructions, as well as project management, respectively. With the further improvement of IT technology, localization technology has become an indispensable trait for future interpreters and translators.

5.2 Optimizing training faculty

With the professionalization of interpreter training educators, it is urgent to build a team of qualified trainers. Qualified interpreting trainers are those who have interpreted for more than 20 international conferences. To improve their interpreting competence, trainers need more training and practice opportunities so as to ensure that they can carry out effective guidance for students.

It is necessary to provide trainers with opportunities for further education in terms of training methodologies and interpretation competence enhancement. The MTI colleges in Xinjiang should encourage educators to attend multilevel translation training programs and carry out systematic study at top translation colleges. MTI colleges are recommended to conduct more exchanges and cooperation in terms of training and scientific research and invite professional interpreters and interpreting trainers from top translation colleges to give lectures on interpretation practices and training methodologies. Academic supervisors and part-time practice supervisors should strengthen communication and exchanges and enhance supervision of students in the whole process of their academic study.

To create a good research atmosphere, trainers should be encouraged to participate in translation academic seminars and integrate training practice with their research, with the aim of producing more academic achievements.

5.3 Improving curriculum design

It is suggested to establish a multimodal Chinese–English, Chinese–Russian translation corpus related to Xinjiang's regional geography and culture contents, based on which trainers can provide a series of related translation and interpretation courses and enable students to better "tell Xinjiang's stories" to the world. Trainers are encouraged to work collaboratively to compile textbooks of local characteristics, including Xinjiang's customs, history, scenic spots, and food culture. Local economic and cultural development serves as a basis for formulating education goals, so professional interpreters should be cultivated to meet the market demand. As of May 2015, translation industries in Xinjiang mainly serve the following areas: economy and trade, culture and media, foreign affairs and diplomacy, communication technology and manufacturing (Huang 2015). Therefore, it is recommended that optional courses in the aforementioned fields be provided for translation and interpretation trainees. Meanwhile, translation and interpretation courses should be open for all the students irrespective of their major.

According to the needs and language proficiency of students in Xinjiang, more optional courses should open for enrollment, such as public speaking and advanced English listening and speaking (Li 2017). Students ought to have a solid foundation in their CI study and sight interpretation before they transfer to SI study.

The big data era calls for new demands on technology application ability of interpreters. Thus, the MTI programs should develop students' interpretation technology competence centering on interpretation equipment operation skills, computer application skills, information retrieval skills, terminology management skills, computer-aided translation skills, machine translation skills, and video and audio processing skills (Wang et al. 2018).

5.4 Innovating training methods

Different training methods should be explored and applied in interpreter training, for example, situated learning approach and interactive training and learning. Training materials should contain varied features, including spontaneous speech, written speech, fast-paced speech, and speech with accents. Trainers can increase the difficulty of the materials gradually according to students' abilities.

The procedure of training can be divided into three steps (Zhang and Chai 2022), namely, vocabulary and background knowledge preparation before the interpreting class, in-class practice with trainers' demonstration and feedback from trainers and peers, and individual and group practice after class. Trainers are advised to make full use of online training resources, such as MOOCs, to make training more efficient.

5.5   *Innovate quality control mechanism*

Demanded by the information technology to translation training, a theoretical model of TPACC (Technological Pedagogical Content Competence) was invented in accordance with the discipline status and pedagogical features (Liu and Wang 2022). This model is composed of three key indices of TC, CC, and PC as well four sub-indices of PPC, TPC, TCC, and TPCC, which provide a matrix to evaluate the quality of interpreting trainers.

Since interpreter training programs aim at producing high-level interpreters, practice-oriented approach and trainee-centric approach must be adopted. Generally speaking, the study quality is reflected by the cognitive achievements of the trainees, such as interpretations, dissertations, competitions, and interpreting certificates (Lü 2019). The interpreter training program should provide adequate opportunities for trainees to participate in competitions, mock or real occasions for interpreting, encouraging trainees to compose dissertations from personal interpreter training experiences.

6   Conclusion

Xinjiang has played a significant role in the cultural and economic communication between China and the West. The cultivation of top translation talents is high on the agenda of Xinjiang's institutions of higher education. This chapter first reviewed the status quo of interpreter training in Xinjiang over the past decade and then proposed the challenges and measures for improving current interpreter training system. The chapter aimed to explore a new path for interpreting education in Xinjiang with distinctive localized characteristics in the new era and improve students' interpreting competence to meet the needs of local market.

References

Cui Qiliang 崔启亮. 2012. "Gaoxiao MTI fanyi yu bendihua kecheng jiaoxue shijian" 高校 MTI 翻译与本地化课程教学实践 [The Practice of MTI Translation Localization in Chinese Universities]. *Zhongguo fanyi* 中国翻译 [Chinese Translators Journal] (1): 29–34.

Huang Wei 黄威. 2015. "Kouyi zhiyehua qushixia xinjiang de yingyu kouyi rencai xuqiu qishi" 口译职业化趋势下新疆的英语口译人才需求及启示 [A Study on Model of Interpreter Training in Xinjiang]. *Haiwai yingyu* 海外英语 [Overseas English] (23): 145–6.

Huang Zhonglian 黄忠廉, and Zhang Bo 张博. 2016. "Woguo fanyi shuoshi zhuanye xuewei shidian jianshe zhanlue sikao" 我国翻译硕士专业学位试点建设战略思考 [Reflection on Strategic Planning of China's MTI Institution Development]. *Waiguoyu wen yanjiu* 外国语文研究 [Foreign Language and Literature Research] (2): 74–8.

Leng Bingbing 冷冰冰. 2012. "Tan MTI peiyang tixizhong de bendihua kecheng shezhi" 谈 MTI 培养体系中的本地化课程设置 [Curriculum Design in MTI Localization]. *Shanghai fanyi* 上海翻译 [Shanghai Journal of Translation] (1): 53–6.

Li Xiaoyan 李晓燕. 2017. "Kouyi kecheng shezhi bentuhua yanjiu – yi xinjiang gaoxiao weili" 口译课程设置本土化研究 – 以新疆高校为例 [Localized Interpreting Curriculum Design: Taking Universities in Xinjiang as Examples]. *Xiaoyuan yingyu* 校园英语 [English on Campus] (37): 12–3.

Liu Hongwei 刘宏伟, and Wang Xiangling 王湘玲. 2022. "Zhenghe jishu de fanyi jiaoshi jiaoxue nengli liangbiaoyanzhi yu jianyan" 整合技术的翻译教师教学能力量表研制与检验 [The Design and Appraisal of TPACK]. *Waiyujie* 外语界 [Foreign Language World] (5): 71–9.

Lü Hongyan 吕红艳. 2019. "Yi shengweiben linian xia MTI jiaoyu zhiliang yingxiang yinsu yanjiu" 以生为本"理念下 MTI 教育质量影响因素研究 [Research on the Factors Influencing the Quality of MTI with Students-Centered Principle]. *Shanghai fanyi* 上海翻译 [Shanghai Journal of Translation] (4): 60–5.

Mu Lei 穆雷, and Li Wen 李雯. 2019. "Fanyi shuoshi zhuanye xuewei lunwen xiezuo moshi de zaisikao – jiyu 704 pian xuewei lunwen de fenxi" 翻译硕士专业学位论文写作模式的再思考 – 基于704篇学位论文的分析 [Re-Consideration of the Dissertation Model for MTI- on the Analysis of 704 Dissertations]. *Xuewi yu yanjiusheng jiaoyu* 学位与研究生教育 [Academic Degrees and Graduate Education] (11): 33–9.

Shi Xingsong 史兴松, and Niu Yilin 牛一琳. 2020. "Guoneiwai fanyi shuoshi rencai peiyang moshi duibi yanjiu" 国内外翻译硕士人才培养模式对比研究 [A Comparative Study of the Models for MTI Education at Home and Abroad]. *Zhongguo fanyi* 中国翻译 [Chinese Translators Journal] (5): 63–70.

Wang Huashu 王华树, Li Zhi 李智, and Li Defeng 李德凤. 2018. "Kouyiyuan jishu yingyong nengli shizheng yanjiu: wenti yu duice" 口译员技术应用能力实证研究:问题与对策 [An Empirical Research on Professional Interpreters' Use of Interpreting Technologies]. *Shanghai fanyi* 上海翻译 [Shanghai Journal of Translators] (5): 70–7,88.

Wang Zhiwei 王志伟, and Cheng Lu 程璐. 2020. "MTI zhuanye xianzhuang fenxi yu tese fazhan" MTI 专业现状分析与特色发展 [Status quo and characteristic of MTI]. *Luoyang shifan daxue xuebao* 洛阳师范大学学报 [Journal of Luoyang Normal University] (39): 76–80.

Zhang Jiliang 张吉良, and Chai Mingjiong 柴明颎. 2022. "Teseban-benke kouyi rencai peiyang moshi xintan" 特色班 – 本科口译人才培养模式新探 [A Special Class: A New Exploration of the Training Model for Undergraduate Interpreting Students]. *Zhongguo fanyi* 中国翻译 [Chinese Translators Journal] (2): 67–74.

12 Problems in MTI conference interpreting education in Gansu, Qinghai, and Ningxia and suggested solutions

Xuejie Bai

1 Introduction

The three provinces of Gansu, Qinghai, and Ningxia Hui Autonomous Region are located in the west of China. They are not politically relevant, like the capital of China, Beijing; they are not economically developed, like Shanghai and its surrounding cities; they are not technology hubs, like the city of Hangzhou; and they are not coastal cities, like the cities in Guangdong province which enjoy advantages in foreign exchange and international trade. However, their importance may grow following President Xi's announcement of building the Silk Road Economic Belt and the 21st-century Maritime Silk Road. China has introduced its "One Belt and One Road Initiative" in recent years, and it will see a boom in the development in green economy, especially in tourism. Gansu, Qinghai, and Ningxia are critical provinces in the initiative, and they all boast rich tourism resources. So they will see a surge in international exchanges, trade, and cooperation.

Xia (2021, 80) argues that MTI (master of translation and interpreting) is established with the aim to alleviate the stress on increasing demand for top-notch professional interpreters and translators, conference interpreters in particular, as China is increasingly opening to the outside world and is increasingly active on the international stage. It is also expected to help build a full-fledged language service industry to serve China's "going global" strategy and its increased international trade, cooperation, and exchange. Nonetheless, it speaks to the shortage of top-notch professional interpreters and translators, especially in China's less-developed regions, such as the provinces in western China.

Interpretation, conference interpretation in particular, plays a crucial role in international exchange, trade, and cooperation; however, MTI conference interpreting education in the three western provinces of Gansu, Qinghai, and Ningxia Hui Autonomous Region is faced with major problems due to the aforementioned reasons. Therefore, this chapter tries to find out some common problems faced by the universities authorized to confer MTI degrees in the three provinces and suggest some possible solutions.

DOI: 10.4324/9781003357629-15

2 Problems in conference interpreting education in higher institutions in the three western provinces

Eight universities in the three provinces are authorized to confer MTI degrees, including Lanzhou University, Northwest Normal University, Northwest Minzu University, Lanzhou Jiaotong University, Lanzhou University of Technology, Ningxia University, Qinghai Nationalities University, and North Minzu University. Geographically speaking, Lanzhou University, Northwest Normal University, Northwest Minzu University, Lanzhou Jiaotong University, and Lanzhou University of Technology are located in the city of Lanzhou in Gansu province; Ningxia University and North Minzu University are based in Ningxia Hui Autonomous Region; and Qinghai Nationalities University is positioned in Qinghai province. Through research and investigation, I found that only four universities have enrolled or are still enrolling candidates for MTI conference interpreting, including Lanzhou University, Northwest Normal University, Lanzhou Jiaotong University, and Ningxia University. The other four universities have never enrolled MTI interpreting students or have stopped enrolling them because they lack qualified teachers who are supposed to be experienced professional interpreters themselves with the knowledge about how to train professional interpreters or because they are not able to enroll enough MTI interpreting students. The four universities that have enrolled and/or are still enrolling MTI conference interpreting candidates are struggling with enrolling interpreting candidates for similar problems. This chapter classifies their problems into the following four categories.

2.1 *Curriculum*

Table 12.1 indicates that there is a lack of diversity and simply the number of related courses in at least two universities. Through an in-depth analysis of the problems in the curriculum design of MTI conference interpreting of the four universities and taking into account the needs of a thriving language service industry which is in need of a large number of high-level conference interpreters to contribute to China's further integration into the international community and reform and opening-up, I discovered the following aspects that still have room to improve: first, teaching content overlaps among the core courses; second, fundamental courses are missing in some universities; third, interpreting training does not cater to the students' internship; fourth, interpreting students are not required to get professional accreditation for the completion of their degree in some universities; and finally, courses in interpreting technology are missing in all four universities in spite of the fact that interpreting services are more and more provided on digital platforms and remote interpreting services are in increasing demand, which requires the help of such new technologies as virtual reality, artificial intelligence, big data, and Internet 5G technology. One possible reason is that the universities lack the necessary human resources and/or facilities to open and administer such

Table 12.1 Conference Interpreting Curricula in the Four Universities

University / Course	Lanzhou University	Northwest Normal University	Lanzhou Jiaotong University	Ningxia University
1	Simultaneous Interpreting 1 (English)	Interpreting Theories and Skills	Interpreting Basics 1	Interpreting on Local Situations
2	Consecutive Interpreting 1	Consecutive Interpreting	Interpreting Basics 2	Simulated Conference Interpreting
3	Interpreting Workshop	Simultaneous Interpreting	Interpreting for Engineering Project Negotiation	Sight Interpreting
4	Interpreting under Various Themes	Conference Interpreting and Exhibition Management	Interpreting under Various Themes	Listening and Speaking Training in Interpreting
5	Interpreting Theories and Skills	Business and Trade Interpreting	Business Interpreting	Liaison Interpreting
6	Simultaneous Interpreting 2 (English)	Tourism Interpreting	Interpreting on Current Politics	Business Interpreting
7	Consecutive Interpreting 2	Diplomatic Interpreting	Conference Interpreting and Exhibition Management	
8		Interpreting Workshop	Interpreting Workshop	
9		Training for CATTI (China Accreditation Test for Translators and Interpreters) Level-C Interpreting		
10		Training for CATTI Level-B Interpreting		

courses. Similar problems can only be solved by finding a way around them, which will be discussed later. But there are also problems that the universities could solve by simply changing their way of thinking or finding a way to take full advantage of the resources they already have. For example, only one course in one university demonstrates that conference interpreting education there caters to or takes advantage of the strong disciplines and features of that university, namely, *Interpreting for Engineering Project Negotiation* in Lanzhou Jiaotong University. The other three universities will surely bring benefits to their MTI conference interpreting students by learning from Lanzhou

Jiaotong University and developing similar courses with their own characteristics. Another thing we can read from the table is that there is little, if any, exchange and cooperation among the four universities in spite of the fact that three of them are in the same city and all of them are not located far away from each other. In this respect, each of the four universities has distinctive features and boasts different strong disciplines, but they are all in shortage of human resources in the field of conference interpreting, advanced facilities and equipment, and funding because of the local economic conditions. If they could cooperate more and share resources with one another, they would all be in a better position to produce high-level professional interpreters to serve the international trade, cooperation, and exchanges between their cities, provinces, or even the country and other countries and regions in the world, which would in turn bring more fundings to the universities.

Li (2022, 97) argues that courses play an essential role in training professional interpreters, as they teach relevant interpreting theories which guide interpreting practice, various interpreting skills, such as note-taking, which directly influence information input, and interpreting delivery, emergency coping techniques which prepare potential interpreters for highly pressured and/or unpredictable occasions. According to Cao (2020, 86), generally speaking, courses for MTI conference interpreting should aim at producing high-level language service talents with a focus on practice, should reflect the development of the modern language service industry, especially new technological development in the field of professional interpreting, and should keep an eye on the demands of the market. Hence, as argued by Dong et al. (2022, 94), a lack of diversity and the number of interpreting courses, core and fundamental courses, as well as courses in new technologies in the field of interpreting may present difficulties in MTI interpreting education and negatively influence the outcome of the MTI interpreting education and training in the relevant universities and, eventually, the students' confidence, thereby further affecting the universities' ability to enroll students and the further development of MTI education of those universities.

2.2 Teaching staff

Shortage of teachers who specialize in interpretation is a common problem among the four universities. For example, the university where the present author is working only has three qualified teachers for MTI interpreting students, who are university teachers and, at the same time, part-time interpreters. As a result, the university has to cut down on interpreting courses for MTI students. In order to solve this problem, some universities adopt a system called "dual-teacher system," in which two teachers, usually a professor or an associate professor and a lecturer or an associate professor, are in charge of one interpreting course. And some universities adopt the "dual-tutor system," where one MTI conference interpreting candidate is supervised by two tutors; one of them is from the relevant university, and the other is hired by the university from government departments, language service agencies, etc. The tutors from outside the university need to be experienced interpreters, high-level management personnel in language service agencies, or government official in charge of foreign affairs. The two systems both appear to be plausible solutions, but they have some innate problems that are often neglected by decision makers. First of all, Zhong (2014, 42) argues that teachers for MTI conference interpreting courses should have much expertise and experience in teaching and interpreting in order to impart interpreting theories and skills and practical advice to students, but the fact that MTI was established in China to meet the need for high-level translators and interpreters speaks to the shortage of such talents, and such talents in China often choose to work in more-developed municipalities, like Beijing and Shanghai, and provinces, like Guangdong and Zhejiang. As a result, professors and associate professors specializing in other fields such as linguistics who, as pointed out by Wang (2016, 16), do not necessarily make qualified teachers for MTI conference interpreting courses or tutors for MTI conference interpreting candidates are invited to teach interpreting courses and guide interpreting students. Furthermore, some of them have never even done interpreting-related work for once, let alone interpreting itself. Secondly, due to red tape in China's universities, tutors from outside universities should have certain credentials, and their agencies or departments should meet certain standards, excluding some really good freelance interpreters and self-employed language service providers who otherwise are capable of showing the students real-world interpreting skills and techniques with case study from their past experiences, which would make learning conference interpreting more effective and interesting. Besides, they may offer more opportunities to students to observe or take part in on-the-spot interpreting, which provides valuable learning experience and material for the students' thesis writing. Besides teachers for interpreting courses, all the formalities in these universities also make it more difficult to secure qualified tutors.

2.3 Theses

I typed the word "interpreting" on of www.cnki.net and limited the results to master's theses. As a result, 10,200 theses came up. Then I proceeded to select the theses from universities in the three provinces, and the theses totaled 153 in number.

Through further analysis, I found that nearly half of the 153 theses are from Ningxia University in Ningxia province, and only 83 theses are from the other three universities in Gansu province. The data start from the year 2003, much earlier than the time when the three universities in Lanzhou were approved to enroll MTI candidates, meaning, some theses with titles containing the word "interpreting" are actually written by potential masters in linguistics and foreign literature. Therefore, even less than 83 MTI candidates in the three universities in Lanzhou have chosen to write theses on interpreting (the field of their study and research). Secondly, I discovered that

Sources of the Theses

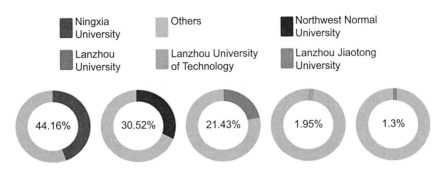

Figure 12.1 Sources for theses with titles containing "interpreting" from the three provinces.

among those 153 theses, 101 are reports on interpreting practices, most of which are simulated interpreting practices with similar titles such as *An Analysis of Problems and Solutions in Escort Interpretation – A Practice Report on the Escort Interpreting for Zhongyouxin Utions Technology Limited Company* and *On Interpreter's Subjectivity from the Perspective of George Steiner's Hermeneutic Motion – A Practice Report on Symposium of US Congressional Delegation*; 46 are research papers on translation studies, such as *A Corpus-Based Research on Simplification of Lexical Patterns of C-E Interpreting of Chinese University Students* and *The Influence of Undergraduates' Language Choice for Note-taking on Quality of Consecutive Interpreting*; 4 are reports on interpreting internship, like *A Report of Strategies for Conference Interpretation Under the Guidance of Interpretive Theory – Ningxia Wolfberry -FDA(USA) Conference*; 1 is a report about an experiment on interpreting, which is titled *An Experimental Study of Interpreting Teaching Based on Sense Theory*; and 1 is a report on a survey about interpreting, which is titled *A Report on the Need for Interpreters in Ningxia*.

The findings reveal that there is a lack of diversity in the candidates' theses. Since 2007, the master of translation and interpreting program (MTI) has been added to the curricula of about 250 universities in China. The guidelines issued by the National Committee for MTI Education allow MTI candidates to graduate with five types of theses. According to Sun (2019, 84), these are translation/interpreting practice report, internship report, survey report, experiment report, and academically oriented research papers. However, most of the 153 theses are interpreting practice reports, and more than three-fourths are simulated interpreting practice reports. There are four possible reasons: firstly, MTI conference interpreting candidates don't have enough opportunities to do actual interpreting, and they also lack the opportunities to do interpreting-related internship; secondly, MTI interpreting students often don't have access to the required data and information for survey-based theses; thirdly, relevant teachers and tutors lack the expertise in experimental research and thus are not able to guide the students to successfully plan for and carry out an interpreting-related experiment in accordance with standard criteria and procedures and write academic papers about it; fourthly, as pointed out by Liu (2013, 54), MTI program aims at developing practice-oriented translation and interpreting talents, so MTI conference interpreting candidates are not encouraged to write academically oriented research papers. In conclusion, the findings further expose problems in MTI conference interpreting education in the four universities in the three provinces of Gansu, Qinghai, and Ningxia Hui Autonomous Region.

2.4 Internships

With China's further connectivity with the international community springs up a thriving language service industry, bringing both challenges and opportunities for MTI education and training. As argued by Li and Fan (2022, 111), the three features of the language service industry, namely, "information conversion at the core, the increasing importance of technology as management elements, and the involvement of more diversified, subdivided, and verticalized fields and occupations," require MTI graduates to acquire a comprehensive set of abilities and skills, as stated by Zhang (2017, 55); of course, the ability to translate and interpret efficiently is the most important one, but the MTI interpreting students need to hone their other abilities and skills. The other necessary abilities and skills include extra-linguistic ability, interpersonal ability, communicative skills, and according to Zhang (2020, 29), the ability to search for information, the ability to use different tools, technologies, and platforms for translation and interpreting, the ability to manage a translation or interpreting project, to name just a few.

Mu (2011, 29) states that according to the guiding policy and as a professional program cultivating high-level translation and interpreting talents who meet the requirements of the language service industry to serve the country in its economic, cultural, and social development, MTI education should be market-oriented and service-oriented. And as argued by Shi (2020, 70), it puts much emphasis on practice and internship and implies that interpreting practice and internship play a bigger role in MTI conference interpreting education than relevant courses. Nonetheless, the four universities in the three provinces have to cope with some common problems in this respect.

On the one hand, international conferences and other international events held in the three provinces of Gansu, Qinghai, and Ningxia Hui Autonomous Region almost always need experienced interpreters, which deprives interpreting students of the opportunities to directly participate in actual interpreting for the conferences and activities. On the other hand, the signed internship bases with the four universities, including government departments, state-owned enterprises, and public institutions, have their own foreign affairs offices with working translators and interpreters. As a result, interns at those places are usually only entrusted with such tasks as answering phone calls and doing some paperwork. They seldom get a chance to do work related, even remotely related, to interpreting.

Liu et al. (2017, 55) demonstrates that internship is supposed to give students insights into what their future career looks like, how to navigate all the competing demands and complexity of their workplace, acquire skills, and abilities that they are unable to obtain in the classroom, like interpersonal skills, and how to learn from veteran professionals in their fields. However, considering the situation of the internship in the four universities, namely, Lanzhou University, Northwest Normal University, Lanzhou Jiaotong University, and Ningxia University, in the three provinces of Gansu, Qinghai, and Ningxia Hui Autonomous Region, I reckon that it would be difficult for the concerning MTI interpreting students to really benefit from their internship. I interviewed some MTI conference interpreting students about the issue. The majority of the students interviewed by myself feel that they would like to do more work related to interpreting, that they don't have enough access to off-campus practice advisers or tutors who may otherwise give them practical advice on their professional skills, their career, even some real-world unspoken rules, and so on and help them find a decent job, and most of the time, that they are just doing internship for the credits in order to graduate.

3   Some possible solutions

On account of the aforementioned problems shared by the four universities in MTI conference interpreting education and taking the economic, cultural, political, and geographical conditions in the three provinces in western China into consideration, I propose the following solutions.

3.1   *Enhancing inter-institutional cooperation and sharing resources*

In order to successfully carry out MTI interpreting program, Li (2011, 96) explains that universities ought to equip themselves with advanced facilities like simultaneous interpreting studios, multimedia interpreting classrooms or labs, VR interpreting training systems, etc. I discovered that all four universities lack state-of-the-art facilities, and the facilities they have are either outdated or nonfunctional. The aforementioned facilities require large funds which all four universities have trouble securing. Also, all four universities lack the human resources to successfully carry out MTI interpreting programs.

Considering these factors, I shall put forward some suggestions. First, the four universities, especially the three in the same city, could join hands in purchasing and constructing the facilities, and they could share limited human resources. This will address the problems in the short run, improve the usage of the facilities, and require less-technical maintenance and support. Second, the four universities may cooperate with local language service companies, those with advanced facilities in particular. This will not only help with the hardware and software shortage of the universities but also provide students with more opportunities to practice, experience real-world working environment, and witness with their own eyes the complete process of executing an interpreting project which, according to Deng (2012, 79), includes signing the contract, dividing up and assigning tasks, quality control, and so on, which could ensure a seamless transition from university to the job market. As for the language service companies, the students will save energy and time of the existing staff, freeing them from routine tasks and chores to do more specialized work. And frankly speaking, the students also help save labor costs of those companies. So it is a win-win cooperation. Last but not the least, the four universities could ask for support from local government and large-scale enterprises; they just need to think of a way to benefit the supporters as well.

A successful example is the University of International Business and Economics. According to Zhang et al. (2022, 69), it has established cooperative partnerships with institutions at home and abroad, including high-end law firms and international organizations, such as the European Union, to provide practicing opportunities for its interpreting students and explore different practice-oriented talent development models, such as "the off-campus practice adviser model, the international practice model and the business interpreting practice model." Of course, it is located in China's capital, Beijing, so its relevant policies and measures only offer limited inspiration to other Chinese universities with the MTI conference interpreting programs. Although other universities may find it difficult to copy its success, they could still draw useful lessons from it. For example, they ought to make good use of the strong disciplines of the universities and seek for opportunities to cooperate with the institutions in these fields, like the aforementioned law firms. And other universities should also search for cooperating opportunities with institutions in other countries, including non-English-speaking countries.

3.2 *Taking advantage of opportunities for practice and internship inside and outside of the universities flexibly and effectively*

All four universities have departments or offices for foreign exchange, cooperation, and other affairs, and they conduct a wide range of international conferences, symposia, and other events and tackle all kinds of affairs for international students, exchange students from other countries, and cooperating universities and colleges in other countries. Therefore, they are almost like the ideal places to provide MTI candidates, especially conference interpreting students, with opportunities to practice what they have learned about interpreting theories and skills. However, the universities need to think flexibly. If the students get to do actual interpreting, it is good. But even observing veteran interpreters at work is an excellent learning opportunity for them, for they could learn some things that they are not able to learn in the classroom, for example, how veteran interpreters deal with an emergency and what techniques they employ. They can record the conference, later do a simulated interpreting, and compare their interpretations with interpretations done by veteran interpreters, and maybe write about it in their theses with a theory to back it up and some in-depth research. In this way, they kill two birds with one stone by practicing their interpreting skills, learning from veteran interpreters, and finding something to write in their theses. Another way to think flexibly is to find a way around the red tape and welcome private enterprises, no matter how small-scale they are, and freelancers aboard as partners. These enterprises, more often than not, do not have the financial and human resources to set up their own foreign affairs office, so they might actually allow the interns to interpret for them. And the universities should not only have their eyes on language service providers. They need to include companies of all types, as long as those companies have the need for international communication. By interning in other types of companies, students may learn about their industry and their daily operation along with honing their skills in interpreting, which will increase the students' chances of finding a job in the future.

Take the university where the present author is working as an example. The university hires scores of foreign experts and teachers, most of whom speak English, at least a little English. Furthermore, the university has two affiliate hospitals, and they hire many foreign experts, both short-term and long-term, to give lectures, carry out cooperative projects, exchange information and views, and so on. The university usually appoints interpreters to help with the lectures, formal meetings, negotiations, and seminars given or attended by those foreign teachers and experts. However, the teachers and experts are pretty much left on their own when it comes to dealing with a variety of affairs in their daily lives, including shopping, seeing doctors, going to banks, and so on. It is terribly inconvenient for the experts and teachers, especially for long-term ones. So if the MTI interpreting students could volunteer to interpret for them on those occasions, the students would practice their oral English and interpreting skills, and the foreign teachers and experts will live a much better and smoother life. In particular, interpreting for those teachers and experts when they see doctors or visit banks may require basic knowledge about finance and medicine and advanced vocabulary; this could really do good to the students. In short, it is a truly win-win situation.

3.3　*Learning from Sichuan University and encouraging students to participate in conference interpreting–related activities*

Sichuan University is located in the neighboring province of Gansu. Sichuan University takes a creative and pragmatic approach to educating MTI interpreting candidates, and the four universities ought to learn from it. The guiding policy of MTI education stipulates that MTI interpreting students should finish 400 hours of interpreting practice in order to graduate. The students in the four universities often finish the required hours by doing simulated interpreting and recording interpreting classes. Comparatively speaking, the measures taken by Sichuan University are more stimulating and useful for students. According to Ren (2012, 50), they allow CATTI Level-B simultaneous interpreting credentials to count as 200 hours of interpreting practice, CATTI Level-B consecutive interpreting credentials as 150 hours, CATTI Level-C interpreting credentials 100 hours; 50,000-word translation or CATTI Level-B translating credentials as 100 hours; the first, second, and third places in national interpreting contests to count as 120, 100, and 80 hours, the first, second, and third places in provincial interpreting contests as 100, 80, and 60 hours, and the first, second, and third places in university-level interpreting contests as 80, 60, and 50 hours; and doing 100 hours of interpreting teaching to count as 50 hours of interpreting practice.

Entrusted by the Ministry of Human Resources and Social Security of the People's Republic of China and implemented and administrated by the China International Publishing Group, the China Accreditation Test for Translators and Interpreters (CATTI) is the most authoritative translation and interpretation proficiency accreditation test, which has been officially included in the list of national occupational qualification tests. Those who pass the CATTI will obtain the Translation and Interpretation Proficiency Qualification Certificate of the People's Republic of China issued by the Ministry of Human Resources and Social Security, which is valid throughout the country. Undoubtedly, to graduate with such a certificate would give students more advantages in securing a decent job than just doing interpreting or simulated interpreting for 400 hours. Furthermore, the process of preparing for the test and actually taking it is somewhat similar to the process during which an interpreter prepares for a conference and actually interprets for the conference. As for interpreting contests at various levels, getting ready for and finishing the contests also resemble actual interpretation. In addition, contestants get to meet other competitors, observe their counterparts' performance, learn from their strength, draw lessons from their mistakes, compare themselves with other contestants and find ways to improve themselves, exchange views and experiences. Most importantly, the judges and commentators invited to attend the contests are, more often than not, experts in the relevant area, so their comments after each contestant's performance are both targeted and extremely instructive; as a result, even if one doesn't win any prize at all, they often leave with much food for thought and valuable advice to help them grow and improve professionally and personally.

In conclusion, this policy not only gives students more incentives to take tests for interpreting credentials and take part in interpreting contests, which in turn will provide them with better resumes, but moreover, in these exams and contests, students' interpreting skills are also put to the test. And the pressure in preparing for and taking the tests and contests is no less than the pressure in preparing for and interpreting for a real conference, so the students will be ready for their future on-the-spot interpreting psychologically.

3.4 *Making good use of online learning opportunities in the post-pandemic era*

The COVID-19 pandemic has resulted in schools and universities shut all across the world. Globally, millions of university students are out of the classroom. As a result, college education has changed dramatically, with the distinctive rise of e-learning, whereby teaching is undertaken remotely and on digital platforms. While some believe that the unplanned and rapid move to online learning – with no training, insufficient bandwidth, and little preparation – will result in a poor user experience that is unconducive to both teaching and learning, others believe that a new hybrid model of education combining online and offline teaching and learning will emerge, with significant benefits. And the assumption is backed up by science, as research suggests that online learning has been shown to increase retention of information and takes less time, meaning, this sudden shift away from the classroom in many parts of the globe will continue to persist after the pandemic and such a shift would impact the worldwide education market in the long run.

In response to significant demand, many online learning platforms are offering free access to their services, including online interpreting training platforms; world-renowned universities are coming up with online interpreting courses which students could take anytime and anywhere they want and maybe for free; experts in the field of conference interpreting and experienced conference interpreters are also giving lectures. Besides, online learning and training platforms are offering teachers and students unlimited videoconferencing time, auto-translation capabilities, real-time coediting of project work, and smart calendar scheduling, among other features. All these make interpreting classes more interesting and interactive.

I believe that the integration of information technology in education will be further accelerated and that online education will eventually become an integral component of school education. This could mean huge changes to MTI conference interpreting education, and teachers and students alike should seize the opportunities brought about by the changes and reap the technological dividends. Take the courses I am running as an example. The combination of online and offline teaching and learning has kept the advantages of traditional classroom education, like face-to-face communication, better monitoring of students' performance, similarities between simulated conference interpreting in classroom and on-the-spot interpreting for real conferences, while allowing for more ways and flexible means of teaching. This enables me to reach out to my students more efficiently and effectively through chat groups, video meetings, voting, and also document sharing, especially during the lockdowns caused by this pandemic. My students also find it easier to communicate on WeChat, QQ, or Tencent Meeting. In addition, MTI conference interpreting students could use the online interpreting training platforms in their spare time to improve. Some of the platforms are offering not only a wide range of practicing materials but also instructive feedbacks and interpretations done by veteran interpreters for comparison. Last but not the least, students are able to get important lessons, advice, tips, and secondhand experience from the experts and veteran interpreters giving lectures and talks online. These were not available before due to time limit, geographical distance, technological restrictions, and so forth.

4 Conclusion

Universities in the provinces of Gansu, Qinghai, and Ningxia Hui Autonomous Region face major obstacles in MTI conference interpreting education due to geopolitical, economic, and cultural disadvantages. This chapter discusses some common problems faced by them in terms of curriculum design, human resources, thesis writing, and internship and puts forward some possible solutions in the hope that it may offer inspiration to universities located in remote places with underdeveloped economy and backward facilities. Universities in similar situations could establish and expand cooperation and partnership and share resources with other institutions, no matter how big or small those institutions are and no matter whether those institutions are state-owned or privately owned, actively search for opportunities both on-campus and off-campus for practice and internship, and use those opportunities flexibly and effectively regardless of whether they directly involve interpreting or are just tasks indirectly related to interpreting, encourage students to sign up for interpreting credentials tests, especially authoritative ones and interpreting-related activities such as interpreting contests, just like Sichuan University is doing, and take advantage of online learning opportunities and new technologies emerged with and boosted by the new online teaching and learning model brought about by the COVID-19 pandemic.

   Nonetheless, this research is only limited to four universities in the three provinces in the west of China. There are many universities in similar localities and with similar conditions in such an enormous and complex country. Therefore, future researches may cover more universities of the same kind and take into consideration more factors in an effort to discover more universal problems, enhance the influence of similar researches, and offer perspectives in relevant policymaking in order to promote a more balanced development of MTI conference interpreting education in China.

References

Cao Xinyu 曹新宇. 2020. "Bawo fanyi shuoshi peiyang neihan tisheng jiaoxue yanjiu zixin-mulei jiaoshou fangtanlu" 把握翻译硕士培养内涵 提升教学研究自信 – 穆雷教授访谈录 [Grasp the Nature of MTI Education and Improving Teaching and Research: An Interview with Professor Mu Lei]. *Zhongguo fanyi* 中国翻译 [Chinese Translators Journal] 41(3): 85–90.

Deng Yuan 邓媛. 2012. "Shengtai fanyixue shijiaoxia yituo xiangmu de MTI kouyi xuexi moshi yanjiu" 生态翻译学视角下依托项目的 MTI 口译学习模式研究

[A Study on the Project-Based Learning and Instruction Mode of MTI Interpretation under the Framework of Eco-Translatology]. *Waiyu dianhua jiaoxue* 外语电化教学 [Technology Enhanced Foreign Language Education] 147(5): 77–80.

Dong Hongxue 董洪学, Chu Shenghua 初胜华, Zhang Kunyuan 张坤媛, and Dong Zhe 董哲. 2022. "MTI xuesheng zhiye fanyi nengli fazhan ji yingxiang yinsu yanjiu" MTI 学生职业翻译能力发展及影响因素研究 [An Empirical Study on MTI Students' Professional Translation Competence and Its Affecting Factors]. *Waiyu dianhua jiaoxue* 外语电化教学 [Technology Enhanced Foreign Language Education] 204(2): 88–95+118.

Li Mingqiu 李明秋. 2022. "MTI shehai keji fanyi jiaoxue moshi de chuangxin shijian-yi dalian haiyang daxue weili" MTI 涉海科技翻译教学模式的创新实践 – 以大连海洋大学为例 [On the Practical Innovation of MTI Sea-Related Scientific Translation Teaching: Taking Dalian Ocean University as an Example]. *Xinan jiaotong daxue xuebao (shehui kexue ban)* 西南交通大学学报（社会科学版）[Journal of Southwest Jiaotong University (Social Sciences)] 23(2): 96–103.

Li Ruilin 李瑞林, and He Ying 贺莺. 2011. "Xuexi kexue shijaoxia de xiangmu fanyi xuexi moshi yanjiu" 学习科学视角下的项目翻译学习模式研究 [A Study on the Project-Based Learning Mode from the Perspective of Learning Sciences]. *Waiyu jiaoxue* 外语教学 [Foreign Language Education] 32(1): 94–98.

Li Yunxin 李芸昕, and Fan Wuqiu 范武邱. 2022. "Mianxiang yuyan fuwu chanye de fanyi shuoshi peiyang tixi goujian tansuo" 面向语言服务产业的翻译硕士培养体系建构探索 [On the Construction of MTI Training System Oriented Toward the Language Service Industry]. *Waiyu dianhua jiaoxue* 外语电化教学 [Technology Enhanced Foreign Language Education] 203(1): 70–74+111.

Liu Heping 刘和平. 2013. "Fanyi jaoxue moshi: lilun yu yingyong" 翻译教学模式：理论与应用 [Translation Teaching Models: Theories and Application]. *Zhongguo fanyi* 中国翻译 [Chinese Translators Journal] 34(2): 50–55.

Liu Yanqin 刘艳芹, Zhu Shan 朱珊, and Guo Hongxia 郭红霞. 2017. "'3+3+1' MTI jiaoxue moshi tansuo yu shijian-yi zhongguo shiyou da xue (Huadong) weili" "3+3+1" MTI 教学模式探索与实践 – 以中国石油大学（华东）为例 [Exploring and Practicing "3+3+1" MTI Teaching Model: Take China University of Petroleum as an Example]. *Shanghai fanyi* 上海翻译 [Shanghai Journal of Translators] (1): 52–57.

Mu Lei 穆雷, and Wang Weiwei 王巍巍. 2011. "Fanyi shuoshi zhuanye xuewei jiaoyu de tese peiyang moshi" 翻译硕士专业学位教育的特色培养模式 [MA and MTI in Translation Education: Divergent Goals, Differentiated Curricula]. *Zhongguo fanyi* 中国翻译 [Chinese Translators Journal] 32(2): 29–32+95.

Ren Wen 任文. 2012. "MTI kouyi fangxiang zhuanye shixi tansuo" MTI 口译方向专业实习探索 [On Internship for MTI Interpreting Candidates]. *Zhongguo fanyi* 中国翻译 [Chinese Translators Journal] 33(6): 46–51.

Shi Xingsong 史兴松, and Niu Yilin 牛一琳. 2020. "Guoneiwai fanyi shuoshi rencai peiyang moshi duibi yanjiu" 国内外翻译硕士人才培养模式对比研究 [A Comparative Study of the Models for MTI Education at Home and Aabroad]. *Zhongguo fanyi* 中国翻译 [Chinese Translators Journal] 41(5): 63–70+192.

Sun Sanjun 孙三军, and Ren Wen 任文. 2019. "Fanyi shuoshi xuewei lunwen moshi tanjiu" 翻译硕士学位论文模式探究 [Types and Structures of the Degree Theses Required of China's MTI Students]. *Zhongguo fanyi* 中国翻译 [Chinese Translators Journal] 40(4): 82–90+189.

Wang Hong 王宏, and Zhang Ling 张玲. 2016. "Zhongguo fanyi zhuanye xuewei jiaoyu: chengji wenti yu duice" 中国翻译专业学位教育：成绩、问题与对策 [BTI

integrate AI technology into machine interpreting, with the aim of continuously optimizing automatic speech recognition and translation results. Technological progress and industrial development have created great confusion among interpreting learners, teachers, and practitioners. Many interpreters fear technology, are passively predisposed to it (Fantinuoli 2019), or even fear that it may harm their work, including by replacing traditional interpreting occupations.

Teachers and students accordingly question if it is necessary to study or teach translation and interpreting, and we, therefore, stress that it is important to undertake related theoretical research. We believe that only the objective understanding of interpreting technology will effectively serve the interpretation cause by promoting its best use. This chapter, therefore, seeks to scientifically describe the panorama of interpreting technology with the aim of contributing to objective understanding. It, therefore, seeks to answer the following research questions by sorting through the literature and does so intending to combine the development history and practice of interpreting technology:

1 What is interpreting technology, and how is it classified?
2 What process has the development of interpreting technology gone through?
3 What is the future development trend of interpreting technology vis-à-vis conference interpreting?

2 A Historical overview of conference interpreting technology

Conference interpreting has a very long history. "Zhou Yu," in *The Discourse of the States* (an ancient book that records the historical events of the Zhou Dynasty's royal family), provides the earliest record of the "she ren" (who acted as interpreters). Conference interpreting technology is relatively new and is very closely related to conference interpreting and information technology. Baigorri-Jalón (1999), Zhao Yihui (2017), and Braun (2019) observe that interpreting technology originated in the 1920s with the first conference interpreting. Braun (2019) contends that the earliest conference simultaneous interpreting in distance interpreting settings can be dated back to the 1970s.

However, many accounts refer back to 1925 and to an earlier and more mature product of conference interpreting technology, when Edward Filene collaborated with Gordon Finley to create the first simple simultaneous interpreting system by using telephone components. However, it was only in the 1940s that simultaneous interpreting officially became a part of the interpreting profession, and this occurred when the technology was sufficiently mature to be used on a large scale. Since then, interpreting activities that use interpreting technology have been fast-tracked. In referring to historical events in interpreting history, we observe that there was still a certain amount of experimentation and preparation in the pre-Filene-Finley system period, and we accordingly denote this as the preparation period of interpreting technology. We roughly divide conference interpreting technology development into four periods, specifically, the preparation, germination, rising, and explosion periods.

The preparation period of conference interpreting technology extended from the end of the 19th century to the 1920s, when audio transmission technology laid the foundation for consecutive interpreting. In order to transmit sound, interpreting technology was initially closely related to the development of modern audio transmission technology. At this time, the emergence and maturation of sound signal transmission (including radio and telephone) established a foundation for the use of consecutive interpreting in large-scale conferences. Since the First World War and the Paris Peace Conference, consecutive interpreting has been widely used.

In the germination period (the 1920s–1950s), consecutive interpreting developed in leaps and bounds, and simultaneous interpreting first appeared on the historical stage. When consecutive interpreting is widely used, its shortcomings (which include substantial time consumption) are exposed. In the 1920s, the concept and implementation of simultaneous interpreting were developed to improve efficiency and save time (Flerov 2013). In 1925, Edward Filene collaborated with Gordon Finley to create the first system that used telephone components. IBM later modified it and named it "Hushaphone" (also known as Hush-A-Phone). Although its functions and appearance were far less advanced than contemporary technologies, it played an important role in conferences of the time. In the period 1945–1946, simultaneous interpreting (in multiple languages) was used in trials in military tribunals, such as the Nuremberg trials, and its application greatly increased the efficiency of international trials and preceded the large-scale use of simultaneous interpreting.

In the rising period (the 1950s to the early 21st century), technological development promoted the steady progress of interpreting technology and contributed to a diversity of interpreting forms and occupations. After the Nuremberg trials, simultaneous interpreting has been widely used in international/multilateral organizations (including both the UN and EEC) and conferences. After 1950, the forms of interpreting were refined, and different technologies, including community, media, remote, and telephone interpreting, began to appear. In 1973, Australia responded to large-scale immigration and multiethnic integration by introducing telephone interpreting to the community interpreting services it provided to immigrants (Mikkelson 2003). In the UK, the National Register of Public Service Interpreters (NRPSI 2022), in acknowledging the use of multiple languages in contemporary UK, provided reliable communication in the period after the 1990s. Telephone interpreting also became popular in the United States and Europe in the 1990s (Mikkelson 2003). In the 1980s, the prototype of machine interpreting appeared in the form of automatic speech recognition (ASR) and machine translation (MT), and both technological innovations anticipated the explosive period that followed. But technologies such as the global Internet and big data had not been popularized on a large scale, and so in this period, interpreting was mainly manual and carried out on machines that provided a carrier for dissemination and presentation.

In the explosive period (2010–present), the interpreting profession entered a new stage as technology and interpreting practice were integrated. Artificial intelligence developed rapidly after 2010, as interpreting technology, the Internet, cloud technology, big data, automatic speech recognition, terminology, and corpus technology grew in a range of areas, including the interpreting of terminology management, remote interpreting systems, global interpreting delivery platforms, AI machine simultaneous interpreting, and the interpreting of corpora. In being driven by a variety of information technologies (including cloud technology, interpreting management systems, interpreting delivery platforms, and bring your own device), technological advances have broken the confinement of interpreters' equipment. These technologies allow interpreters to go out of the simultaneous interpreting booth and move to the "virtual simultaneous interpreting room" – this does not only break geographical restrictions and reduce travel risks (Wang and Li 2022) but also makes it possible to access and retrieve interpreting-related resources anywhere, anytime.

3   The basic concepts of conference interpreting technology

The history and integration of conference interpreting and technology show the concept was not formed at one time but was instead jointly produced by the continuous evolution and development of technology and the conference interpreting profession.

In referring to the germination and rising stages of conference interpreting technology, scholars noted the impact of technology on conference interpreting but also recognized that the immaturity of the technology resulted in the definition and research remaining fragmented and incomplete. Researchers only focused on a certain form of interpreting with related technology, including interpreting terminology management (Moser-Mercer 1992), telephone interpreting technology (Oviatt and Cohen 1992; Böcker and Anderson 1993; Rosenberg 2007), and remote interpreting (Mouzourakis 1996; Moser-Mercer 2005). At this stage, there was no concrete or unified definition of conference interpreting technology.

During the rising and explosion periods, many scholars realized it was necessary to clarify the technology's definition and related concepts. As a result, definitions expanded beyond conference interpreting, and many different modes of interpreting began to appear. Although many terms, including computer-aided interpreting or computer-assisted interpreting (CAI) (Qian 2011; Costa et al. 2014a; Fantinuoli 2016) and technical-assisted interpreting (Costa et al. 2014b), began to emerge, a constant definition remained elusive. As technology and related research matured, the family of interpreting technology gained more members. As a result, scholars realized that the term "interpreting technology" needed, in both a broad and narrow sense, to be studied in more detail. For example, Wang and Zhang (2015) and Fantinuoli (2019) discussed the concept of CAI, Orlando (2014) discussed simultaneous consecutive (SimConsec), and Braun (2019) described and defined interpreting technology in accordance with different forms of interpreting, and including telephone interpreting (OPI) technology, remote video interpreting (VRI) technology, and remote video simultaneous interpreting (RSI) technology. Zhao (2017), in engaging from the perspective of technical philosophy, analyzed the intellectual, substantive, and collaborative elements of interpreting technology and provided definitions. Meanwhile, Wang and Yang (2019) combed through a large number of literatures and provided a descriptive definition of interpreting technology. Li and Li (2019) and Wang and Li (2022) classified and defined interpreting technology by undertaking a questionnaire survey, which produced a classification.

This study applies Wang and Li's (2022) definition of "interpreting technology." It is used in interpreting practice, and especially in conference interpreting, training, and researching. It is defined as a variety of technologies that interpreters apply in undertaking interpreting and seeking to ensure the fulfillment of conference interpreting tasks that include decoding, memorizing, coding, delivering, and sharing information.

4   Classifications of conference interpreting technology

The classification of interpreting technology is closely related to its function and different interpreting forms, and this reflects the fact that the original purpose of interpreting technology is to maintain the normality of interpreting activities. The available technology, therefore, serves specific types of interpreting activities. Consider the example of telephone interpreting devices. This device allows the client's voice to be transmitted to two different lines (one for the receiver and one for an interpreter). After answering the phone, the receiver informs the interpreter what their client needs. The receiver also needs an interpreter to reply in the language the client understands. A further example is when the speaker's language is translated into multiple languages at international conferences, and the audience listens to the speeches by using handheld devices to switch between different channels.

Braun (2019) "distinguishe[s] between different types of technology in interpreting" by referring to three categories, specifically, technology-mediated (distance interpreting), technology-supported, and technology-generated (machine interpreting) interpreting. In comparison to other research, this is a more general classification that provides more of a "macro" perspective of technology. Strictly speaking, the different types cannot be considered to be "golden rules." For example, in referring to the first category (technology-mediated interpreting), Braun placed distance interpreting within it. In addition, this kind of technology (including online meeting software and systems and online delivery platforms for interpreters) functions in the same way as technology-supported interpreting that provides technical support to interpreters. Some technology-generated interpreting technology functions in a similar way, and the technology-supported interpreting category overlaps with others.

Braun's classification and the features of technology shed light on follow-up research, and based on her research, we believe it may not be possible to classify by using one single rule. In this study, we, therefore, apply Wang and Li's (2022) multiple classifications approach and do so in order to describe the whole picture of interpreting technology

Wang and Li (2022) took other characteristics into consideration (see Figure 13.1), which can be roughly divided into (1) hardware (such as applied interpreting devices) or software (such as the apps interpreters use); (2) the different functions of a tool or resource; (3) the degree of automation in machine (completely automatic) or computer-aided (semiautomatic) interpreting; (4) the process of interpreting: technology used before, during, and after interpreting; (5) the different roles of technology (technology-mediated, technology-supported, and technology-generated interpreting – see Braun 2019); (6) and different users (interpreters, customers, and service providers).

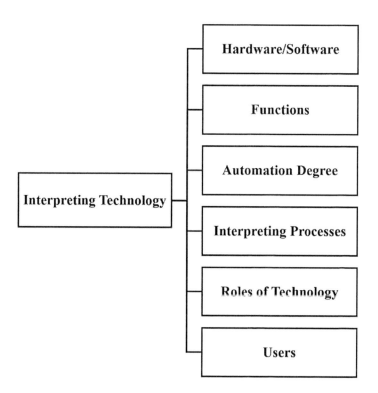

Figure 13.1 The classifications of interpreting technology.

5   The future development trends of conference interpreting technology

In the traditional conference interpreting industry, it is the distinguished performance of interpreters that mainly enables them to gain a competitive advantage in the career market. However, in the future, this mode may gradually be replaced by a human-technology counterpart that is a more competitive service type. Advances in AI technology further reiterate the indispensable role of technology, whose effects and implications extend to all parts of the interpreting industry. In addition to the aforementioned concepts, categories, and other features, conference interpreting technology contributes to a trend characterized by various features, namely, customization, intelligence, ubiquity, platform as a service, and standardization.

5.1   *Customization*

In the era of artificial intelligence, software and technology have become increasingly user-friendly. This trend has been recognized by technology providers, interpreters, and other users. For example, machine interpreting or translation plays a key role in embedding with other technologies. Together with speech recognition and production, machine interpreting is customized mainly dependent on the function of machine translation.

Machine translation, in drawing on the neural network and deep learning and being equipped with high-quality corpus, has achieved outstanding results and accuracy that far exceeds the scopes of the first two generations. Special training enables the customized translation system to be provided in accordance with the needs of customers in specific fields and scenarios related to expansion and certain features. In this respect, it exceeds the general machine translation and can satisfy the entire translation needs of clients or interpreters in areas such as medicine and politics.

In addition to machine interpreting, other conference interpreting technology has, as part of a "customizing turn," sought to meet industry needs in multiple fields and scenarios. Technology can make the material more user-friendly by reducing the complexity of dealing with multimodal data forms, including text, images, audio, video, or web pages. For example, before the conference, interpreters usually need to prepare terms and fixed sentence pairs. Terminology management (such as InterpretBank, Intragloss, and Termbox) assists interpreters by making it possible to rapidly prepare conference material – it does this by helping to undertake automated term extraction, identification, searching, adding, and deleting.

5.2   *Intelligence*

Artificial intelligence has developed rapidly over the past 5–10 years, as technologies such as speech recognition, image recognition, AR/VR, and blockchain have increasingly begun to be integrated into the translation and interpreting industry. Multi-expert system technology, machine learning, hardware and software integration, and parallel distributed processing technology promote the rapid development of automatic speech recognition, machine translation, and machine interpreting. Enhanced automated machine learning will be more intelligent, and powerful algorithms can find patterns in complex interpretation data and evolve into more advanced intelligence systems. They will show a human-like ability to observe, understand, judge, and generate various emotional characteristics and will also demonstrate the ability to communicate naturally like interpreters. AI conference interpreting technology integrates emotional computing. When delivering interpreting, this technology exceeds traditional performance by adding a new dimension (data of emotion, facial expression, and body language) that improves the accuracy of interpreting. In grasping the user's emotional state, it is able to issue the most appropriate response to the user's emotional changes. For example, Google Assistant integrates deep learning, machine learning, cognitive computing, and other technologies. In the process of interacting in real scenes, its pronunciation is natural and its speed of speech is smooth, and it even includes human prosodic features (such as pauses and "um") that indicate thinking. The intelligent interpreting system will develop rapidly because it has been deeply optimized by integrating translation memory, terminology technology, and various decoding algorithms, such as statistics and neural networks. The interpreting technology will have a higher degree of intelligence, and this will enable it to fit a broader range of scenarios.

5.3 Ubiquity

Technologies such as the Internet of Things, Internet+, and ubiquitous networks have spawned the emergence of "hypermedia," "omni-media," "pan-media," and "BYOD (bring your own device)," and this has, in turn, contributed to ubiquity in interpreting. The mobile Internet equipment for conference interpreting has, in combination with customer needs and services, enabled interpreters to break the shackles imposed by traditional devices and on-the-scene interpreting. When the technology and working environment permit, they will be able to offer interpreting services anywhere, anytime.

Three types of technology mainly help guarantee the ubiquity of conference interpreting. The first type is meeting or remote interpreting systems. In court interpreting, the interpreter may not be present at the court sometimes. This problem has been perfectly solved by using remote interpreting technology, such as Zoom and Tencent Meeting. This kind of technology resolves the problems associated with the global deployment of interpreters, including the risks associated with extreme situations, such as wars or pandemics.

The second category is the location-based service with a positioning system. This technology (e.g., FindYee and the BEasy) can accurately locate professional interpreters in certain fields. It does not only help interpreters and language service providers (LSPs) to locate more interpreting demands but also helps clients quickly locate professional interpreters. It provides a bridge between interpreters, LSPs, and clients.

The third technology, 5G networks, provides a strong foundation that helps sustain the interpreting technology used in conference interpreting. Theoretically, the peak transmission rate of 5G ultrahigh wireless speed can reach 10 Gbps+, which can provide ultra-high-definition streaming media services (such as cloud VR/AR interpreting, remote conference interpreting, and cloud live broadcast interpreting) and wireless high-speed broadband access in specific scenarios. In seeking to maintain transmission stability, interpreters may establish a broadband connection to the computers or other devices. In preparation, they may use fast online networks to look up references and terms. The efficient and fast network that the 5G network has constructed can, when combined with ubiquitous network technology, better assist efforts to cope with resource scarcities and remote environment challenges and will surely help produce an upgrading revolution in the interpreting industry that will enable it to be promoted across the globe.

The ubiquity of interpreting technology can make it possible to quickly locate available interpreters and match-make the language service on the basis of the client and LSPs locations. It will also contribute to the overall arrangement of interpreters and services across the world and will promote the sharing and utilization of interpreting resources. The implications will extend beyond conference interpreting, as ubiquity also impacts interpreting modes in some way, including crowdsourced interpreting, mobile interpreting services, precision interpreting marketing, LBS interpreting equipment services, and online and offline man-machine coupling.

5.4 Platform as a service

In the new era of the digital economy, innovative language service platforms with interpreting technology have been developed by LSPs, Internet tech giants, newborn translation or interpreting platform companies, and transformed translation or interpreting companies; in addition, they are seeking to achieve platform-based collaborative services by integrating valuable language service resources, conducting big data knowledge mining, and inspiring customers and users. International enterprises with a large member system, rich technology accumulation, and substantial financial strength (including Google, Microsoft, Baidu, Tencent, Sougou, New Tranx Tech, Yunyi, etc.) are currently seeking to create diversified and multifunctional products by providing machine translation API (application program interface) that reshapes the service model and gradually builds a perfect resource-gathering ecological platform. The competition in the interpreting technology supply chain has gradually evolved into a platform-based ecosystem competition. In large-scale interpreting activities, a comprehensive, collaborative platform that integrates personnel management, resource management, and knowledge management will be able to meet the increasing demand for the collaborative management of interpreting. In complex future scenarios, individual interpreting technology will be transformed into a platform (such as thebigword, Plunet, Primaxis, and other interpreting management systems). Most may connect every interpreting service participant (customers, interpreters, services providers, and even the third party of equipment providers) through the platform. For example, Boostlingo, operating through the platform website and app, can enable clients to make appointments for conference interpreting services anywhere in the world and can also make it possible to obtain remote interpreting services (such as videoconferences) anywhere. LSPs can also use the platform to inform interpreters when there is a demand for online conference interpreting or on-site interpreting services and can also use it to make related arrangements. Interpreters, meanwhile, can undertake projects, complete the job, receive project information and resources, obtain payments, give feedback, and record working logs.

5.5 Standardization

Interpreting and translation associations and standardization organizations have, in recognizing the importance of technology in conference interpreting, also acknowledged an ongoing need for standardization. The International Organization for Standardization (ISO) has accordingly put forward a series of technological standards.[3] In addition to these standards, worldwide interpreting and translation associations have also strongly emphasized professional conference interpreter guidelines or ethical codes related to the use of technology – examples include those provided by the Translators Association of China (2017, 2018, 2019) and the American Translators' Association (ATA) (2010).

The International Association of Conference Interpreters (AIIC), as one of the most authoritative organizations involved in conference interpreting, has provided the most thorough guidelines (AIIC 2020) for "extreme" situations. They cover the specific requirements of distance interpreting (including video remote conference interpreting in both simultaneous and consecutive modes) and extend to the working/technical conditions of sign language interpreting, including equipment and media. AIIC also provided "best practice" guidance to distance interpreters during the pandemic.

Organizations and associations, as the upper layer of the whole language service industry, make every effort to keep pace with ongoing development and shoulder responsibility for making the rules. They provide guidance and direction to the middle (technology providers) and downstream (interpreters who use the technology) layers and thereby help maintain the sound development of the entire chain. This ensures technology providers compete on an equal footing when designing new platforms for conferences. And it obliges interpreters to observe ethical codes when interpreting (e.g., maintaining liability, privacy, and confidentiality) and to follow regulations when using technology.

6. Case study

In treating Cymo technology as a typical conference interpreting technology, this case study uses it to explain how the technology functions in conference interpreting.

6.1   *Cymo and its technology*

Cymo is an interpreting technology company whose mission is to enable and facilitate excellence in human interpreting by leveraging technology that supports human interpreters in specific interpretation engagements and more generally over the course of their professional careers. Its first product was launched in 2019, and since then, it has continually focused on solving specific pain points within the interpreter's workflow and professional development path – to achieve this, it has used technology solutions to build a number of scenarios. This has produced solutions that enhance interpreter training and practice and augment the efficiency and quality of the interpreter's day-to-day workflow, including the output from preparation, interpreting delivery, and post-project closeout stages.

Its key offerings include Cymo Meeting, Classroom and Practicum, Booth, and Note. Cymo Booth has a user base that spans over 50 countries, and Cymo Note has become a groundbreaking CAI tool used by many leading interpreters. Cymo has constructed an ecosystem with various cutting-edge technology products that include remote simultaneous interpreting, video simultaneous interpreting, audio simultaneous interpreting, and computer-assisted interpreting.

6.2   *The use of integrated technology by conference interpreters*

Cymo has a wide array of products and has integrated a number of technologies, including virtual booth, online simultaneous interpreting classroom, CAI, speech recognition, terminology management, note-taking, machine translation, and remote interpreting system (see Figure 13.2).

In order to understand how Cymo's offerings work together, it is helpful to see how its offerings facilitate excellence at each stage of an interpreter's career. It is necessary to begin with initial skill acquisition, proceed to professional practice, and concurrently consider continuous skill development.

Cymo Classroom and Practicum were developed for the education and training scenario, irrespective of accredited or in-house training. It was designed to recreate the on-site lecture, exercise, feedback, and debrief loop that is commonly applied in most interpreting pedagogy, along with the in-booth teamwork, sense of camaraderie, and peer-learning environment that is necessary to prepare students for real-world engagements.

As the trainee becomes a newly minted professional, Cymo Meeting provides a platform that will enable new interpreters to gain real-world experience

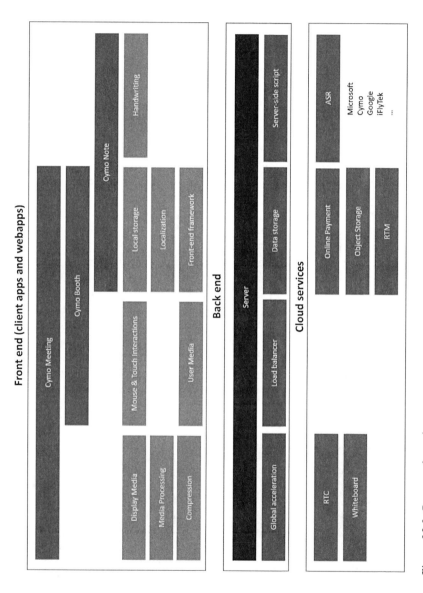

Figure 13.2 Cymo tech stack.

by starting with virtual engagements. Cymo Meeting is designed for a classic remote simultaneous interpreting (RSI) scenario, but its proprietary virtual booth design enables it to surpass competing solutions. Cymo's virtual booth was designed on the basis of the principle of "physical booth parity" and was intended to create a user experience that would cultivate the behaviors expected in a physical booth. Partnering interpreters can hear and see each other but will not start "broadcasting" interpreting unless an "on air" button (which is similar to the "MIC" button in any in-booth interpreter console) is pressed. This unique design completely replicates the physical booth experience and has been proven to enhance collaboration and reduce stress and mishandling during the handover process, and this will ultimately lead to higher-quality interpreting and a better audience experience.

Cymo's most unique feature can be identified in Cymo Note, its industry-pioneering computer-assisted interpreting (CAI) solution that was developed with the interpreter's day-to-day workflow in mind. It leverages a host of automatic speech recognition (ASR) technologies and dictates speech to text live while highlighting numbers and looking for terms that are present within the interpreter's terminology database. When the engine recognizes a term that is present within the database, Cymo Note will highlight them and prompt the interpreter with their second language equivalent, which they will be able to reference if needed. When an important term is not part of the user's custom database, the interpreter will be able to immediately highlight the term to get its second language translation and add it to their database for future prompts and recordkeeping, which can be obtained with the click of a button. Cymo Note also enables the interpreter to locally correct recognition errors in a way that will minimize recognition mistakes, export the recognition results for their review, or offer additional values to their clients. These capabilities make Cymo Note a powerful tool that the interpreter can use throughout the entire life cycle of an interpreting project, extending from preparation to delivery and closeout.

6.3   Interpreter workflow with Cymo

Pre-interpreting

At this stage, interpreters usually prepare their materials and populate their terminology database before a meeting. Cymo Note can help meet their needs. This is achieved by opening files and referring to researched articles (on related subjects) from the Internet. Cymo Note will then recognize when they read the content out loud. After they read through a paragraph or entire file, they will be able to select terms of interest, obtain their machine translation, and save it for CAI use. Interpreters can also, if they are in spreadsheet format and accept and act in accordance with related terms, import previously prepared terms. Cymo Note can benefit the workflow in three ways: (1) by facilitating the memorization of important terms, (2) by eliminating the need to manually type terms into search engines or dictionaries (the biggest time sink in the preparation phase), and (3) by testing the voice recognition engine for commonly misrecognized words. The interpreter can take this opportunity to create Force Replace rules for commonly misrecognized words, which are often proper nouns, abbreviations, and slang.

Interpreting

We will now consider Cymo Note, Meeting, and Booth, which are the most important parts of the technology.

Interpreters can use Cymo Note for whole-text autonomous speech recognition. It highlights number and database terms and their translations; allows instant term lookup and saves to the database; follows interpreter-defined rules; and enables collaboration with boothmate(s).

In referring to a consecutive scenario and using a tablet, the interpreter will be able to enable Cymo Note's consecutive layout with live handwriting annotation capability. This will enable them to take consecutive notes and use Cymo Note to dictate the speech for reference. At the beginning of each section, the interpreter will be able to drop a time-stamped consecutive line break that the interpreter can quickly return to when the speaker stops. Interpreters can use it on a Mac or PC, in consecutive and simultaneous interpreting modes, and also in both remote and on-site settings.

As previously noted, interpreters can also use Cymo Meeting, a professional online videoconferencing platform, to deliver their service. If they are asked to use Zoom, WebEx, or any other widely recognized web conferencing platform, they can use Cymo Booth, a platform agnostic back-channel built under the same principle of "physical booth parity," to facilitate handover and communication with their boothmates. Cymo Booth is now used by professional interpreters in more than 50 countries across the world – it has been proven to ease the difficulty of collaborating in remote environments and has been demonstrated to improve the entire team's performance.

Post-interpreting

Interpreters sometimes neglect this stage. As language assets become one of the most valuable resources of interpreters and language service companies, it has increasingly been recognized that the completion of the on-the-scene task is not the end of the process. There is still work to do, such as saving or storing resources that may be used in the future. The interpreter can export the transcript of the entire event with a glossary for later review and study. And the transcript can serve as a blueprint for subtitling or captioning that the client can use. Linguistic assets can also be archived in the interpreters' usual terminology management database and reused in future events.

Cymo Practicum, a powerful tool that students can use to test their skills in mock conferences, can also be used by professional interpreters to continuously develop skills in groups. Here, the Cymo suite of tools closes the loop of a professional interpreter's career and appears as a never-ending process of continuous skill development that is augmented by technology. It will enable interpreters to focus on what they do best by crafting faithful, expressive, and elegant messages, which will help build cultural bridges necessary for human advancement.

6.4   Meet future needs

As one of the typical technologies, Cymo systems show the five characteristics of future perspectives mentioned: customization, intelligence, ubiquity, platform as a service, and standardization.

Customization

By using Cymo Note, interpreters will be able to accumulate their own linguistic assets for future reuse and batch-import a large number of linguistic assets, which will in turn enable a more customized CAI experience.

Intelligence

Cymo Note can leverage AI technologies such as automatic speech recognition and machine translation and support multiple AI technology providers, which will enable interpreters to use the correct one in the appropriate scenario. Cymo Note also has its own proprietary glossar-matching algorithm that can be used to highlight specific terminologies.

Ubiquity

Cymo Note can also be used on mobile ends. In addition to this CAI tech product, it also provides Cymo Live, a live streaming web app that allows its audience to access a remote event by using multilingual audio channels with a URL or a QR code. Cymo Meeting can be accessed on a Mac/PC with a Chrome/Edge browser.

Platform as a service

Although Cymo does not provide interpreting liaisoning services and is a pure tech player, it does provide access to Cymo Booth users in over 50 countries. The company is still currently focusing on expanding and serving its interpreter users, although it has not yet been established if it will adopt the platform strategy and leverage its interpreter base.

Standardization

Cymo's audio transmission quality meets ISO quality standards, and all its operations are protected by AES 256-bit encryption technology that protects customer data and privacy.

7 Conclusion

This chapter comprehensively reviewed the history of the development of interpreting technology, provided an in-depth discussion of its connotation and classification, and predicted future development by referring to customization, intelligence, ubiquity, platform as a service, and standardization. It selected Cymo systems, a cutting-edge conference interpreting technology, as a case and used it to explain how technology functions in the whole procedure of conference interpreting.

Technological development will inevitably occur as time progresses. From the initial audio transmission onward, interpreting technology has been gradually integrated with artificial intelligence and interpreting services and applied to a great variety of technology that assists in interpreting. It is only by mastering, applying, and improving technology, while working to become a skillful technology user, that we will be able to guide the future development of interpreting in a new era.

Acknowledgments

This research is one of the achievements of the National Social Science Foundation Project of China (Project No. 22BYY043) and the Youth Foundation of Humanities and Social Sciences of Heilongjiang Province, China (Project No. 19YYC149).

Notes

1 Some of the contents are translated from the paper "Interpreting Technologies in the Era of Artificial Intelligence: Concepts, Influences and Trends" published by Wang Huashu and Yang Chengshu in the 6th issue of *Chinese Translators Journal*, pages 69–79, in 2019.

The translated content is noted in the following list:

In 2. History of conference interpreting technology, the third, fourth, part of fifth, and sixth paragraphs are translated from the paper.
In 3. Basic concepts of conference interpreting technology, the second and third paragraphs are translated from the paper.
In 5.2 Intelligence is translated from the paper.
In 5.3 Ubiquity, the first, and part of the fourth and fifth paragraphs are translated from the paper.
5.4 Platform as a service is translated from the paper.

2 For instance, see *Preparing for the Future of Artificial Intelligence* and *National Artificial Intelligence Research and Development Strategic Plan* (US) (National Science and Technology Council 2016a), *Artificial Intelligence: Opportunities and Implications for the Future of Decision Making* (US) (National Science and Technology Council 2016b), *New Generation of Artificial Intelligence Development Plan* (China) (The State Council of the PRC 2017), *Three-year Action Plan to Promote the Development of the New Generation of Artificial Intelligence Industry (2018–2020)* (China) (The Ministry of Industry and Information Technology of the PRC 2017), and put forward *Key points of Artificial Intelligence of the Federal Government Strategy* (Germany) (Federal Ministry of Education and Research of Germany 2018).
3 "Simultaneous interpreting – Equipment – Requirements" (ISO 20109 2016) (ISO 2016a), "Simultaneous Interpreting – Mobile Booths – Requirements" (ISO

4043 2016) (ISO 2016b), "Simultaneous interpreting – Permanent booths – Requirements" (ISO 2603 2016) (ISO 2016c), "Conference systems – Equipment – Requirements" (ISO 22259 2019).

References

AIIC. 2020. "Reference Guide to Remote Simultaneous Interpreting." Accessed November 13, 2022. https://aiic.ch/wp-content/uploads/2020/05/aiic-ch-reference-guide-to-rsi.pdf.

American Translators Association. 2010. "American Translators Association Code of Ethics and Professional Practice." Accessed November 13, 2022. https://member.atanet.org/governance/code_of_ethics_commentary.pdf.

Baigorri-Jalón, Jesús. 1999. "Conference Interpreting: From Modern Times to Space Technology." *Interpreting* 4(1): 29–40.

Böcker, Martin, and Donald S. Anderson. 1993. "Remote Conference Interpreting Using ISDN Video Telephony: A Requirements Analysis and Feasibility Study." In *Proceedings of the Human Factors and Ergonomics Society, 37th Annual Meeting*, 235–9.

Braun, Sabin. 2019. "Technology and Interpreting." In *The Routledge Handbook of Translation and Technology*, edited by Minako O'Hagan, 271–89. London and New York: Routledge.

Costa, Hernani Pereira, Gloria Corpas Pastor, and Isabel Durán Muñoz. 2014a. "A Comparative User Evaluation of Terminology Management Tools for Interpreters." In *Proceedings of the 4th International Workshop on Computational Terminology (Computerm)*, edited by Patrick Drouin, Natalia Grabar, Thierry Hamon and Kyo Kageura, 68–76. Dublin: Association for Computational Linguistics and Dublin City University.

Costa, Hernani Pereira, Gloria Corpas Pastor, and Isabel Durán Muñoz. 2014b. "Technology-Assisted Interpreting." *Multilingual* 25(3): 27–32.

Fantinuoli, Claudio. 2016. "InterpretBank. Redefining Computer-Assisted Interpreting Tools." In *Proceedings of the Translating and the Computer 38 Conference in London*, edited by AsLing, The International Association for Advancement in Language Technology, 42–52. Geneva: Editions Tradulex.

Fantinuoli, Claudio. 2019. *Interpreting and Technology*. Berlin: Language Science Press.

Federal Ministry of Education and Research of Germany. 2018. "Key Points of the Federal Government for an Artificial Intelligence Strategy (Eckpunkte der Bundesregierung für eine Strategie künstliche Intelligenz)." Accessed November 13, 2022. www.bmbf.de/files/180718%20Eckpunkte_KI-Strategie%20final%20Layout.pdf.

Flerov, Cyril. 2013. "On Comintern and Hush-a-Phone: Early History of Simultaneous Interpretation Equipment." Accessed November 13, 2022. https://aiic.net/page/6625/early-history-of-simultaneous-interpretation-equipment/lang/1.

ISO. 2016a. "ISO 20109: 2016 Simultaneous Interpreting: Equipment: Requirements." Accessed November 13, 2022. www.iso.org/standard/67063.html.

ISO. 2016b. "ISO 2603: 2016 Simultaneous Interpreting: Permanent Booths: Requirements." Accessed November 13, 2022. www.iso.org/standard/67065.html.

ISO. 2016c. "ISO 4043: 2016 Simultaneous Interpreting: Mobile Booths: Requirements." Accessed November 13, 2022. www.iso.org/standard/67066.html.

ISO. 2019. "ISO 22259:2019 Conference systems: Equipment: Requirements." Accessed November 13, 2022. www.iso.org/standard/72988.html.

Li Zhi 李智, and Li Defeng 李德凤. 2019. "Rengong zhineng shidai kouyiyuan xinxi jishu suyang yanjiu" 人工智能时代口译员信息技术素养研究 [A Study on Interpreters' Information Technology Literacy in the Era of Artificial Intelligence]. *Zhongguo Fanyi* 中国翻译 [Chinese Translators Journal] 40(6): 80–7.

Mikkelson, Holly. 2003. "Telephone Interpreting: Boon or Bane?" In *Speaking in Tongues: Language across Contexts and Users*, edited by L. Pérez González, 251–69. València: Universitat de València.

Moser-Mercer, Barbara. 1992. "Banking on Terminology: Conference Interpreters in the Electronic Age." *Meta: Translators' Journal* 37(3): 507–22.

Moser-Mercer, Barbara. 2005. "Remote Interpreting: Issues of Multi-Sensory Integration in a Multilingual Task." *Meta: Translators' Journal* 50(2): 727–38.

Mouzourakis, Panayotis. 1996. "Videoconferencing: Techniques and Challenges." *Interpreting* 1(1): 21–38.

National Register of Public Service Interpreters. "Our History." Accessed November 13, 2022. www.nrpsi.org.uk/about-us/our-history.html.

National Science and Technology Council. 2016a. "National Artificial Intelligence Research and Development Strategic Plan." Accessed November 13, 2022. https://obamawhitehouse.archives.gov/sites/default/files/whitehouse_files/microsites/ostp/NSTC/national_ai_rd_strategic_plan.pdf.

National Science and Technology Council. 2016b. "Preparing for the Future of Artificial Intelligence." Accessed November 13, 2022. https://obamawhitehouse.archives.gov/sites/default/files/whitehouse_files/microsites/ostp/NSTC/preparing_for_the_future_of_ai.pdf.

Orlando, Marc. 2014. "A Study on the Amenability of Digital Pen Technology in a Hybrid Mode of Interpreting: Consec- Simul with Notes." *Translation and Interpreting* 6(2): 39–54.

Oviatt, Sharon L., and Cohen, Philip R. 1992. "Spoken Language in Interpreted Telephone Dialogues." *Computer Speech and Language* 6(3): 277–302.

Qian Duoxiu 钱多秀. 2011. "Shixi jisuanji fuzhu gongju zai kouyi zhong de yingyong" 试析计算机辅助工具在口译中的应用 [An Analysis of the Application of Computer-Aided Tools in Interpretation]. *Minzu Fanyi* 民族翻译 [Minority Translators Journal] 4: 76–80.

Rosenberg, Brett Allen. 2007. "A Data Driven Analysis of Telephone Interpreting." In *The Critical Link 4: Professionalisation of Interpreting in the Community*, edited by C. Wadensjö, B. Englund Dimitrova, and A. L. Nilsson, 65–76. Amsterdam: Benjamins.

Zhongguo fanyi xiehui 中国翻译协会 [Translators Association of China]. 2017. *Koubiyi renyuan jiben nengli yaoqiu* 口笔译人员基本能力要求 [Competence of Translators and Interpreters]. Beijing: Zhongguo biaozhun chubanshe 中国标准出版社 [Standards Press of China].

Zhongguo fanyi xiehui 中国翻译协会 [Translators Association of China]. 2018. *Fanyi fuwu kouyi fuwu yaoqiu* 翻译服务 口译服务要求 [Translation Services: Requirements for Interpreting Service]. Beijing: Zhongguo biaozhun chubanshe 中国标准出版社 [Standards Press of China].

Zhongguo fanyi xiehui 中国翻译协会 [Translators Association of China]. 2019. *Fanyi fuwu caigou zhinan di'er bufen: kouyi* 翻译服务采购指南 第二部分:口译 [Guideline on Procurement of Translation Services: Part 2: Interpretation]. Beijing: Zhongguo biaozhun chubanshe 中国标准出版社 [Standards Press of China].

Zhonghua renmin gongheguo gongye he xinxihuabu 中华人民共和国工业和信息化部 [The Ministry of Industry and Information Technology of the PRC]. 2017. "Gongye he xinxihuabu fabu cujin xinyidai rengong zhineng chanye fazhan sannian xingdong jihua (2018–2022nian)" 工业和信息化部发布《促进新一代人工智能产业发展三年行动计划（2018–2020 年）》 [The Ministry of Industry and Information Technology Released the Three Year Action Plan for Promoting the Development of the New Generation AI Industry (2018–2020)]." Accessed November 13, 2022. www.miit.gov.cn/jgsj/kjs/jscx/gjsfz/art/2020/art_291b5e6bc13f415494e84a0e9eac78f1.html.

Zhonghua renmin gongheguo guowuyuan 中华人民共和国国务院 [The State Council of the PRC]. 2017. Guowuyuan guanyu yinfa xinyidai rengong zhineng fazhan guihua de tongzhi 国务院关于印发新一代人工智能发展规划的通知 [The State Council Prints and Distributes the Document of New Generation of Artificial Intelligence Development Plan]. Accessed November 13, 2022. www.gov.cn/zhengce/content/2017-07/20/content_5211996.htm.

Wang Huashu 王华树, and Yang Chengshu 杨承淑. 2019. "Rengong zhineng shidai de kouyi jishu fazhan: gainian, yingxiang yu qushi" 人工智能时代的口译技术发展：概念、影响与趋势 [Interpreting Technologies in the Era of Artificial Intelligence: Concepts, Influences and Trends]. *Zhongguo Fanyi* 中国翻译 [Chinese Translators Journal] 40(6): 69–79.

Wang Huashu 王华树 and Zhang Jing 张静. 2015. "Xinxihua shidai kouyi yiyuan de jishu nengli yanjiu" 信息化时代口译译员的技术能力研究 [A Study on Interpreters' Technical Competence in the Information Age]. *Beijing di'er waiguoyu xueyuan xuebao* 北京第二外国语学院学报 [Journal of Beijing International Studies University] 37(10): 25–32.

Wang, Huashu, and Zhi Li. 2022. "Constructing a Competence Framework for Interpreting Technologies, and Related Educational Insights: An Empirical Study." *The Interpreter and Translator Trainer* 16(3): 367–90. doi: 10.1080/1750399X.2022.2101850.

Zhao Yihui 赵毅慧. 2017. "Kouyi jishu de huisu yu qianzhan: gongjuhua, jiaohuahua ji zhinenghua de yanbian" 口译技术的回溯与前瞻:工具化、交互化及智能化的演变 [A Review of the Development of Interpreting Technologies: A Shift from Instrumentality to Interactivity and to Intelligence]. *Waiwen yanjiu* 外文研究 [Foreign Studies] 5(4): 65–71, 105.

14 Multimodal videoconference interpreting

Technical challenges and opportunities

Jie Lü and Xiaojun Zhang

1 Introduction

The evolution of communication technologies such as telephony, video-conferencing, and web conferencing has created plentiful opportunities for real-time distance communication and has led to new ways of delivering interpreting services in China. Conferences/meetings, as one of the main activities which make use of videoconferencing, are an appropriate focus for this chapter since they play a crucial role in the generation of ideas, documents, relationships, and actions within an organization. Conference interpreting deals exclusively with oral communication: rendering messages from one language into another naturally and fluently, with the interpreter adopting the delivery, tone, and convictions of the speaker while speaking in the first person.

In recent decades, videoconferencing has slowly established itself as a tool for verbal and visual interaction in real time between two or more sites. When such videoconferencing involves interpretation, this is called remote interpreting. Specifically, remote interpreting refers to the use of communication technologies to gain access to an interpreter in another room, building, city, or country. With regard to videoconferences, the term most commonly used for remote interpreting via videoconference and interpreter-mediated videoconferencing is videoconference interpreting (Braun 2015). Videoconference interpreting, either spoken-language interpreting or sign-language interpreting, is best described as a way to deliver interpreting remotely. It can be used for simultaneous, consecutive, and dialogue interpreting.

In this chapter, we propose a prototype computer-aided conference interpreting system (CACIS) which integrates video, audio, and text translation technologies into a single platform to help conference interpreters undertake their work (Zhang 2015). The chapter will focus on the technical issues relating to this prototype system. In particular, our analysis relies not only on the techniques that we have implemented in our previous experiments but also some other innovative ideas which we intend to implement in the future.

DOI: 10.4324/9781003357629-17

2 Motivation

Like other business processes, conferences are also going digital. Increasingly, computer technology is being used both on its own and in conjunction with broadband networks to support meeting objectives. Information retrieval is used to find domain-related texts for interpreters to read in advance of meetings. Collaborative workspaces in corporate networks and on the Internet offer geographically distributed collaborators a virtual repository for documents related to a particular project or conference. Electronic meeting support systems, such as interactive network-connected whiteboards and videoconferencing appliances, are available for those who are located in the same meeting room as well as those who are in remote locations.

Traditionally, Chinese interpreters will take whatever style of notes they prefer or use needed information from the official written minutes of previous meetings created by others. Whatever the form of the written record, it will be subjective and incomplete. Even with the best note-taking skills/procedures, interpreting errors often occur, and such errors can only be resolved by reviewing what actually happened in the meeting. The technology now exists to capture the entire meeting process, recording the text and graphics that are generated during a meeting alongside the audio and video signals.

If interpreters can use the multimedia recordings of meetings to find out or recall what they need to know about the outcome of the meeting, then such recordings can act as a valuable complement to their note-taking. However, this can only happen when it is possible to recognize, structure, index, and summarize meeting recordings automatically so that they can be searched efficiently. One of the long-term goals of meeting support technology is to make it possible to capture and analyze meeting participants' speech and actions using portable equipment and to create a wide range of applications to support meeting participants. This can be done using different systems, a unique platform, or web services. It will allow tasks like recognizing speech, summarizing, and analysis of the interaction among meeting participants to be undertaken. Another key benefit is that it will enable other interpreters to make use of the archives of recorded meetings in their subsequent work. Taken together, these possibilities indicate that videoconference interpreting in China is at the cusp of a major technological breakthrough.

The first core technology that will shape the future of videoconference interpreting will be audio and visual processing that provides interpreters basic facts, such as who is presenting and what words are being said. This audio and visual information processing will help make sense of meetings in human terms. Combining different sources of information into a meeting record of who said what, when, and to whom is often also useful for interpreting studies. For instance, by applying models of group dynamics from the behavioral and social sciences, it is possible to reveal how a group interacts, or to abstract and summarize a meeting's overall content.

However, finding ways to integrate the varying analyses required for a particular meeting support application has emerged as a major new challenge. Moreover, modeling and analyzing multimodal human-to-human communication to real-world applications require careful interface and systems design which is both user-centric and demand-captured. Finally, deciding how to evaluate such systems breaks new ground, whether it is done intrinsically or from an end user's point of view.

3   Remote interpreting flowchart

It is clear that technologies are playing increasingly important roles in interpreting practice and studies in China. In this section, we will firstly introduce a flowchart (Figure 14.1) that sets out typical remote interpreting technologies, including meeting content analysis, multimodal content conversion, and videoconference interpreting. We will then review each of these in more detail.

3.1   Meeting content analysis

Combining the theoretical goal of artificial intelligence (AI) and the practical value of information access, the computer-assisted understanding of human communication does not have a long history. Our understanding of this area accelerated in the 1990s when larger and larger amounts of audiovisual recordings became available in digital formats. Furthermore, during the 1990s, separate advances in the audio and video analysis of recordings led to the first

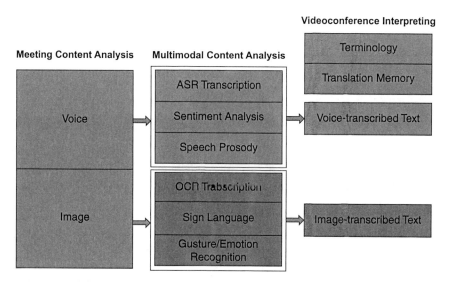

Figure 14.1 Flowchart of remote interpreting.

systems for interaction capture, analysis, and retrieval. For instance, the early Filochat system (Whittaker et al. 1994) was able to process handwritten notes to provide access to recordings of conversations, while BBN's Rough'n'Ready system (Kubala et al. 1999) enhanced audio recordings with structured information from speech transcription supplemented with speaker and topic identification. Video indexing of conferences was also considered in an early study by Kazman et al. (1996). Multichannel audio recording and transcription of business or research meetings were applied on a considerably larger scale in the Meeting Recorder project at ICSI, Berkeley (Morgan et al. 2003), which produced a landmark corpus that was reused in many subsequent projects.

Around the year 2000, it became obvious that meeting content analysis technologies needed to address a significant subtask of the modalities used for all human communication. This, in turn, required appropriate capture devices, which needed to be placed in instrumented meeting rooms, due to constraints on their position, size, and connection to recording devices. This was exemplified by the MIT Intelligent Room with its multiple sensors (Coen 1999). Moreover, Classroom 2000 (Abowd 1999) was an instrumented classroom that sought to capture and render all aspects of the teaching activities that constitute a lecture, while Microsoft's Distributed Meetings system (Cutler et al. 2002) supported the live broadcast of audio and video meeting data, alongside recording and subsequent browsing. Experiments with lectures, for example, for distance learning, indicated the importance of video editing based on multimodal cues (Rui et al. 2003). Instrumented meeting or conference rooms were also developed by Ricoh Corporation, along with a browser for audiovisual recordings (Lee et al. 2002), and by Fuji Xerox at FXPAL, where the semiautomatic production of meeting minutes, including summaries, was investigated (Chiu et al. 2001). However, while the technology seemed sufficiently mature for corporate research centers to engage in the design of such rooms and accompanying software, with potential end-user applications seeming not far from reach, it became clear that a finer-grained level of meeting content analysis and abstraction, that is, technology for remote audiovisual conferencing, was required to provide intelligent access to multimedia and multimodal human interaction.

Thanks to the capabilities of deep neural networks that have emerged in computer science since the 2010s, a series of new approaches which can fuse information from different modalities in hidden space at the intermediate level has successfully become a part of multimodal analysis. Today, there are new methodologies and techniques which stem from AI and natural language processing (NLP), which are suitable for handling the integration of multimodal data and domain knowledge. These methods can fully utilize multimodal data through learning correlational representations (i.e., the multimodal fusion of data across different modalities) and achieve multimodal data and knowledge fusion (multimodal fusion of data with domain knowledge). However, it should be noted that quite a few methods, including deep learning, can be used to learn hidden representations, while further correlational mining techniques are necessary for data-driven correlational representations (Zhu et al. 2020).

Regarding CACIS systems, the main task for meeting content analysis is to distinguish the speaker's *voice* from meeting *images* (professionally referred to as *frames*). Speech transcription can be generated from separated voice data for interpreters' reference, and interpreters can also uncover speakers' attitudes or emotions via sentiment analysis and speech prosody. While the characters or words in an image can be recognized by an optical character reader from the image dataset of a speech and the frozen frames of sign language, the gestures or facial emotions of the speaker will be recognized as well. All these recognized items will be converted into text from voice or image data, which allows the next step of the flowchart, multimodal content conversion.

3.2   Multimodal content conversion

The need for advanced multimodal signal processing for content abstraction and access has been addressed via several collaborative initiatives in the past decade. Such collaborative undertakings are vital, as only this approach can address the full complexity of human interaction in meetings. Moreover, as they are needed for training powerful machine learning algorithms, only such consortia have the means to collect large amounts of data and to provide reference annotations in several modalities. The public nature of most of the funding involved in such initiatives has ensured the public availability of their data. This section will now briefly review some of these collaborative initiatives.

Two projects at Carnegie Mellon University (CMU), the Informedia project (Wactlar et al. 1996) and its Interactive Systems Laboratory (ISL) project (Waibel et al. 2001), were among the first to receive public funding to study multimodal capture, indexing, and retrieval, with a focus on meetings. These projects were designed to record and browse meetings based on audio and video information, and they emphasized the role of speech transcription and summarization for information access (Burger et al. 2002). In Europe, the FAME project developed the prototype of a system that made use of multimodal information streams from an instrumented room to facilitate cross-cultural human–human conversation (Rogina and Schaaf 2002). A second prototype, the FAME Interactive Space (Metze et al. 2006), provided access to recordings of lectures via a tabletop interface that accepted voice commands from a user. The M4 European project introduced a framework for the integration of multimodal data streams and for the detection of group actions (McCowan et al. 2005). That project also proposed solutions for multimodal tracking of the focus of attention of meeting participants, multimodal summarization, and multimodal information retrieval. The IM2 National Centre of Competence in Research (Switzerland) is a large long-term initiative in the field of interactive multimodal information management. In particular, it is focused on multimodal meeting processing and access. The CHIL European project has explored the use of computers to enhance human communication in smart environments, especially within lectures and post-lecture discussions, building on several innovations from the CMU/ISL and FAME projects mentioned previously (Waibel et al. 2009). The US CALO project has developed, among other things, a meeting assistant focused on advanced analysis of spoken meeting recordings, along with related documents, including emails (Tür et al. 2010). Its primary goal was to learn to detect high-level aspects of human interaction which could serve to create summaries based on action items.

Typical multimodal content conversion scenarios in translation and interpreting fields include audiovisual translation and respeaking (where interpreters produce live subtitles via speech recognition software). In terms of multimodality, dubbing, subtitling, and respeaking transcend the mere transposition of written words or speech in a screenplay and instead bring other multimodal elements that make up a video product into the equation. Multimodal content conversion can also be applied to dialogue systems, virtual assistants, and machine interpreting. Moreover, this model of interaction can also be successfully applied to videoconference interpreting as it involves (i) processing of different input modalities, such as speech recognition, lip-reading, eye-tracking, gesture recognition, and handwriting recognition (cf. Oviatt et al. 2017), as well as (ii) various levels of integrations, including leveraging visual modality for speech recognition (Choe et al. 2019), integrating simultaneous lip movement sequences into speech recognition (Lin et al. 2021), isolating target speech from a multispeaker mixture signal with voice and face references (Qu et al. 2020), and grounding speech recognition with visual objects and scene information (Gupta et al. 2017).

Following the flow of meeting content analysis, multimodal content of the separated voice and image modalities can be converted into text modality.

In Figure 14.1, **automatic speech recognition (ASR)** synchronously transcribes text streams from speech input and shows them on a whiteboard or interpreters' computer screens. It is suggested that ASR-generated texts can greatly help interpreters attain a better understanding of a speech and undertake simultaneous note-taking during a speech. Furthermore, ASR transcriptions can be employed as an additional text confirmation of what is being said, and that they aid comprehension in cases when interpreters forget some of the main points from a speech. **Sentiment analysis** is the use of natural language processing, text analysis, computational linguistics, and biometrics to systematically identify, extract, quantify, and study affective states and subjective information. Sentiment analysis is widely applied to customer materials such as reviews and survey responses, online and social media, and health-care materials. This is done to underpin applications that range from marketing and customer service to clinical medicine. Moreover, with the rise of deep language models, more difficult data domains can be analyzed, for example, speech texts where speakers express their opinions/sentiments less explicitly. **Speech prosody** is not concerned with elements of speech that are individual phonetic segments (vowels and consonants) but instead focuses on the properties of syllables and larger units of speech, including linguistic functions, such as intonation, stress, and rhythm. Prosody may reflect features of the speaker or the utterance. For instance, this may include their emotional state, the form of their utterance (statement, question, or command), the presence of irony or sarcasm, and emphasis, contrast, and focus.

In terms of **optical character recognition (OCR)**, this is the electronic or mechanical conversion of images of typed, handwritten, or printed text into machine-encoded text. The source text can come from a scanned document, a photo of a document, a scene-photo or subtitle text superimposed on an image. With the help of artificial intelligence, accuracy concerns are mitigated because OCR engines are now sufficiently sensitive to read low-resolution and non-original documents. **Sign language recognition** is a computational task that involves recognizing actions from sign languages. This task is essential in tackling the communication gap faced by people with hearing impairments in the digital environment (Cooper et al. 2011). Solving this problem not only usually requires annotated color (RGB) data, but various other modalities like depth, sensory information, etc. are also useful. In contemporary society, a increasing numbers of organizations and institutes are committed to providing sign language services for public events, including video meetings and remote interpreting. For example, the Scottish Borders Council released "BSL Plan 2018–2024," stating "support the use of British Sign Language in University activities."[1] **Gesture/emotion recognition** is a topic in computer science and language technology that has the goal of interpreting human gestures/emotions via mathematical algorithms. Gestures can originate from any bodily motion or state, while emotions are most commonly evident from the face. Many approaches have been made to interpret sign language. However, the identification and recognition of posture, gait, proxemics, and human behavior are also the subject of gesture recognition techniques. Therefore, gesture recognition can be conceived of as a way for computers to begin to understand human body language.

Based on converted text from both voice and image video meeting datasets, alongside inputting interpreters' collected terminologies and prepared parallel topic-related texts, a video-meeting interpreting system can be built.

3.3 Video-meeting interpreting

The development of video-meeting interpreting was originally driven by the interest of supranational institutes such as the United Nations (UN) and the European Union (EU). The earliest documented experiment was conducted in 1976. The experiment linked the UNESCO headquarters in Paris with a conference center in Nairobi and involved three different methods: remote interpreting by telephone, remote interpreting by video link, and interpreting of a videoconference between Paris and Nairobi, with the interpreters situated in Paris (UNESCO 1976). Further similar experiments were subsequently organized by the UN in the 1970s and 1980s (Viaggi 2011; Mouzourakis 1996). The reports from these early tests indicated that interpreting via a videoconference link seemed feasible, but unfortunately, the remote interpreting was perceived to either be too challenging or to produce unacceptable results.

When videoconferencing over digital telephone lines became available in the 1990s, a series of studies into the feasibility of remote interpreting was conducted by various institutions, including the European Telecommunications Standard Institute, the European Commission, the UN, the International Telecommunications Union, the European Council, and the European Parliament (Braun 2015).

More recently, the EU has promoted the use of videoconferencing in legal proceedings, and many European countries have implemented videoconferencing facilities in courtrooms using the Internet. Compared to telephone line–based systems, the Internet provides better video and audio quality. Together with high-end peripheral equipment such as cameras and microphones, these systems can provide better support for video-meeting interpreting than older systems. However, at the same time, the availability of web-based videoconference services, which provide more but comparatively unstable sounds and images and access via tablets and other mobile devices, especially in health-care settings, raises new questions about the feasibility of remote interpreting using such systems.

Next, we will demonstrate how CACIS systems work in remote conference interpreting scenarios.

4 Remote conference interpreting technologies

Figure 14.2 shows the infrastructure of a prototype CACIS system.

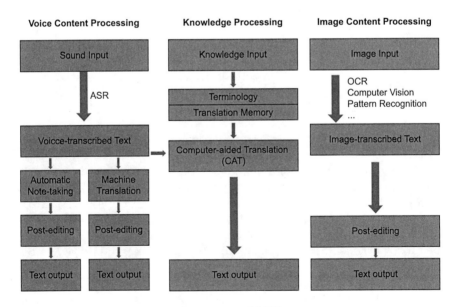

Figure 14.2 The infrastructure of a prototype CACIS system.

In this system, knowledge relating to the speech that is to be interpreted, including terminology and translation memory, is the priority input. As normal, such data would be created and collected by the interpreters based on their previous work and their preparation for this speech. The audiovisual content of the live speech will be inputted and processed in real time. In the audio content processing module, the speech will be transcribed by the automatic speech recognition (ASR) tool, and the transcription can be translated by a professional translator with computer-aided translation (CAT) technology. This can either be done in a consecutive interpreting scenario or translated automatically by a machine translation (MT) system in simultaneous/consecutive interpreting scenarios. The CACIS will extract interpreting keywords, such as numerals, proper names, terminology, and thematic phrases, from the transcription and analyze their logical relationship within discourse, that is, automatic note-taking. The automatic outputs of MT and note-taking can be accepted, rejected, or revised by human interpreters. This is called post-editing (PE). In the video content processing module, the speaker's gestures and emotions can be recognized and grasped automatically, and his/her speech prosody and sign language can be transcribed alongside the text. In this section, we will introduce the aforementioned videoconference-based translation technologies in a CACIS, including CAT, MT, and PE.

4.1 Computer-aided translation (CAT) tools

CAT tools are software applications which have been created to support translators in their daily work. CAT tools use databases of previous translations with specific parallel source language and target language to aid the translation process. This is called translation memory. Visually, a CAT tool interface usually displays across three zones: one for translation memory, one for terminology, and the final one for editing, with two columns or panels; one shows the source text, and the other is for editing the target text. Typically, the tool will segment the source text into sentences or paragraphs to make it easier for the translator to keep track of the flow of information. CAT tools are widely used in written translation, but they are infrequently applied in the interpreting scenario in China. However, this does not mean that there is no space for CAT in consecutive conference interpreting: there is a sufficient time gap for the spare interpreter (ideally, an interpreter off-mike or professional translator who is assisting the interpreter on-mike) to conduct computer-aided translation with the ASR transcription as the source text. Thus, the spare interpreter will transfer the CAT output to the consecutive interpreter on-mike and undertake the without-text interpreting with text.

CAT tools have a large number of functions, such as:

a. Translation memories, which allow translators to reuse previous translations.
b. Term bases or glossaries, which can be used to search for brand-specific or project-specific terminology.

c. The option to click through to secondary resources for additional context, such as images or comments left by other translators, the project manager, or other stakeholders.
d. Advanced search and navigation tools.
e. Reports detailing how much of the translation has been completed.
f. Auto-completion of segments if they are an exact match to previously translated content.
g. Quality assurance tools to search for errors in the translation, such as untranslated segments, missing numbers, or instances where the same word has two different translations.
h. The possibility of generating a final translated document that automatically mirrors the original document's format.
i. Integration with other translation technologies, such as neural machine translation engines.

Most of these functions can be utilized in consecutive conference interpreting. Besides the translation memories we mentioned earlier, term bases or terminology retrieval also provides the interpreter valuable help when s/he encounters an unfamiliar term in an utterance.

CAT tools have revolutionized translation technology, making it easier for companies to optimize the translation process and handle large amounts of content in a more efficient way, saving both time and money. For translators, the main benefit is that they can use the time saved on repetitive tasks to focus on the translation itself. For interpreters, they enjoy similar benefits in terms of being relieved from repetitive interpreting and being able to focus more on new and creative speeches.

4.2   *Machine translation (MT)*

Machine translation (MT) is an automated approach that produces translated content without human intervention. As described in the previous section concerning CAT tools, MT can be integrated with those tools. However, MT differs from CAT tools in that it doesn't rely on human input but produces translation entirely on its own. In conference interpreting, the target of MT is ASR transcription text or speech text.

Normally, MT engines fall into one of three categories: rule-based machine translation (RBMT), where the engine translates words and sentences based on a set of rules that can be adjusted by the user; statistical machine translation (SMT), where the system translates based on a corpus (a large body of parallel texts) to train the engineer; and neural machine translation (NMT), where the engine is AI-powered and capable of mimicking the way a human brain works when processing language. In a nutshell, thanks to machine learning technology, these engines are capable of understanding entire sentences and even paragraphs at once instead of translating word by word. Until 2016, MT systems adopted the statistical approach. Today, most MT engines are neural in nature.

The quality of MT output varies depending on different factors. Languages of dissimilar syntax such as English and Chinese may be harder to translate accurately than languages with similar grammar, such as Spanish and French; a general language document tends to translate more accurately than a specified domain translation, for example, a legal text; if the source text undergoes pre-processing to eliminate certain "noisy" elements, this may improve the translation output; and more training data results in better MT. Thus, some engines perform better than others as a result of having access to more data.

Considering the issues discussed earlier, interpreters can choose whether to use raw or unedited MT output or to refine the output, depending on their goals and needs. The latter is called "machine translation post-editing (MTPE)," and it can be either light or full.

4.3   Post-editing (PE)

Some types of transcribed texts will be more suitable for a lower level of editing. For example, Q&A session conversational texts may require light editing; however, a press release that will directly impact a speaker's reputation or that of his/her organization should go through a full PE process. By the same logic, sensitive content such as financial statements should always be handled by human translators. Given this, interpreters always use raw machine translation for low-impact, quickly perishable, and unambiguous content. Examples include internal documentation, user-generated content like product reviews (where consumers generally expect low quality), customer inquiries, or frequently amended content, like features and information updates.

Because MT is nowadays integrated into most modern CAT tools, interpreters can assist the work of post-editors with features such as glossaries, term bases, and translation memories, as well as brand books and style guides. This makes it more feasible to maintain brand voice and consistency of key messages across cultures and languages with MTPE.

It is important to note that the term "post-editing" can actually be employed beyond MT. For instance, interpreters can also edit the output of ASR, automatic note-taking, and video transcriptions.

4.4   Automatic note-taking

Different to keyword extraction, the notes that interpreters make during consecutive interpreting include not only keywords such as terminology, high-frequency content words, or the most important words in a text but also numerals and proper names, which are decisive for the interpretation quality of an utterance. Furthermore, automatic note-taking needs to frame the event involved in a speech where NLP summarization technology could be introduced to automatic note-taking. Alternatively, the interpreter might organize the notes made by the machine with his/her own understanding of the

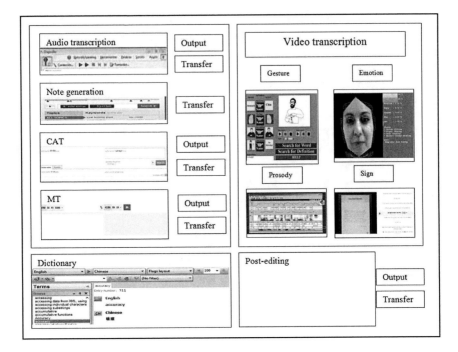

Figure 14.3 CACIS UI design.

speech, an approach which at least saves interpreters' time compared to writing down the interpreting keywords manually.

The previous technologies used in the prototype CACIS system are also highly scalable and customizable. This makes them invaluable for any business which is seeking to streamline its interpreting process based on the specific needs of its content and target audience. We have designed the user interface of our CACIS specialized for English and Chinese language pair as shown in Figure 14.3.

5   Remote interpreting – opportunities and challenges

5.1   *Opportunities*

Due to the COVID-19 pandemic, videoconferencing has become increasingly popular in China as well as other countries and regions across the world. For many companies and organizations, videoconferencing is now a preferred form of communication for both financial and convenience reasons. Consequently, videoconferencing systems have become a mainstream means of distant communication, and they play a crucial role in the generation of ideas, documents, relationships, and actions within many organizations.

Online meetings are less costly and time-consuming compared to in-person meetings. Conducting an in-person meeting often necessitates hotel accommodation costs, the arrangement of facilities, travel expenses, etc. When attendees need to come from different locations, this may lead to a delay in a meeting being arranged. In contrast, virtual/online conferences only need a computer or smart device with a stable Internet connection. They therefore save time by avoiding travel and allowing participants to continue to work from their normal location. Furthermore, enhanced accessibility, easier joining and leaving arrangements, increased attendance, and the ability to record discussions are additional benefits arising from online conferences.

Similarly, remote conference interpreting saves time because it can be completed in just a few hours, whereas managing on-site conference interpreting takes much more time. Therefore, online conference interpreting is more cost-effective and saves time compared to in-person conference interpreting.

One of the most significant changes for conference interpreting concerns the ease of sharing information with team members. For in-person conference interpreting, it is necessary to create numerous copies of documents. However, when using a computer-assisted conference system, such prepared materials can be stored electronically in advance and can be retrieved at any time by the interpreter on or off the mike. CACIS needs teamwork if some post-editing jobs are necessary. Using virtual conferencing tools like Zoom, Skype, Teams, etc. makes it easier to share documents and information with other team members. This ease of sharing information allows interpreters to raise any issues in real time and make changes to documents when necessary. This enhances collaboration and makes conference interpreting more effective, as a conference can only be effective when all team members are involved.

5.2 Challenges

During on-site conference interpreting, face-to-face communication between the interpreter and the speaker is extremely important. Specifically, it promotes healthy engagement while also building a trustworthy working environment among participants. With the help of a computer-assisted conference interpreting system and/or in a virtual conference environment, interpreters sit in front of a computer in a booth and are only able to communicate with the speaker and audience virtually. The reduced face-to-face contact can make interaction between participants difficult, especially in terms of understanding emotions even though a gesture/emotion recognition module can be used to address this issue. Speakers use emotions, tone of voice, gestures, and facial expressions as part of communication. Only the improvement of speech prosody, sign language, and gesture emotion recognition will provide interpreters the chance to fully express speakers' emotions. The insufficiency of multimodal processing can also limit the level of understanding that the interpreter wants to get from other participants, as their emotions and passion cannot be understood.

There are other technical challenges which include poor Internet connections and the cost of software. Our prototype CACIS and similar platforms will eventually be commercialized, and users will have to pay for their services. Paying for the software requires money. Furthermore, if more features are required, this will cost more. With monthly or yearly subscription renewals and other packages, paying for effective computer-assisted interpreting software may entail high costs, and in some circumstances, this could lead to virtual and computer-assisted conference interpreting being more expensive than on-site interpreting.

As for the interpreters themselves, it may be difficult for them to handle the technological infrastructure due to a lack of relevant expertise. For instance, many interpreters in China still don't understand remote connectivity, virtual technology, or how new platforms work. Because some people do not understand how to use technology, this will limit the acceptance of computer-assisted interpreting and remote conference interpreting. Consequently, introducing new software and technology for virtual meetings could have a negative impact on organizations or individuals who struggle to master new technology.

6   Conclusion

For videoconference interpreting, in order to interpret naturally and to enable computers to support interaction between interpreters, it is necessary to develop new models and algorithms which can extract both explicit and implicit information from meetings. Human communication is centered on information exchange, but the words that people say are never the whole story: non-verbal cues also play a key role. Indeed, when people talk to each other, facial expressions, posture, and voice quality (i.e., non-verbal communication) tell us how those around us are disposed toward what we say.

Although the research areas covered in the literature often relate to different levels of interpreting studies, it is clear that natural multimodal interaction will be required in many future applications, in particular, for mobile settings, like remote interpreting in videoconferencing. Automatic analysis and understanding of communication scenes form a significant part of the field.

The CACIS discussed in this chapter remains a prototype, which is not only designed for English/Chinese translation but also extendable to other language pairs. In the future, we believe that it will also be necessary to develop algorithms for this system to automatically analyze a group's social processes. At the same time, there is also a significant trend toward deeper collaboration between technology specialists and interpreters in China and all over the world to inspire new tools for interpreting.

Acknowledgments

This research is one of the achievements of Innovative Projects of Colleges and Universities under the Department of Education of Guangdong

Province (Project No. 2019WTSCX024). It is supported by the Institute of Hermeneutics of Guangdong University of Foreign Studies (Fund No. CSY-2021-YA-04) and funded by the Center for Translation Studies of Guangdong University of Foreign Studies (Fund No. CTS201501)

Notes

1 www.scotborders.gov.uk/downloads/file/5154/british_sign_language_bsl_plan_2018_-_2024_stage_1.

References

Abowd, Gregory D. 1999. "Classroom 2000: An Experiment with the Instrumentation of a Living Educational Environment." *IBM Systems Journal* 38(4): 508–30.

Braun, Sabine. 2015. "Remote Interpreting." In *The Routledge Handbook of Interpreting*, edited by Holly Mikkelson and Renée Jourdenais, 352–67. New York: Routledge.

Burger, Susanne, Victoria MacLaren, and Hua Yu. 2002. "The ISL Meeting Corpus: The Impact of Meeting Type on Speech Style." In *Proceedings of the 7th International Conference on Spoken Language Processing (ICSLP2002)*, edited by Nicoletta Calzolari, Khalid Choukri, Bente Maegaard, Joseph Mariani, Jan Odijk, Stelios Piperidis, Mike Rosner and Daniel Tapias, 301–4. Valletta: European Language Resources Association (ELRA).

Chiu, Patrick, John Boreczky, Andreas Girgensohn, and Don Kimber. 2001. "LiteMinutes: An Internet-Based System for Multimedia Meeting Minutes." In *Proceedings of the 10th International Conference on World Wide Web (WWW2001)*, edited by Vincent Y. Shen, Nobuo Saito, Michael R. Lyu and Mary Ellen Zurko, 140–9. New York: Association for Computing Machinery.

Choe, Sang K., Quanyang Lu, Vikas Raunak, Yi Xu, and Florian Metze. 2019. "On Leveraging Visual Modality for Speech Recognition Error Correction." Accessed November 24, 2022. https://srvk.github.io/how2-challenge/assets/authors/TH2_paper_7.pdf.

Coen, Michael H. 1999. "The Future of Human-Computer Interaction, or How I Learned to Stop Worrying and Love My Intelligent Room." *IEEE Intelligent Systems* 14(5): 8–10.

Cooper, Helen, Eng-Jon Ong, Nicolas Pugeault, and Richard Bowden. 2011. "Sign Language Recognition." In *Visual Analysis of Humans: Looking at People*, edited by Thomas B. Moeslund, Adrian Hilton, Volker Krüger and Leonid Sigal, 539–62. London: Springer.

Cutler, Ross, Yong Rui, Anoop Gupta, J. J. Cadiz, Ivan Tashev, Liwei He, Alex Colburn, Zhengyou Zhang, Zicheng Liu, and Steve Silverberg. 2002. "Distributed Meetings: A Meeting Capture and Broadcasting System." In *Proceedings of the 10th ACM International conference on Multimedia*, edited by Lawrence Rowe, Bernard Merialdo, Max Muhlhauser, Keith Ross and Nevenka Dimitrova, 503–12. New York: Association for Computing Machinery.

Gupta, Abhinav, Yajie Miao, Leonardo Neves, and Florian Metze. 2017. "Visual Features for Context-Aware Speech Recognition." In *Proceedings of 2017 IEEE International Conference on Acoustics, Speech and Signal Processing (ICASSP 2017)*, edited by Magdy A. Bayoumi, Tulay Adali and Eli Saber, 5020–4. Piscataway: IEEE Press.

Kazman, Rick, Reem Al-Halimi, William Hunt, and Marilyn Mantei. 1996. "Four Paradigms for Indexing Video Conferences." *IEEE multimedia* 3(1): 63–73.

Kubala, Francis, Sean Colbath, Daben Liu, and John Makhoul. 1999. "Rough'n'Ready: A Meeting Recorder and Browser." *ACM Computing Surveys* 31(2es): 7.

Lee, Dar-Shyang, Berna Erol, Jamey Graham, Jonathan J. Hull, and Norihiko Murata. 2002. "Portable Meeting Recorder." In *Proceedings of the 10th ACM International Conference on Multimedia*, edited by Lawrence Rowe, Bernard Merialdo, Max Muhlhauser, Keith Ross and Nevenka Dimitrova, 493–502. New York: Association for Computing Machinery.

Lin, Zhijie, Zhou Zhao, Haoyuan Li, Jinglin Liu, Meng Zhang, Xingshan Zeng, and Xiaofei He. 2021. "SimulLR: Simultaneous LipReading Transducer with Attention-Guided Adaptive Memory." In *Proceedings of the 29th ACM International Conference on Multimedia* (MM' 2021), edited by Heng T. Shen, Yueting Zhuang, John R. Smith, Yang Yang, Pablo Cesar, Florian Metze and Balakrishnan Prabhakaran, 1359–67. New York: Association for Computing Machinery.

McCowan, Iain, Daniel Gatica-Perez, Samy Bengio, Guillaume Lathoud, Mark Barnard, and Dong Zhang. 2005. "Automatic Analysis of Multimodal Group Actions in Meetings." *IEEE Transactions on Pattern Analysis and Machine Intelligence* 27(3): 305–17.

Metze, Florian, Petra Gieselmann, Hartwig Holzapfel, Tobias Kluge, Ivica Rogina, Alexander H. Waibel, Matthias Wölfel, James L. Crowley, Patrick Reignier, Dominique Vaufreydaz, François Bérard, Bérangère Cohen, Joëlle Coutaz, Sylvie Rouillard, Victoria Arranz, Manuel Bertrán, and Horacio Rodríguez. 2006. "The 'Fame' Interactive Space." In *Machine Learning for Multimodal Interaction*, edited by Andrei Popescu-Belis and Rainer Stiefelhagen, 285–96. Berlin: Springer.

Morgan, Nelson, Don Baron, Sonali Bhagat, Hannah Carvey, Rajdip Dhillon, Jane Edwards, David Gelbart, Adam L. Janin, Ashley Krupski, Barbara Peskin, Thilo Pfau, Elizabeth Shriberg, Andreas Stolcke, and Chuck Wooters. 2003. "Meetings about Meetings: Research at ICSI on Speech in Multiparty Conversations." In *Proceedings of IEEE International Conference on Acoustics, Speech, and Signal Processing (ICASSP2003)*, edited by Billene Mercer, 740–3. Piscataway: IEEE Press.

Mouzourakis, Panayotis. 1996. "Videoconferencing: Techniques and Challenges." *Interpreting* 1(1): 21–38.

Oviatt, Sharon, Björn Schuller, Philip Cohen, Daniel Sonntag, Gerasimos Potamianos, and Antonio Krüger. 2017. *The Handbook of Multimodal-Multisensor Interfaces, Volume 1: Foundations, User Modeling, and Common Modality Combinations*. Broadway: ACM and Morgan & Claypool.

Qu, Leyuan, Cornelius Weber, and Stefan Wermter. 2020. "Multimodal Target Speech Separation with Voice and Face References." In *Proceedings of Interspeech 2020*, edited by Hellen Meng, Bo Xu and Thomas Zheng, 1416–20. Baixas: ISCA.

Rogina, Ivica, and Thomas Schaaf. 2002. "Lecture and Presentation Tracking in an Intelligent Meeting Room." In *Proceedings of the 4th IEEE International Conference on Multimodal Interfaces*, edited by Danielle C. Martin, 47–52. Piscataway: IEEE Press.

Rui, Yong, Anoop Gupta, and Jonathan T Grudin. 2003. "Videography for Telepresentations." In *Proceedings of the SIGCHI Conference on Human Factors in Computing Systems*, edited by Philippe Palanque, Matt Jones, Albrecht Schmidt and Tovi Grossman, 457–64. New York: Association for Computing Machinery.

Tür, Gökhan, Andreas Stolcke, L. Lynn Voss, Stanley Peters, Dilek Z. Hakkani-Tür, John Dowding, Benoît Favre, R. Fernández, Matthew Frampton, Michael W.

Frandsen, Clint Frederickson, Martin Graciarena, Donald Kintzing, Kyle Leveque, Shane Mason, John Niekrasz, Matthew Purver, Korbinian Riedhammer, Elizabeth Shriberg, Jing Tien, Dimitra Vergyri, and Fan Yang. 2010. "The CALO Meeting Assistant System." *IEEE Transactions on Audio, Speech, and Language Processing* 18(6): 1601–11.

UNESCO. 1976. *A Teleconference Experiment*. Paris: UNESCO.

Viaggio, Sergio. 2011. "Remote Interpreting Rides Again." *The AIIC Webzine*. Accessed January 1, 2016. http://aiic.net/page/3710/remote-interpreting-rides-again/lang/1.

Wactlar, Howard D, Takeo Kanade, Michael A. Smith, and Scott M. Stevens. 1996. "Intelligent Access to Digital Video: Informedia Project." *Computer* 29(5): 46–52.

Waibel, Alexander H., Michael Bett, Florian Metze, Klaus Ries, Thomas Schaaf, Tanja Schultz, Hagen Soltau, Hua Yu, and Klaus Zechner. 2001. "Advances in Automatic Meeting Record Creation and Access." In *Proceedings of IEEE International Conference on Acoustics, Speech, and Signal Processing (ICASSP2001)*, edited by Behrouz Farhang-Boroujeny, 597–600. Piscataway: IEEE Press.

Waibel, Alexander, Rainer Stiefelhagen, Rolf Carlson, Josep Ramon Casas, Jan Kleindienst, Lori Lamel, Oswald Lanz, Djamel Mostefa, Maurizio Omologo, Fabio Pianesi, Lazaros Polymenakos, Gerasimos Potamianos, John Soldatos, Gerhard Sutschet, and Jacques M. B. Terken. 2009. *Computers in the Human Interaction Loop*. London: Springer.

Whittaker, Steve, Patricia A. Hyland, and Myrtle Wiley. 1994. "Filochat: Handwritten Notes Provide Access to Recorded Conversations." In *Proceedings of the SIGCHI Conference on Human Factors in Computing Systems*, edited by Beth Adelson, Susan Dumais and Judith Olson, 271–7. New York: Association for Computing Machinery.

Zhang, Xiaojun. 2015. "The Changing Face of Conference Interpreting." In *New Horizon of Translation and Interpreting Studies*, edited by Gloria C. Pastor, Miriam Seghiri, Rut Gutierrez Florido and Miriam Urbano, 255–63. Lisbon: Editions Tradulex.

Zhu, Wenwu, Xin Wang, and Hongzhi Li. 2020. "Multi-Modal Deep Analysis for Multimedia." *IEEE Transactions on Circuits and Systems for Video Technology* 30(10): 3740–64.

15 Interpreter training and related research in virtual reality

The Chinese experience

Yu Jiang and Hui Jia

1 Introduction

As we enter an era witnessing the booming development of science and technology, the role that technology plays in modern education and research cannot be simply ignored. In China, a number of documents issued by the Chinese government since 1980s have clearly stated that information and communications technologies (ICT) application in education is an important and strategic direction. In the *Action Plan 2.0 to Promote ICT Integration in Education*, Internet, big data, artificial intelligence (AI), and virtual reality (VR) are encouraged to be used to explore future teaching/learning modes and facilitate teaching/learning reforms.

It is acknowledged that VR and other technological developments are gradually integrated into interpreter training and related research. EU has funded two projects – Interpreting in Virtual Reality (IVY) and Evaluating the Education of Interpreters and Their Clients through Virtual Learning Activities (EVIVA) – to foster the acquisition and application of interpreting skills and develop innovative evaluation methods by using virtual environments. Similarly, in China, VR interpreting simulation labs and projects start to flourish with the policy support from the Ministry of Education to develop simulation projects, and VR has become an important tool in interpreting research.

2 Why adopt VR in interpreter training and related research?

2.1 Interpreting as a situated communicative activity

Interpreting is widely recognized as an immediate, complex transfer of meaning across languages. The seemingly linear relationship between speakers, receivers, and interpreters has long restricted interpreting research to issues such as information processing and code-switching. Nevertheless, a growing number of scholars remind that the communicative nature of interpreting should not be neglected, because interpreters actually work as intermediaries or mediators between communicators of different cultural backgrounds (Pöchhacker 2008, 11–14; Wadensjö 2014, 61–68). To be more specific, "interpreting is a service of interlingual, intercultural and interpersonal communication situated

DOI: 10.4324/9781003357629-18

in and constrained by a professional context" (Li 2015, 324), and interpreters could both influence and be influenced by this dynamic process of communication (Baraldi 2017, 372–75; Schäffner 2015, 436–47). The shift of emphasis from linguistic to contextual stimuli highlights the importance of contextual embedding in interpreting practice and particularly in the training for novice interpreters.

In addition to being contextualized, interpreting is a highly situated activity, given that it is always carried out on-site, and interpreters are likely to be affected by a variety of extra-lingual factors, including working conditions, psychological pressure, etc. (Kurz 2003, 54–58). Therefore, scholars suggest that interpreter training should focus not only on fostering linguistic skills but also on bridging the gap between training and reality, allowing students to get better prepared for the real working scenarios (Chmiel 2015, 166; Li 2015, 324). This appeal is in line with the concept of social constructivism, which advocates that knowledge construction should be situated in authentic settings and achieved through social interaction (Vygotsky and Cole 1978, 79–91).

2.2 Progress and problems of current interpreter training

Despite the fact that interpreter trainers and researchers have agreed on the importance of situated learning, the mainstream of current training mode is still teacher-centered and lacks interactivity with trainees doing in-class exercises, instructors introducing interpreting skills and commenting on the exercise renditions.

Looking back over the past few decades, it is noticeable that interpreter training methods have mainly evolved with advancements in technology and educational theory. On one hand, the progress of ICT has encouraged innovation in interpreting teaching materials, from outdated, static textbooks with a limited number of exercises to constantly updated, abundant digital audio/video repositories of speeches and dialogues taped in real-world working settings (Braun et al. 2013, 95). In addition, training facilities have advanced from tape recorders to interpreting laboratories equipped with professional conference interpreting systems (Lim 2020, 145), which helps improve training efficiency and facilitate after-class self-directed practice. However, the "social" elements, which are assumed quite important as discussed earlier (Vygotsky and Cole 1978, 79–91), are still somewhat missing in ICT-based training.

Theoretical advancement in the education area, on the other hand, motivated reforms of methods and techniques in interpreter training. Since Kiraly (2014, 34–50) first introduced social constructivist approaches in the translation and interpreting field, increasingly more scholars have stressed on "the authentic situated action, the collaborative construction of knowledge, and personal experience," thus giving rise to mock conferences as a form of situated learning. In mock conferences, the traditional teacher-centered method gives way to the situated, trainee-centered approach: trainees have to independently prepare and work for lifelike interpreting tasks. Advantages of such situated learning are obvious and have been reported in several studies (Defrancq et al. 2022, 48–55; Li 2015, 336–37). In addition to enabling trainees to better understand and adapt to real, complex interpreting work scenarios, mock conferences provide a safe environment for them to make mistakes, thus serving as a bridge between the classroom and the market. However, even though it is generally accepted that mock conferences are beneficial, due to time and space constraints, this form of situated learning is hardly employed in after-class exercises and mostly carried out in final years only as a supplement to conventional classes.

2.3   One step further: adopting VR in interpreter training

To create a situated training platform which features flexibility, authenticity, autonomy, and peer collaboration has become the demand of the new era. Thanks to the vigorous development of computer-aided learning, it is possible to find solutions to the aforementioned problems in conventional interpreting classes. One of the cutting-edge computer technologies that has recently been applied in interpreter training is VR, which, according to Gayeski (1993, 76), can be defined as "a form of human-computer interface characterized by an environmental simulation."

Although VR seems to be a notion that has only lately gained popularity, its application in education and vocational training can be traced back to as early as 1960s, when a flight simulator was developed for pilot training (Page 2000, 11). However, it wasn't until the first decade of the 21st century that VR-integrated learning and related research began to draw attention as the technology grew more advanced and its commercial application gained fast momentum. Early educational VR implementation mainly concentrated in STEM-related fields, such as medical and surgical education, engineering, and science (Kavanagh et al. 2017, 88). Tentative exploration in these areas has yielded positive results for further application of VR in other disciplines, indicating that VR is effective in enhancing learners' motivation (Garris et al. 2017, 455–57; Parong and Mayer 2018, 791–93) and enjoyment (Makransky et al. 2019, 698–99; Sung et al. 2021, 206), encouraging interaction (Roussou 2004, 8–11), benefiting for knowledge acquisition and long-term retention (Yildirim et al. 2019, 25), and thus boosting learning outcomes (Slavova and Mu 2018, 686). One of the reasons that VR-integrated training is more effective in improving learning performance than traditional teaching techniques is probably that VR is able to give users an immersive experience, namely, "the feeling of 'being there'" (Psotka 1995, 405), which is also the key factor that sets VR apart from other technologies. The immersive feature of VR learning environment enables learners to actively participate in the learning process and interact with the environment, transforming passive learning such as listening to lectures into an active exploratory mode (Chen 2016, 638).

With these unique advantages, VR's pedagogical application has soon caught the attention of linguists interested in language acquisition. Simulated environment, strong interactivity, and self-regulating learning in the VR training mode are just in line with language acquisition's needs of an authentic context, sociality, and autonomy (Li 2018, 49–51). Empirical evidence indicates that in addition to better learning experience and positive emotional influence (Lin and Wang 2021, 4498–99), VR tools can significantly improve L2 learning outcomes by enhancing vocabulary learning and retention (Legault et al. 2019, 32–35; Santos et al. 2016, 19–20; Tai et al. 2020, 912–13), written and oral language skills (Xie et al. 2021, 236–37), and learners' ability to communicate across cultural boundaries (O'Brien and Levy 2008, 677–80). Since interpreting has a close relationship with language learning, these encouraging results confirm the potential of VR in interpreter training. Furthermore, the rise of remote interpreting in the post-pandemic era also necessitates pedagogical innovation to better prepare novice interpreters for the digital communication environment (Braun 2015, 364). It is thus not surprising that scholars have soon attempted to incorporate VR into interpreting classes.

The majority of VR-based interpretation training trials are conducted in Europe and rely on Second Life (Şahin 2013, 97), one of the largest 3D multi-user virtual worlds that has already seen extensive use in L2 learning, business, engineering, and other fields. Among various interpreting projects, the most influential one so far is probably the IVY (Interpreting in Virtual Reality) project (Braun et al. 2013, 93) funded by the European Commission.

According to its introduction (Ritsos et al. 2012, 191), the IVY virtual environment offers prospective clients a tool to gain a firsthand experience of interpreting service as well as a 3D platform for trainee interpreters to learn and practice interpreting skills in an almost-real environment. With a focus on community and business settings, the working modes mainly practiced in the IVY environment are consecutive and liaison interpreting. In order to examine IVY's pedagogical effectiveness, researchers have conducted a *post hoc* evaluation with e-diaries, questionnaire, observation, and direct interaction with IVY users. Results indicate that despite some technique issues that may cause users' perspectives to differ, the "sense of presence" in IVY and feasibility of VR in interpreter training are confirmed (Braun et al. 2015, 51).

In general, although VR-based training mode and the guidance for users need to be further improved, this innovative technology has unique advantages in providing an immersive environment and high flexibility and could be better tailored to individual preferences. Therefore, VR is gradually recognized as a valuable tool for transforming conventional interpreting classes into student-centered and contextualized ones free from temporal and spatial constraints.

3　Interpreter training in VR settings: the Chinese cases

It is estimated that Chinese universities offer the largest number of BTI (Bachelor of Translation and Interpreting) programs and MTI (Master of

Translation and Interpreting) programs in the world. According to the *2022 Report on the Development of Translation and Language Service Industry in China* published by the Translators Association of China, there are now 301 BTI programs and 316 MTI programs across Chinese universities. These programs, especially the MTI programs, are designed to provide adequate training for those would-be professional interpreters and translators. Therefore, it is fair to say that universities play a major role in providing and transforming interpreter training with cutting-edge technologies like VR in China. Public information (public news, bid announcements, bid results, etc.) shows that to reinvigorate interpreter training by embracing VR and other modern technological elements, Chinese universities usually choose to build VR labs and develop VR-aided interpreting simulation projects.

3.1   VR labs

Some universities embed VR in interpreter training by building VR interpreting platforms or labs. Renmin University of China (中国人民大学) has devoted more than 2 million *yuan* (about $280 thousand) to build a multilingual VR interpreting simulation training platform (Renmin University of China, np).[1] It is said that the preparatory work for the platform, like system debugging, script-writing for interpreting scenarios, has finished, and the platform will "provide students with simulated interpreting experience, enabling them to improve their language skills and acquire professional knowledge" (Renmin University of China, np)[2] when finished. One tangible result of the platform is a granted patent named "a computer-aided interpreter training simulation system" including subsystems of logging, preview, teaching, evaluation, and database filed by the project team (Patentstar, np).[3] But to build a VR platform or lab dedicated for interpreter training is not often seen in Chinese universities.

A more cost-effective and commonly used approach by Chinese universities is to build a multifunctional VR foreign language lab or studio in which VR interpreting is an essential component. Currently, English is the most frequently seen foreign language applied in many VR language labs or studios in Chinese universities. A multifunctional VR foreign language lab or studio is generally designed to offer different types of training and accommodate students learning various courses, such as English public speaking, English listening, business English, business negotiation, intercultural communication, interpreting and translation, etc. The VR foreign language simulation training center of Hangzhou Normal University (杭州师范大学), built in 2018 with functions like English public speaking and pronunciation training and scenarios including cross-border e-commerce, business negotiation, and international exhibition, is claimed to be the first VR foreign language lab in Chinese universities (CASRZ, np).[4] VR interpreting modules are included in the VR foreign language labs in universities like Ningbo University (宁波大学), Xi'an International Studies University (西安外国语大学), Luoyang Normal

University (洛阳师范学院), etc. Students can wear VR headsets to experience different interpreting scenarios created by VR.

3.2 *VR-aided interpreting simulation projects*

The second commonly used approach by Chinese universities is to develop VR-aided interpreting simulation projects. There are mainly three types of projects, namely, projects based on courses, projects for general purposes, and projects with specific themes. Some projects are developed based on courses in a way that VR helps visualize the scenarios in a specific course and upgrade its learning/teaching environment, for example, the business English interpreting course of Shanghai University of Finance and Economics (上海财经大学), and Spanish communication and interpreting course of Guangdong University of Foreign Studies (广东外语外贸大学). It is worth noting that these two aforementioned courses both won the award "China's First-Class Simulation Course" according to public information.

Another type is projects for general purposes. A representative example is the immersive VR interpreting simulation training and intelligent evaluation project developed by University of Electronic Science and Technology of China (电子科技大学) (UESTC, np).[5] This project can provide VR-aided interpreter training with 15 cases in CI/SI modes, like "Belt and Road Initiative" "sustainable development" "China–Britain financial cooperation" "speech delivered by UN Secretary General" set at three difficulty levels (basic, medium, and advanced) in three scenarios (international conference, news release, and public speaking). After each experiment, students' recordings are stored, transcribed, and evaluated by the cloud platform. The AI-supported automatic grading system evaluates students' performance from three dimensions (fluency, completeness, and accuracy). Teachers can retrieve data from the platform and grade for the second time. A questionnaire is designed to collect feedback and suggestions from participants in order to further optimize the algorithm of the whole system.

The third type is projects with specific themes. A common feature of this type is that the theme of the VR simulation project is quite closely related to the distinctive characteristics of the university or local/regional economic development. For example, Fujian Medical University (福建医科大学) has developed a VR-aided interpreting simulation project with the theme of acupuncture diagnosis and treatment in Botswana in which acupuncture knowledge is integrated into interpreter training (Fujian Medical University, np);[6] Beijing Language and Culture University (北京语言大学) has developed a VR simulation project of UN conference interpreting (iLab-X.com, np)[7] since the university is known as "the Mini-United Nations," with more than 6,000 international students from more than 140 countries and regions every year studying there Sichuan International Studies University (四川外国语大学) has developed a VR emulation experiment project for liaison and conference interpreter training based on business exchanges in areas along the

Chongqing-Xinjiang-Europe International Railway, which "serves as a profound transformation on the concepts, models and pedagogies of traditional interpreting teaching and learning, as well as a response to the development trends of ICT and the 'Belt and Road Initiative'" (Qin and Qin 2022, 131).

With the spread of COVID-19 around the world, it becomes more obvious that there is a lack of qualified and competent bilingual/multilingual professionals that can provide language service in emergency scenarios. Against such backdrop, Wuhan University (武汉大学) has developed a VR simulation project as an upgraded version of the "Interpreting and Social Service" course based on multilingual services in emergency cases in which students are assigned the role of "emergency language service providers" and participate in the whole process of emergency handling in a highly simulated environment (iLab-X.com, np).[8] Hunan Normal University (湖南师范大学) has also developed a similar project with the focus on emergency language services (iLab-X.com, np).[9]

In general, changes of teaching modes and assessments can be seen in VR interpreting/foreign language labs and VR-aided interpreting simulation projects. VR creates a "decentralized" teaching/learning environment. Teachers become "facilitators" in the whole teaching/learning process, and students are freer to explore different scenarios with the help of VR. In terms of assessment, students' performance can be evaluated from different dimensions, namely, AI, self-evaluation, peer review, and feedback from teachers, which enables students to identify their advantages and problems in interpreting in a more scientific and diverse manner. Though a growing number of VR interpreting labs or projects have been established in Chinese universities, VR application in interpreting and even foreign language teaching still lags behind when compared to VR projects in other disciplines like science and engineering in China.

4 Integrating VR tools into research: the Chinese perspectives

Research on ICT-based interpreter training has always been an academic focus whether in China or abroad. The development of big data and AI has led to the widespread use of corpus, machine translation, automatic speech recognition, and VR in translation and interpreting learning. In comparison to other technologies, particularly corpus technology, employment of VR is quite new. While the preceding section has introduced VR application cases in interpreter training in China, this section mainly focuses on related research.

4.1 Descriptive research

Successful cases of VR application in L2 learning and the call for improving computer-aided interpreting both encouraged scholars to explore the feasibility of VR integration in interpreter training. Deng and Xu (2020, 62–64) reviewed digitalized interpreting classes in Europe and found that the e-resources under study come in a variety of forms, place an emphasis on authenticity, and cater to trainees' demands. Their review sheds light on ICT-based reform of interpreter training and constitutes a background for incorporating VR in Chinese interpreting classes. Liu (2016, 74) focused on VR *per se* and examined the theory background, technology application, and concrete functions of the IVY project. In another paper, Liu (2018, 79–81) provided a detailed introduction to the IVY platform's operation in various interpreting modes (i.e., consecutive and liaison interpreting), at different phrases (preparation before the task, working during the task, and reflection after the task), as well as how trainees and clients interact through the platform. Jiang and Peng (2018) went into more detail on the value of IVY in continuing education, which is important for professional interpreters.

Drawing on European practices and experience, Chinese scholars started to explore VR-based platforms suitable for interpreter training in the Chinese context. Zhang and Chou (2021, 80–83) introduced their Platform of Immersion Interpreting Teaching in Virtual Reality with AI Assessment (PIIT), which incorporates both VR and AI into interpreting teaching process. PIIT adopts VR to simulate the context and situation of real consecutive interpreting activities in international conferences and press conferences. In the after-interpreting phrase, AI technologies are employed to evaluate trainees' performance. This innovative platform is thought to have the potential to compensate for shortcomings in traditional interpreting classes by enhancing the flexibility, interactivity, and individualization of both in-class and after-class activities and enabling each learner to receive feedback of their performance. Since the Chinese cases have already been introduced earlier, we won't go through them in detail here.

4.2 Empirical studies

In addition to descriptive studies that introduce VR platforms, another important research branch of VR application in interpreting is to investigate its effectiveness and users' attitudes. The most frequently used methods in these empirical investigations include experiments, surveys, and pre- and post-tests. Kang's (2012, 39–40) preliminary examination into the perceptions of 209 undergraduate students on the use of VR in interpreting learning reveals a high level of satisfaction with this new technology. The survey, however, primarily looks at students' general attitudes and skips over thoughts about how well VR works in specific areas, such as the immersive experience, learning efficacy, engagement, student motivation, etc.

The effectiveness of VR was examined experimentally by Zhai (2019, 154–55) and Nai and Hassan (2022), with the latter's research focused on simultaneous interpreting while the former's on consecutive interpreting and public speaking. Both studies were carried out with senior undergraduates, using questionnaires and pre- and post-tests. Results of the five-point Likert questionnaires indicate an overall positive experience of VR-based training, as most students agree or fully agree that VR helps them better acquire interpreting skills, understand real interpreting tasks and procedures, enhance their learning motivation, and bring a more interactive experience. The pre- and post-test results show a significantly higher score in the VR-based training group than in the group receiving traditional teaching, demonstrating VR's effectiveness in enhancing teaching efficacy.

Chao (2021, 95) further narrowed down the research scope, focusing on the effect of VR in pre-task preparation on the cognitive load during consecutive interpreting. Twelve master students majoring in translation and interpreting were asked to prepare to interpret an English interview into Chinese: six adopted the traditional method, including collecting background information and preparing for the terminology, while the others used VR for preparation. Examination of students' outputs reveals that those who have prepared with VR significantly outperform their peers in terms of accuracy, completeness, and fluency of renditions. In addition, results of the NASA Task Load Index scores and the retelling outputs of the source text show that VR is effective in lowering trainee interpreters' cognitive load.

It is obvious that the empirical evidence has supported the feasibility and effectiveness of VR-based interpreter training, which constitutes a basis for pedagogical reform in the future. Nevertheless, the application of VR in interpreting and relevant research are still in their infancy. Further efforts are needed to investigate issues, such as how to better integrate it into interpreting classes, VR's influence on skill acquisition, etc. Furthermore, research methods can also be more diversified rather than being confined with questionnaires and tests. A toolkit of methods such as corpus and eye movement analysis can also be used to shed light on the impact and nature of VR-based interpreter training.

5   Conclusion

VR is reshaping the interpreting and translation industry with both opportunities and challenges. With VR, innovation in interpreter training can be realized and trainees can experience various working scenarios with just a few clicks. VR-supported interpreting research promotes interdisciplinary studies, which help researchers and practitioners better understand the process of interpreting. Surely, there will be more results in the future by applying VR to interpreter training and research in China and globally. But there are still more areas for us to explore, like the efficiency of VR-aided interpreter training and the ethics of applying VR in interpreter training and research.

Notes

1 "中国人民大学口译虚拟仿真实验教学平台项目中标（成交）结果公告," Renmin University of China, accessed Nov. 23, 2022, http://cgzx.ruc.edu.cn/index/index/news_cont/id/1058.html.

2 "杜鹏副校长到外国语学院智能虚拟仿真实验室调研," Renmin University of China, accessed Nov. 23, 2022, https://news.ruc.edu.cn/archives/305500.
3 "一种计算机口译教学仿真系统," Patentstar, accessed Nov. 23, 2022, https://cprs.patentstar.com.cn/Search/Detail?ANE=7EBA6GAA9DFB4ADA9BHA4CCA9IBG9AEB9EFG9GAACEHA9FIF.
4 "杭州师范大学外国语学院VR虚拟仿真外语实训中心," CASRZ, accessed Nov. 23, 2022, www.casrz.com/h-nd-160.html.
5 "沉浸式外语虚拟仿真实训与智能测评研究中心," UESTC, accessed Nov. 23, 2022, http://vrenglish.uestc.edu.cn/dist/#/VirtualSimulation.
6 "援博茨瓦纳针灸诊疗口译虚拟仿真项目," Fujian Medical University, accessed Nov. 23, 2022, www.tduvr.club/vrInterpret.
7 "模拟联合国会议口译虚拟仿真实验教学," iLab-X.com, accessed Nov. 23, 2022, www.ilab-x.com/details/page?id=5995&isView=true.
8 "多语种应急服务能力虚拟仿真实训实践课程," iLab-X.com, accessed Nov. 23, 2022, www.ilab-x.com/details/page?id=6299&isView=true.
9 "新文科背景下应急语言服务虚拟仿真实验," iLab-X.com, accessed Nov. 23, 2022, www.ilab-x.com/details/page?id=6176&isView=true.

References

Baraldi, Claudio. 2017. "Language Mediation as Communication System: Language Mediation as Communication System." *Communication Theory* 27(4): 367–87. https://doi.org/10.1111/comt.12118.

Braun, Sabine. 2015. "Remote Interpreting." In *The Routledge Handbook of Interpreting*, edited by Holly Mikkelson and Renée Jourdenais, 364–79. London: Routledge.

Braun, Sabine, Catherine Slater, and Nicolas Botfield. 2015. "Evaluating the Pedagogical Affordances of a Bespoke 3D Virtual Learning Environment for Interpreters and Their Clients." In *Digital Education in Interpreter Education*, edited by Suzanne Ehrlich and Jemina Napier, 39–67. Washington: Gallaudet University Press. https://doi.org/10.2307/j.ctv2rcnmhs.

Braun, Sabine, Catherine Slater, Robert Gittins, Panagiotis D Ritsos, and Jonathan C Roberts. 2013. "Interpreting in Virtual Reality: Designing and Developing a 3D Virtual World to Prepare Interpreters and Their Clients for Professional Practice." In *New Prospects and Perspectives for Educating Language Mediators*, edited by Don Kiraly, Silvia Hansen-Schirra, and Karin Maksymski, 93–120. Tübingen: Narr.

CASRZ. "杭州师范大学外国语学院 VR 虚拟仿真外语实训中心." Accessed November 23, 2022. www.casrz.com/h-nd-160.html.

Chao Yue 巢玥. 2021. "3D xuni xianshi jishu jieru de yiqian zhunbei yu jiaoti chuanyi renzhi fuhe de xiangguanxing yanjiu" 3D 虚拟现实技术介入的译前准备与交替传译认知负荷的相关性研究 [Correlation between 3D Virtual Reality Based Pre-Task Preparation and the Cognitive Load of Consecutive Interpreting]. *Waiyu Jiaoxue* 外语教学 [Foreign Language Education] 42(5): 93–7.

Chen, Yu-Li. 2016. "The Effects of Virtual Reality Learning Environment on Student Cognitive and Linguistic Development." *The Asia-Pacific Education Researcher* 25(4): 637–46. https://doi.org/10.1007/s40299-016-0293-2.

Chmiel, Agnieszka. 2015. "Contextualising Interpreter Training through Simulated Conferences." In *Constructing Translation Competence*, edited by Paulina Pietrzak and Mikołaj Deckert, 159–75. Frankfurt: Peter Lang.

Defrancq, Bart, Sarah Delputte, and Tom Baudewijn. 2022. "Interprofessional Training for Student Conference Interpreters and Students of Political Science through

Joint Mock Conferences: An Assessment." *The Interpreter and Translator Trainer* 16(1): 39–57. https://doi.org/10.1080/1750399X.2021.1919975.

Deng Juntao 邓军涛, and Xu Mianjun 许勉军. 2020. "Shuzihua kouyi jiaoxue ziyuan jianshe: Ouzhou jingyan yu qishi" 数字化口译教学资源建设：欧洲经验与启示 [Developing Digital Resources for Interpreting Teaching: Implications of European Experience]. *Shanghai Fanyi* 上海翻译 [Shanghai Journal of Translation] (3): 62–6.

Fujian Medical University. "援博茨瓦纳针灸诊疗口译虚拟仿真项目." Accessed November 23, 2022. www.tduvr.club/vrInterpret.

Garris, Rosemary, Robert Ahlers, and James E Driskell. 2017. "Games, Motivation, and Learning: A Research and Practice Model." In *Simulation in Aviation Training*, edited by Florian Jentsch and Michael Curtis, 475–501. Abingdon, UK: Routledge.

Gayeski, Diane Mary. 1993. *Multimedia for Learning: Development, Application, Evaluation*. Englewood Cliffs, NJ: Educational Technology Publications.

iLab-X.com. "模拟联合国会议口译虚拟仿真实验教学." Accessed November 23, 2022. www.ilab-x.com/details/page?id=5995&isView=true.

iLab-X.com. "多语种应急服务能力虚拟仿真实训实践课程." Accessed November 23, 2022. www.ilab-x.com/details/page?id=6299&isView=true.

iLab-X.com. "新文科背景下应急语言服务虚拟仿真实验." Accessed November 23, 2022. www.ilab-x.com/details/page?id=6176&isView=true.

Jiang Lihua 蒋莉华, and Peng Xuejiao 彭雪姣. 2018. "Fanyi jixu jiaoyu lingyu kouyi jiaoxue xinmoshi tansuo – Laizi IVY xiangmu de qishi" 翻译继续教育领域口译教学新模式探索 – 来自IVY项目的启示 [Virtual-Reality-Based Continuing Education of Translators and Interpreters: An EU Model]. *Zhongguo Fanyi* 中国翻译 [Chinese Translator Journal] (6): 41–6.

Kang Zhifeng 康志峰. 2012. "Litilun yu duomotai kouyi jiaoxue" 立体论与多模态口译教学 [The All-Encompassing Theory and Interpreting Teaching with Multimodalities]. *Waiyujie* 外语界 [Foreign Language World] (5): 34–41.

Kavanagh, Sam, Andrew Luxton-Reilly, Burkhard Wuensche, and Beryl Plimmer. 2017. "A Systematic Review of Virtual Reality in Education." *Themes in Science and Technology Education* 10(2): 85–119.

Kiraly, Donald. 2014. *A Social Constructivist Approach to Translator Education: Empowerment from Theory to Practice*. London: Routledge.

Kurz, Ingrid. 2003. "Physiological Stress during Simultaneous Interpreting: A Comparison of Experts and Novices." *The Interpreters' Newsletter* 12: 51–67.

Legault, Jennifer, Jiayan Zhao, Ying-An Chi, Weitao Chen, Alexander Klippel, and Ping Li. 2019. "Immersive Virtual Reality as an Effective Tool for Second Language Vocabulary Learning." *Languages* 4(1): 13–44. https://doi.org/10.3390/languages4010013.

Li, Xiangdong. 2015. "Mock Conference as a Situated Learning Activity in Interpreter Training: A Case Study of Its Design and Effect as Perceived by Trainee Interpreters." *The Interpreter and Translator Trainer* 9(3): 323–41. https://doi.org/10.1080/1750399X.2015.1100399.

Li, Xiangdong. 2018. "Self-Assessment as 'Assessment as Learning' in Translator and Interpreter Education: Validity and Washback." *The Interpreter and Translator Trainer* 12(1): 48–67. https://doi.org/10.1080/1750399X.2017.1418581.

Lim, Lily. 2020. "Interpreting Training in China: Past, Present, and Future." In *Key Issues in Translation Studies in China*, edited by Lily Lim and Defeng Li, 143–59. Singapore: Springer.

Lin, Yu-Ju, and Hung-chun Wang. 2021. "Using Virtual Reality to Facilitate Learners' Creative Self-Efficacy and Intrinsic Motivation in an EFL

Classroom." *Education and Information Technologies* 26(4): 4487–505. https://doi.org/10.1007/s10639-021-10472-9.

Liu Menglian 刘梦莲. 2016. "Oumeng IVY yingyong tedian ji qi dui jizhu kouyi jiaoxue de qishi" 欧盟 IVY 应用特点及其对机助口译教学的启示 [The European Union IVY Project and Its Inspiration to Computer Assisted Interpreter Training]. *Xiandai Jiaoyu Jishu* 现代教育技术 [Modern Educational Technology] 26(6): 74–9.

Liu Menglian 刘梦莲. 2018. "IVY xuni kouyi xunlian moshi yanjiu" IVY 虚拟现实口译训练模式研究 [On the IVY Virtual Reality Interpreting Training Model]. *Shanghai Fanyi* 上海翻译 [Shanghai Journal of Translation] (5): 78–83.

Makransky, Guido, Stefan Borre-Gude, and Richard E Mayer. 2019. "Motivational and Cognitive Benefits of Training in Immersive Virtual Reality Based on Multiple Assessments." *Journal of Computer Assisted Learning* 35(6): 691–707. https://doi.org/10.1111/jcal.12375.

Nai, Ruihua, and Hanita Hassan. 2022. "Multi-Modal Simultaneous Interpreting Teaching: Based on Situated Learning in Virtual Reality." In *International Conference on Innovative Computing*, 494–501. Singapore: Springer.

O'Brien, Mary Grantham, and Richard M Levy. 2008. "Exploration through Virtual Reality: Encounters with the Target Culture." *Canadian Modern Language Review* 64(4): 663–91. https://doi.org/10.3138/cmlr.64.4.663.

Page, Ray L. 2000. "Brief History of Flight Simulation." *SimTecT 2000 Proceedings*: 11–7. https://doi.org/10.1.1.132.5428.

Parong, Jocelyn, and Richard E Mayer. 2018. "Learning Science in Immersive Virtual Reality." *Journal of Educational Psychology* 110(6): 785–97. https://doi.org/10.1037/edu0000241.

Patentstar. "一种计算机口译教学仿真系统." Accessed November 23, 2022. https://cprs.patentstar.com.cn/Search/Detail?ANE=7EBA6GAA9DFB4ADA9BHA4CCA9IBG9AEB9EFG9GAACEHA9FIF.

Pöchhacker, Franz. 2008. "Interpreting as Mediation." In *Crossing Borders in Community Interpreting: Definitions and Dilemmas*, edited by Carmen Valero-Garcés and Anne Martin, 9–26. Amsterdam and Philadelphia: John Benjamins.

Psotka, Joseph. 1995. "Immersive Training Systems: Virtual Reality and Education and Training." *Instructional Science* 23(5): 405–31. https://doi.org/10.1007/BF00896880.

Qin Yong 秦勇, and Qin Qin 秦勤. 2022. "Goujian jiyu yidaiyilu yanxian quyu jingji fazhan tese de xuni fangzhen kouyi shixun xitong" 构建基于"一带一路"沿线区域经济发展特色的虚拟仿真口译实训系统 [Building a VR Emulation Interpreting Training System Based on the Regional Economic Development Characteristics of the Areas Along the Belt and Road]. *Waiguo Yuwen* 外国语文 [Foreign Languages and Literature] 38(2): 124–31.

Renmin University of China. "中国人民大学口译虚拟仿真实验教学平台项目中标（成交）结果公告." Accessed November 23, 2022. http://cgzx.ruc.edu.cn/index/index/news_cont/id/1058.html

Renmin University of China. "杜鹏副校长到外国语学院智能虚拟仿真实验室调研." Accessed November 23, 2022. https://news.ruc.edu.cn/archives/305500.

Ritsos, Panagiotis D., Robert Gittins, Jonathan C. Roberts, Sabine Braun, and Catherine Slater. 2012. "Using Virtual Reality for Interpreter-Mediated Communication and Training." In *2012 International Conference on Cyberworlds*, 191–8. Darmstadt, Germany: IEEE. https://doi.org/10.1109/CW.2012.34.

Roussou, Maria. 2004. "Learning by Doing and Learning through Play: An Exploration of Interactivity in Virtual Environments for Children." *Computers in Entertainment (CIE)* 2(1): 1–23. https://doi.org/10.1145/973801.973818.

Şahin, Mehmet. 2013. "Virtual Worlds in Interpreter Training." *The Interpreter and Translator Trainer* 7(1): 91–106. https://doi.org/10.1080/13556509.2013.107 98845.

Santos, Marc Ericson C., Takafumi Taketomi, Goshiro Yamamoto, Ma Rodrigo, T. Mercedes, Christian Sandor, Hirokazu Kato, and others. 2016. "Augmented Reality as Multimedia: The Case for Situated Vocabulary Learning." *Research and Practice in Technology Enhanced Learning* 11(1): 1–23. https://doi.org/10.1186/s41039-016-0028-2.

Schäffner, Christina. 2015. "Speaker Positioning in Interpreter-Mediated Press Conferences." *Target: International Journal of Translation Studies* 27(3): 422–39. https://doi.org/10.1075/target.27.3.06sch.

Slavova, Yoana, and Mu Mu. 2018. "A Comparative Study of the Learning Outcomes and Experience of VR in Education." In *2018 IEEE Conference on Virtual Reality and 3D User Interfaces (VR): Tübingen/Reutlingen, Germany, 18–22 March 2018*, 685–6. Piscataway, NJ: IEEE. https://doi.org/10.1109/VR.2018.8446486.

Sung, Billy, Enrique Mergelsberg, Min Teah, Brandon D'Silva, and Ian Phau. 2021. "The Effectiveness of a Marketing Virtual Reality Learning Simulation: A Quantitative Survey with Psychophysiological Measures." *British Journal of Educational Technology* 52(1): 196–213. https://doi.org/10.1111/bjet.13003.

Tai, Tzu-Yu, Howard Hao-Jan Chen, and Graeme Todd. 2020. "The Impact of a Virtual Reality App on Adolescent EFL Learners' Vocabulary Learning." *Computer Assisted Language Learning* 35(4): 892–917. https://doi.org/10.1080/09588221.2020.1752735.

UESTC. "沉浸式外语虚拟仿真实训与智能测评研究中心." Accessed November 23, 2022. http://vrenglish.uestc.edu.cn/dist/#/VirtualSimulation.

Vygotsky, Lev Semenovich, and Michael Cole. 1978. *Mind in Society: Development of Higher Psychological Processes*. Cambridge, MA: Harvard university press.

Wadensjö, Cecilia. 2014. *Interpreting as Interaction*. London and New York: Routledge.

Xie, Ying, Yan Chen, and Lan Hui Ryder. 2021. "Effects of Using Mobile-Based Virtual Reality on Chinese L2 Students' Oral Proficiency." *Computer Assisted Language Learning* 34(3): 225–45. https://doi.org/10.1080/09588221.2019.1604551.

Yildirim, Gurkan, Serkan Yildirim, and Emrah Dolgunsoz. 2019. "The Effect of VR and Traditional Videos on Learner Retention and Decision Making." *World Journal on Educational Technology: Current Issues* 11(1): 21–9.

Zhai Jiayu 翟佳羽. 2019. "Xuni xianshi jishu fuzhu xia qingjinghua jiaochuan yuyanjiang yitihua jiaoxue yanjiu yu shijian" 虚拟现实技术辅助下情景化交传与演讲一体化教学研究与实践 [Integrated and Situated Teaching of Consecutive Interpreting and Public Speaking in Virtual Reality]. *Waiguo Yuwen* 外国语文 [Foreign Language and Literature] 35(6): 150–7.

Zhang Yijun 张轶骏, and Isabelle Chou 周晶. 2021. "VI yu AI funeng de chenjinshi qingjing kouyi jiaoxue moshi yanjiu" VR 与 AI 赋能的沉浸式情境口译教学模式研究 [Platform of Immersion Interpreting Teaching in Virtual Reality with AI Assessment: An Exploration towards the Situated Interpreting Learning]. *Waiyu Dianhua Jiaxue* 外语电化教学 [Technology Enhanced Foreign Language Education] 1: 78–84.

Index

Printed in Canada

PGCA2024